P9-CCR-671

lonely planet

Rio de Janeiro

"All you've got to do is decide to go and the hardest part is over.

So go!"

TONY WHEELER, COFOUNDER – LONELY PLANET

Property of
HUNTSVILLE PUBLIC LIBRARY

Regis St Louis

Contents

Plan Your Trip 4

Welcome to Rio de Janeiro 4
Rio de Janeiro's Top 10 6
What's New 13
Need to Know 14
First Time Rio de Janeiro 16
Top Itineraries 18
If You Like... 20
Month by Month 22
With Kids 26
For Free 28
Carnaval 29
Eating 35
Drinking & Nightlife 39
Entertainment 42
Samba 45
Shopping 49
Sports & Activities 51

Explore Rio de Janeiro 54

Ipanema & Leblon 58
Gávea, Jardim Botânico & Lagoa 78
Copacabana & Leme ... 90
Botafogo, Humaitá & Urca 101
Flamengo & Around 112
Centro & Praça Mauá 121
Santa Teresa & Lapa ... 135
Zona Norte 148
Barra da Tijuca & Western Rio 155
Sleeping 161

Understand Rio de Janeiro 171

Rio de Janeiro Today ... 172
History 174
The Sounds of Rio 185
The Beautiful Game 191
Architecture 195

Survival Guide 199

Transportation 200
Directory A–Z 205
Language 211
Index 219

Rio de Janeiro Maps 226

LAZYLLAMA/SHUTTERSTOCK ©

IGOR ALECSANDER/GETTY IMAGES ©

(left) **Santa Teresa p135** This neighborhood is home to a vibrant arts scene.

(above) ***Chorinho* performance p42** Rio has a thriving music scene.

(right) **Ipanema Beach p60** The city's most famous beach.

MICHAEL HEFFERNAN/LONELY PLANET ©

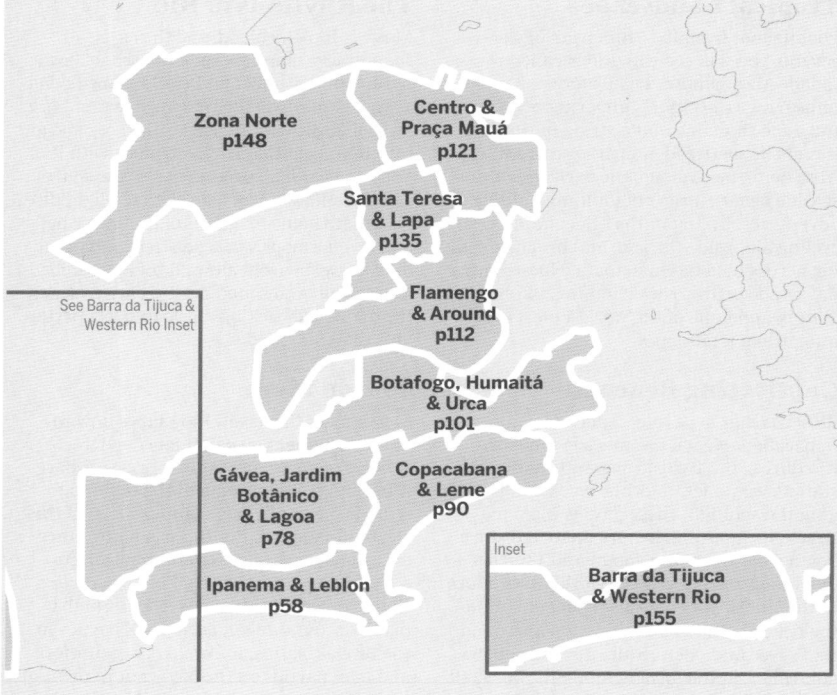

Welcome to Rio de Janeiro

Golden beaches and lush mountains, samba-fueled nightlife and spectacular football matches: welcome to the Cidade Maravilhosa (Marvelous City).

Tropical Landscapes

Looking out from the 710m peak of Corcovado, you will see why Rio is called the Cidade Maravilhosa. Lushly forested mountains fringe the city, shimmering beaches trace the shoreline and a string of tiny islands lie scattered along the seafront. Far from being mere cinematic backdrop, this seaside beauty hosts outstanding outdoor adventures: hiking in the Tijuca rainforest, cycling alongside the lake and beaches, sailing across Baía de Guanabara (Guanabara Bay), and surfing, rock climbing and hang gliding amid one of the world's most stunning urban landscapes.

Captivating Beaches

Rio's beaches have long seduced visitors. Copacabana Beach became a symbol of Rio during the 1940s, when international starlets would jet in for the weekend. Hogging the spotlight these days is Ipanema Beach, its fame and beauty unabated since bossa nova stars Tom Jobim and Vinícius de Moraes introduced the world to its allure in the 1960s. For *cariocas* (residents of Rio), the beach is Rio's backyard – a playground that's free and open to all, offering endless enjoyment in the form of football, volleyball, surfing, snacking, drinking or simply relaxing amid the passing parade of people.

The Rhythms of Rio

Music is Rio's lifeblood, and the city's soundtrack comprises rock, old-school bossa nova, hip-hop, funk and Brazil's many regional styles. Above all there's samba, a rapid-fire style of music with African influences and an infectious beat that is synonymous with Rio. You can hear it all over town, but the soul of samba resides in Lapa, an edgy red-light district that's home to dozens of live-music halls and an enormous weekend street party that draws revelers from all walks of life. Samba is also the integral sound during Carnaval, and the danceable backing music to street parties and all-night parades.

Joie de Vivre

Speaking of Carnaval, Rio knows how to party. Whether you call it joie de vivre, *Lebensfreude* or lust for life, *cariocas* have it in spades. Carnaval, and the buildup to it, is the most obvious manifestation of this celebratory spirit. But Rio has many other occasions for revelry: celebrations after a big Flamengo (or Vasco, Fluminense or Botafogo) soccer match; weekend samba parties around town; *baile* funk parties in the favelas (slums, informal communities); and boat parties on the bay – not to mention major fests such as Réveillon (New Year's Eve) and the Festas Juninas.

RAFA BAHIENSE/500PX ©

Why I Love Rio de Janeiro

By Regis St Louis, Writer

There's no other place like Rio. It's a combination of many things that I find so captivating: walking through parks inside the city and seeing monkeys and toucans; spending the evening catching music jams around Lapa; joining a few friends amid the roaring crowds at Maracanã; or greeting the sunrise (after an early morning or late night) from Copacabana Beach. In moments like these you realize you're hooked. I also love the *carioca* spirit: spontaneous and good-natured, with the urge to live life to the fullest.

For more about our writer, see p256

Top: Copacabana Beach (p92)

Rio de Janeiro's Top 10

Carnaval *(p29)*

1 Get plenty of sleep before you board the plane to Rio, because Carnaval means nonstop revelry until Ash Wednesday (sort of) brings it all to a close. With nearly 500 street parties happening in every corner of town, you will not lack for options. For the full experience, join a samba school and parade amid pounding drum corps and mechanized smoke-breathing dragons before thousands of roaring fans in the Sambódromo (p152). Or assemble a costume and hit one of the Carnaval balls around town. The buildup starts weeks in advance.

Carnaval

Copacabana Beach *(p92)*

2 The Copacabana experience is about many things: rising early and going for a run along the sands; playing in the waves on a sun-drenched afternoon; or whiling away the evening over cocktails and appetizers at a beachfront kiosk. Regardless, you'll probably notice the incredibly seductive view: 4km of wide, curving sands framed by Rio's ubiquitous green peaks. Head uphill for even better views; rooftop bars and forts at either end of the beach make great settings for taking it all in.

Copacabana & Leme

MIRALEX/GETTY IMAGES ©

LAZYLLAMA/SHUTTERSTOCK ©

3

4

Pão de Açúcar *(p103)*

3 Some will tell you to arrive around sunset for the best views from this absurd confection of a mountain. But in truth, no matter what time you come, you're unlikely to look at Rio in the same way again. From up here on Sugarloaf Mountain the landscape is one of undulating green hills and golden beaches lapped by blue sea, with rows of skyscrapers sprouting along the shore. The ride up on an all-glass aerial tram is good fun, too. Adventurous visitors can rock climb their way to the summit.

Botafogo, Humaitá & Urca

Cristo Redentor *(p114)*

4 The open-armed savior has stood atop his lofty perch (710m-high Corcovado), gazing peacefully over Rio, since 1931. The statue of Christ the Redeemer is a remarkable work of artistry, but most people don't come up here to admire the art deco design. They come for the mesmerizing panorama, a combination of tropical rainforest, beaches, islands, ocean, bay and verdant peaks, that surrounds this unlikely metropolis. There are various ways to reach the top, including a memorable (and steep!) ascent on a cog train.

Flamengo & Around

Ipanema Beach *(p60)*

5 This enchanting beachfront attracts a wide mix of *cariocas* (Rio residents). Different crowds – surfers, volleyballers, bohemians, muscle boys – congregate at each *posto* (section), including famous *posto* 9, where Ipanema's young and beautiful frolic. The principal activities of the day are people-watching, surf-side walks and sunset-watching – best from Arpoador, at Ipanema's east end. You can also eat and drink on the sand. Roaming vendors will come to you, and *barracas* (beach stalls) will set you up with chairs, umbrellas and caipirinhas. All you need do is show up.

Ipanema & Leblon

Nightlife in Lapa *(p142)*

6 The Lapa Arches form the gateway to Rio's most animated nightlife. Pass through the 64m-high portal and stroll the packed, bar-lined streets while the rhythms of samba spill out of 19th-century facades. While there are drinks (curbside beer and caipirinha vendors) and music (impromptu jam sessions) all around, venture inside an old-school dance hall to see the city at its most dynamic. From the band on stage comes the rhythms of samba – one of the world's most infectious beats. Grab a partner and join the mayhem on the dance floor. BELOW: CLUBE DOS DEMOCRÁTICOS (P144)

☆ ***Santa Teresa & Lapa***

Santa Teresa *(p135)*

7 Overlooking downtown Rio, the hilltop neighborhood of Santa Teresa – where people live in houses rather than high-rises – has a village-like vibe. Its aging 19th-century mansions and bohemian spirit offer a dramatic counterpoint to Rio's better-known seaside persona. Here you'll find old-school bars, art-loving B&Bs and lush backyards where marmosets often roam, with magical views over downtown and the bay. The downside: it's still rough around the edges. But the locals and expats who live here wouldn't have it any other way.

Santa Teresa & Lapa

Lagoa Rodrigo de Freitas *(p80)*

8 'Saltwater lagoon' may not be the first thing you think of when you hear the words 'Rio de Janeiro,' but this picturesque body of water plays a key role in the city's psyche. By day *cariocas* cycle, jog and stroll the 7km path that loops around it. At nightfall a different crowd arrives to eat and drink in the open-air kiosks scattered along the shore. In December Lagoa is home to a massive floating Christmas tree, its glittering lights and nightly displays pure magic for kids and adults alike.

Gávea, Jardim Botânico & Lagoa

Floresta da Tijuca *(p158)*

9 New York has Central Park; Rio has the Floresta da Tijuca, a vast swath of rainforest with hiking trails, sparkling waterfalls and abundant greenery. There are a number of fine walks, as well as climbs up rocky 900m peaks, where rewarding views await. If you prefer flying to walking, take a hang-gliding flight from Pedra Bonita inside the Tijuca boundaries for a magnificent (if somewhat terrifying) view over Rio's wondrously green backyard.

Barra da Tijuca & Western Rio

Maracanã Football Stadium *(p150)*

10 Rio's famous stadium, Maracanã, is hallowed ground among Brazilians. It has been the site of both triumph (Pelé's 1000th goal) and catastrophe (losing to Uruguay in the final match of the 1950 World Cup). Games here are simply spectacular, with tens of thousands of cheering fans sending up an earth-shaking roar when the home team (and Rio has four of them) scores. Whether or not you're a football fan, don't pass up the chance to see a game inside this historic arena.

Zona Norte

What's New

Boulevard Olímpico

A formerly run-down section of docklands north of Centro has been reborn as the Boulevard Olímpico, a pretty pedestrian (and light-rail) thoroughfare lined with colorful murals. (p128)

Botafogo

For the latest in cutting-edge culture in Rio, head to Botafogo, replete with new microbrew bars, creative, market-oriented eateries and an indie vibe. (p107)

Craft Beer

Rio's craft-beer scene continues to expand, with small producers popping up around the city. Sample brews from around town at new hot spots like Brou. (p117)

Bike Sharing

Rio has overhauled its bike-sharing network, making access easier for casual users. There are now nearly 260 stations across the city, and getting around is a breeze, particularly on the many dedicated bike lanes. (p201)

Wine Bars

In a city devoted to beer and caipirinhas, wine bars have been slow to arrive on the scene. Botafogo's new WineHouse, however, has become the talk of the town, with quality pours from Brazil and abroad. (p107)

Casa Camolese

Casa Camolese has become the new neighborhood hot spot, with a great restaurant, a microbrewery and an intimate concert venue. Next door are two new art galleries. (p83)

Hotel Emiliano

One of Copacabana's most eye-catching new arrivals, the Hotel Emiliano combines luxury with high design in an imaginative interior by Brazilian architect Arthur Casas. The tropical-plant-filled courtyard is a living work of art. (p166)

Explorer Bar

The hot new destination in Santa Teresa, the Explorer Bar serves up imaginative cocktails and creative fusion fare. There's also a guesthouse if you really want to be close to the action. (p142)

Museu da Imagem e do Som

Work on Rio's architecturally stunning Museu da Imagem e do Som was slated to restart in early 2019, with an estimated completion date of late 2020. The project will bring a new film and sound museum to one of the world's great music centers. (p93)

AquaRio

In Rio's former port district, a new 26,000-sq-meter aquarium with 350 marine species is a draw for all ages. The highlight is a 3.5-million-liter tank complete with sharks, rays and massive tropical fish. (p128)

For more recommendations and reviews, see **lonelyplanet.com/rio-de-janeiro**

Need to Know

For more information, see Survival Guide (p199)

Currency
Real (R$)

Language
Portuguese

Visas
Many nationalities require them, including citizens of the US, Canada and Australia.

Money
ATMs widely available. Credit cards accepted in most mid-range and top-end hotels and restaurants.

Cell Phones
Local SIM cards can be used in unlocked European and Australian phones, and in US phones on the GSM network.

Time
Brasília Time (GMT/UTC minus three hours)

Tourist Information
Riotur (www.visit.rio) has offices and kiosks for getting maps, transport info and tips on attractions and events.

Daily Costs

Budget: Less than R$200

- Hostel bed: R$40–70
- Sandwich and drink in a juice bar: R$18
- Coconut water on the beach: R$5-8

Midrange: R$200–600

- Standard double room in Copacabana: R$300
- Dinner for two: R$100–180
- Guided bicycle tour: R$100–150
- Admission to a samba club: R$20–50

Top End: More than R$600

- Boutique hotel room: from R$600
- Dinner for two at top restaurant with drinks: R$350
- Hang gliding off Pedra Bonita: R$500

Advance Planning

Nine months before Book a room if visiting during Carnaval or at New Year's Eve.

Three months before Organize your visa (if you need one) and book accommodations.

Two weeks before Book guided tours and activities such as rock climbing, rainforest tours and tandem gliding.

One week before Book a table at top restaurants. Check concerts and events on www.visit.rio.

Useful Websites

Lonely Planet (www.lonelyplanet.com/rio-de-janeiro) Destination information, hotel bookings, traveler forum and more.

Riotur (www.visit.rio) Rio's official tourism authority.

Rio Times (www.riotimesonline.com) English-language resource on current events.

Carioca Guide to Rio (www.ipanema.com) Tips and planning info, with special sections on Carnaval and gay Rio.

WHEN TO GO

High season runs from December to March, when Rio is festive, pricey and hot. To beat the crowds and higher prices, visit from May to September.

Rio De Janeiro

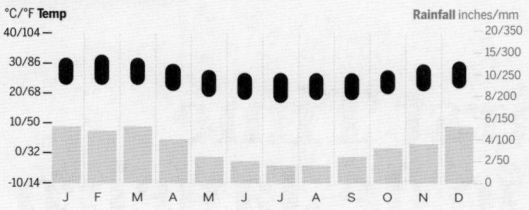

Arriving in Rio de Janeiro

Aeroporto Internacional Antônio Carlos Jobim Most international flights arrive at this airport (also called Galeão), located 15km north of the city center. Premium Auto Ônibus operates buses approximately every 30 to 40 minutes to Flamengo, Copacabana, Ipanema, Leblon and other neighborhoods (bus 2018; R$16). The trip takes one to two hours depending on traffic. Radio taxis charge a set fare of R$130 to Copacabana and Ipanema (45 to 90 minutes). Less-expensive metered yellow-and-blue *comum* (common) taxis cost between R$82 and R$100. Ride-sharing services cost around R$60. There's also shuttle service (R$25).

For much more on **arrival** see p200

Getting Around

Metro The most convenient way to get around. Trains run from 5am to midnight Monday through Saturday, and from 7am to 11pm on Sunday and holidays. Single rides cost R$4.30.

Bus Buses are frequent and cheap; destinations are listed above the windscreen. Fares are around R$3.50.

Taxi Useful at night. Fares start at R$5.50, plus R$2.50 per kilometer. Rates rise to R$3 per kilometer at night and on Sunday.

Bike Rio's bike-share scheme has numerous stations around town. Use an app, or simply a credit card at many stations, to release a bike.

For much more on **getting around** see p201

Sleeping

Rio has a wide range of lodging, including B&Bs, hostels and guesthouses; there are scores of luxury hotels, particularly in Copacabana. Prices are comparable to what you'd expect in a North American oceanside city such as Miami or LA; an abundance of options keeps rates from going sky high, except during Carnaval and other major events.

Book at least two or three months ahead during high season.

Useful Websites

Blame It on Rio 4 Travel (www.blameitonrio4travel.com) Excellent agency that rents apartments in Copacabana and Ipanema.

Lonely Planet (lonelyplanet.com/brazil/rio-de-janeiro/hotels) Recommendations and bookings.

For much more on **sleeping** see p161

First Time Rio de Janeiro

For more information, see Survival Guide (p199)

Checklist

➡ Make sure you have your Brazilian visa if you need one.

➡ Purchase travel insurance (or ensure that your home policy covers you in Brazil).

➡ Make arrangements to be able to use your mobile phone upon arrival.

➡ Download essential smartphone apps, including WhatsApp (used by nearly everyone in Brazil, including tour operators, guesthouse owners and some restaurants).

What to Pack

➡ Good walking shoes

➡ Lightweight rain jacket (for those unexpected tropical downpours)

➡ Brazilian electrical adapter

➡ Sunscreen, hat and sunglasses

➡ A sarong (handy for the beach and as an extra towel)

➡ Language phrasebook, or useful translation apps on your phone

Top Tips for Your Trip

➡ Download WhatsApp and set up your profile. Tour operators, guides, restaurants, guesthouses and everyone else uses it.

➡ Don't try to pack too much into your day. Pick a neighborhood or two, and leave time to wander or just take in the city from a cafe or bar in between sightseeing.

➡ Using a ride-sharing app (like Uber, 99Taxis or Easy Taxi) to get around is generally faster and cheaper than using a traditional taxi.

➡ Be sure to pencil some 'nature time' into your itinerary, whether it's taking a hiking tour in Parque Nacional da Tijuca or simply looking for monkeys in Parque Lage.

➡ Plan at least one outdoor adventure: cycling the beaches, stand-up paddle boarding, hang gliding, or jogging around the lake.

What to Wear

The dress code is very casual in Rio, but it's a good idea to bring along some dressy clothes for a night out (a dress or skirt-and-top ensemble for women, pants and a collared shirt for men). Given the heat and humidity, lightweight, natural, breathable fabrics are best.

On the beach, women generally wear tiny bikinis, and men wear tight swim trunks. Everyone flaunts it all, regardless of body shape and size.

Be Forewarned

Crime is a concern in Rio, but if you take basic precautions, you'll minimize your risk of becoming a target.

➡ Dress down and leave expensive jewelry, watches and sunglasses at home.

➡ Don't take anything of value with you to the beach.

➡ Don't walk around deserted areas or on any of the beaches at night.

➡ Carry only the money you'll need for the day. Cameras and backpacks attract a lot of attention. Plastic shopping bags disguise whatever you're carrying.

➡ If you have the misfortune to be robbed, calmly hand over the goods.

Planning Your Days

Before hitting the streets of Rio, make sure you've thought about what days you want to visit certain areas. The beaches get packed on weekends, so come on weekdays to beat the crowds. Weekdays are also the best time to visit Centro (though keep in mind that on Mondays some museums are closed). Weekends are the best time to visit Santa Teresa, when most shops and restaurants are open, and there's a fair bit of street life.

Taxes & Refunds

Value-added tax (VAT), levied on most goods, is 19% in Rio; this is always included in the ticketed price. Hotel-room tax is 5%, which may not be included in the quoted price; double-check when booking. A 10% service charge is added to rates at many hotels; this is rarely included in the quoted price.

There's no system of VAT refunds for purchases made in Brazil.

Tipping

Restaurants *Serviço* (service charge) usually included in bills and mandatory; when *serviço* not included, leave 10%, more if a waiter is friendly and helpful.

Juice stands, bars, coffee corners, street and beach vendors Tipping not customary but a welcome gesture.

Parking assistants Usually about R$4 (these workers receive no wages and are dependent on tips).

Taxi drivers Not usually tipped; round up the fare.

Language

English is not widely spoken in Rio. Most midrange and top-end hotels as well as hostels have English-speaking staff on hand, and the city's better restaurants also have English-speaking staff. Aside from this, it helps to master a few basic Portuguese phrases. You'll have a head start if you've studied Spanish, as Portuguese and Spanish share many words and grammatical structures. The pronunciation, however, is completely different, and very few Brazilians speak Spanish.

1 **Do you speak English?**
Você fala inglês?
vo•se *faa*•laa eeng•*gles*

Staff at hostels, midrange and top-end hotels and high-end shops will often speak some English.

2 **What's the score?**
Quanto está o jogo?
kwang•to es•*taa* o *zho*•go

On big international game days, Rio residents pack into neighborhood *botecos* (small, open-air bars) to watch the game.

3 **What would you recommend?**
O que você recomenda?
o ke vo·se he·ko·*meng*·daa

Brazilian dishes are normally quite large – and some dishes are meant for two. When in doubt, ask the server to clarify.

4 **How much is it?**
Quanto custa?
kwang•to *koos*•taa

A little bargaining is expected at markets, but sellers generally don't inflate their prices so often aren't willing to haggle.

5 **Where's the best beach?**
Onde fi ca a melhor praia?
ong•de *fee*•kaa aa me•*lyorr prai*•aa

The beaches of Rio are the city's wondrous and carefree backyard and have long seduced visitors.

Etiquette

Cariocas (residents of Rio) are pretty informal, but there are a few unspoken rules of etiquette.

Greetings When greeting or bidding goodbye to women, an air kiss is exchanged on each cheek (start to her left). Men shake hands with one another.

Dining Use a napkin or toothpick when dealing with finger foods. Brazilians tend to eat pizza with a knife and fork.

Politics Brazilians are exasperated by their country's corruption but can be defensive if foreigners begin criticizing their government.

Top Itineraries

Day One

Ipanema & Leblon (p58)

Spend the first day soaking up the rays on **Ipanema Beach**. Be sure to hydrate with *maté* (cold, sweetened tea) and *agua de côco* (coconut water), sample a few beach snacks (or a sandwich at **Uruguai**) and take a scenic stroll down to Leblon.

Lunch Quitéria (p63) spreads an excellent Brazilian lunch buffet.

Ipanema & Leblon (p58)

In the afternoon, have a wander through the streets of Ipanema, doing some window-shopping on Rua Garcia d'Ávila, stopping for ice cream at **Vero**, and getting a coffee fix at **Cafeína**. Later, stroll over to **Ponta do Arpoador**, and watch the sunset behind Dois Irmãos.

Dinner Creative dishes amid tropical splendor at Casa Camolese (p83).

Gávea, Jardim Botânico & Lagoa (p78)

After dinner, enjoy drinks or microbrews in the spacious new entertainment complex of **Casa Camolese**, then head to the downstairs **Clube Manouche** to hear some high-quality jazz or Brazilian beats. If you're still not ready to call it a night, head over to **Palaphita Gávea** for a nightcap in a lush outdoor setting.

Day Two

Flamengo & Around (p112)

Start the morning with a dose of history by visiting the atmospheric **Museu da República**. Next door, the **Museu de Folclore Edison Carneiro** has an intriguing folk-art collection well worth a look. Afterwards, head to Cosme Velho and take the cog train up Corcovado to admire the view beneath the open-armed **Cristo Redentor**.

Lunch Have lunch at Bar do Mineiro (p140), a Santa Teresa classic.

Santa Teresa & Lapa (p135)

Afterwards, wander through Santa Teresa, Rio's most atmospheric neighborhood. Browse for handicrafts at **La Vereda**, admire the views from the **Parque das Ruínas**, and check out the eclectic art collection and lush gardens of **Museu Chácara do Céu**. Stop for a late-afternoon cocktail and snack at **Explorer Bar**.

Dinner Feast on beautiful Amazonian dishes at Espírito Santa (p140).

Santa Teresa & Lapa (p135)

Take a taxi downhill to Lapa for a late night of samba and caipirinhas. Start the evening by taking in the street party around the **Arcos da Lapa** before making your way to **Rio Scenarium**, a beautiful antique-filled club where you can join samba-loving crowds on the dance floor or simply watch the evening unfold from an upper balcony.

Day Three

Barra da Tijuca & Western Rio (p155)

In the morning, go for a hike in **Floresta da Tijuca**, which has rainforest-lined hiking trails, refreshing waterfalls and spectacular views from craggy summits.

Lunch Indulge in grilled dishes at Leblon's Giuseppe Grill (p68).

Copacabana & Leme (p90)

In the afternoon, take in the sun and surf on **Copacabana Beach**. If you're feeling active, try your hand at stand-up paddle boarding. After a few hours in the sun, stroll to the southern end of the neighborhood, where you can visit the **Forte de Copacabana**. Here you'll find a small museum and several relaxing open-air cafes with memorable views across the sweep of Copacabana Beach.

Dinner Enjoy tapas and sangria at El Born (p94) in buzzing Baixo Copa.

Gávea, Jardim Botânico & Lagoa (p78)

After dinner, go for creative cocktails and serene views at the open-air lakeside bar of **Palaphita Kitch**. Then head to the other side of the lake for a concert at the **Blue Note Rio**.

Day Four

Centro & Praça Mauá (p121)

Start the morning in the newly redesigned streets around Praça Mauá. Admire the view from the **Museu de Arte do Rio** and check out the futuristic exhibits inside the **Museu do Amanhã**. Peek inside the lavish **Mosteiro de São Bento** en route to Praça XV (Quinze) de Novembro and check out other impressive colonial sights, including **Paço Imperial** and the **Igreja de Nossa Senhora do Carmo da Antiga Sé**.

Lunch Enjoy creative Asian fusion and panoramic bay views at Xian (p130).

Botafogo & Urca (p101)

Spend the afternoon down in Urca. Take the cable car to the top of **Pão de Açúcar**, from where Rio spreads before you in a stunning panorama. Afterwards, enjoy a drink and a snack at waterfront **Bar Urca**.

Dinner Experience high-end gastronomy at the celebrated Oteque (p106).

Botafogo & Urca (p101)

Stick around Botafogo for libations in some of the neighborhood's creative new drinking dens. Sip bespoke cocktails and join locals over DJ sets at **CoLAB**; follow it up with drinks at buzzing **Comuna**; later, catch some casual sidewalk jam sessions at **Fuska 2.0**.

If You Like...

Activities & Sports

Bike in Rio Three- to five-hour bicycle tours showcase Rio's parks and beaches. (p201)

Jungle Me Knowledgeable guides offer hikes through Parque Nacional da Tijuca. (p51)

Crux Eco Choose from a range of climbing, rappelling (abseiling) and hiking adventures. (p52)

Asa Delta Flight in Rio Take to the skies for a hang gliding experience with an experienced and safety-conscious pro pilot. (p52)

Fundição Progresso Salsa, tango and capoeira classes can be found at this cultural center. (p145)

Lagoa Aventuras Rock climbing and zip-line adventures for adults and kids. (p87)

Universo Paddle Surf Ride the waves on a stand-up paddle board. (p100)

Sail in Rio Superb sailing tours offer bay and island views. (p203)

Art & Architecture

Museu de Arte do Rio The city's best new art museum is a showcase for great photography, painting and sculpture. (p127)

Museu do Amanhã The spectacular new science museum designed by Santiago Calatrava. (p128)

Museu Nacional de Belas Artes An impressive collection of 19th- and early 20th-century paintings in the heart of downtown. (p124)

DIEGO GRANDI/SHUTTERSTOCK ©

Museu da República (p116)

Museu de Arte Moderna A massive postmodern building that houses works by some of Brazil's best-known 20th-century artists. (p124)

Theatro Municipal One of Rio's most striking buildings, this theater was recently restored to its former splendor. (p124)

Museu Chácara do Céu You'll pass through lush gardens en route to this small museum with an outstanding modern-art collection. (p138)

OM.art A striking new gallery that presents thought-provoking art exhibitions. (p82)

Beaches

Ipanema Rio's most famous beach has volleyball games, food and drink vendors, and inviting waves. (p60)

Copacabana Planted with high-rises and framed by mountains, curving Copacabana Beach is truly magnificent. (p92)

Praia Vermelha Hidden near the cable-car station to Pão de Açúcar, this tiny beach boasts a magnificent panorama. (p104)

Barra da Tijuca A picturesque, seemingly endless stretch of sand located west of Leblon. (p157)

Prainha Good surf and a striking setting of rainforest-backed beachfront with little development in sight. (p157)

Free Stuff

Centro Cultural Banco do Brasil Massive arts center home to some of the city's top exhibits. (p127)

Centro de Arte Hélio Oiticica A little-visited gem that has cutting-edge contemporary exhibitions. (p125)

Parque das Ruínas High up in Santa Teresa, the site of a ruined mansion has magnificent views over Rio. (p138)

Museu de Folclore Edison Carneiro A small but worthwhile collection of Brazilian folk art next to the former presidential palace. (p116)

Instituto Moreira Salles Fascinating gallery of temporary exhibits in a restored villa. (p81)

Centro Cultural Justiça Federal The handsome building that once housed Brazil's Supreme Court today hosts diverse exhibitions. (p124)

Historical Sights

Museu da República The former presidential palace has historical artifacts and an eerie room where one president died by suicide. (p116)

Igreja de Nossa Senhora do Carmo da Antiga Sé Magnificently restored church where several Portuguese kings were crowned. (p126)

Museu do Índio A celebration of Brazil's indigenous culture, both past and present. (p104)

Pedra do Sal Celebrate samba in the open-air setting where the music was born in the heart of Brazil's former 'Little Africa.' (p133)

Museu Histórico Nacional The former colonial arsenal provides a fascinating glimpse of Rio's royal days. (p123)

Instituto de Pesquisa e Memória Presto Novos Learn about the tragic era of slavery in Brazil. (p128)

Outdoor Adventures

Parque Nacional da Tijuca Lush rainforest, waterfalls, scenic views atop rocky cliffs – Tijuca is a must for outdoor-lovers. (p158)

Hang gliding Take the plunge off Pedra Bonita for an unforgettable airborne adventure. (p52)

Pão de Açúcar For an adrenaline rush, sign up for a rock-climbing excursion to the top of Sugarloaf Mountain. (p103)

Lagoa Rodrigo de Freitas By day, jog or cycle around the picturesque lake; by night, enjoy cocktails at waterfront kiosks. (p80)

Parks & Gardens

Jardim Botânico This beautifully set botanical garden makes a refreshing escape from the city. (p81)

Parque Lage Home to a historic mansion and rainforest-lined walking trails, including one challenging trail that ascends Corcovado. (p81)

Parque do Flamengo A long, narrow park with magnificent bay views; a great place for a bike ride. (p116)

Parque da Catacumba Trails lead to a peak with magnificent views over the lake and the mountains beyond. (p82)

Sítio Burle Marx It's a long journey to get here, but this beautifully landscaped 35-hectare estate is a verdant wonderland. (p157)

For more top Rio de Janeiro spots, see the following:

- Eating (p35)
- Drinking & Nightlife (p39)
- Entertainment (p42)
- Shopping (p49)
- Sports & Activities (p51)

Month by Month

TOP EVENTS

Carnaval, February

Festas Juninas, June

Festival do Rio, November

Réveillon, December

January

Following the excitement of New Year's Eve, Rio starts the year in high gear, with steamy beach days, open-air concerts and the buzz of pre-Carnaval revelry.

Dia de São Sebastião

The patron saint of Rio is commemorated on January 20 with a procession that carries the image of São Sebastião from Igreja de São Sebastião dos Capuchinos (Rua Haddock Lobo 266) in Tijuca to the Catedral Metropolitana in Lapa.

February

High season is in full swing, with people-packed beaches, sold-out hotel rooms and the unbridled revelry of Carnaval. Periodic thunderstorms bring some relief from the sweltering humidity.

Carnaval

Brazil's biggest fest is celebrated with abandon in Rio, with hundreds of street parties, as well as costume balls and elaborate samba-fueled parades that attract revelers from all corners of the globe.

Rio Music Carnaval

Arriving in the midst of Carnaval, this big February fest (http://riomusiccarnival.com.br) features a stellar lineup of electronic-music gurus. Past guests at the five-night event have featured Diplo, Fatboy Slim and Bob Sinclair. Headliners appear in the Marina da Glória.

March

After Carnaval the visiting crowds disperse somewhat, though the weather remains hot and the tropical rain showers continue on. Ongoing summer concerts and events make it a festive time to visit the city.

Dia da Fundação da Cidade

The city commemorates its 1565 founding with a March 1 Mass in the church of its patron saint, Igreja de São Sebastião dos Capuchinos (Rua Haddock Lobo 266, Tijuca). A procession, concerts, a children's parade and a massive birthday cake are part of the festivities.

Sexta-Feira da Paixão

In March or April (depending on when Easter falls), Good Friday is celebrated throughout the city. The most important ceremony re-enacts the Stations of the Cross under the Arcos da Lapa (p139), with more than 100 actors.

Festival é Tudo Verdade

Latin America's most important documentary film festival (http://etudoverdade.com.br/br/home) takes place over 10 days in March or April; more than 100 films from Brazil and abroad are screened at theaters in Rio and São Paulo.

April

After the sweltering heat of summer, April remains warm but pleasant, with slightly cooler temperatures and fewer rainstorms. Following the festive January-to-March period, *cariocas* (Rio residents) return to work, and the kids are back in school.

Dia do Índio

April 19 pays homage to Brazil's indigenous cultures, with special events, including indigenous songs, dancing and art exhibitions. Locations vary, but the event has recently been held in Parque Lage (p81).

Dia de São Jorge

On April 23 the city pays its respects to St George, an important figure in the Afro-Brazilian community. There's a Mass at Igreja de São Jorge (Rua da Alfândega 382, Centro), followed by a procession. Food vendors abound.

May

May is another excellent month to visit Rio, with good low-season prices, fewer crowds and generally appealing weather (low humidity but warm days).

June

June brings milder weather, with temperatures in the low 20s (Celsius) and little rainfall. Although it's low season, there's much merriment in the air during the fun-loving Festas Juninas.

Rio das Ostras Jazz e Blues Festival

Located 170km east of Rio, en route to Búzios, pretty Rio das Ostras hosts one of Brazil's best jazz and blues fests (www.riodasostrasjazzeblues.com), with four days of concerts by international performers on outdoor stages.

Festas Juninas

Spanning the month of June, the feast days of various saints mark some of the most important folkloric festivals in Brazil. Celebrations are held in various public squares, with food stands, music, fireworks and bonfires. The big days are June 13, 24 and 29.

Rio Marathon

Set along the coast, with the ocean always at your side, this marathon course ranks among the world's loveliest. The event (www.maratonadorio.com.br) typically happens in June or July (but sometimes as early as late May), when the weather's mild. Also has 6km and 21km runs.

July

The cooler days of winter arrive, with little rainfall, clear blue skies and mild temperatures. There aren't many visitors in town, and accommodations prices are near their lowest.

Portas Abertas

Artists in Santa Teresa open their studios for a week in the winter during this lively annual festival. Expect music, a diverse crowd and inventive installations that make good use of the atmospheric bohemian 'hood.

Festa da São Pedro do Mar

The fishing fraternity pays homage to its patron saint in late June. A maritime procession of decorated boats leaves from the fishing community of Caju and sails to the statue of São Pedro in Urca.

Festa Literária Internacional de Paraty

This important literary festival (www.flip.org.br) brings authors from around the world to Paraty (four hours west of Rio) for five days in July or August. Writers Jhumpa Lahiri, Colm Tóibín and Richard Flanagan have been among the featured guests in past years.

August

With continuing cool weather but sunny skies, it's an excellent time to take advantage of outdoor activities such as cycling, rock climbing, and hiking in the Tijuca forest.

Festa de NS da Glória do Outeiro

On August 15 the historic church (p117) overlooking Glória and the bay holds a procession, stages a concert and hosts colorful stalls. Festivities start early and continue all day.

Rio Gastronomia

For several days in August, Rio hosts Brazil's biggest culinary event (www.riogastronomia.com.br). The focal point of all the action is out on Pier Mauá, with special tastings, workshops and cooking lessons, plus concerts.

September

Temperatures are rising, and although Carnaval is still months away, samba-school rehearsals begin, making for a great opportunity to get a taste of the excitement out of season.

Mondial de la Biere

This four-day event draws brew-lovers from far and wide to an extravaganza of food and beer tasting currently held on Praça Mauá (www.mondialdelabiere rio.com).

Dia de Independência do Brasil

Independence Day is celebrated on September 7 with a large military parade down Av Presidente Vargas in Centro. It starts at 8am at Igreja de Nossa Senhora de Candelária (p127) and goes down just past Praça XI.

Rock in Rio

One of the biggest rock festivals on earth has recently returned to Rio (after alternating between Lisbon and Madrid). Expect a stellar lineup of bands and huge, celebratory crowds. Scheduled to happen in Rio in 2019 and 2021; check out www.rockinrio.com.br.

October

October brings more beach days and a touch more daylight; Rio also pushes

(Top) Lagoa Christmas Tree
(Bottom) Festas Juninas (p23)

DONATAS DABRAVOLSKAS/SHUTTERSTOCK ©

TED SOMERVILLE/ALAMY STOCK PHOTO ©

the clock ahead for one hour from mid-October (till mid-February). Comfortable temperatures make this an excellent time to be in the tropics.

Festa da Penha

Held on Sundays in October, this religious fest draws thousands of pilgrims who ascend the 365 steps to the dramatically set Basílica da Penha in the northern suburb of Penha. In the plaza below, food and drink stalls and live music create a festive environment.

Gay Pride Rio

Although not as large as São Paulo's massive parade, the Rio Gay Pride event (www.gaypridebrazil.org) gets bigger each year, with more than a million people turning out in recent years. It usually takes place in October or November.

November

Summer has nearly arrived and the city begins to gear up for the festive days and nights ahead, with a dance festival, a film fest and more activities on the city's sands.

Festival do Rio

Rio's international film festival (www.festivaldorio.com.br) is one of the biggest in Latin America. Some 400 films from more than 60 countries are shown at 30 theaters. Running over two weeks, it typically kicks off in November.

SAMBA-SCHOOL REHEARSALS

From September until Carnaval, Samba schools host open gatherings once a week (usually on Friday or Saturday nights). In spite of the name, these are less a dress rehearsal than an excuse to dance (to samba, of course) and to celebrate. All are welcome. Things get decidedly livelier (with higher admission prices to match), the closer you get to Carnaval.

Festival Panorama de Dança

Spanning two weeks in November, the Festival Panorama (www.panoramafestival.com) showcases the work of dozens of contemporary dance groups from across the globe, bringing together a mix of experimental troupes as well as traditional performers.

December

While the northern hemisphere shivers, *cariocas* strip down to the bare essentials for hot days on the beach and steamy nights at samba parties around town.

Lighting of the Lagoa Christmas Tree

Throughout December the world's largest floating Christmas tree (85m) glows brightly on Lagoa Rodrigo de Freitas (p80). To celebrate its lighting, the city throws a concert in Parque Brigadeiro Faria Lima on the west side of the lake. It's usually held on the first Saturday in December.

Festa de Iemanjá

This December 31 Candomblé festival celebrates the feast day of Iemanjá, the goddess of the sea. Celebrants dress in white and place their petitions on small boats, sending them out to sea. If their petitions return, their prayers will not be answered.

Reveillon

The city's biggest holiday after Carnaval takes place on Copacabana Beach, when some two million people pack the sands to welcome in the New Year. Fireworks light up the sky as top musical groups perform on stages built on the sands.

With Kids

There are plenty of activities to keep kids amused in Rio: sandy fun on the beach; bike rides around Lagoa; aerial cable-car rides; boat trips and rainforest walks; and plenty of great treats – fresh juices, ice creams and pastries – along the way.

DANIELA FERRAZ/EYEEM/GETTY IMAGES ©

Ilha Fiscal (p127)

Sights

AquaRio

Get up close to a marvelous variety of marine life at this aquarium (p128), South America's largest.

Museu do Amanhã

Learn about evolution, sustainability and climate change and much more at this futuristic and interactive science museum (p128).

Ilha Fiscal

A Cinderella-esque castle (p127), reached by short boat ride.

The Bonde

Ride the little yellow streetcar (p138) up to Santa Teresa, and enjoy the views along the way.

Markets

You'll find fruit markets all across town; they're the perfect spot to assemble a picnic, while sampling delicacies you may not find back home.

Planetário

Astronomical fun and stargazing (p81).

Green Spaces

Jardim Botânico

These verdant gardens (p81) offer a fine break from the sun on a hot day. Explore a lily-filled pond, a playground, a cafe and shaded walking trails.

Parque Lage

About 1km northeast of the Jardim Botânico, Parque Lage (p81) has extensive walking trails, plus a playground, a small fish pond and a good outdoor cafe; it's also a great spot to see monkeys, so keep your eyes peeled.

Floresta da Tijuca

At this vast wilderness (p158) northwest of the Zona Sul you can take short or long hikes, enjoy picturesque views and take a dip in a waterfall.

Panoramas

Cristo Redentor

Most kids will get a huge kick out of the steep cog train that takes visitors through dense forest to the massive Christ the Redeemer statue (p114).

Pão de Açúcar

The journey by aerial gondola to the summit of Sugarloaf Mountain (p103) is probably the best part of the experience for kids; afterwards, you can walk to the small, pretty beach of Praia Vermelha.

The Beach

If traveling with younger kids, check out **Baixo Bebê Leblon**. The family-friendly beach area between *postos* (posts) 11 and 12 in Leblon has a netted-off play area with slides.

Older kids will find lots to see and do on the beach: football and volleyball games, boogie boarding and stand-up paddling, and sampling snacks from roaming food vendors.

The Lake

At **Parque dos Patins**, on the west side of Lagoa Rodrigo de Freitas, you can hire bikes, scooters, tricycles, toys and huge family-size pedal bikes for a spin along the lakeside path.

On the east side of the lake, at **Parque do Cantagalo**, you can hire pedal boats for a glide around the lake (in a swan boat, no less).

If you're around in December, pay a visit to the lake at night, when a giant floating Christmas tree lights up the lakeside.

Climbing Adventures

Near the east side of Lagoa Rodrigo de Freitas you'll find Parque da Catacumba (p82), which is a great spot for older kids. The outfit known as Lagoa Aventuras (p87) has a zipline, a rock-climbing wall, treetop walks and rappelling (abseiling). There are also short but steep hiking trails that take you to a lookout with pretty views over the lake.

NEED TO KNOW

Admission At most sights, kids under 13 years pay half-price; those under five or six typically get in for free.

Attitudes Brazilians are very family-oriented; you'll be welcomed with open arms at most restaurants. High chairs are readily available.

Accommodations Many hotels let children stay for free, although the age limit varies.

Boat Trips

Older kids might enjoy a boat ride out on the bay. For a full-day outing you can take the ferry to Ilha de Paquetá (p130). Once you're on the car-free island, you can get around by bicycle or horse-drawn carriage. There are also shorter cruises most days, as well as the ferry to Niterói, which offers great views of the bay.

Rio Snacks

Sorvete

Treat the kids to ice cream, especially from Vero (p62) or **Felice Caffè** (Map p228, F5; ☎21 2522-7749; Gomes Carneiro 30; mains R$38-73; ⏲noon-1am Mon-Fri, 10am-1am Sat & Sun; ❄📶).

Agua de Côco

Drink coconut water straight from the nut at beachside kiosks.

Pão de Queijo

This small, round, cheese-filled bread is available at any juice bar.

Pastel de Nata

Sample these tasty custard tarts at beautiful art deco Confeitaria Colombo (p130).

Sucos

Try creamy *açaí* and many other juice flavors.

For Free

Aside from lounging on the beach and strolling around historic parts of town, Rio has numerous fine ways to experience the city without spending a single centavo. You'll save by planning ahead, particularly when it comes to visiting museums on their free days.

ALEKSANDAR TODOROVIC/SHUTTERSTOCK ©

Palácio Tiradentes (p126)

Sights

Centro is a great place for bargain sightseeing. Top galleries that are always free include the Centro de Arte Hélio Oiticica (p125), the Centro Cultural Banco do Brasil (p127) and the Centro Cultural Justiça Federal (p124). Up in Santa Teresa, the Parque das Ruínas (p138) offers magnificent views over the city.

On Sundays several museums are free: the Museu Nacional de Belas Artes (p124) and the Museu Histórico Nacional (p123). Just north of Centro, two of Rio's blockbuster new museums are free on Tuesdays: the Museu de Arte do Rio (p127) and the Museu do Amanhã (p128).

Live Music

You can catch live samba and other Brazilian sounds throughout the week at free shows happening across town. A few good options include Pedra do Sal (p133) on Monday and Friday, Bip Bip (p99) Sunday through Friday, Vaca Atolada (p142) Tuesday through Saturday, and weekends at Galeria Bazá (p139). Santa Teresa's Favela Hype (p143) throws some of the best free live-music parties on Fridays, Saturdays and Sundays.

Walking Tours

There are several free walking tours around town, including a historical tour in Centro and a Copacabana and Ipanema tour offered by Free Walker Tours (p204).

For a dose of political history, take a free guided tour through the Palácio Tiradentes (p126).

Carnaval

If you haven't heard by now, Rio throws one of the world's best parties, with music and dancing filling the streets for days on end. Officially, Carnaval is just five days of revelry – from the Friday to the Tuesday before Ash Wednesday – but the city begins partying months in advance.

A.PAES/SHUTTERSTOCK ©

amba school parade (p31)

Experiencing Carnaval

The culmination of the big fest is the brilliantly colorful parade through the Oscar Niemeyer-designed Sambódromo (p152) arena, with giant mechanized floats, pounding drummers and whirling dancers. But there's lots of action in Rio's many neighborhoods for those seeking more than just the stadium experience.

Out-of-towners add to the mayhem, joining *cariocas* (residents of Rio) in the street parties and costumed balls that erupt throughout the city. There are free concerts to be found (in Largo do Machado, Arcos da Lapa and Praça General Osório, among other places), while those seeking a bit of decadence can head to the various balls.

Whatever you do, prepare yourself for sleepless nights, ample doses of caipirinhas (cocktails consisting of lime, sugar and rum) and samba, and plenty of mingling with the joyful crowds spilling out of the city.

Joining the *bandas* and *blocos* (street parties) is one of the best ways to have a *carioca* experience. These marching parades consist of a procession of brass bands (in the case of *bandas*) or drummers and vocalists (in the case of *blocos*), and are followed by anyone who wants to dance through the streets. Some *bandas* suggest costumes (such as drag, Amazonian attire etc), while others expect people simply to show up and add to the good cheer.

History

Although the exact origins of Carnaval are shrouded in mystery, some believe the festival originated as a pagan celebration of spring's arrival some time during the Middle Ages. The Portuguese brought the celebration to Brazil in the 1500s, but it took on a decidedly local flavor by adopting indigenous costumes and African rhythms. The origin of the word itself probably derives from the Latin *'carne vale'* – 'farewell, meat' – whereby the Catholic population would give up meat and other fleshly temptations during the 40 days of Lent.

The first festivals in Rio de Janeiro were called *entrudo,* during which locals danced through the streets in colorful costumes, throwing mud, flour and various

CP DC PRESS/SHUTTERSTOCK ©

Samba school float, Sambódromo (p152)

suspect liquids at one another. In the 19th century Carnaval meant attending a lavish masked ball or participating in the orderly and rather vapid European-style parade. Rio's poor citizens, bored by the finery but eager to participate in a celebration, began holding their own parades, dancing through the streets to African-based rhythms. Then, in the 1920s, the new sound of samba emerged in Rio. It was music full of African flavors, brought to the city by former slaves and their descendants – a sound that would forever more be associated with Carnaval.

Since those days Carnaval has grown in leaps and bounds, and its elaborate parades have spread from Rio de Janeiro to other parts of Brazil. It has also become a huge commercial enterprise: visitors to the city spend in excess of R$1 billion each year.

Carnaval on the Streets

Rio's street parties – the *bandas* and *blocos* – have exploded in recent years. Ten years ago there were only a handful of these events, but these days there are around 500 street parties, filling every neighborhood in town with the sound of pounding drums and old-fashioned Carnaval songs – not to mention thousands of merrymakers. For many *cariocas,* this is the highlight of Carnaval. You can don a costume (or not), learn a few songs and join in; all you have to do is show up. For Zona Sul fests, don't forget to bring your swimsuit for a dip in the ocean afterwards.

For complete listings, pick up a free *Carnaval de Rua* guide from **Riotur** (http://visit.rio) or check www.ipanema.com/carnival, which lists the times, dates and meeting spots of Rio's best *bandas*. The following are some of the better-known street parties, and each attracts anywhere from 1000 to hundreds of thousands. Although the dates are usually reliable, the times sometimes change, so it's wise to confirm before heading out.

AfroReggae (Av Atlântica, Copacabana; ⏲9am Carnaval Sun) A massive and hugely popular *bloco* with a heavy rhythm section that celebrates along the beachfront Av Atlântica near Rainha Elizabeth in Copacabana.

Banda de Ipanema (www.facebook.com/bandadeipanema; Praça General Osório, Ipanema; ⏲4pm 2nd Sat before Carnaval, Carnaval Sat & Carnaval Tue) This long-standing *banda* attracts a wild crowd, complete with drag queens and others in costume. Don't miss it.

Banda Simpatia é Quase Amor (www.facebook.com/bloco.simpataquaseamor; Praça General Osório, Ipanema; ⏲4pm Sat before Carnaval & Carnaval Sun) Another Ipanema favorite, with a 50-piece percussion band.

Barbas (www.facebook.com/blocodobarbas oficial; cnr Assis Bueno & Arnaldo Quintela, Botafogo; ⏲3:30pm Carnaval Sat) One of the oldest *bandas* of the Zona Sul parades through the streets with a 60-piece percussion band. A water truck decked out in red and white follows along to spray the crowd.

Carmelitas (cnr Dias de Barros & Ladeira de Santa Teresa, Santa Teresa; ⏲1pm Carnaval Fri & 8am Carnaval Tue) A crazy mixed crowd (some dressed as Carmelite nuns) parades through Santa Teresa's streets.

Céu na Terra (www.facebook.com/ceunaterra carnaval; Curvelo, Santa Teresa; ⏲8am Carnaval Sat) Follows the tram tracks on a memorable celebration through Santa Teresa en route to Largo das Neves.

Cordão do Bola Preta (www.facebook.com/cordaodabolapreta; Primeiro de Março, Centro;

⏲9am Carnaval Sat) The oldest and biggest *banda* still in action. Costumes are always welcome, especially those with black-and-white spots. More than two million join the festivities.

Dois Pra Lá, Dois Pra Cá (www.facebook.com/blococarnavalescodoispraladoispraca; Carlinhos de Jesus Dance School, Rua da Passagem 145, Botafogo; ⏲10am Carnaval Sat) This fairly long march begins at Carlinhos de Jesus Dance School and ends at the Copacabana Palace.

Monobloco (www.facebook.com/monobloco oficial; Av Rio Branco, Centro; ⏲7am 1st Sun after Carnaval) Rise and shine! This huge *bloco* attracts upwards of 400,000 revelers. Nursing hangovers (or perhaps still inebriated), they gather in Centro for a final farewell to the Carnaval mayhem.

Que Merda É Essa? (Garcia d'Ávila, Ipanema; ⏲1pm Carnaval Sun) This playful gathering (which means 'What the shit is this?') is yet another big draw in Ipanema. Beginning near Nascimento da Silva, it eventually makes its way along the beach.

Suvaco de Cristo (Rua Jardim Botânico, Jardim Botânico; ⏲9am Sun before Carnaval) Very popular *bloco* whose name means 'Christ's armpit,' in reference to the open-armed Redeemer looming overhead. It also meets on Carnaval Saturday but doesn't announce the time (to avoid overcrowding), so ask around.

Carnaval Balls

Carnaval balls are giant, sometimes costumed, parties with live music and dancing, and an ambience that runs the gamut from staid and formal to wild and a bit tawdry. The most famous and formal ball (there's a black-tie dress code) is held at the Copacabana Palace (p167), where you'll have the opportunity to celebrate with Rio's glitterati as well as international stars. Tickets cost upwards of R$1600.

Popular but less pricey (under R$150) balls and themed parties are held at Rio Scenarium (p143), the Jockey Club (p86) and at Circo Voador (p144), among other venues. These are good places to don a costume to help get in the mood.

Tickets go on sale about two weeks before, and balls are held nightly during Carnaval. The 'Veja Rio' insert in *Veja* magazine has details.

Samba School Parades

The highlight of any Carnaval experience is attending (or participating in) a parade at the Sambódromo (p152). There, before a crowd of some 90,000 (with millions more watching on TV), each of 12 samba schools has its 80 minutes to dance and sing through the open Oscar Niemeyer–designed stadium. The pageantry is not simply eye candy for the masses. Schools are competing for top honors in the parade, with winners announced (and a winners' parade held) on the Saturday following Carnaval.

The Big Event

Here's what to expect: each school enters the Sambódromo with amped energy levels, and dancers take things up a notch as they move through the stadium. Announcers introduce the school, the group's theme colors and the number of *alas* (literally, wings – subgroups within a school, each playing a different role). Far away the lone voice of the *puxador* (interpreter) starts the samba. Thousands more voices join him (each school has 3000 to 5000 members), and then the drummers kick in: 200 to 400 per school. The pounding

NEED TO KNOW

Carnival Dates 2020–22

Carnaval 2020 February 21–25

Carnaval 2021 February 12–16

Carnaval 2022 February 25–March 1

Resources

Riotur (Map p236; ☎21 2541-7522; Av Princesa Isabel 183; ⏲9am-6pm Mon-Fri) The tourist organization in charge of Carnaval.

LIESA (Map p246; ☎21 3213-5151; http://liesa.globo.com; Av Rio Branco 4, Centro; ⏲10am-4pm Mon-Fri Sep-Carnaval) For information on buying tickets to the big parades in the Sambódromo.

Ipanema.com (ipanema.com/carnival) For dates and times of street parades.

drums drive the parade. Next come the main wings of the school, the big allegorical floats, the children's wing, the drummers, the celebrities, and the bell-shaped *baianas* (women dressed as Bahian aunts) twirling in elegant hoop skirts. The *baianas* honor the history of the parade itself, which was brought to Rio from Salvador da Bahia in 1877. Costumes are fabulously lavish, with 1.5m feathered headdresses; long, flowing capes that sparkle with sequins; and rhinestone-studded G-strings.

Crowning a Winner

The whole procession is an elaborate competition. A handpicked set of judges chooses the best school on the basis of many components, including percussion; the *samba do enredo* (theme song); harmony between percussion, song and dance; and choreography, costumes, story line, floats and decorations. The dance championship is hotly contested, with the winner becoming the pride not just of Rio but of all Brazil.

Watching the Parade

Most visitors stay for three or four schools, and come to see their favorite in action (every self-respecting *carioca* has a school they support, just as they have a favorite football team). If you're really gung-ho, wear your school's colors and learn the theme song (the words are found on the website of each school), so you can sing along when it marches through the Sambódromo. Mangueira (pink and green) and Salgueiro (red and white) are two of the most popular schools.

Parade Nights

The Sambódromo parades start with the *mirins* (young samba-school members) on the evening of Carnaval Friday, and continue on through Saturday night, when the Group A samba schools strut their stuff. Sunday and Monday are the big nights, when the 12 best samba schools in Rio (the Grupo Especial) parade: six of them on Sunday night and into the morning, and six more on Monday night. The following Saturday, the six top schools strut their stuff again in the Parade of Champions, which generally has more affordable tickets than the big nights do. Each event starts at 9pm and runs until 4am.

Tickets

Getting tickets for the parades at legitimate prices can be tough, even for locals. LIESA (p31), the official samba school league, begins selling tickets in December or January, most of which are immediately snatched up by travel agencies and then later resold at higher prices. Check with **Riotur** (www.visit.rio) about where you can get tickets, as the official outlet can vary from year to year.

Prices At face value, tickets run from R$150 to R$500, though you'll probably have to pay about twice that (or more) if you buy just before Carnaval.

Where to sit The best seating areas, in order of preference, are sectors 9, 7, 11, 5 and 3. The first two (9 and 7) have great views and are in the center, which is the liveliest place to be.

Last-minute options By Carnaval weekend, most tickets will have sold out, but there are lots of scalpers. If you buy a ticket from a scalper (no need to worry about looking for them – they'll find you!), make sure you get both the plastic ticket with the magnetic strip and the ticket showing the seat number. The tickets for different days are color coded, so double-check the date as well.

If you haven't purchased a ticket but still want to go, you can show up at the Sambódromo during Carnaval at around midnight, three or four hours into the show, when you can get grandstand tickets for about R$50 from scalpers outside the gate. Make sure you check which sector your ticket is for. Most ticket sellers will try to sell their worst seats.

And if you can't make it during Carnaval proper, there's always the cheaper Parade of Champions the following Saturday.

Getting to the Sambódromo

The best way to get to the Sambódromo is by metro; several stations are within walking distance of the arena. The metro runs

A PAES/SHUTTERSTOCK ©

Samba school dancer, Sambódromo (p152)

around the clock during Carnaval, from Saturday morning until Tuesday evening. This is also a great opportunity to check out the paraders commuting in costume.

If you take the metro, the stop at which you get off depends on the location of your seats. For sectors 2, 4 and 6, exit at Praça Onze. Once outside the station, turn to the right, take another right and then walk straight ahead on Júlio Carmo to sector 2. For sectors 4 and 6, turn right at Carmo Neto and proceed to Av Salvador de Sá. You'll soon see the Sambódromo and hear the roar of the crowd. Look for signs showing the entrance to the sectors. If you are going to sectors on the other side (1, 3, 5, 7, 9, 11 and 13), exit at metro stop Central. You'll then walk about 700m along Av Presidente Vargas until you see the Sambódromo.

If you go by taxi, make sure you tell your driver which side of the stadium your seats are on.

Joining a Samba School

Those who have done it say no other part of Carnaval quite compares to donning a costume and dancing through the Sambódromo before roaring crowds. Anyone with the desire and a little extra money to spare can march in the parade. Most samba schools are happy to have foreigners join one of the wings. To get the ball rolling, you'll need to contact your chosen school in advance; it will tell you the rehearsal times and when you need to be in the city (usually it's a week or so before Carnaval). Ideally, you should memorize the theme song as well, but it's not essential (you can always lip sync). The biggest investment, aside from the airfare to Rio, is buying a *fantasia* (costume), which will cost upwards of R$600. If you speak some Portuguese, you can contact a school directly; many Rio travel agencies can also arrange this.

Those seeking an insider's perspective on samba schools should read Alma Guillermoprieto's excellent book, *Samba*.

Rio Folia

Lapa becomes one of the city's major focal points during Carnaval. Rio Folia consists of open-air concerts held in front of the Arcos da Lapa on the Praça Cardeal Câmara. About half a dozen bands play each night (samba, of course). The music starts at 10pm and runs until after 2am, though revelers pack Lapa until well past sunrise.

Samba Land & Samba City

Another festive space for concerts is the Terreirão do Samba (Samba Land), an open-air courtyard next to the Sambódromo's sector 1, where bands play to large crowds throughout Carnaval (beginning the weekend before). There are also dozens of food and drink vendors. The action starts around 8pm and continues until 5:30am. Admission is R$15.

For a behind-the-scenes look at Carnaval, plan a visit to **Cidade do Samba** (Samba City; Map p253, E1; ☎21 2213-2503; http://cidadedosambarj.globo.com; Rivadávia Correa 60, Gamboa). Located north of Centro near the port, the 'samba city' is actually made up of 14 large buildings in which the top schools assemble the Carnaval floats.

Visitors can take a tour through the area or attend a live show, which features costumed dancers, live music and audience participation, and comes with free drinks

CP DC PRESS/SHUTTERSTOCK ©

Salgueiro (p154) samba-school parade

and appetizers. It's touristy and pricey, but some visitors enjoy the Carnaval-style show nonetheless. Confirm times and prices with Cidade do Samba, or check with Riotur.

Samba Glossary for Parade-Goers

Alas Literally the 'wings.' These are groups of samba-school members responsible for a specific part of the central *samba do enredo* (theme song). Special *alas* include the *baianas* (women dressed as Bahian aunts in full skirts and turbans). The *abre ala* of each school is the opening wing or float.

Bateria The drum section is the driving beat behind the school's samba and is the 'soul' of the school.

Carnavalesco The artistic director of each school, responsible for the overall layout and design of the school's theme.

Carros alegóricos The dazzling floats, usually decorated with near-naked women. The floats are pushed along by the school's maintenance crew.

Desfile The parade. The most important samba schools *desfilar* (parade) on the Sunday and Monday night of Carnaval. Each school's *desfile* is judged on its samba, drum section, master of ceremonies and flag bearer, floats, leading commission, costumes, dance coordination and overall harmony.

Destaques The richest and most elaborate costumes. The heaviest ones usually get a spot on one of the floats.

Diretores de harmonia The school organizers, who usually wear white or the school colors; they run around yelling and 'pumping up' the wings, making sure there aren't any gaps in the parade.

Enredo The central theme of each school. The *samba do enredo* is the samba that goes with it. Radio stations and dance halls prime *cariocas* with classic *enredos* in the weeks leading up to Carnaval.

Passistas The best samba dancers of a school. They roam the parade in groups or alone, stopping to show off some fancy footwork along the way. The women are usually dressed in short, revealing skirts, and the men usually hold tambourines.

Puxador The interpreter of the theme song. He (a *puxador* is invariably male) works as a guiding voice, leading the school's singers at rehearsals and in the parade.

LAZYLLAMA/SHUTTERSTOCK ©

Açaí (berry-like fruit prized for its nutritional value and addictive taste) with strawberries

Eating

Despite top-notch chefs, ethnically diverse cuisine and a rich bounty from farm, forest and sea, Rio hasn't earned much of a culinary reputation abroad. Within Brazil, however, it's a different story, with cariocas (residents of Rio) convinced that there's no place quite like home for sitting down to a first-rate meal.

The Dining Scene

Variety comes in many forms in Rio, which is unsurprising given the large immigrant population. Lebanese, Japanese, Spanish, German, French and Italian cuisines are among the standouts, though there's an equally broad selection of regional Brazilian restaurants.

Diners can sample rich, shrimp-filled *moqueca* (seafood stew cooked in coconut milk) from Bahia or tender *carne seca* (jerked meat) covered in *farofa* (manioc flour), a staple in Minas Gerais. Daring palates can venture north into Amazonia, enjoying savory *tacacá* (manioc paste, lip-numbing leaves of the vegetable *jambú* and dried shrimp) or *tambaqui* (a large Amazonian fish) and other meaty fishes from the mighty Amazon. Cowboys and the *gaúcho* from the south bring the city its *churrascarias,* Brazil's famous all-you-can-eat barbecue restaurants, where crisply dressed waiters bring piping-hot spits of freshly roasted meats to your table.

Wherever you end up, try to pace yourself. Brazilian dishes are normally quite large – and some dishes are meant for two. When in doubt, ask the server to clarify.

Juice Bars

Most *cariocas* start their morning with a stop at the local juice bar, where they can enjoy

NEED TO KNOW

Price Ranges

The following price ranges refer to the cost of a main course.

$ less than R$30

$$ R$30–75

$$$ more than R$75

Opening Hours

Most restaurants open from noon to 3pm and 6pm to 11pm. On Sunday many restaurants open only for lunch, if at all. Juice bars open around 7am or 8am and close at midnight or later.

Tipping

A 10% tip is usually included in restaurant bills. When it isn't included, it's customary to leave 10%. Some higher-end restaurants recommend a 13% gratuity.

Reservations

Most restaurants accept reservations for both lunch and dinner, so call ahead to avoid a wait. Reservations are essential at high-end restaurants, and the answering host will usually speak English.

Lunch Specials

Some restaurants serve multicourse lunch specials, which often provide decent value for money. Prices hover around R$35 but can be upwards of R$60 for more elaborate offerings.

Dress Code

Cariocas (residents of Rio) are quite casual when it comes to dress, and dining out is no exception. Even at the nicest places, a pair of smart jeans and a collared shirt or blouse will do just fine.

Etiquette

Brazilians can be fastidious when it comes to eating. Use a knife and fork when eating pizza. In fact, never touch your food with bare hands: always use a napkin when eating sandwiches, bar snacks etc.

two or three dozen varieties of vitamin-filled elixir, including the very popular *açaí* (healthful juice made from an Amazonian berry and whipped to a thick consistency – it's eaten with a spoon).

Other unique flavors to try include *cupuaçu* (Amazonian fruit), *caju* (fruit from the cashew-nut tree), *acerola* (tropical cherry), *carambola* (star fruit), *graviola* (custard apple), *fruta do conde* (sugar apple) and *cacau* (made from the creamy pulp of the cocoa pod; nothing like cocoa). More traditional fruits include *maracujá* (passion fruit), *manga* (mango), *goiaba* (guava) and *tomate de árbol* (tamarillo).

Juices are made from frozen pulp, with sugar added. To order yours without sugar, request *'sem açúcar.'*

Juice bars also serve snacks (on display in the counters), hot sandwiches such as *misto quente* (ham and cheese) and other quickly prepared bites.

Per-Kilo Restaurants

At lunchtime, locals favor pay-by-weight restaurants, which range from simple, working-class affairs to sumptuous buffets lined with fresh salads, grilled meats, pastas, seafood dishes and copious desserts. These are found all across the city, and are a great way to sample a wide variety of Brazilian dishes.

Most places charge around R$60 to R$100 per kilogram, with a sizable plate of food costing about R$40 to R$60.

Snacks

Snack stands, juice bars and *botecos* (small open-air bars) serve a wide variety of delicious, if utterly unhealthy, *salgados* (snacks). After a day at the beach they go quite nicely with a few rounds of *chope* (draft beer). A few top picks:

Pão de queijo Bite-size cheese-filled rolls.

Esfiha Triangular pastry filled with meat and spices, spinach or other fillings.

Kibe Deep-fried Middle Eastern snack with a thin whole-wheat crust and a filling of ground beef and spices.

Bolinho de bacalhau Deep-fried codfish balls.

Coxinha Pear-shaped cornmeal balls filled with shredded chicken.

Pastel de carne/camarão/queijo Square of deep-fried dough filled with meat, shrimp or cheese.

Tapioca A crepe made from manioc flour, filled with chicken, cheese, fruit preserves and more. Found primarily at food markets.

Food Markets

The *feiras* (produce markets) that pop up in different locations throughout the week are the best places to shop for juicy mangoes, papayas, pineapples and other fruits. For an authentic slice of homegrown *carioca* commerce, nothing beats wandering through a market and taking in the action. The best time to go is from 9am to noon; the *feiras* end by 2pm or 3pm.

You can also stop in at Ipanema's Hippie Fair (p73) on Sunday for delectable Bahian fare.

Cobal do Humaitá (Map p244; Voluntários da Pátria 446, Botafogo; ⏲8am-10pm), the city's largest farmers market, sells plenty of veggies and fruit; it also has cafes and restaurants, and a huge open-air pavilion for alfresco dining.

Cobal do Leblon (Map p232; ☎21 2529-2222; Gilberto Cardoso; ⏲6pm-1am Tue-Sun) has fruit stalls, as well as indoor-outdoor restaurants and bars.

Copacabana Markets are held Wednesday on Praça Edmundo Bittencourt, Thursday on Ministro Viveiros de Castro and Ronald de Carvalho, Saturday on General Azevedo Pimentel and Sunday on Praça Serzedelo Correia.

Gávea Friday market on Praça Santos Dumont.

Glória Sunday market on Av Augusto Severo.

Ipanema Markets are held Monday on Henrique Dumont, Tuesday on Praça General Osório and Friday on Praça NS da Paz.

Jardim Botânico Saturday market on Frei Leandro.

Leblon Thursday market on General Urquiza.

Leme Monday market on Gustavo Sampaio.

Santa Teresa Friday market on Felicio dos Santos.

Urca Sunday market on Praça Tenente Gil Guilherme.

Feijoada

As distinctively *carioca* as Pão de Açúcar (Sugarloaf Mountain) or Cristo Redentor (Christ the Redeemer), the *feijoada completa* is a dish that constitutes an entire meal, and often begins with a caipirinha aperitif.

A properly prepared *feijoada* consists of black beans slowly cooked with a great variety of meat – including dried tongue and pork offcuts – seasoned with salt, garlic, onion and oil. The stew is accompanied by white rice and finely shredded kale, then tossed with croutons, fried *farofa* (manioc flour) and pieces of orange.

Feijoada has its origins in Portuguese cuisine, which uses a large variety of meats and vegetables; fried *farofa* (an ingredient in indigenous dishes) and kale are also Portuguese favorites. The African influence comes with the spice and the tradition of using pork offcuts, which were the only part of the pig given to slaves.

Traditionally, *cariocas* eat *feijoada* for lunch on Saturday, though a few restaurants serve it on other days. Among the top places to sample the signature dish is Casa da Feijoada (p65), which is one of the few places in Rio that serve *feijoada* daily. Vegetarians can sample tasty meat-free versions of *feijoada* at Vegetariano Social Club (p66).

Eating by Neighborhood

Ipanema & Leblon (p62) Best assortment of dining from inexpensive juice bars and per-kilo places to award-winning restaurants.

Gávea, Jardim Botânico & Lagoa (p83) Charming upscale neighborhood options, plus dining with views at open-air lakeside kiosks.

Copacabana & Leme (p93) Humble rotisseries, ethnic fare and beachfront kiosks, plus delights tucked away on side streets.

Botafogo, Humaitá & Urca (p104) Creative, high-end eateries along Conde de Irajá; casual open-air options along Nelson Mandela.

Flamengo & Around (p117) Small selection of midrange and down-market options, and a few well-concealed surprises (Lebanese, Japanese and Rio's best pizzas).

Centro & Praça Mauá (p130) Atmospheric lunch options on cobblestone streets near Praça XV, but few dinner options.

Santa Teresa & Lapa (p139) Small but enticing collection of eateries, with the densest concentration around Largo do Guimarães.

Lonely Planet's Top Choices

Giuseppe Grill (p68) Meals are always memorable at this Leblon icon.

Zazá Bistrô Tropical (p65) Handsomely converted Ipanema mansion with contemporary Asian-inspired fare.

Aprazível (p140) In a beautiful Santa Teresa setting with magical views over the city.

Oteque (p106) Haute cuisine in an atmospheric spot in Botafogo.

Ferro e Farinha (p118) Wonderful pizza in an atmospheric but hard-to-find space in Catete.

Espírito Santa (p140) Superb Amazonian dishes and creative cocktails in Santa Teresa.

Best by Budget

$

Talho Capixaba (p68) Delectable sandwiches and antipasti.

Slow Bakery (p104) The best bakery (and pastries) in Rio.

Vezpa (p66) Satisfying, creatively topped pizza served by the slice.

$$

TT Burger (p96) Outstanding burgers a short stroll from the beach.

Mironga (p132) Stylish and good-value lunch spot in Centro.

Frontera (p64) Excellent per-kilo joint in Rio, with a huge variety of dishes.

$$$

Churrascaria Palace (p96) Rio's best all-you-can-eat joint, with sizzling cuts of meat in an elegant setting.

Olympe (p85) An imaginative fusion of Brazilian and French cooking.

Térèze (p140) French decadence at the plush Hotel Santa Teresa.

Zuka (p68) Brilliantly executed dishes on Leblon's main eat street.

CT Boucherie (p69) Juicy grilled dishes and limitless servings of creative sides.

Best for Seafood

La Carioca Cevicheria (p85) Mouthwatering ceviche and other Peruvian fare.

Laguna Restaurante (p158) Seafood in a lush island setting reached by boat.

Sushi Leblon (p69) Famous for its inventive dishes and delectable sashimi.

Best for Views

Xian (p130) Asian jewel with mesmerizing views over the bay.

Espaço 7zero6 (p65) Top-floor restaurant overlooking Ipanema Beach, with amazing brunches.

Bar Urca (p107) Sit on the sea wall, nibble great snacks and admire the view.

Best for Atmosphere

Plage Café (p83) Outdoor dining in an elegant courtyard with views of Corcovado.

Bar do Mineiro (p140) An old-fashioned favorite for traditional Brazilian cooking and lively ambience.

Cais do Oriente (p131) Delicious fare in a stylish 19th-century setting.

Formidable (p69) A classy bistro that evokes a bit of old Paris.

Best for Vegetarians

Prana Vegetariano (p83) The best vegetarian cooking (and juices) in town.

Govardhana Harí (p130) Beautifully prepared vegetarian dishes served by Hare Krishnas.

Galeria Bazá (p139) Creative vegetarian eatery, shop and cultural spot.

Vegetariano Social Club (p66) A small, elegant favorite.

Best for Snacks

Sírio Libaneza (p118) Rio's best Middle Eastern snacks.

Tacacá do Norte (p117) Lunch counter with mind-blowing *tacacá* (an Amazonian soup).

Bibi Sucos (p73) Sandwiches and snacks, and a huge variety of Brazilian juices.

Vero (p62) Creamy, rich gelato in Ipanema.

Best for Sharing Plates

Venga! (p63) Buzzing atmosphere and satisfying tapas.

El Born (p94) Great tapas and beer that pay homage to Barcelona.

Casa Momus (p141) Delicious Mediterranean fare in a picturesque Lapa setting.

Meza Bar (p106) A trendy spot in Rio's most food-centric neighborhood.

Stuzzi (p67) Italian *stuzzichini* (sharing plates), great wine and a festive atmosphere.

Drinking & Nightlife

Any night of the week you'll find plenty of ways to experience Rio's electrifying nightlife: open-air bars by the lake; festive outdoor drinking spots on the colonial streets of Centro; beachfront kiosks; stylish lounges and nightclubs; and warm and welcoming botecos (small open-air bars) that are scattered all across the city.

The Scene

As in most places in the world, there are a few different subcultures (models and modelizers, surfers, hipsters and hippies) within the nightlife circuit, though there's plenty of crossover between groups. The well-heeled crowd from the Zona Sul tends to favor high-end bars in Gávea and Barra, while an alternative crowd heads to the drinking dens in Botafogo. Lapa's mix of bars and dance halls attracts a range of people from all backgrounds, who may have little in common aside from a love of samba.

Venues come and go – and the best parties are often one-off events in unique spots – so it helps if you can get the latest from a local source. If you can read a bit of Portuguese, pick up the 'Veja Rio' insert in *Veja* magazine, which comes out each Sunday. 'Rio Show,' the entertainment insert that comes in the Friday edition of *O Globo,* also has extensive listings.

Botecos & Brewhouses

For an insight into Rio's drinking culture, familiarize yourself with one of the great sociocultural icons of the city: the *boteco.* These casual, open-sided bars are found all over town, and draw in a broad cross-section of society. Young and old, upper class and working class, men and women, black and white mix over ice-cold *chope* (draft beer) or caipirinhas (cocktails made from lime, sugar and sugarcane alcohol), flirting and swapping the latest gossip as bow-tied waiters move deftly among the crowd.

Just as most *cariocas* (Rio residents) have a favorite team, nearly every local has a favorite *boteco.* These range from hole-in-the-wall joints where canned beer is handed out to drinkers slouched over plastic tables to classic, wood-paneled bar rooms with murals on the walls, expertly mixed drinks and a history dating back several generations. Wherever you go in the city, you'll find that food is an important part of the experience, as *cariocas* rate bars not just on the drinks and the vibe but on the menu as well.

Lately the beer scene has improved immensely thanks to the rise of the craft-brewing industry across Brazil. New bars featuring top microbrews from within the state and beyond have opened all across Rio, and *cariocas* are discovering their inner beer nerd.

Nightclubs

Rio has some great places to shake your *bunda* (booty). DJs pull from the latest house, drum and bass and hip-hop favorites, as well as uniquely Brazilian combinations such as electro-samba and bossa-jazz. In addition to local DJs, Rio attracts a handful of vinyl gurus from São Paulo, New York and London to spin at bigger affairs. Flyers advertising dance parties can be found in boutiques in Ipanema and Leblon, and in the surf shops in Galeria River (p100) by Praia Arpoador. You'll save money by getting on the guest list – this usually means adding your name to the club's event-listing page on Facebook.

NEED TO KNOW

Opening Hours

Bars From 6pm to 2am Monday to Friday, from noon on Saturday and Sunday. Most places stay open later (typically till 4am) on Friday and Saturday nights.

Nightclubs From 11pm to 5am Thursday to Saturday.

Prices

Drinks A draft beer costs R$8 to R$12; cocktails cost R$15 to R$25, up to R$40 at pricier lounges. Most bars tack on a 10% service charge.

Club admission Fridays and Saturdays are the most expensive nights, with admission averaging around R$50. Women sometimes pay less than men.

Club Entry

➡ The dress code at clubs isn't strict in Rio. Neat shorts and sneakers are fine, though flip-flops and swimsuits are no-nos.

➡ Groups of single men will have a harder time getting in. Try to join up with a few women.

➡ Go before midnight to beat the crowds.

CONSUMPTION CARD

At many clubs in Rio you'll receive a control card when you enter. Rather than paying for individual drinks, your card will be marked each time you order. At the end of the night, you'll head to the cashier and pay for your food and drinks, plus the admission charge. Don't lose the card, as you'll be hit with a hefty fee (upwards of R$200).

LGBT+ Rio

Rio has been a major destination for gay travelers since the 1950s. Back then the action was near the Copacabana Palace, which is still popular with a slightly older crowd (look for the rainbow-hued flag). Today, however, the party has mostly moved on, with the focal point of the LGBT scene, especially for visitors, being in Ipanema. The gay beach at the end of Rua Farme de Amoedo (again, look for the rainbow flag) is the stomping ground of some of Rio's buffest men, sometimes known as 'barbies' in *carioca* slang. The bars and cafes of nearby streets – Rua Teixeira de Melo and Rua Farme – attract a mixed crowd and are a good spot to explore if you're not quite ready to jump into the beach scene.

Rio also hosts an enormously popular Gay Pride festival. For more info on the gay scene in Rio, including recommendations on nightclubs, bars, cafes and guesthouses, visit **Rio Gay Guide** (www.riogayguide.com).

Drinking & Nightlife by Neighborhood

Ipanema & Leblon (p69) Lots of *botecos*, a handful of lounges and nightclubs.

Gávea, Jardim Botânico & Lagoa (p85) Romantic lakeside drinking spots popular with couples.

Copacabana & Leme (p97) Beach kiosks, *botecos*, nightclubs and bars with views in the favela above Leme.

Botafogo, Humaitá & Urca (p107) Several popular spots in Urca; great *botecos* and creative bars and drinking dens in Botafogo.

Centro & Praça Mauá (p132) Atmospheric after-work drinking spots on pedestrianized streets in Centro.

Santa Teresa & Lapa (p141) Old-fashioned bars and bohemian haunts in Santa Teresa; riotous street parties and samba clubs in Lapa.

Lonely Planet's Top Choices

Explorer Bar (p142) Imaginative cocktails in a beautiful Santa Teresa setting.

Palaphita Kitch (p86) Amazonian-tinged cocktails and serene lakeside views.

Canastra (p69) A friendly French-run neighborhood bar with great food and drinks.

Bar dos Descasados (p142) Romantic outdoor lounge with hilltop views.

Comuna (p107) Creative gathering space for art, music and microbrews.

WineHouse (p107) Rio's most atmospheric wine bar.

Best Socializing

Antônio's (p143) A fine spot for taking in the Lapa street scene.

Jobi (p72) Tiny, much-loved watering hole in Leblon open very late.

Champanharia Ovelha Negra (p108) A festive meeting spot for champagne-lovers.

Ponto da Bossa Nova (p98) A mainstay of Baixo Copa's outdoor drinking scene.

Hipódromo (p85) Outdoor drinking fest that happens most nights in Gávea.

Best Dancing

Palaphita Gávea (p203) A fun, wildly decorated space, with an adjoining dance club that opens weekends.

Fosfobox (p99) Long-running downstairs dance club in Copacabana.

Barzin (p203) The go-to spot for big nights out, especially on Tuesday.

Bar Bukowski (p108) A party house in Botafogo with a dance floor, an upstairs stage and a games room.

Leviano Bar (p143) Outdoor tables on Lapa's wildest street and dancing upstairs.

Best Botecos

Pavão Azul (p98) Cold beer and great snacks always draw a festive crowd.

Boteco Belmonte (p98) A tranquil beachfront bar in Leme.

Bar do Gomes (p142) Old-fashioned neighborhood charmer in Santa Teresa.

Best Beer Selection

Brewteco (p72) A masculine beer-lovers' gathering spot in Leblon.

Hocus Pocus (p107) Top brews from a much-loved Rio-based microbrewer.

Booze Bar (p142) Sip your way through local craft beers in the heart of Lapa.

As Melhores Cervejas do Mundo (p98) A friendly place for beer nerds of all stripes.

Escondido (p98) A casual place to start the night, with good microbrews on tap.

Delirium Cafe (p71) Great global selections for beer lovers in Ipanema.

Best LGBT+ Clubs & Bars

Week (p133) One of the best Saturday-night party spots in Rio.

Buraco da Lacraia (p143) A trashy good time for adventure seekers in Lapa.

Tô Nem Aí (p71) Buzzing bar on Ipanema's most gay-friendly street.

TV Bar (p99) A good-time crowd against a backdrop of TV screens and DJs.

Galeria Café (p71) A staple of the Ipanema scene.

Best Atmosphere

Bar Léo (p132) Raise a glass over the cobblestones of Rio's oldest neighborhood.

Baretto-Londra (p70) Very swanky party space inside Ipanema's Hotel Fasano.

Bar do Zé (p119) Atmospheric and well-hidden bar tucked away in Glória.

Bar Astor (p70) Luscious cocktails and a great location across from Ipanema Beach.

Bar Urca (p108) Drinking in the open air with views over the bay.

Entertainment

Rio has a celebrated music scene, with enchanting settings in which to catch live performances, from cutting-edge concert halls to intimate neighborhood venues. Dance, theater, classical concerts and opera also have their small but loyal local followings, while cinema is an even bigger deal – Rio is one of the leading film centers in Latin America.

Live Music

In addition to samba, Rio is a showcase for jazz, bossa nova, Música Popular Brasileira (MPB), rock, hip-hop and fusions of these styles. Brazil's many regional styles – *forró* (traditional Brazilian music from the Northeast), *chorinho* (romantic, intimate samba) and *pagode* (relaxed and rhythmic samba) – are also a part of the music scene.

Venues range from modern concert halls seating thousands to intimate samba clubs in edgy neighborhoods. Antiquated colonial mansions, parks overlooking the city, old-school bars, crumbling buildings at the edge of town and hypermodern lounges facing the ocean are all part of the mix. Rio has a few large concert halls that attract Brazilian stars such as Gilberto Gil and Milton Nascimento, and well-known international bands visiting Rio on world tours.

Major music festivals include the Rio Music Conference (www.riomusicconference.com.br), held in the Marina da Glória. In addition to established venues, during the summer months concerts sometimes take place on the beaches of Copacabana, Botafogo, Ipanema and Barra da Tijuca.

Dance

Rio has produced a number of successful dance troupes, including the contemporary Companhia de Dança Deborah Colker, which spends much of its time touring abroad. One homegrown talent you might catch in town is the Cia de Dança Dani Lima, an avant-garde troupe that weaves provocative pieces together through dance and aerial gymnastics. Also keep an eye out for the Lapa-based Intrépida Trupe, whose talented acrobat-dancers bring surreal works to the stage.

There is no space dedicated solely to dance; performances can take place at many venues around the city.

Rio's biggest dance festival, Festival Panorama de Dança (www.panoramafestival.com), is held in November. For classical dance, try to see a production by the Ballet do Theatro Municipal, which puts on highly professional performances at Rio's most venerable theater.

Theater

Brazil has a long history of theater. Literary greats from the 19th century, including the highly imaginative *carioca* (Rio resident) Joaquim Machado de Assis, lent their vision to the stage. Talents from the 20th century, such as the great Nelson Rodrigues and more recently Gerald Thomas, have kept the flame alive, and you may be able to catch some of their work in Rio's theaters. There are more than two dozen venues in town. Unfortunately, if you don't speak Portuguese, you won't get a lot out of an evening at the theater.

Classical Music

Rio has several symphony orchestras, and irregular appearances are made by chamber groups and soloists. The best new venue is Barra da Tijuca's excellent Cidade das Artes (p159), where the Brazilian Symphony Orchestra plays. Other first-rate places to catch a performance include the Sala

Cecília Meireles (p144), which has excellent acoustics, and the magnificent Theatro Municipal (p133). You might also attend a performance at the Centro Cultural Banco do Brasil (p127) or the Fundação Eva Klabin (p82), both of which host orchestral works periodically.

The biggest classical-music festival is **Música no Museu** (Music in the Museum; www.musicanomuseu.com.br; ⏲Jan-Sep), held in museums, churches and cultural centers around town.

MUSIC IN THE MUSEUM

Classical-music lovers should try to attend a concert held during the ongoing Música No Museu (p43). Held annually over a number of months, this event features dozens of free concerts each month at museums and cultural spaces around the city, including the Museu de Arte Moderna (p124), Museu da República (p116), Centro Cultural Banco do Brasil (p127) and Parque das Ruínas (p138). Most concerts are held during the day (typically starting some time between noon and 3pm), making them an alternative to the beach if you need a break. Visit the website or pick up a brochure from any tourist office for the current schedule.

Cinema

There's plenty of variety at Rio's many cinemas. The market here is remarkably open to foreign and independent films, documentaries and avant-garde cinema. The latest American blockbusters get ample airtime at movie megaplexes, while cultural centers, museums and old one-screen theaters offer a more diverse repertoire. Films are shown in the original language with Portuguese subtitles. At weekends, popular shows often sell out, so buy your ticket early. Prices range from R$20 to R$34 per ticket, with cheaper matinee prices from Monday to Thursday and the highest prices (and longest lines) from Friday to Sunday.

The Rio film fest is one of the biggest in Latin America; more than 400 films representing 60 countries show at theaters all across Rio, and there are occasional screenings at the Marina da Glória and other open-air spots around town. In past years the two-week festival has attracted more than 300,000 attendees. Although it screens a wide variety of international fare, the festival often sets the stage for the success of Brazilian films aimed at wide release. For more info, visit www.festivaldorio.com.br.

NEED TO KNOW

Tickets & Reservations

Tickets for Fun (http://premier.ticketsforfun.com.br) Sells tickets to big shows at Citibank Hall and Arena HSBC. Also sells through various stores, including Lojas Saraiva in **Rio Sul Shopping** (p109).

Ingresso Rápido (www.ingressorapido.com.br) Sells tickets to the Theatro Municipal.

Listings

Visit Rio (www.visit.rio) The city's tourism authority maintains listings of major events.

Rio Show (http://rioshow.oglobo.globo.com) Published inside the Friday edition of *O Globo* newspaper; has extensive listings in Portuguese.

Veja (http://veja.abril.com.br)The 'Rio' insert included with this magazine, which comes out on Sunday, is a good (Portuguese only) source of info.

Entertainment by Neighborhood

Ipanema & Leblon (p73) A handful of theaters, cinemas and live-music venues.

Gávea, Jardim Botânico & Lagoa (p86) Live-music spots at lakeside kiosks.

Botafogo, Humaitá & Urca (p108) Several cinemas and creative venues.

Flamengo & Around (p120) Small concert halls in arts spaces.

Centro & Praça Mauá (p133) Large selection of concert halls and theaters.

Santa Teresa & Lapa (p143) Many live-music venues in Lapa.

Barra da Tijuca & Western Rio (p159) Home to mega-sized concert halls.

Lonely Planet's Top Choices

Theatro Municipal (p124) Grande dame of a theater that showcases some of Rio's best performing arts.

Clube Manouche (p86) Intimate downstairs club reminiscent of NYC jazz dens.

Teatro Riachuelo (p133) Architecturally stunning new downtown theater with a fabulous lineup of concerts.

Cidade das Artes (p159) Massive R$500-million home to the Brazilian Symphony Orchestra.

Teatro Odisséia (p144) A Lapa mainstay with rock and MPB bands.

Best Cinemas

Cine Odeon (p133) Classic old-fashioned cinema and performing-arts venue on Praça Floriano in Centro.

Estação Net Rio (p109) Good location near the metro.

Estação Net Ipanema (p73) Perfect rainy-day escape in Ipanema.

Cine Museu da República (p120) Contemporary and classic films.

Best Jazz & Bossa Nova

Blue Note (p86) Fabled new space beside Lagoa.

Maze Inn (p120) Fabulous setting for a monthly jazz-concert party high up in Tavares Bastos favela.

TribOz (p143) Some of Rio's best jazz shows take place in a beautifully decorated house in Lapa.

Beco das Garrafas (p99) An intimate club in the legendary birthplace of bossa nova.

Best Rock

Circo Voador (p144) Creative open-air space for top concerts; in the heart of Lapa.

Barzin (p203) In addition to DJs, this Ipanema spot hosts an eclectic lineup of live music.

Wood's (p72) Leblon club where bands sometimes play.

Fundição Progresso (p144) A Lapa showcase for top names and up-and-coming groups.

Teatro Rival Petrobras (p133) Downtown venue where you can eat, drink and catch MPB.

Best Theaters

Teatro do Leblon (p73) Stages thought-provoking fare.

Casa da Cultura Laura Alvim (p73) Diverse works showcased in a restored mansion facing Ipanema Beach.

LUIZSOUZA/SHUTTERSTOCK ©

Samba jam session at Pedra do Sal (p133)

Samba

Samba is the great soundtrack of Rio. It plays all across town, but if you're looking for its heart, you'll probably find it in the bohemian neighborhood of Lapa. In this neighborhood, addictive rhythms spill out of old-fashioned dance halls, drawing music lovers from far and wide. Samba also takes center stage during Carnaval, where percussive beats and singsong lyrics are essential to the big fest.

Samba Clubs

Gafieiras (dance halls) have risen from the ashes of the once-bombed-out neighborhood of Lapa and reinvigorated it with an air of youth and song. After years of neglect, Lapa has reclaimed its place as Rio's nightlife center. In the 1920s and '30s it was a major destination for the bohemian crowd, who were attracted to its decadent cabaret joints and *gafieiras*. Today its vintage buildings hide beautifully restored interiors set with wide dance floors.

Inside you'll find some of Rio's top samba groups, playing to crowds that often pack the dance floor. The clubs' nostalgic decor adds to the appeal, and even if you don't feel like dancing, the music and the festive crowd set the scene for a great night out.

Samba da Mesa

by Carmen Michael

On Friday night Rio's samba community congregates in front of the faded colonial facades of Rua do Mercado under a canopy of tropical foliage to play *samba da mesa* (literally, 'samba of the table'). On the worn cobblestones, a long table stands, altar-like. Around it the musicians sit and the crowd

NEED TO KNOW

Opening Hours

There's always something going on in Lapa, though many clubs are closed on Sunday and Monday. Typical opening times are from about 8pm to 1am during the week, and till 3am or 4am at weekends.

When to Go

At weekends Lapa packs in huge crowds, and many people come for the festive ambience on the streets. If you plan to visit a samba club on a Friday or Saturday, go early to beat the lines and have a few backup options just in case.

Cover Charges

Cover charges typically range from R$20 to R$50, and women generally pay less than men. Often a portion of the charge covers drinks. As with other clubs, you'll be given a consumption card to keep track of your drinks, which you'll pay for at the end of the night.

Security

Lapa is still scruffy around the edges, so keep your wits about you. Stick to well-trafficked streets, be mindful of pickpockets in crowded areas and leave valuables at home.

Resources

Visit Rio (www.visit.rio) Lists samba venues and upcoming concerts.

Rio Carnival (www.rio-carnival.net) A decent website for checking times and reading up on other Carnaval-related activities.

gyrates, paying homage to their favorite religion. *Samba da mesa* in Rio today is a grassroots movement of musicians and appreciators passionately committed to keeping their music on the street and in an improvised form.

This form of samba typically involves a table, at least one person playing a *cavaquinho* (small, ukulele-like instrument), an assortment of *tambores* (drums), and any number of makeshift instruments such as soda cans, knives and forks that will make a rattle. The standard of the music can be outstanding, and it's not uncommon to catch sight of a samba *bamba* (big-name samba performer) keeping the beat for the group or belting out one of its tunes. Depending on which bohemians have blown in for the night, you might even catch a duel, in which two singers pit their wits against each other in a battle of rhymes. It's a challenge of the intellect, and the topics include everything from love to poverty to the opponent's mother. Even if you speak some Portuguese, you probably won't understand the slang or the local references, but the delight of the crowd is infectious.

Street samba has taken a battering from the commercialization of music and space, the rising popularity of funk in the favelas (slums, informal communities) and the police clampdown on 'noise pollution' in public spaces. However, for those still interested in a little piece of bohemian Rio, there are several established places that support free, improvised street music. On Friday nights Rua do Mercado and Travessa do Comércio near Praça XV (Quinze) de Novembro in Centro attract a younger, radical-chic set. On Sunday and Thursday nights, Bip Bip (p99), a tiny bar in Copacabana, caters for hard-core *sambistas* (samba singers). If you're around on December 2, Dia de Samba (Samba Day), you can join the samba train bound for Oswaldo Cruz with the rest of Rio's samba community. The musicians disembark in the dusty backstreets of this working-class suburb, which is transformed every year into a labyrinth of makeshift bars and stages that host a 24-hour marathon of *samba da mesa*.

Impromptu street gatherings in Rio are more elusive at other times and finding them can sometimes be challenging. But it's an unforgettable experience when you do discover one. There are few fixed places for these parties, and they move from one week to the next. Lapa, in particular Rua Joaquim Silva, generally has something going on, but if not, keep your ears open for the unmistakable sound of the *samba bateria* (percussive-style samba) – follow that sound and you will find a party. Heed the local etiquette: ensure you don't talk over the music; don't use a camera with a flash; and don't sit down unless you're a contributing musician.

Samba Schools

In preparation for Carnaval, most big samba schools open their weekly rehearsals to the public, starting around September. An *escola de samba* (samba school) is a professional troupe that performs in the grand samba parade during Carnaval. Schools typically charge between R$10 and R$30 at the door (admission can go upwards of R$50 as Carnaval nears), and you'll be able to buy drinks. These are large dance parties, not specific lessons in samba (although you may learn to samba at some of them); they're fun to watch and visitors are always welcome to join in. Confirm that there's going to be a rehearsal before you visit.

Keep in mind that many samba schools are in the favelas, so use common sense and consider going with a *carioca* (resident of Rio) for peace of mind. It's best to take a taxi. Mangueira and Salgueiro are among the easiest schools to get to (and the most popular with visitors). All schools get incredibly packed as Carnaval approaches.

Beija-Flor (☎21 2791-2866; www.beija-flor.com.br; Praçinha Wallace Paes Leme 1025, Nilópolis; ⏲10pm Thu) Founded in 1948 this samba school has won more than a dozen parades over the years – most recently in 2018. It's located way out in Nilópolis (38km northwest of downtown Rio).

Grande Rio (☎21 2671-3585; www.academicosdogranderio.com.br; Almirante Barroso 5, Duque de Caxias; ⏲midnight Sat) Located northwest of Ilha do Governador, Grande Rio has been crowned parade champions only once (in 1992) but has lots of devoted followers, especially in its home suburb of Duque de Caxias.

Imperatriz Leopoldinense (☎21 2560-8037; www.imperatrizleopoldinense.com.br; Professor Lacê 235, Ramos; ⏲8pm Sun) Located 15km northwest of Centro, Imperatriz Leopoldinense is named after Empress Maria Leopoldina, archduchess of Austria and wife of Pedro I.

Mangueira Map p253 (☎21 2567-3419; www.mangueira.com.br; Visconde de Niterói 1072, Mangueira; ⏲10pm Sat) One of Rio's most famous samba schools, Mangueira has many followers all across the city. They come out en masse in their green and pink (Mangueira's colors), when the school parades on Carnaval weekend.

Mocidade Independente de Padre Miguel (☎21 3291-8700; www.mocidadeindependente.com.br; Av Brasil 31146, Padre Miguel; ⏲11pm Sat) Located 38km west of downtown, this samba school vaulted to fame in 2017 when it (along with Portela) was crowned parade champion of Rio's Carnaval.

Portela (☎21 3207-1604; www.gresportela.org.br; Clara Nunes 81, Oswaldo Cruz; ⏲10pm Fri) Portela is a highly successful samba school with creative themes and brilliant costumes. It has been crowned Carnaval champion nearly two dozen times since its founding back in the 1920s.

Salgueiro (☎21 2238-9226; www.salgueiro.com.br; Silva Teles 104, Andaraí; ⏲10pm Sat) One of the best samba schools for foreigners to visit, Salgueiro hosts big Saturday-night parties from late August until Carnaval. Expect live music, ever-flowing caipirinhas and lots of fiery footwork.

Unidos da Tijuca Map p253 (☎21 2516-2749; www.unidosdatijuca.com.br; Francisco Bicalho 47, Santo Cristo; ⏲10pm Sat) Going strong since 1931, this samba school has staged many dazzling parades over the years. Unidos da Tijuca has been crowned champion three times since 2010 (and vice-champion twice).

Vila Isabel (☎21 2578-0077; www.facebook.com/unidosdevilaisabeloficial; Blvd 28 de Setembro 382, Vila Isabel; ⏲10pm Sat) One of Rio's best-loved samba schools has won a few parade titles over the years. Vila Isabel is deeply connected to famed samba singer Martinho da Vila, who wrote some well-known hits for the school that still receive airtime today (especially during Carnaval season).

DANCE CLASSES

Given samba's resurgence, it's not surprising that there are several places where you can learn the moves. You can also find places to study *forró* (dance accompanied by the traditional, fast-paced music from the Northeast) and other styles. A dance class is a good setting in which to meet other people while getting those feet to step in time.

A few good places to learn:

Casa de Dança Carlinhos de Jesus (p206)

Fundição Progresso (p145)

Rio Samba Dancer (p206)

Lonely Planet's Top Choices

Salgueiro (p154) Wonderfully festive, well-located samba school.

Rio Scenarium (p143) Touristy, but still a fantastic setting for live samba.

Clube dos Democráticos (p144) Long-running club with first-class musicians.

Bip Bip (p99) Copacabana gem famed for its *samba de roda* (informal samba played in a circle).

Pedra do Sal (p133) Twice-weekly outdoor samba jam sessions in a historic locale north of Centro.

Best Samba Spots

Carioca da Gema (p143) Long-running favorite, especially on Monday night.

Fundição Progresso (p143) Top *sambistas* and much more in a massive industrial space that was once a foundry.

Lapa 40 Graus (p144) Dance to samba and play pool, all in one multistory complex.

Vaca Atolada (p142) Small, brightly lit bar with a lively *samba de roda* most nights.

Sarau (p143) Great people-watching on the outdoor plaza with live samba and *forró* groups in the background.

Beco do Rato (p144) Low-key and welcoming spot; there's never a cover charge.

Best Live Samba Outside Lapa

Trapiche Gamboa (p133) Atmospheric music club in Gamboa with addictive samba beats.

Renascença Clube (p154) Open-air celebration in Andaraí that draws samba fans from across Rio.

Fuska 2.0 (p108) Fun neighborhood gathering spot in Botafogo.

Cariocando (p118) Head to Catete on Saturday for live bands and feasting on *feijoada* (bean-and-meat stew).

Shopping

Unsurprisingly, beach and casual wear are a big part of the shopping scene in Rio. Less well known is the great variety of stores selling antiques, custom-made handicrafts, wine and spirits, handmade jewelry, records and CDs, coffee-table books and one-of-a-kind goods found only in Rio.

Markets of Rio

Rio's many markets are ideal places to explore the subcultures beneath the city's surface, whether that means you're brushing elbows with antique-lovers, recent migrants from the Northeast or youthful flocks of fashionistas from the Zona Sul. Several markets, such as the Feira Nordestina and the monthly Feira do Rio Antigo, are as much about food and music as they are about shopping.

A few top markets:

Hippie Fair (p73)

Av Atlântica Fair (p100)

Feira do Rio Antigo (p145)

Feira Nordestina (p152)

Praça do Lido Market (p100)

Praça Santos Dumont Antique Fair (p86)

Rio Souvenirs

Music Expand your collection with local favorites such as singers Maria Rita, Diogo Nogueira or Mart'nália.

Cachaça Buy quality *cachaça* (high-proof sugarcane alcohol) from Minas from around R$35.

Swimwear Flaunt your new tan in a tiny *sunga* (Speedo) or *fio dental* (string bikini). Ipanema, along Rua Visconde de Pirajá, is the place to look.

Maracatu drums If the massive Northeastern instrument won't fit on your coffee table, consider the smaller ukulele-like *cavaquinho*.

Havaianas Find a pair for every mood at shops all across town, including the spacious emporium in **Copacabana** (p100).

Paintings Artists showcase their work at the Sunday Hippie Fair (p73).

Soccer jerseys Score a jersey for one of Rio's teams. Loja Fla (p100) is the go-to place for Flamengo fans.

Folk art Tap into Brazil's handicraft traditions at stores scattered about town.

Shopping by Neighborhood

Ipanema & Leblon (p73) Loads of boutiques; high prices.

Gávea, Jardim Botânico & Lagoa (p86) Several small-scale but atmospheric shopping streets.

Copacabana & Leme (p99) Countless stores, a few markets and tourist fare.

Centro & Praça Mauá (p133) Wine shops, bookstores and down-market clothing shops; medina-like browsing in the pedestrian streets of Saara.

Santa Teresa & Lapa (p144) A few handicrafts shops and galleries near Largo do Guimarães.

NEED TO KNOW

Opening Hours

Stores From 9am to 6pm Monday to Friday, to 1pm Saturday.

Malls From 10am to 10pm Monday to Saturday, 3pm to 10pm Sunday.

Taxes

All stores list their prices with the tax already included, so what you see on the tag is the total price you'll pay for the goods.

Language

Many sales assistants in high-end shops speak some English.

Bargaining

A little bargaining is expected when making purchases at markets, but keep in mind that sellers generally don't inflate their prices and so aren't willing to haggle very much.

Lonely Planet's Top Choices

Gilson Martins (p99) Wallets, bags and other accessories with iconic Rio imagery.

Maria Oiticica (p75) Elegant jewelry made from Amazonian seeds and fibers.

Chocolate Q (p73) Exquisite, beautifully wrapped chocolate produced from the cacao beans of a sustainable Brazilian grower.

Osklen (p74) Attractive men's and women's fashion from Brazil's best-known designer.

CRAB (p134) Beautifully displayed crafts from across Brazil.

Hippie Fair (p73) Have fun browsing – and eating street food – in Ipanema.

Best Handicrafts

La Vereda (p145) Unique gift ideas with a local focus.

Pé de Boi (p120) Eye-catching handicrafts made by artists from around Brazil.

O Sol (p87) Folk art that benefits a social-welfare organization.

Tucum (p145) Small store with Amazonian jewelry, pottery, baskets and wall hangings with pre-Columbian motifs.

Best Fashion Boutiques

Dona Coisa (p87) Fun, high-end browsing in Jardim Botânico.

Lenny Niemeyer (p73) Rio's best place to browse women's swimwear.

Isabela Capeto (p75) Lovely one-of-a-kind garments sold from the studio in Jardim Botânico.

Redley (p74) Eye-catching clothing for the summer.

Best Bookshops

Livraria da Travessa (p134) Locations all around town, including a much-loved Centro branch.

Argumento (p75) Browse books and music, and nibble crepes.

Baratos de Ribeiro (p109) Botafogo favorite with books and vinyl.

Best Music

Toca do Vinícius (p74) A must for bossa nova fans.

Pleidisco (p134) Well known for its guitars and stringed instruments.

Baratos de Ribeiro (p109) Atmospheric place to browse for records in Botafogo.

Best Shopping Malls

Shopping Cidade Copacabana (p100) Quirky place with used books, plus galleries and antique stores.

Shopping Leblon (p75) A great place to shop and while away a rainy day.

Village (p159) Rio's most lavish mall.

Botafogo Praia Shopping (p109) A fine place to browse, plus a food court with incredible views.

Best Unusual Stores

Gabinete (p87) Full of elegant objects for the home.

Granado (p134) High-end skin-care products in an old-fashioned pharmacy.

Maracatu Brasil (p120) Many percussion instruments, and it's possible to take classes upstairs.

Sports & Activities

Tropical rainforest, towering peaks and sparkling beaches set the stage for a wide range of adventures in this outdoors-loving city. Hiking, rock climbing, hang gliding, surfing and cycling are only a few ways to spend a sun-drenched afternoon. Rio is also a great place to watch sport; nothing quite compares to seeing the mad spectacle of a football match at hallowed Maracanã.

Walking, Jogging & Cycling

Splendid views and the sounds of the ever-present ocean are just two features of the many good walking and jogging paths of the Zona Sul. Parque do Flamengo (p116) has plenty of paths stretching between city and bay. Further south, Lagoa Rodrigo de Freitas (p80) has a 7.2km track for cyclists, joggers and in-line skaters. At the lakeside Parque dos Patins you can rent bicycles (R$15 per hour), tricycles or quadricycles (around R$30 per hour). A popular option is to take the seaside path from Leme to Barra da Tijuca. You can also cycle along paths from Copacabana up to Parque do Flamengo. Sunday is the best day to go, as the road is closed to traffic but open to the city's many outdoor enthusiasts.

The short Pista Cláudio Coutinho (p109), between the mountains and the sea at Praia Vermelha in Urca, is closed to bikes but open to walkers and joggers. It's open from 7am to 6pm daily.

Rio by Bike (p201) offers excellent tours that combine scenery and cultural insights, with guides pointing out key landmarks and describing events that have shaped Rio. Tours last three to four hours and travel mostly along bike lanes.

Hiking

Rio has some outstanding hikes along the trails coursing through the Floresta da Tijuca. You can also go for hikes through wilderness areas around Corcovado, Morro da Urca and Pão de Açúcar (p103).

Jungle Me (☎21 4105-7533; www.jungleme.com.br; tours from R$195; 👪) This top-notch outfit offers excellent hiking tours through Parque Nacional da Tijuca led by knowledgeable guides. The eight-hour Tijuca Circuit (Peaks & Waterfalls tour) offers challenging walks up several escarpments with stunning views of Rio, followed by a refreshing dip in a waterfall. The Prainha & Grumari tour consists of a hike between scenic beaches in Rio's little-visited western reaches.

Rio Adventures (☎21 3587-3282; www.rioadventures.com; hiking/climbing/rafting tours from R$180/370/450) Offering a range of outdoor activities, Rio Adventures leads hikes through Parque Nacional da Tijuca, including short treks up Pico Tijuca and more challenging ascents up Pedra Bonito. It also runs sightseeing tours, rock climbs, rafting excursions to Paraibuna River (175km northwest of Rio), and parachuting and paragliding trips.

Rio Natural (☎21 99992-1666; www.rionatural.com.br; hikes from R$210) Reputable Rio Natural offers seemingly every type of outdoor adventure you can think of. You can go hiking (up Pico Tijuca, Pão de Açúcar, Corcovado, Pedra Bonita and Dois Irmãos), abseiling, paragliding, kayaking or rafting (on rivers outside Rio).

Trilha Dois Irmãos (☎21 98394-4928; www.trilhadoisirmaos.com.br; tour from R$100) Based in Vidigal, this small outfit leads tours up to an overlook near the top of Dois Irmãos. The views are mesmerizing. It also offers culturally themed walking tours inside Vidigal favela. The outfit keeps abreast of the latest security situation in the area, and will cancel tours when warranted.

NEED TO KNOW

Football at Maracanã

Getting to Maracanã You can take the metro to Maracanã station and buy tickets at the stadium gate, or go with a group organized by Brazil Expedition (p203), Be a Local (p204) or Sergio Manhães (p151).

Game days Games take place year-round on Saturday or Sunday, and less frequently on Wednesday or Thursday.

Rock Climbing

Rio is the center of rock climbing in Brazil, with 350 documented climbs within 40 minutes of the city center. In addition to organized outings, you can also try your hand at the rock-climbing wall in Parque da Catacumba (p82).

Crux Eco (☎21 3322-8765, 21 99392-9203; www.cruxeco.com.br;) This reputable outfit offers a huge range of excursions and outdoor adventures. You can arrange a mountaineering adventure up Pão de Açúcar (R$470) or climb Corcovado, go rappelling (abseiling) down waterfalls, head off on full-day hikes through Floresta da Tijuca, or go on cycling and kayaking trips.

Climb in Rio (☎21 99328-5904; www.climbinrio.com; half-/full-day climbs from R$350/600) This respected agency offers half- and full-day climbing trips led by experienced guides. Navigating more than 400 routes around Rio and the state, this is a good pick for climbing junkies.

Hang Gliding

If you weigh less than 100kg (about 220lb) and have a spare R$500, you can do the fantastic hang glide off 510m Pedra Bonita – one of the giant granite slabs that tower above Rio – onto Pepino Beach in São Conrado. Flights last about seven to 10 minutes, and no experience is necessary. Guest riders are secured in a kind of pouch that is attached to the hang glider. The winds are quite safe here and accidents are rare.

The price includes pickup and drop-off at your hotel.

Tandem Fly (☎21 9996-6341, 21 2422-0941; www.riotandemfly.com.br; flight R$500) Two brothers – both very experienced pilots – run this outfit; they also give lessons for those who want to learn how to fly solo.

Just Fly (☎21 3593-4362; www.justflyinrio.blogspot.com; R$520) Go hang gliding with Paulo Celani, a highly experienced tandem flyer with more than 6000 flights to his credit.

Asa Delta Flight in Rio (☎21 99693-8800; www.facebook.com/asadeltaflightrio; tandem flight R$490) With more than 20 years' experience, Ricardo Hamond has earned a solid reputation as a safety-conscious and extremely professional pilot; he has flown more than 12,000 tandem flights.

Capoeira

The only martial art native to the Americas, capoeira was invented by Afro-Brazilian slaves about 400 years ago. In its original form the grappling style of combat developed as a means of self-defense against slave owners. Unsurprisingly, once capoeira was discovered, it was quickly banned. However, slaves continued to hone their fighting skills out of sight, practicing secretly in the forest. Later the sport was disguised as a kind of dance, allowing it to emerge into the open. This is the form of capoeira that exists today.

Referred to as a *jogo* (game), a bout of capoeira is accompanied by hand clapping and the plucking of the *berimbau* (a long, single-stringed instrument). Initially the music was used to warn fighters of the boss's approach; today it guides the *jogo*'s rhythm. Fast tempos dictate the players' exchange of rapid, powerful kicks and blows, while slower tempos bring the pace down to a quasi-dance. The *berimbau* is accompanied by the *atabaque* (floor drum) and the *pandeiro* (Brazilian tambourine).

You can see musicians and spectators arranged in a *roda de capoeira* (capoeira circle) at the weekly Feira Nordestina (p152) in São Cristóvão. If you're in town for a while, you can also sign up for classes; Fundição Progresso (p145) in Lapa offers them three nights a week.

Surfing & Paddle Boarding

Rio has some fine options when it comes to surfing, with great breaks just outside the city. If you're not ready to leave the Zona Sul, there are a few options, including fairly consistent breaks in front of *posto* (post) 10 in Ipanema and *posto* 11 in Leblon. Copacabana gets an OK break between *postos* 4 and 5. You'll find better waves near the spit of land dividing Copacabana from Ipanema.

On the east side, off Praia do Diabo, there are right and left breaks that can reach up to 2m high, but it's not a good spot for beginners. On the other side of the rocks is Arpoador, which is generally more consistent, with fast, hollow breaks to the left ranging from 0.5m to 3m. The big drawback here is that the place gets crowded, making maneuvering extremely difficult. To beat the crowds, go early on weekday mornings.

If you're serious about surfing, you'll want to head down to the beaches west of Rio. Just past Barra da Tijuca and Recreio is **Macumba Beach**; its left and right breaks draw both longboarders and beginners. After Macumba is pretty **Prainha**, which is widely considered the best surf spot in the area, with waves reaching 3m on good days. If it's too packed, you can continue to **Grumari**, where the swell isn't as good but the crowds are thinner.

You can also get out on the water on a stand-up paddle board.

SURF ESSENTIALS

Surf conditions Find detailed information on all the breaks around Rio at www.wannasurf.com.

Boards For boards and other gear, visit Galeria River (p100). Some hostels also rent boards.

Classes Beginners who want to learn to surf can take classes through informal *escolinhas* (schools) off Ipanema Beach and off Barra. Rio Surf 'N Stay (p170) offers lessons (in English) and overnight accommodation.

Activities by Neighborhood

Ipanema & Leblon (p75) Cycling or jogging the beach path.

Gávea, Jardim Botânico & Lagoa (p87) Cycling or jogging the lakeshore path. Hikes in Parque Lage.

Copacabana & Leme (p100) Cycling or jogging the beach path; stand-up paddle boarding off the beach.

Botafogo, Humaitá & Urca (p109) Rock climbing up Pão de Açúcar. Walking the short Pista Cláudio Coutinho.

Flamengo & Around (p120) Cycling or jogging through Parque do Flamengo.

Zona Norte (p150) Watching a football game at Maracanã.

Barra da Tijuca & Western Rio (p160) Hikes and climbs in Floresta da Tijuca.

LONELY PLANET'S TOP CHOICES

Maracanã Football Stadium (p150) Attending a match here is an unmissable part of a visit to Rio.

Bike Rio (p201) Pick up a bike from a self-hire kiosk and go for a memorable ride along the beachside path from Leblon to Leme.

Pão de Açúcar (p103) The mountaineering ascent up this mountain offers unforgettable views.

Parque Nacional da Tijuca (p158) Scramble through rainforest and up craggy overlooks.

Prainha (p157) With waves up to 3m, this beach is Rio's best for those looking to catch waves.

Tandem Fly (p53) Hang glide off the giant granite slab of Pedra Bonita.

Explore Rio de Janeiro

Ipanema & Leblon . . . 58
Top Sights 60
Sights 61
Eating 62
Drinking & Nightlife 69
Entertainment 73
Shopping 73
Sports & Activities 75

Gávea, Jardim Botânico & Lagoa 78
Top Sights 80
Sights 81
Eating 83
Drinking & Nightlife 85
Entertainment 86
Shopping 86
Sports & Activities 87

Copacabana & Leme 90
Top Sights 92
Sights 93
Eating 93
Drinking & Nightlife 97
Entertainment 99
Shopping 99
Sports & Activities 100

Botafogo, Humaitá & Urca 101
Top Sights 103
Sights 104
Eating 104
Drinking & Nightlife 107
Entertainment 108
Shopping 109
Sports & Activities 109

Flamengo & Around 112
Top Sights 114
Sights 116
Eating 117
Drinking & Nightlife 119
Entertainment 120
Shopping 120
Sports & Activities 120

Centro & Praça Mauá 121
Top Sights 123
Sights 124
Eating 130
Drinking & Nightlife 132
Entertainment 133
Shopping 133
Sports & Activities 134

Santa Teresa & Lapa 135
Top Sights 137
Sights 138
Eating 139
Drinking & Nightlife 141
Entertainment 143
Shopping 144
Sports & Activities 145

Zona Norte 148
Top Sights 150
Sights 152
Eating 152
Drinking & Nightlife 153
Entertainment 154

Barra da Tijuca & Western Rio 155
Sights 157
Eating 157
Drinking & Nightlife 159
Entertainment 159
Shopping 159
Sports & Activities 160

Sleeping 161

RIO DE JANEIRO'S **TOP SIGHTS**

Ipanema Beach 60

Lagoa Rodrigo de Freitas 80

Copacabana Beach 92

Pão de Açúcar 103

Cristo Redentor.....114

Museu Histórico Nacional 123

Escadaria Selarón..... 137

Maracanã Football Stadium.....150

Neighborhoods at a Glance

1 Ipanema & Leblon p58

Ipanema and Leblon share the same stretch of south-facing shoreline. Rio's beautiful people flock to these beaches, while the tree-lined streets located just inland hide some of the best eating, drinking and shopping offerings to be found in the whole city.

2 Gávea, Jardim Botânico & Lagoa p78

The northern border of Ipanema and Leblon is formed by the Lagoa Rodrigo de Freitas, a saltwater lagoon fronted by the high-rent districts of Gávea, Jardim Botânico and Lagoa. Here you'll find open-air dining and drinking at lakeside restaurants, and verdant botanical gardens to the west.

3 Copacabana & Leme p90

The scalloped beach of Copacabana begins northeast of Ipanema. Once a destination for international jet-setters, Copacabana is the city's somewhat ragged tourist magnet, with dozens of oceanfront hotels and sidewalk restaurants. The population density is high here and mixes old-timers, favela kids and tourists, and high and low culture.

4 Botafogo, Humaitá & Urca p101

Just north of Copacabana, Botafogo and Humaitá are desirable neighborhoods with vibrant nightlife, cutting-edge restaurants and a few intriguing museums and galleries in the area's old mansions. East of Botafogo, Urca retains a peaceful vibe, and is famed for Pão de Açúcar (Sugarloaf Mountain), which shadows its quiet streets.

5 Flamengo & Around p112

To the north of Botafogo, residential neighborhoods include low-key Flamengo, leafy Laranjeiras and, further west, Cosme Velho, above which looms Cristo Redentor (Christ the Redeemer) atop Corcovado. Following the curve of the bay north is Parque do Flamengo, home to cycling trails, sports fields, and several monuments and museums. Inland from there, Catete and Glória hide history in their battered streets, including the former presidential home.

6 Centro & Praça Mauá p121

Centro is Rio's business hub and also one of Rio's oldest areas; it houses baroque churches, historic sites, scenic plazas and lavish theaters. Its wide boulevards are crisscrossed with narrow pedestrian streets sprinkled with colonial buildings. History aside, Centro has atmospheric open-air cafes and bars that draw the happy-hour crowd. North of Centro, Praça Mauá is the center of Rio's revitalized port district and has some outstanding new museums.

7 Santa Teresa & Lapa p135

On the southwestern edge of Centro, Lapa is a ramshackle district that's also the epicenter of Rio's nightlife, with dozens of samba-filled bars and clubs, and late-night street parties. Uphill from Lapa, Santa Teresa is a picturesque neighborhood of winding streets and old mansions that have been restored by the many artists and bohemian characters who have settled there.

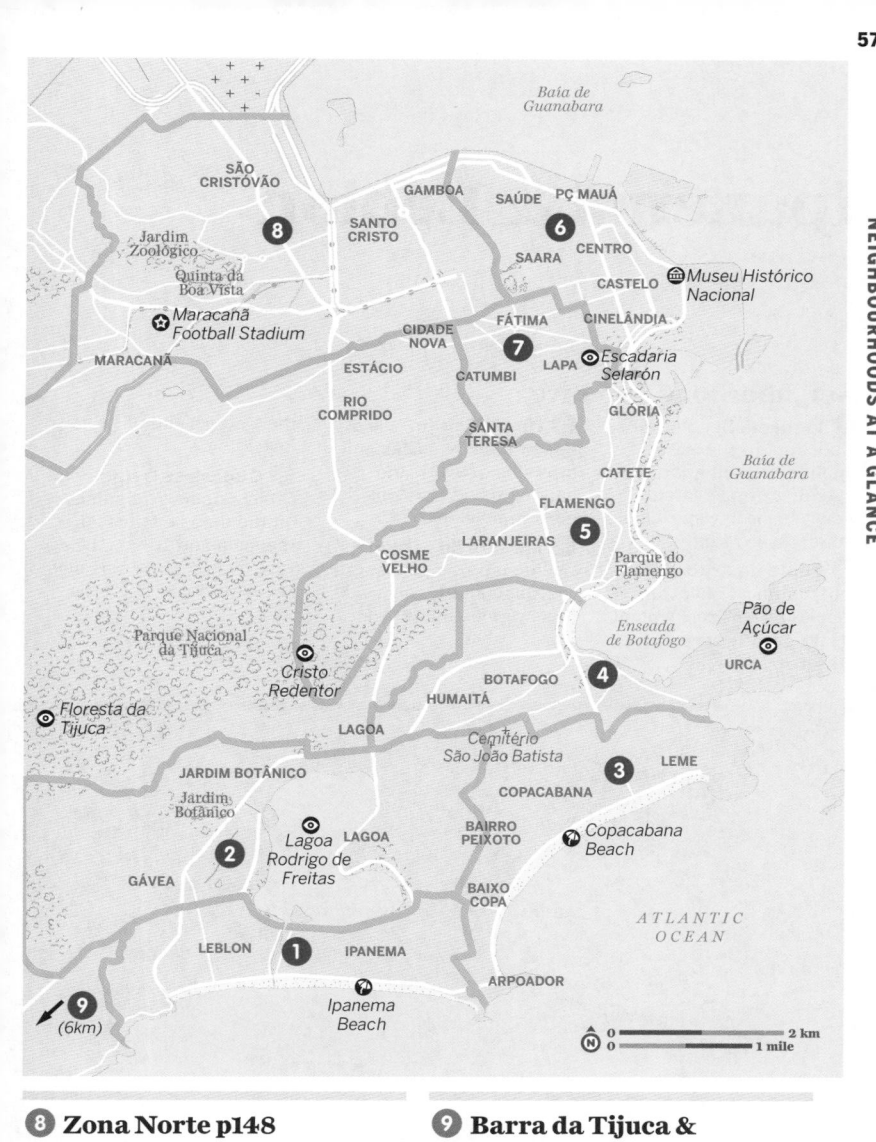

8 Zona Norte p148

The big draws in Rio's northern zone are Maracanã football stadium, the Feira Nordestina (Northeastern Fair) and the Quinta da Boa Vista, former residence of the Portuguese imperial family. Aside from its key sights, the Zona Norte draws few visitors. Those wanting to get off the beaten track here will find some surprises, however, including a growing eating and drinking scene in the Praça da Bandeira neighborhood.

9 Barra da Tijuca & Western Rio p155

West of Leblon you'll find great hiking amid the rainforest of Floresta da Tijuca. Nearby, hang gliders make their soaring descent. Further out, Barra da Tijuca is a sprawling suburb with a long, pretty beach. Apart from the area near the new Jardim Oceânico metro stop, to get around here you'll generally need a car. Other beaches dot the coast, and get wilder and less populated the further west you go.

Ipanema & Leblon

IPANEMA | LEBLON

Neighborhood Top Five

1 Ipanema Beach (p60) Frolicking in the waves, sipping refreshing *maté* and watching people parade along this iconic stretch of sun-drenched sand.

2 Ponta do Arpoador (p61) Joining fishers and couples on this rocky point for the nightly spectacle of sunset.

3 Hippie Fair (p73) Feasting on Bahian snacks and browsing artwork and handicrafts at the Zona Sul's most famous market.

4 Mirante do Leblon (p61) Gazing out over the length of Leblon and Ipanema at this overlook uphill from the western end of Leblon Beach.

5 Chocolate Q (p73) Going window-shopping on the upscale streets of Ipanema and Leblon, being sure to stop for refreshment at this serious chocolatier.

For more detail of this area see Map p228 and p232

Explore Ipanema & Leblon

The favored address for young, beautiful and wealthy *cariocas* (residents of Rio), these twin neighborhoods boast magnificent beaches and tree-lined streets full of enticing open-air cafes, restaurants and bars. They're also the epicenter of the city's high-end shopping, with dozens of colorful boutiques and multistory *galerias* (shopping centers) selling pretty things that can quickly deplete a budget. While there are few traditional sights here, you can just bask on the beach and explore the leafy streets. Ipanema is also Rio's gay district, which revolves around the cafe and bar scene on and near Rua Farme de Amoedo.

Ipanema acquired international fame in the early '60s as the birthplace of the bossa nova hit song 'The Girl from Ipanema.' The neighborhood became the hangout of artists, intellectuals and wealthy liberals, who frequented the sidewalk cafes and bars. These days the artists and intellectuals have moved on, and the area is better known for its high-priced apartments and luxury lifestyle. This is, after all, Rio's most affluent district. While few *cariocas* can afford to live here, the streets and beach attract a wide cross-section of society, from surf kids from the outskirts to long-time residents and fashion-conscious twenty- and thirty-somethings who pack the open-sided bars by night. Ipanema and Leblon are also among the city's top destinations for dining and drinking.

Local Life

Markets Hit a fruit market (p37) for fresh mangoes, passion fruit and snacks (such as the crepe-like tapioca).

Restaurant strips Rua Dias Ferreira in Leblon is packed with high-end restaurants that serve sushi, Italian tapas, Brazilian fusion and more.

Hangouts Ipanema and Leblon have many lively neighborhood bars. Good starting points: Belmonte (p72) in Leblon and Barzin (p70) in Ipanema.

Rainy-day escapes Shopping Leblon (p75) has plenty of rainy-day amusement including top-end shops, a movie theater and decent restaurants – some with views.

Getting There & Away

Bus Botafogo (574); Corcovado train station (570); Urca (512); Copacabana (570); São Conrado (177); Centro (132); Novo Rio bus station (474).

Metro General Osório and NS da Paz in Ipanema; Jardim de Alah and Antero de Quental in Leblon.

Lonely Planet's Top Tip

On Sundays the east-bound lane of the beach road closes to traffic and fills with cyclists, joggers and in-line skaters. The car-free stretch goes all the way up through Copacabana to Leme.

Best Places to Eat

- Giuseppe Grill (p68)
- Zazá Bistrô Tropical (p65)
- Zuka (p68)
- Formidable (p69)
- CT Boucherie (p69)
- La Carioca Cevicheria (p63)

For reviews, see p62

Best Places to Drink

- Canastra (p69)
- Nosso (p70)
- Bar Astor (p70)
- Academia da Cachaça (p72)
- Brewteco (p72)
- Barzin (p70)

For reviews, see p69

Best Places to Shop

- Hippie Fair (p73)
- Gilson Martins (p73)
- Osklen (p74)
- Lenny Niemeyer (p73)
- Maria Oiticica (p75)
- Chocolate Q (p73)

For reviews, see p73

PHILIPPE COHAT/GETTY IMAGES ©

TOP SIGHT
IPANEMA BEACH

You've probably seen the photos and heard the theme song ('The Girl from Ipanema'), but nothing quite compares to the experience of strolling along the golden sands of Rio's most famous beach. It's the city's great backyard, with amusements of all kinds, from surfing and jogging to sitting back, *agua de côco* (coconut water) in hand, and watching Rio at play.

DON'T MISS

- *Globos* and *maté*
- Rehydrating *agua de côco*
- Watching *cariocas* show off their skills at volleyball and *futevôlei* (volleyball played without hands)

PRACTICALITIES

- Map p228, A5
- Av Vieira Souto

The Scene

One long stretch of sun-drenched sand, Ipanema Beach is demarcated by *postos* (posts), which mark off subcultures as diverse as the city itself. *Posto* 9, near Rua Vinícius de Moraes, is Garota de Ipanema, where Rio's most lithe and tanned bodies tend to migrate. The area is also known as the Cemetério dos Elefantes because of the handful of old leftists, hippies and artists who sometimes hang out there. In front of Rua Farme de Amoedo the beach is known as Praia Farme, and is the stomping ground for gay society. *Posto* 8 further east is mostly the domain of favela (slum, informal community) kids. Arpoador, between Ipanema and Copacabana, is Rio's most popular surf spot.

Whatever part you choose, you'll enjoy cleaner sands and sea than in Copacabana. Keep in mind that if you go on a Saturday or Sunday, the sands get crowded.

Relaxation & Refreshment

Once on the beach, head to your favorite *barraca* (beach stall), where you can hire chairs and a sun umbrella. There are also food and drink stalls, though roving vendors will come to you, proffering cold drinks (try the sweet tea-like *maté*) and snacks (such as crunchy *globos* – a crispy biscuit made from manioc flour).

If you're in the mood for something more substantial, head up to one of the kiosks lining the beachfront. The best are on the western end of Leblon.

SIGHTS

The beach is the all-encompassing draw here, and the area's other attractions are somewhat secondary compared to this captivating shoreline. However, when you need to head indoors (due to rain or perhaps sunburn), there are a few things to do here without leaving the area. You can take a gemological tour through H Stern, arrange a special chocolate tasting at Chocolate Q, or take a peek at some of the art galleries, such as Lurixs: Arte Contemporânea.

Ipanema

IPANEMA BEACH — BEACH

See p60.

PONTA DO ARPOADOR — VIEWPOINT

Map p228 (Av Vieira Souto) At the far eastern end of Av Vieira Souto, this rocky point juts out into the water and serves as one of Rio's best places for watching the sunset. Throughout the day, you'll spot fishers casting off the rock, couples stealing a few kisses and photographers snapping that iconic length of Ipanema Beach that stretches off toward the towering peaks of Dois Irmãos.

You'll also see large flocks of surfers jockeying for position offshore. Around the western edge of the rock is the tiny, secluded Praia do Diabo (Devil's Beach); it's a fine place to take in the views, but swim with caution. A very rustic gym is built into the rocks (wtih Fred Flintstone–style barbells with concrete weights and chin-up bars).

MUSEU AMSTERDAM SAUER — MUSEUM

Map p228 (☎21 2512-9601; www.amsterdamsauer.com; Garcia d'Ávila 105; ⏲10am-7pm Mon-Fri, to 4pm Sat) **FREE** On the most upscale street in Ipanema, the Amsterdam Sauer Museum houses an impressive collection of precious stones: more than 3000 items in all. Visitors can also take a peek at the two replicas of mines.

H STERN — MUSEUM

Map p228 (☎21 2274-8897; www.hsterninrio.com; Garcia d'Ávila 113; ⏲9am-6pm Mon-Fri, to 2pm Sat) **FREE** The famous jeweler H Stern allows visitors to get a glimpse behind the scenes at these gemological headquarters. A 12-minute audio tour shows the process of turning the rough stones into flawlessly cut jewels, and you can peer behind the laboratory windows to see craftspeople, cutters, goldsmiths and setters at work. There's a free shuttle service to and from major hotels in Rio.

While there you can also ask to visit the small museum with its display of rare mineral specimens and large collection of tourmalines. Following the tour, you'll meet with a sales rep, which some people find uncomfortable. A polite 'No, thank you,' will usually see you to the next level (the showroom) and then on to the exit.

PARQUE GAROTA DE IPANEMA — PARK

Map p228 (off Francisco Otaviano, near Bulhões Carvalho; ⏲7am-7pm) This small park next to Ponta do Arpoador features a tiny playground, a concrete area popular with skaters, and a lookout with a view of Ipanema Beach. On weekends in summer occasional concerts are held here.

ELEVADOR DO MORRO DO CANTAGALO — VIEWPOINT

Map p228 (Barão da Torre & Teixeira de Melo; ⏲6am-11pm) **FREE** Connected to the metro station off Praça General Osório, this elevator whisks passengers up to Cantagalo, a favela that's wedged between Ipanema and Copacabana. The sparkling sea views from the elevator are quite fine, though local residents are happy simply to have a convenient way to get home that doesn't mean ascending hundreds of steps.

As far as security goes, Cantagalo has been safe to visit since the police pacification units arrived in 2009. High-profile visitors have included Lady Gaga, Carla Bruni and Brazil's former president, Dilma Rousseff.

Leblon

PRAIA DE LEBLON — BEACH

Map p232 (Av Delfim Moreira) Separated from Ipanema by the gardens and canal of Jardim de Alah, Leblon Beach attracts families and has a slightly more sedate vibe than its eastern counterpart. Parents with little ones may want to check out Baixo Bebê, between *postos* 11 and 12, where you'll find a small playground on the sand as well as other young families.

MIRANTE DO LEBLON — VIEWPOINT

Map p232 (Av Niemeyer) A few fishers casting out to sea mingle with couples admiring the view at this overlook uphill from the western end of Leblon Beach. The luxury Sheraton hotel looms to the west, with the photogenic favela of Vidigal nearby.

LURIXS: ARTE CONTEMPORÂNEA GALLERY
Map p232 (☎21 2541-4935; www.lurixs.com; Dias Ferreira 214; ⏲noon-8pm Mon-Fri, to 4pm Sat) One of Rio's top contemporary galleries moved to this Leblon location in 2017, and it continues to stage captivating exhibitions inside a four-story custom-built art space. Lurixs represents some of Brazil's best-known artists, and you might see pieces by Hélio Oiticica, Lygia Clark and Cildo Meireles, depending upon what's on display.

EATING

Rio's best restaurants lie in the neighborhoods of Ipanema and Leblon. Along the tree-lined side streets abutting the major thoroughfares you'll find a mix of trendy eating spots, outdoor cafes and juice bars. Price and quality generally run high here, though whatever the latest stylish flavor of the month is won't always live up to the hype.

Ipanema

VERO ICE CREAM $
Map p228 (☎21 3497-8754; Visconde de Pirajá 229; ice creams R$11-16, pizza slices R$13-16; ⏲10am-12:30am; ✎) This artisanal Italian-run gelateria whips up Rio's best ice cream. You'll find more than two dozen rich and creamy temptations, including *gianduia* (chocolate with hazelnut), *caramelo com flor de sal* (caramel with sea salt), *figo com amêndoas* (fig with almond) and classic flavors such as *morango* (strawberry).

A counter out back serves delicious thin-crust pizzas, with creative options like caramelized pear or a cheese-free vegan option, as well as the classic margherita.

JOANA PIZZA $
Map p228 (☎21 98201-8044; www.facebook.com/joanapizzabar; Joana Angélica 47; pizzas R$24-30; ⏲6pm-midnight Tue-Sun; 📶✎) One block up from Ipanema Beach, this hip little spot with a small terrace fires up some of the best thin-crust pizzas in the Zona Sul. The creative toppings steal the show: grilled pumpkin and eggplant with cherry tomatoes (the Veggie), or thin slices of marinated steak with fresh goat cheese and mint (the Churrasco Turco).

You can match the pizzas with great cocktails shaken up at the small side bar.

DELÍRIO TROPICAL BRAZILIAN $
Map p228 (☎21 3624-8164; www.delirio.com.br; Garcia d'Ávila 48; salads R$18-27; ⏲11am-9pm Mon-Sat; ✎) Delírio Tropical serves a tempting array of salads, which you can enhance by adding grilled trout, salmon carpaccio, filet mignon and other items. The open layout has a pleasant, casual ambience, but you'll need to go early to beat the lunchtime crowds.

VEZPA PIZZA $
Map p228 (Farme de Amoedo 75; pizza slices from R$11; ⏲noon-1am Sun-Thu, to 2am Fri & Sat) Great for a quick slice when your energy levels are low, Vezpa serves satisfying New York–style pizza slices and lasagna from a tiny storefront. There are a few outdoor tables for you to sit at while you munch.

BARRACA DO URUGUAI SNACKS $
Map p228 (Posto 9, Ipanema Beach; sandwiches R$14-20; ⏲noon-5pm) Of the many *barracas* (food stalls) on Ipanema Beach, Uruguai is a long-term favorite and serves scrumptious grilled chicken, beef and sausage sandwiches, plus *agua de côco* (coconut water), caipirinhas, beers and other refreshments. Look for the blue-and-white striped Uruguayan flag flying high over the beach.

As with other *barracas*, the friendly Uruguai folks rent out chairs and umbrellas for the day.

LA VERONESE PIZZA $
Map p228 (☎21 2247-3152; Visconde de Pirajá 29; mini pizzas from R$5; ⏲8:30am-7pm Tue-Fri, to 6pm Sat, 9am-2:30pm Sun) If Rio is destroying your budget, head to this friendly stand-up snack counter for one of the best deals in the Zona Sul: the R$5 mini pizza with crispy crust is excellent value, and you can top it off with a few strangely addictive *palmeiras* (palm-shaped cookies).

MIL FRUTAS ICE CREAM $
Map p228 (☎21 2521-1384; www.milfrutas.com.br; Garcia d'Ávila 134; ice cream 1/2/3 scoops R$14/23/30; ⏲11am-midnight) On chic Gar-

cia d'Ávila, Mil Frutas serves ice cream that showcases fruits from the Amazon and abroad. *Abacaxí* (pineapple), *goiaba* (guava), *maracujá* (passion fruit) and *açaí* (berry-like fruit) are among the several dozen varieties.

KONI STORE JAPANESE $

Map p228 (☎21 2521-9348; Maria Quitéria 77; hand rolls R$16-22; ⏲11am-midnight Sun-Thu, to 2am Fri & Sat) The Koni craze shows no sign of abating. The recipe is simple: *temakis* (seaweed hand rolls) stuffed with salmon, tuna, shrimp, roast beef or a combination of ingredients, which are then devoured at one of the tiny bistro tables.

It's healthy, tasty and cheap, which are a few of the reasons why you'll have to wait in line among the bar-hopping crowd for a roll at 1am on a Friday. There are numerous other branches around town.

ZONA SUL SUPERMARKET SUPERMARKET $

Map p228 (Prudente de Morais 49; ⏲24hr, except 9pm Sun to 6am Mon) An excellent supermarket across from Praça General Osório.

LA CARIOCA CEVICHERIA PERUVIAN $$

Map p228 (☎21 2522-8184; www.lacarioca.com.br; Garcia d'Ávila 173; sharing plates R$31-51; ⏲6:30pm-1am Mon, noon-1am Tue-Sun) True to its name, this Peruvian place specializes in ceviche and serves more than a dozen varieties of the tangy, tender seafood dish. Other great plates for sharing include the *pulpo andino* (crispy octopus with potato salad and baked red pepper), *tiraditos* (fresh, thinly sliced fish) and *lomo saltado* (stir-fried steak and spices).

Take a seat on the inviting front terrace and don't forget to order a pisco sour; they're the best you'll find this side of Machu Picchu.

QUITÉRIA BRAZILIAN $$

Map p228 (☎21 2267-4603; www.ipanemainn.com.br/en/quiteria; Maria Quitéria 27; mains around R$53, lunch buffet weekday/weekends R$39/53; ⏲7am-11pm) Inside the Ipanema Inn, this humble-looking place serves delectable contemporary Brazilian cooking. Seasonal, high-quality ingredients feature in the extensive lunch buffet, which draws mostly locals. By night the à la carte menu offers hits such as nicely turned out pork ribs with mashed baroa potatoes and cashew sauce, or grilled catch of the day with creamy rice and black-eyed beans.

EMPÓRIO JARDIM NA PRAIA BISTRO $$

Map p228 (☎21 2513-5151; www.emporiojardimrio.com.br; Maria Quitéria 62; mains R$36-68; ⏲8am-10pm; 📶) This charming cafe, which arrived in Ipanema in 2018, was an instant hit thanks to its excellent anytime menu of rich quiches, huge ingredient-packed salads and mouthwatering sandwiches on Empório's house-baked breads. You can start off the morning (or take an afternoon coffee break) over flaky croissants, éclairs and fruit-topped tarts at the bakery counter. Excellent vegetarian options too.

GURUMÊ JAPANESE $$

Map p228 (☎21 2540-7065; www.japagurume.com.br; Anibal de Mendonça 132; sharing plates R$25-54; ⏲noon-11pm Mon-Sat, to 10pm Sun) Gurumê is a Zen-like restaurant turning out creative, beautifully presented dishes that blend flavors from East and West. Among the many temptations are tender salmon topped with guacamole, tuna sashimi with fresh burrata cheese, slices of mouthwatering Wagyu beef with ponzu sauce, and grilled octopus with pesto sauce. Order a handful of sharing plates to experience the works.

VENGA! SPANISH $$

Map p228 (☎21 2247-0234; www.venga.com.br; Garcia d'Ávila 147; small plates R$20-46; ⏲noon-midnight; 🍸) A festive spot to eat and drink, Venga! was Rio's first authentic tapas bar when it opened back in 2009. Classic wood details and a good soundtrack set the scene for noshing on *patatas bravas* (spicy potatoes), *pulpo a la Gallega* (grilled octopus), *gambas al ajillo* (garlic prawns) and other Iberian hits. Match those small plates with a glass of Spanish rioja.

There are other Venga! locations in town, including in Leblon, Copacabana and Jardim Botânico.

AZTEKA MEXICAN $$

Map p228 (☎21 3489-8900; www.azteka-rio.com; Visconde de Pirajá 156; mains R$32-48; ⏲noon-11pm) A few steps from Praça General Osório, this small open-sided eating spot fills a much lacking niche in Rio's food world: Mexican cuisine! Nibble on tortilla chips and guacamole before feasting on quesadillas and burritos. Try the Morelia (pulled pork in *tomatillo* sauce).

The chef-owner hails from Mexico and worked in the US before bringing his cooking to Rio.

MERCEARIA DA PRAÇA BRAZILIAN $$

Map p228 (☎21 3986-1400; www.facebook.com/merceariadapracaipanema; Praça General Osório; mains R$45-80; ⏲11am-midnight Mon, 9am-midnight Tue-Sun) This photogenic newcomer evokes more than a hint of old-world Portugal with its tiled walls, bottle-filled shelves and gourmet items tantalizingly displayed in glass counters. Creamy *bacalhau* (codfish), duck with rice and octopus salad are best followed by a rich *pastel de nata* (custard tart). The buzzing space also functions as a deli and a wine shop.

FRONTERA BUFFET $$

Map p228 (☎21 3289-2350; www.frontera.com.br; Visconde de Pirajá 128; food per kg R$65-70; ⏲11:30am-11pm) Run by a Dutch chef, Frontera offers more than 60 plates at its lunch buffet, which features a mouthwatering assortment of grilled meats, baked casseroles and seafood pastas, plus grilled vegetables, salads, fresh fruits and desserts. Sushi and the dessert counter costs extra. Dark woods and vintage travel posters give it a cozier feel than most per-kilo places.

After 6pm Frontera offers all-you-can-eat pizzas (served *rodizio*-style), for R$20 to R$30, depending on the day (it's cheapest on Wednesdays).

CAPRICCIOSA PIZZA $$

Map p228 (☎21 2523-3394; www.capricciosa.com.br; Vinícius de Moraes 134; pizzas R$56-92; ⏲noon-4pm & 6:30pm-1am Mon-Thu, 6am to 2am Fri & Sat, 5am-1am Sun) This trendy, high-end pizzeria serves tasty thin-crust pizzas made with fresh ingredients. Prices are higher than at other pizza joints, but the chefs – working in an open kitchen next to the brick oven – are generous with the toppings. Among many flavorful combinations is the signature *capricciosa* (ham, bacon, egg, artichoke hearts and mushrooms).

The menu also features flavor-packed pastas, risottos and good-value lunch specials (R$28 to R$32).

VIA SETE INTERNATIONAL $$

Map p228 (☎21 2512-8100; Garcia d'Ávila 125; mains R$46-92; ⏲noon-midnight; 📶) This restaurant on upscale Garcia d'Ávila serves a good selection of salads, burgers and unique appetizers such as calamari in manioc crust, as well as excellent grilled dishes like tuna steak, rump steak, Black Angus and a fish of the day. You choose the side dishes and sauce to accompany your meal.

Via Sete uses 100% organic ingredients, beef included. The pleasant front-side patio is a prime spot for sipping on tropical cocktails while practicing the discreet art of people-watching.

CAFEÍNA CAFE $$

Map p228 (☎21 2521-2194; www.cafeina.com.br; Farme de Amoedo 43; pastas R$35-57, sandwiches R$25-46; ⏲8am-10pm; 📶) In the heart of Ipanema, this inviting cafe with sidewalk tables is a fine spot to have an espresso while watching the city stroll by. You'll also find freshly made sandwiches, salads, pastas, quiches and some very rich desserts.

It's also a good breakfast spot, with omelets, waffles and *açaí* with granola.

FARAJ MIDDLE EASTERN $$

Map p228 (☎21 2247-2705; www.restaurantefaraj.com.br; Gomes Carneiro 131, Ipanema; snacks from R$5, mains R$37-59; ⏲9am-10pm Tue-Sun) A much-loved neighborhood favorite, Faraj is the go-to spot for both satisfying snacks like a *kibbe* (meat croquette), *esfiha* (triangular spinach or meat pastry) or juice. For something more substantial, there's zesty tabbouleh, creamy hummus and daily lunch specials such as lamb kebabs with rice and lentils. Excellent value.

GAROTA DE IPANEMA BRAZILIAN $$

Map p228 (☎21 2522-0340; Vinícius de Moraes 49; mains R$64-133; ⏲noon-2am) A mix of visitors and neighborhood regulars pack the tables at the former bar where 'The Girl from Ipanema' composers Tom Jobim and Vinícius de Moraes once held court. Although the food is fairly standard Brazilian fare, one dish stands out: the *picanha Brasileira* (R$133 for two), a scrumptious skillet of sliced sirloin brought sizzling to your table.

Wash it down with a few glasses of ice-cold *chope* (draft beer) and you'll realize why Garotas have been springing up all over the city.

ALESSANDRO E FEDERICO ITALIAN $$

Map p228 (☎21 2521-0828; www.alessandroefrederico.com.br; Garcia d'Ávila 134; mains R$66-85; ⏲8am-midnight; 📶) This inviting restaurant on Ipanema's most upscale shopping street serves freshly made panini, salads, creamy risottos and creative pastas as well as excellent thin-crust pizzas. Go early to score a sidewalk table and enjoy the passing people parade.

GRINGO CAFE CAFE $$

Map p228 (☎21 3813-3972; www.gringocafe.com; Barão da Torre 240; mains R$29-57; ⏲8:30am-10pm Mon-Sat, to 9pm Sun;) Tired of eating *feijoada*? This open-sided American-run diner dishes up remedies in spades for the homesick gringo: waffles, pancakes, hash browns, mac and cheese, chili (both meat and vegetarian), barbecue ribs, milkshakes etc. It even smells like a US diner.

AMAZÔNIA SOUL AMAZONIAN $$

Map p228 (☎21 2247-1028; www.facebook.com/amazoniasoul; Teixeira de Melo 37; mains R$25-65; ⏲11am-9pm Tue-Sun, 2-8pm Mon;) This tiny cafe doles out rich dishes of *maniçoba* (Amazon-style *feijoada* stew made with manioc leaves instead of beans), *vatapá* (a puree of manioc, dried shrimp, coconut and *dendê* oil) and *tacacá* (a complicated soup made of tapioca, shrimp, lip-numbing jambu leaves and manioc root). For something a little less daring, try the *caranguejo society* (sautéed crab meat with toasted manioc flour).

The small shop inside sells handicrafts and edible items from the Amazon.

NEW NATURAL HEALTH FOOD, BRAZILIAN $$

Map p228 (☎21 2287-0301; Barão da Torre 167; food per kg R$55; ⏲8am-10:30pm;) Featuring an excellent lunch buffet of organic and vegetarian fare, New Natural was the first health-food restaurant to set up in Ipanema. The windowless atmosphere is decidedly uninspiring, but lunchtime crowds don't seem to mind, given all of the excellent options, including salads, soups, grilled veggies and baked dishes, at the healthy buffet.

★ZAZÁ BISTRÔ TROPICAL FUSION $$$

Map p228 (☎21 2247-9101; www.zazabistro.com.br; Joana Angélica 40; mains R$65-87; ⏲7pm-midnight Mon-Thu, from noon Fri-Sun) Inside an art-filled and whimsically decorated converted house, Zazá serves beautifully prepared dishes with Asian accents, and uses organic ingredients when possible. Favorites include chicken curry with jasmine rice, flambéed prawns with risotto, and grilled fish served with caramelized plantain. Don't miss brilliantly creative cocktails like the Caramba Carambola, with Amazonian gin (or vodka), carambola (star fruit), ginger, mint and lemon.

Upstairs, diners lounge in shoeless comfort on throw pillows amid flickering candles. You can also sit at one of the tables out the front.

ESPAÇO 7ZERO6 BRAZILIAN $$$

Map p228 (☎21 2141-4992; www.espaco7zero6.com.br; Av Vieira Souto 706; set brunch R$100; ⏲noon-midnight Mon-Thu, 8am-2pm & 6pm-midnight Fri-Sun) From its location on the top floor of the Hotel Praia Ipanema (p164), this place has a jaw-dropping view of Ipanema Beach. The dinner menu features Brazilian classics, but the best time to come is for the weekend brunch, when the restaurant spreads a banquet of tropical fruits, yogurt, freshly baked breads and pastries, egg dishes and even waffles.

BAZZAR INTERNATIONAL $$$

Map p228 (☎21 3202-2884; www.bazzar.com.br; Barão da Torre 538; mains R$63-98; ⏲noon-11pm Mon-Sat, to 7pm Sun;) Set on a peaceful tree-lined street, this nicely designed restaurant with a relaxing front terrace serves creative, beautifully executed dishes. Start off with oysters from Santa Catarina or crabmeat with fennel puree then move on to tuna with wild chicory and mushrooms, or duck confit with risotto.

There are also seafood pastas and a few meat-free dishes, including a vegetarian heart-of-palm *moqueca* (Bahian fish stew cooked in a clay pot with *dendê* oil, coconut milk and spicy peppers).

CASA DA FEIJOADA BRAZILIAN $$$

Map p228 (☎21 2247-2776; www.restaurantecasadafeijoada.com.br; Prudente de Morais 10B; feijoada R$95; ⏲noon-midnight Mon-Sat, to 11pm Sun) Admirers of Brazil's iconic *feijoada* (black bean and salted pork stew served with rice) needn't wait until Saturday, the time it's traditionally eaten, to experience this meaty meal. The casual Casa da Feijoada serves the rich dish every day of the week.

It comes with the requisite orange slices, *farofa* (garnish of manioc flour sautéed with butter) and grated kale, and goes nicely with a caipirinha.

Leblon

PETIT FORMIDABLE CAFE $

Map p232 (www.formidablebistrot.com.br; João Lira 148; pastries from R$10; ⏲cafe 8am-6pm, bakery 7am-6pm) Next to the Formidable bistro (p69), this tiny bakery and cafe fires up delicious croissants, pains au chocolat, éclairs, mille-feuilles and other delicacies. The cafe also serves eggs Benedict, croque monsieurs (toasted ham and cheese sandwiches) and other light fare.

VEGETARIANO SOCIAL CLUB — VEGAN $

Map p232 (☎21 2294-5200; www.vegetarianosocialclube.com.br; Conde Bernadotte 26L; buffet lunch R$38, mains R$28-36; ⏲noon-11pm Mon-Sat, to 5:30pm Sun; ✍) Vegetarians interested in sampling Brazil's signature dish should visit this small charmer on a Wednesday or a Sunday, when tofu *feijoada* is served. At other times, this 100% vegan eatery serves a 10-dish lunch buffet, while the evening à la carte menu features pizzas, vegetable sandwiches, oat pancakes with shiitake mushrooms and delicious salads.

KURT — DESSERTS $

Map p232 (☎21 2294-0599; www.confeitariakurt.com.br; General Urquiza 117B; desserts R$14-17; ⏲8am-7pm Mon-Fri, 9am-6pm Sat) Extremely popular and going strong since 1942, Kurt has an array of irresistible temptations: flaky strudels, berry crumbles, and palm-sized tortes with strawberries and kiwifruit. There are a few outdoor tables where you can nibble on pastries and take in the street scene.

MOMO — ICE CREAM $

Map p232 (☎21 2294-1965; www.momogelato.com.br; Dias Ferreira 147; ice cream small/large R$16/22; ⏲noon-11pm Sun-Thu, to midnight Fri & Sat) One of the best places in Leblon for a creamy gelato, Momo whips up delectable tropical flavors (guava, mango, avocado) as well as Italian classics such as pistachio or *stracciatella* (vanilla with chocolate chunks).

ARMAZÉM DO CAFÉ — CAFE $

Map p232 (☎21 3874-3678; www.armazemdocafe.com.br; Rita Ludolf 87B; snacks R$8-16; ⏲8am-10pm) Dark-wood furnishings and the aroma of fresh-ground coffee lend authenticity to this Leblon coffeehouse. It serves waffles, snacks and desserts, and connoisseurs rate the aromatic roasts here more highly than at neighboring cafes.

VEZPA — PIZZA $

Map p232 (Av Ataúlfo de Paiva 1063; pizza slices from R$11; ⏲noon-2am Sun-Thu, to 4am Fri & Sat) Vezpa is a New York–style pizza place in Leblon, with brick walls and high ceilings, where you can order pizza by the slice. The crusts are thin and crunchy and there are decent selections on hand – try the mozzarella with tomatoes and basil. Vezpa also has many other locations, including in Ipanema (on Farme de Amoedo) and Copacabana (on Djalma Ulrich).

Don't miss the self-serve artisanal beer (and cocktail) taps. They're a fun way to sample different drink options – in whatever size you want (100mL from R$3.50).

COFFEETOWN — CAFE $

Map p232 (☎21 3798-4484; www.coffeetown.com.br; Bartolomeu Mitre 297; snacks R$12-20; ⏲8am-8pm; 📶) This place aims to create a vibe that evokes an old-fashioned American-style coffeehouse. There's a happy buzz (more chatter than laptop clatter), it serves smoothies, sandwiches, waffles and fluffy pancakes, and the coffee selection is decent. The desserts (temptingly arranged atop the front counter) are almost irresistible, particularly the carrot cake.

BIBI CREPES — CREPES $

Map p232 (☎21 2259-4948; Cupertino Durão 81; crepes R$24-38; ⏲noon-1am Sun-Thu, to 2am Fri & Sat) This small, open-sided restaurant attracts a young, garrulous crowd who enjoy the more than two dozen sweet and savory crepes available, as well as design-your-own salads (choose from 40 different toppings). Come early to beat the lunch crowds.

ZONA SUL SUPERMARKET — SUPERMARKET $

Map p232 (☎21 2259-4699; Dias Ferreira 290; ⏲24hr, except 9pm Sun to 6am Mon) A Rio institution for over 50 years, Zona Sul Supermarket has branches all over the city. This one in Leblon is the best of the bunch, with fresh-baked breads, imported cheeses and olives, wines, cured meats and other items. The adjoining pizza and lasagna counter serves decent plates. There's also a handy Ipanema branch (p63) near Praça General Osório.

PABU IZAKAYA — JAPANESE $$

Map p232 (☎21 3738-0416; www.facebook.com/pabuizakayario; Humberto de Campos 827; sharing plates R$16-38, mains R$48-78; ⏲noon-3pm & 6pm-midnight Mon-Sat, 1-11pm Sun) Tucked away on a quiet Leblon backstreet, this low-lit space brings a dose of creativity to the Rio dining scene, with sharing plates like pork dumplings with house-made mayonnaise, grilled scallops on a bed of sweet potato fries, or eggplant tempura. There's a fine selection of sushi and sashimi, plus refreshing and/or heartwarming sake to accompany your mini feast.

The intimate setting means you'll need to go early to score a table: it has just a few tables outside and a U-shaped counter around the bar.

OKANOSSA CAFE $$

Map p232 (☎21 3204-4055; www.facebook.com/okanossa; Cupertino Durão 79; mains R$22-36; ⏲9am-7:30pm Tue-Sat, 10am-5pm Sun & Mon; ✎) This tiny cafe has a loyal local following for its excellent coffees, all-organic fare and decent vegetarian and vegan dishes – not to mention the friendly welcome. Try a tapioca with goat cheese and pesto (they're made with beet, so they're pink!) or for something more filling, opt for a tartine (open-faced sandwich), heart-of-palm ravioli or the day's changing special (like falafel with tahini).

There's also kombucha and green juice – a favorite with the health-conscious Zona Sul crowd.

CAFÉ DE LA MUSIQUE CAFE $$

Map p232 (☎21 97273-7467; www.facebook.com/cafedelamusiquebeach; Av Delfim Moreira; mains R$32-64; ⏲8am-10pm Sun-Thu, to midnight Fri & Sat) Bringing a dash of style to the Leblon beachfront, the Café de la Musique serves high-end cocktails (R$35 to R$40) to a fashionable crowd. You can sit and watch the surf roll in from well-placed lounge chairs, or grab a table and dine alfresco on salads, sandwiches and seafood (ceviche, marinated octopus, *moqueca*).

You can also come for breakfast fare (eggs Benedict, omelets with Camembert, yogurt with granola).

MASSA ITALIAN $$

Map p232 (☎21 3985-8191; www.massarestaurante.com.br; Dias Ferreira 617; mains R$52-79, lunch menu R$49; ⏲12:30-5pm & 7pm-midnight Mon-Sat, 12:30-10pm Sun) Chef Pedro Siqueira made waves in 2015 with the opening of his excellent restaurant Puro (p84) in Jardim Botânico. Building on that success, Siqueira opened Massa in 2016, offering inventive pasta dishes and other modern Italian-inspired dishes. Considering the location (Rua Dias Ferreira is home to many of Rio's most expensive restaurants) the prices are reasonable – especially the set-menu lunch deal.

VOKOS GREEK $$

Map p232 (☎21 3205-6792; www.vokos.com.br; Dias Ferreira 135; mains R$45-75; ⏲7pm-midnight Mon, noon-midnight Tue-Sun; ✎) Greek fare has at last reached the tropical shores of Rio, with this classy but inviting eatery on restaurant-lined Rua Dias Ferreira. Start off with spanakopita (spinach and cheese pasty) or crispy squid with paprika-dusted yogurt, then continue the feast over tender octopus with truffle oil or lamb with mushroom risotto.

Match your food with Greek wines by the glass and creative cocktails, before finishing with baklava, and cap it all off with a touch of ouzo.

LE BLOND FRENCH $$

Map p232 (☎21 3321-1440; Av Ataúlfo de Paiva 1321; mains R$52-68; ⏲noon-4pm & 6:30pm-midnight Tue-Fri, noon-midnight Sat, noon-6pm Sun) French chef Claude Troisgros adds another hit to his culinary empire with this classic French bistro, opened in 2018, near the western end of Leblon. Globe lights, oversized mirrors and checkered floors evoke a touch of old France, while the menu blends bistro favorites with Latin accents: pork cutlet with guava sauce, foie gras with eggplant and honey, and ceviche with sweet potatoes.

NOLA INTERNATIONAL $$

Map p232 (☎21 2274-5590; Dias Ferreira 247; 3-course lunch menus R$49; ⏲noon-midnight; ✎) A newcomer to Leblon's top culinary strip, Nola has a stylish contemporary design and a creative menu that hits the right notes no matter what you're in the mood for. You'll find comfort fare such as rice with lamb and caramelized onions or roast chicken and Moroccan couscous, as well as pastas, ingredient-packed salads and decent sharing plates (tabbouleh, ceviche, herb-roasted potatoes).

The three-course lunch menus are good value and generally change daily.

STUZZI ITALIAN $$

Map p232 (☎21 2274-4017; Dias Ferreira 48; sharing plates R$29-55, mains R$52-76; ⏲7pm-1am Tue, to 3am Wed-Sat, to midnight Sun) This buzzing, uberpopular Leblon spot specializes in creative Italian tapas (such as roast lamb croquettes, and goat cheese, fig and honey bruschetta) and expertly mixed cocktails. The lively, candelit tables on the sidewalk are the place to be; come early to score one.

GRAVIOLA INTERNATIONAL **$$**

Map p232 (Av Ataúlfo de Paiva 1240; mains R$30-57; noon-10pm;) Graviola started out as a food truck but became such a success that brick-and-mortar eateries quickly followed. The Leblon branch has a tranquil setting amid ferns and hanging plants, with white brick walls and a wooden deck out front that's well placed for taking in the street scene. The wide-ranging menu has veggie burgers, fresh tuna with tropical sauces, and roast organic chicken with creative sides.

Graviola is a popular vegan destination, with vegan lasagna, heart-of-palm spaghetti with pumpkin, and cauliflower risotto with mushroom sauce.

TALHO CAPIXABA SANDWICHES **$$**

Map p232 (21 2512-8760; www.talhocapixaba.com.br; Av Ataúlfo de Paiva 1022; sandwiches R$21-40, mains R$38-60; 7am-10pm;) This deli and gourmet grocer is one of the city's best. In addition to lunchtime specials (roast duck, lasagna, grilled salmon), you'll find pastas, salads and antipasti here. The star of the show is Talho's sandwich selection, with quality ingredients piled high on house-baked baguettes, ciabattas and rye bread. You can dine inside or at the sidewalk tables in front.

PRIMA BRUSCHETTERIA ITALIAN **$$**

Map p232 (21 3592-0881; Rainha Guilhermina 95; bruschetta R$10-17, mains R$48-67; noon-midnight) Prima showcases Italian delicacies not often seen in these parts, using imaginative ingredients such as goat cheese, olive tapenade, prosciutto and smoked salmon to top its chargrilled bread. You'll also find fresh salads, antipasto plates and various risottos and pasta dishes, plus heartier Italian-inspired plates of roast chicken, tuna with couscous and pork with white beans.

YALLA MIDDLE EASTERN **$$**

Map p232 (21 2540-6517; www.facebook.com/pg/yallabistro; Dias Ferreira 45; mains R$37-55, sandwiches R$27-32; 11:30am-midnight;) One of the few casual dining options on the upscale culinary street of Dias Ferreira, Yalla is a small, quick-serving restaurant where you can pick up fresh tabbouleh or couscous salads, sandwiches on lavash bread (shawarma, falafel and shish kebab), or pasties filled with ricotta, beef or spinach. For something heartier, opt for lamb with couscous or moussaka (an eggplant and beef dish).

RÁSCAL ITALIAN **$$**

Map p232 (21 2259-6437; 4th fl, Av Afrânio de Melo Franco 290, Shopping Leblon; all you can eat R$75-84; noon-3pm & 7-10:30pm Mon-Fri, noon-midnight Sat, noon-10pm Sun) This popular São Paulo chain arrived in Rio some years back and quickly earned top marks for its fantastic buffet. The huge spread of Italian cuisine includes salads, bruschetta, pizzas, pastas (six different kinds) and a few juicy grilled choices.

GIRO CHICKEN **$$**

Map p232 (21 2274-0348; Aristides Espinola 101; mains R$35-50; noon-10pm) Bringing a touch of class to the humble rotisserie chicken, Giro has earned a following for its delectable, organic birds. Expect crispy on the outside, juicy tenderness on the inside, served with a choice of creative sauces (try mustard with honey and thyme). Antipasti (like oven-baked potatoes, mushrooms in wine sauce or eggplants with cherry tomatoes) make satisfying accompaniments.

Wash it all down with a craft beer or wines by the glass.

★GIUSEPPE GRILL BRAZILIAN **$$$**

Map p232 (21 2249-3055; www.bestfork.com.br; Bartolomeu Mitre 370; mains R$88-150; noon-4pm & 7pm-midnight Mon-Thu, noon-1am Fri & Sat, noon-11pm Sun) One of Rio's best restaurants, Giuseppe Grill aims for perfection and it rarely disappoints. Chargrilled meat and fish plates are outstanding, as are Brazilian classics like *bobó de camarão* (shrimp and coconut stew). The setting is all class, with black-garbed waitstaff, dark-wood tables and artful touches (an open kitchen, a soaring bar that reaches to the ceiling and a Zen-like wall of water near the entrance).

Wine lovers should ask to take a peak at the magnificent *adega* (cellar) below, with its 500 different varieties of wine (bottles cost from R$98 to upward of R$40,000).

★ZUKA INTERNATIONAL **$$$**

Map p232 (21 3205-7154; www.zuka.com.br; Dias Ferreira 233; mains R$76-120; 7pm-1am Mon, noon-4pm & 7pm-1am Tue-Fri, 1pm-midnight Sat & Sun) One of Rio's best restaurants, Zuka prepares mouthwatering cuisine. Try zingy ceviche with Brazilian *piquinho* pepper or the confection-like delicacy of Zuka's original foie gras to start, followed by tender octopus over a roast potato crisp, honey-glazed duck breast with Moroccan couscous, grilled fish of the day with truffle sauce, or one of many other outstanding dishes.

All the grilling action happens at the open kitchen; you can sit at the counter and watch the chefs in action. The desserts and cocktails, particularly the litchi saketinis, are also excellent.

FORMIDABLE BISTRO **$$$**

Map p232 (☎21 2239-7632; www.formidablebistrot.com.br; João Lira 148; mains R$56-86; ⏲noon-11pm) Something of a secret culinary spot in Leblon, Formidable is a charming bistro with only a handful of tables inside (and a few tables out front). It has a chalkboard menu featuring beautifully executed French bistro classics such as *bœuf bourguignon* (beef stew braised in red wine), *magret de canard* (seared duck breast) and *thon béarnaise* (grilled tuna with *béarnaise* sauce).

Aside from the excellent main courses, don't skimp on dessert (profiteroles, crème brûlée). There are good wine selections as well. Come early to avoid a long wait.

CT BOUCHERIE FUSION **$$$**

Map p232 (☎21 2529-2329; www.ctboucherie.com.br; Dias Ferreira 636; mains R$94-124; ⏲noon-4pm & 7pm-midnight) Created by Claude Troisgros, Rio's most famous chef, this innovative Leblon restaurant takes the idea of the *churrascaria* (traditional barbecue restaurant) and turns it on its head. Instead of all-you-can-eat meat, you order a main course – say a beautifully turned out rack of lamb, duck breast or grilled fish – and you get as many sides as you wish, served *rodizio*-style fresh from the kitchen.

Polenta with passion fruit, chargrilled vegetables, oven-roasted tomatoes, ratatouille with quinoa, and sweet potato mash are among the many offerings. The setting is lively, and nicely designed (subway tiles, whimsical prints) with a welcome lack of pretension.

SUSHI LEBLON JAPANESE **$$$**

Map p232 (☎21 2512-7830; Dias Ferreira 256; mains R$68-122, sushi rolls R$25-38; ⏲noon-4pm & 7pm-midnight) Leblon's top sushi destination boasts a Zen-like ambience, with a handsome dark-wood sushi counter setting the stage for succulent cuisine. In addition to sashimi and sushi, you'll find grilled *namorado* (a type of perch) with passion fruit *farofa*, sea-urchin ceviche and refreshing sake to complement your meal.

NAM THAI THAI **$$$**

Map p232 (☎21 2259-2962; www.namthai.com.br; Rainha Guilhermina 95B; mains R$72-90; ⏲7pm-midnight Mon, noon-midnight Tue-Sat, noon-10:30pm Sun) Thai cuisine is a rarity in Rio, which makes charming Nam Thai even more of a star. The French colonial interior is a cozy setting for the eclectic Thai cooking. Favorites include squid salad and spicy shrimp curry with pineapple. No less intoxicating are Nam Thai's tropical drinks, such as the *caipivodca de lychee* (litchi vodka caipirinha).

At lunchtime, you can score Thai specials for R$58.

DRINKING & NIGHTLIFE

Ipanema has a mix of stylish and classic bars attracting a twenty- and thirty-something crowd. For alfresco drinks, you will find peacefully set tables along the east side of Praça General Osório. Leblon has even more bars on offer than Ipanema, with venerable *botecos* (small open-air bars) and a few lounges as well. One of Leblon's liveliest drinking spots is along Rua Dias Ferreira, with open-sided restaurants transforming into drinking dens as the evening progresses.

Ipanema

★CANASTRA WINE BAR

Map p228 (Jangadeiros 42; ⏲6:30pm-1am Tue-Sat) Run by a trio of Frenchmen, Canastra has become one of the top nightlife destinations in Ipanema. Most nights, the crowd spills out onto the streets, and plenty of socializing *cariocas* never even make it inside. This, however, would be a mistake, as the food (cheese and charcuterie plates, grilled squid and octopus) and drinks (Brazilian wines, sangria, creative caipirinhas) are outstanding.

There's also a hidden bar downstairs – an artfully decorated speakeasy where you can escape the chattering crowds. The big night is Tuesday, when fresh oysters from Santa Catarina arrive (a fine deal at R$40 a dozen).

THE GIRL FROM IPANEMA

Her name was Helô Pinheiro. Tall, tanned, young (she was 17 at the time) and quite lovely, she went frequently to the beach of Ipanema back in 1962. Her route from her home a few blocks away took her past the small Bar Veloso, where several men made overtures to her, though she hardly noticed them.

In August 1962 inside a cramped club in Copacabana, musician and composer Tom Jobim takes the stage along with João Gilberto. They play a song composed by Jobim and poet Vinícius de Moraes. It's a nostalgic, sorrowful tune, with unusual chord progressions and a jazzy beat, and titled 'Garota de Ipanema' (The Girl from Ipanema). The song becomes a smash hit and helps launch the sound of bossa nova, at the time a still-budding movement barely known even in Rio.

When Pinheiro later heard the tune, she never suspected that she was the inspiration for the song. She heard rumors, but didn't believe them – at least until 1965, when de Moraes declared in a press conference that Helô was indeed the inspiration behind the song. Pinheiro got to know de Moraes and Jobim – who both proposed to her. She was impressed with their musical gifts, but never became involved with either of them. In an interview with the *Guardian* in 2012, Pinheiro said, '...The two of them drank too much. They were always at the bar drinking whiskey, caipirinhas, beer.' She shirked fame, marrying her high-school sweetheart and living a sedate life as a homemaker – there was pressure from her father, an army general, to settle down.

Years later, however, circumstances changed, and Pinheiro returned to the spotlight. She became a model, posing for *Playboy* (once alongside her daughter, in 2003), as well as a radio host and TV announcer, and wrote her autobiography in 1996. Although she never earned money directly from the song, it helped pave the way to success in a variety of enterprises, including a swimwear boutique (named Garota de Ipanema, naturally) located on the street next to the former Bar Veloso (now also called the Garota de Ipanema). Rua Montenegro has been renamed Vinícius de Moraes in honor of the songwriter. Today Pinheiro lives in São Paulo, but for bossa nova fans she'll always be the girl from Ipanema.

NOSSO — COCKTAIL BAR

Map p228 (☎21 99619-0099; www.facebook.com/nossoipanema; Maria Quitéria 91, Ipanema; ⏲7pm-1am Tue-Thu, to 2am Fri & Sat, 6-11pm Sun) Located in the heart of Ipanema, this supremely stylish cocktail bar and restaurant, complete with swanky rooftop terrace, feels like it has been plucked directly from downtown Manhattan. The meticulously crafted cocktails are made with high-quality spirits and often arrive adorned with foams and dehydrated fruit slices. The menu offers equally intricate yet delicious dishes.

BAR ASTOR — BAR

Map p228 (☎21 2523-0085; www.barastor.com.br; Av Vieira Souto 110, Ipanema; ⏲6pm-1am Mon-Thu, 1pm-2am Fri, noon-2am Sat, noon-10pm Sun) Not visiting São Paulo? No problem. One of Sampa's best bars has now become a mainstay of post-beach revelry on prime real estate along the Ipanema shorefront. This gorgeous art deco bar does meticulously prepared caipirinhas, as well as Astor's own creative cocktails – try a Tiki Brasil, featuring mango, rangpur and Brazil nut syrup, plus *cachaça* (sugarcane alcohol).

BARZIN — BAR

Map p228 (www.facebook.com/barzinriolive; Vinícius de Moraes 75; ⏲noon-1am Sun, Mon, Wed & Thu, noon-4am Tue, Fri & Sat) Barzin is a popular spot for post-beach drinks; its open-sided ground-floor bar fills with animated chatter at all hours. Upstairs you can catch a changing lineup of bands playing surf rock, hip-hop and other popular Brazilian music (cover charge from R$30 to R$80). The Tuesday night parties hosted by Bem Brasil (p203) are all the rage.

BARETTO-LONDRA — LOUNGE

Map p228 (☎21 3202-4000; www.fasano.com.br/gastronomia/baretto-londra; Av Vieira Souto 80, Hotel Fasano; ⏲8pm-2am Thu-Sat) You'll find one of Rio's most glam bars here inside the Hotel Fasano (p164), offering a vision of decadence matched by few of the city's night spots. The intimate space, designed by Philippe Starck, has an enchantingly illuminated bar, leather armchairs and divans, and a DJ spinning world electronica.

GAROTA DE IPANEMA BAR

Map p228 (☎21 2523-2787; www.bargarotadeipanema.com; Vinícius de Moraes 49; ⏲noon-1am) During its first incarnation, this small, open-sided bar was called the Bar Veloso. Its name and anonymity disappeared once two scruffy young regulars – Tom Jobim and Vinícius de Moraes – penned the famous song, 'The Girl from Ipanema' (p70). It changed history, and the name of the street, too.

Today you'll find a mix of tourists and *cariocas* here, as well as sizzling platters of grilled steak.

BLUE AGAVE BAR

Map p228 (☎21 3592-9271; www.facebook.com/blueagave; Vinícius de Moraes 68; ⏲noon-2am) On a lively bar-lined street, this small drinking den gathers a mix of locals and gringos who come for margaritas, bottles of Sol and a small selection of Tex-Mex fare (tacos, enchiladas and burritos). TVs over the bar show soccer and American football games.

GALERIA CAFÉ GAY, BAR

Map p228 (☎21 2523-8250; www.galeriacafe.com.br; Teixeira de Melo 31; ⏲11pm-4am Wed-Sat, to 8pm Sun) While many other LGBT bars have closed in Rio, Galeria keeps going strong, with a fun mixed crowd, nice decor and a throbbing dance floor in a great location in Ipanema. Go early (at opening time) to avoid the frequently long lines. Entry is R$20 to R$60.

SHENANIGAN'S IRISH PUB

Map p228 (☎21 2267-5860; www.facebook.com/shenanigansrj; Visconde de Pirajá 112A; ⏲6pm-1am Tue-Thu, to 3am Fri & Sat, 4pm-1am Sun) Overlooking the Praça General Osório, Shenanigan's is a friendly, Irish-style pub with imported beers, exposed brick walls and a couple of tiny balconies perched above the street. Gringos and *cariocas* mix it up over games of pool and darts to the backdrop of major games on TV (Brazilian football, American football and basketball).

TAP HOUSE BAR

Map p228 (☎21 3795-4594; www.instagram.com/taphouseipanema; Nascimento Silva 51; ⏲noon-1am Mon-Sat, 5pm-1am Sun) Set in a bright blue house with a small front veranda, the Tap House lives up to its name with a rotating selection of 20 or so microbrews on draft, from Rio and further afield. Good snacks (and a first-rate lunch buffet) as well as live music (blues, folk, rock) several nights a week round out the offerings.

DELIRIUM CAFE BAR

Map p228 (☎21 2502-0029; www.deliriumcafe.com.br; Barão da Torre 183; ⏲5pm-1am Mon-Sat, 4pm-midnight Sun) This small and cozy pub has more than 300 brew varieties, with labels from across Europe, the US, Australia and beyond. If you've been to the original Delirium in Brussels, you might be a bit disappointed by this modest sister enterprise. Nevertheless, it's a great destination for beer lovers.

BAR VELOSO BOTECO

Map p232 (☎21 2274-9966; Aristides Espínola 44; ⏲noon-1am) Named after the original bar, now the Garota de Ipanema, where Tom Jobim and Vinícius de Moraes penned the famous song 'The Girl from Ipanema,' the open-sided Bar Veloso attracts a young, good-looking crowd, who spill out onto the sidewalk on busy weekends.

BARTHODOMEU BOTECO

Map p228 (☎21 2247-8609; www.barthodomeu.com.br; Maria Quitéria 46; ⏲5pm-2am Mon, noon-2am Tue-Sun) Barthodomeu is a friendly, open-sided bar that has *boteco* charm. It has wooden tables, minimal decor and waiters that bustle about under trays of *chope* (draft beer), *feijoada* (bean-and-meat stew), grilled meats and piping-hot appetizers.

EMPÓRIO 37 BAR

Map p228 (☎21 3813-2526; Maria Quitéria 37; ⏲8:30pm-5am) A young mix of *cariocas* and gringos stirs things up over cheap cocktails at this battered old favorite in Ipanema. A porch out the front overlooks the street; it's a fine spot to stake out when the air gets too heavy with dubious '80s music. Don't come early; Empório doesn't get lively until after midnight.

TÔ NEM AÍ BAR

Map p228 (☎21 2247-8403; www.facebook.com/tonemairestaurante; cnr Farme de Amoedo & Visconde de Pirajá; ⏲5pm-2am Mon-Fri, noon-3am Sat & Sun) Located on Rua Farme de Amoedo, Ipanema's most gay-friendly street, this popular bar is a great after-beach spot. It draws a mostly gay crowd, though all are welcome.

POLIS SUCOS JUICE BAR

Map p228 (☎21 2247-2518; www.polissucos.com.br; Maria Quitéria 70; ⏲7am-midnight) One of Ipanema's favorite spots for a dose of fresh-squeezed vitamins, this juice bar facing the Praça NS da Paz has dozens of flavors (juices R$12). You can pair these tangy beverages with sandwiches, burgers or *pão de queijo* (balls of cheese-stuffed tapioca bread).

WOOD'S CLUB

Map p232 (☎21 99193-1134; www.woodsbar.com.br/riodejaneiro; General San Martin 1219; ⏲11pm-4am Thu-Sun) Wood's gathers a young, attractive crowd, who sip brightly colored elixirs amid disco lights while mingling on the dance floor. A mix of DJs and bands keep things going. Live music leans toward *sertanejo,* a somewhat countrified sound from the Northeast. Entry is R$30 to R$50.

Leblon

BREWTECO BAR

Map p232 (☎21 3217-8280; www.brewteco.com.br; Dias Ferreira 420; ⏲10am-4pm Mon, to midnight Tue-Sat, 3:30pm-midnight Sun) A pillar of Rio's growing microbrew-loving community, Brewteco has nearly two dozen taps featuring unique craft beers – nearly all of which are from Rio. Among the rotating selections, you'll find plenty of variety: wheat beers, IPAs, American IPAs, Belgian-style Tripels, and even Russian Imperial stout.

Note that Brewteco is tiny, with only a few seats. The 'bar' is essentially the sidewalk in front of the place, where beer-sipping crowds gather.

ACADEMIA DA CACHAÇA BAR

Map p232 (☎21 2529-2680; www.academiadacachaca.com.br; Conde Bernadotte 26G; ⏲noon-1am) Although *cachaça* has a sordid reputation in some parts, at this bar the fiery liquor is given the respect it (nearly) deserves. Along with dishes of traditional Brazilian cooking, this pleasant indoor-outdoor spot serves more than 100 varieties of *cachaça;* you can order it straight, with honey and lime, or disguised in a fruity caipirinha.

BELMONTE BAR

Map p232 (☎21 2294-8249; Dias Ferreira 521; ⏲11am-2am) An icon in Leblon, Belmonte always draws huge crowds: it's pretty much a massive street party every night, with beer-drinking revelers spilling onto the sidewalk from 8pm onward. If you can score a table, don't miss the delicious, well-priced *pasteis* (dough that's filled then deep-fried), stuffed with crab, jerked beef with cheese, shrimp, heart of palm and other tasty ingredients.

BRACARENSE BOTECO

Map p232 (☎21 2294-3549; www.facebook.com/barbracarense; José Linhares 85B; ⏲10am-midnight Mon-Sat, to 10pm Sun) Opened in 1948, Bracarense is a classic *carioca* watering hole, famous for its simple, unpretentious ambience and its heavenly *salgados* (bar snacks). A steady stream of neighborhood regulars enjoy more than 20 *salgado* varieties, accompanied by ice-cold *chope* (draft beer). Try the *aipim com camarão* (cassava with shrimp).

JOBI BOTECO

Map p232 (☎21 2274-0547; Av Ataúlfo de Paiva 1166; ⏲9am-5am) A favorite since 1956, Jobi has served a lot of beer in its day, and its popularity hasn't waned. The unadorned *botequim* (bar with table service) still serves plenty; grab a seat by the sidewalk and let the night unfold. If hunger beckons, try the tasty appetizers; the *carne seca* (jerked beef) and the *bolinhos de bacalhau* (codfish croquettes) are tops.

NOI CRAFT BEER

Map p232 (☎21 2259-4561; www.cervejarianoi.com.br; Conde Bernadotte 26; ⏲noon-midnight Sun-Thu, to 2am Fri & Sat) A fine contender in Rio's burgeoning craft-beer scene, Noi creates some satisfying brews that go down nicely with snacks like *bolinhos de feijoada* (croquettes of black bean and sausage) or *pasteis* stuffed with shiitake mushrooms. The nine different beers on tap come from Noi's brewery across the bay in Niterói.

LORD JIM PUB

Map p228 (☎21 2249-4881; www.facebook.com/lordjimpub; Paul Redfern 44; ⏲5pm-2am Mon-Thu, to 4am Fri, 11am-4am Sat, noon-2am Sun) Something of a novelty for *cariocas,* Lord Jim is one of several English-style pubs scattered about the Zona Sul. Darts, English-speaking waiters and a few expat beers – Guinness, Harp, Bass etc – are on hand to complete the ambience. Come on weekends to catch live bands playing rock and indie music.

BIBI SUCOS JUICE BAR
Map p232 (☎21 2259-0000; www.bibisucos.com.br; Av Ataúlfo de Paiva 591A; ⏲8am-11pm Sun-Thu, to 1am Fri & Sat) Among Rio's countless juice bars, Bibi Sucos is a long-standing favorite. Here you'll find more than 40 juice varieties (R$8 to R$21), and a never-ending supply of the favorite *açaí* (berry-like fruit). Sandwiches (from R$15 to R$33) will quell greater hunger pangs.

PIZZARIA GUANABARA BAR
Map p232 (☎21 2294-0797; www.pizzariaguanabara.com.br; Av Ataúlfo de Paiva 1228; ⏲noon-6am) One of the pillars of Baixo Leblon, this popular drinking spot serves lousy pizza, but that hasn't stopped patrons from packing it out at all hours of the night. Expect simple ambience and a young, flirtatious, beer-drinking crowd.

ENTERTAINMENT

CASA DA CULTURA LAURA ALVIM ARTS CENTER
Map p228 (☎21 2332-2016; www.casadeculturalauraalvim.rj.gov.br; Av Vieira Souto 176, Ipanema; ⏲1-10pm) Across from the beach in Ipanema, this small center stages plays, screens films and hosts art exhibitions. The atrium cafe is a pleasant spot for a bite.

TEATRO DO LEBLON PERFORMING ARTS
Map p232 (☎21 2529-7700; www.facebook.com/teatrodoleblon; Conde Bernadotte 26, Leblon) This nicely located theater shows a mix of drama, cutting-edge and children's performances on three different stages. In front of the same complex is an assortment of lively eating and drinking spots.

ESTAÇÃO NET IPANEMA CINEMA
Map p228 (☎21 2279-4603; www.grupoestacao.com.br; Visconde de Pirajá 605, Ipanema) On the ground floor of a tiny shopping complex in Ipanema, this two-screen cinema shows popular contemporary films from Brazil and abroad.

SHOPPING

Ipanema and Leblon are the best hunting grounds for top fashion designs, both homegrown and foreign labels. You'll also find curio and novelty stores, galleries, bookshops, liquor stores and lots of cafes for refueling along the way. There's a lot going on along the main thoroughfares of Rua Visconde de Pirajá in Ipanema and Av Ataúlfo de Paiva in Leblon.

Ipanema

★HIPPIE FAIR MARKET
Map p228 (Praça General Osório; ⏲9am-6pm Sun) The Zona Sul's most famous market, the Hippie Fair (aka Feira de Arte de Ipanema) has artwork, jewelry, handicrafts, clothing and souvenirs for sale. Stalls in the four corners of the plaza sell tasty plates of *acarajé* (croquettes made from mashed black-eyed peas, with a sauce of *vatapá* – manioc paste, coconut and *dendê* oil – and shrimp), plus excellent desserts. Don't miss it.

LENNY NIEMEYER FASHION & ACCESSORIES
Map p228 (☎21 2227-5537; www.lennyniemeyer.com; Garcia d'Ávila 149; ⏲10am-8pm Mon-Fri, to 6pm Sat) When it comes to swimwear, few designers have earned a following like Lenny Niemeyer. She creates beautiful, form-fitting bikinis and one-pieces in both classic and avant-garde styles. You'll also find plenty of other essentials for street and beach, including dresses, tops, caftans and sarongs.

You'll find eight other Lenny stores around Rio and nearly a dozen other stores scattered around Brazil.

CHOCOLATE Q CHOCOLATE
Map p228 (☎21 2274-1001; www.chocolateq.com; Shop B, Garcia d'Ávila 149; ⏲10am-8pm Mon-Sat) This is serious chocolate. Cacao beans, harvested from a single, environmentally conscious grower in Bahia, are processed into a range of exquisite dark-chocolate products (milk chocolate fans be advised, there is nothing for you here). All the bars and pastilles are beautifully packaged, with colorful illustrations of Brazilian wildlife, making them eminently gift-worthy.

The chocolates come in a range of cocoa strengths, from a mild 50% all the way up to a challenging 95%. True chocolate obsessives can sign up to the one-hour 'Q Experience' to learn more about the chocolate production process.

GILSON MARTINS FASHION & ACCESSORIES
Map p228 (☎21 2227-6178; www.shop.gilsonmartins.com.br; Visconde de Pirajá 462; ⏲9am-8pm Mon-Fri, to 7pm Sat) Designer Gilson

Martins transforms the Brazilian flag and silhouettes of Pão de Açúcar (Sugarloaf Mountain) and Corcovado into eye-catching accessories in his flagship store in Ipanema. This is the place for unique glossy handbags, wallets, passport covers, key chains and iPad covers. Products are durable and use recycled and sustainable materials – and are not available outside Rio.

You can also design your own bag in the studio in the back of the store. You choose the bag, the embellishments and the layout, then it gets professionally sewn and sent back to the store where you can pick it up in a few days. Gilson also has several other branches, including a spacious showroom in Copacabana (p99).

OSKLEN CLOTHING

Map p228 (☎21 2227-2930; Maria Quitéria 85; ⏲9am-8pm Mon-Fri, 10am-7pm Sat, 11am-5pm Sun) One of Brazil's best-known fashion labels outside the country, Osklen is notable for its stylish and well-made beachwear (particularly men's swim shorts and graphic T-shirts), sneakers and outerwear. The company was started in 1988 by outdoor enthusiast Oskar Metsavaht, the first Brazilian to scale Mont Blanc.

TOCA DO VINÍCIUS MUSIC

Map p228 (☎21 2247-5227; www.facebook.com/casadabossanova.tocadovinicius; Vinícius de Moraes 129; ⏲11am-7pm Mon-Fri, 10am-6pm Sat, 3-6pm Sun) Bossa nova fans shouldn't miss this store. In addition to its ample CD and vinyl selection (starting at R$40) of contemporary and old performers, it also sells music scores and composition books. Around the store you'll find memorabilia from great songwriters including Vinícius de Moraes and Chico Buarque.

CASA IPANEMA SHOES

Map p228 (Garcia d'Ávila 77; ⏲10am-8pm Mon-Fri, 11am-6pm Sat) This stylish, open-sided boutique sells one-of-a-kind flip-flops (thongs) costing R$30 to R$140. It's a creative space with an upstairs gallery where you can catch the occasional art exhibition, workshop, and book and CD launches.

LIVRARIA DA TRAVESSA BOOKS, MUSIC

Map p228 (☎21 3205-9002; www.travessa.com.br; Visconde de Pirajá 572; ⏲9am-11pm Mon-Sat, 10am-11pm Sun) One of several branches around town, this Livraria da Travessa has a small selection of foreign-language books and periodicals, and some CDs upstairs. The buzzing 2nd-floor cafe (a branch of Bazzar) serves salads, sandwiches, quiches and desserts. There's an even larger Livraria da Travessa inside the Shopping Leblon mall.

CATHERINE LABOURÉ VINTAGE

Map p228 (☎21 2227-3375; 2nd fl, Visconde de Pirajá 207, Galeria VIP Center; ⏲12:30-6:30pm Tue-Fri, 11am-4pm Sat) Tucked away inside an otherwise humdrum shopping center, this intriguing shop sells vintage dresses, skirts, silk scarves, handbags, shoes and sunglasses, with labels by top international designers. There's a smaller selection for men – mostly T-shirts and button-downs – as well as a few small antiques and collectibles for the home.

GAROTA DE IPANEMA FASHION & ACCESSORIES

Map p228 (☎21 2521-3168; Vinícius de Moraes 53; ⏲10am-7pm Mon-Sat, noon-6pm Sun) Located next to the famous restaurant of the same name, this tiny boutique is an excellent place to browse for attractive, reasonably priced bikinis and beachwear. There are also eye-catching T-shirts (for men and women), trucker hats, bags and other accessories.

HAVAIANAS SHOES

Map p228 (☎21 3437-1479; Visconde de Pirajá 111; ⏲9am-8pm Mon-Fri, 10am-7pm Sat & Sun) This small shop is a great place to stock up on Brazil's iconic rubber sandals. You'll find a colorful variety of Havaianas for men, women and children, covering all price points (from R$35 to R$96).

DRACO STORE CLOTHING

Map p228 (☎21 2287-7341; Visconde de Pirajá 111, Ipanema; ⏲9am-8pm Mon-Sat, 11am-5pm Sun) This menswear store specializes in stylish beachwear, including well-made swim shorts. You'll also find jeans, button-downs and T-shirts (from R$65 to R$110), the best of which bear the names of Rio neighborhoods (Copacabana, Ipanema, Arpoador etc).

REDLEY CLOTHING

Map p228 (☎21 2267-1573; Maria Quitéria 99; ⏲9am-8pm Mon-Sat, noon-6pm Sun) In the heart of Ipanema, this multilevel fashion store is a fine place to browse for couture beach clothing and streetwear. Unlike most other Ipanema boutiques, this one's aimed at men, and it has an excellent assortment of T-shirts, shorts and swimsuits.

Leblon

MARIA OITICICA JEWELRY
Map p232 (☎21 3875-8025; www.mariaoiticica.com; Av Afrânio de Melo Franco 290, Shopping Leblon; ⏲10am-10pm Mon-Sat, 1-9pm Sun) Using native materials found in the Amazon, Maria Oiticica has created some lovely handcrafted jewelry inspired by indigenous art. Seeds, plant fibers and tree bark are just some of the ingredients of her bracelets, necklaces, earrings and sandals. There are even sandals and handbags made from fish 'leather.'

ISABELA CAPETO CLOTHING
Map p232 (☎21 2540-6640; www.isabelacapeto.com.br; General Venâncio Flôres 481C, Leblon; ⏲10am-8pm Mon-Sat) One of Brazil's rising fashion stars, Isabela Capeto creates colorful apparel that is both flattering and playful. Many of her pieces are embroidered and feature add-ons of vintage lace, sequins or fabric trims. Her new shop here in leafy Leblon is the best place to see dresses and skirts that have earned her accolades in *O Globo*, *Vogue* and other publications.

ELIANE CARVALHO FASHION & ACCESSORIES
Map p232 (☎21 2540-5438; www.facebook.com/loja.elianecarvalho; Dias Ferreira 242; ⏲10:30am-6pm Tue-Sat, 1-6pm Sun) A dapper women's store in a high-end part of Leblon, Eliane Carvalho sells flattering, one-of-a-kind hats in all shapes and styles as well as a smaller selection of scarves, handbags, dresses and jewelry. Its location on restaurant-lined Dias Ferreira makes it a fine spot for a browse before or after a meal.

VOID GENERAL STORE FASHION & ACCESSORIES
Map p232 (☎21 3592-7719; www.avoid.com.br; Av Ataúlfo de Paiva 1166; ⏲10am-1am Mon-Wed, to 3am Thu-Sat, 11am-1am Sun) The go-to spot for all your underground hipster needs, the tiny Void is a shop by day and a lively beer-drinking spot by night. You'll find unique jewelry, graphic T-shirts, baseball caps, sneakers (Converse, Vans) and CDs. It tends to attract a young, alternative crowd.

SHOPPING LEBLON SHOPPING CENTER
Map p232 (☎21 2430-5122; www.shoppingleblon.com.br; Av Afrânio de Melo Franco 290; ⏲10am-10pm Mon-Sat, 1-9pm Sun) This glittering multistory shopping center packed with top-name Brazilian and foreign labels is the best shopping destination in Leblon. It has plenty of tempting stores that will drain your vacation funds, as well as good restaurants and a cinema.

ARGUMENTO BOOKS, MUSIC
Map p232 (☎21 2239-5294; www.livrariaargumento.com; Dias Ferreira 417; ⏲9am-midnight Mon-Sat, 10am-11pm Sun) One of Leblon's fine neighborhood bookstores, Argumento stocks a small but decent selection of foreign-language books and magazines. The charming cafe in the back is the perfect place to disappear with a book.

WÖLLNER OUTDOOR FASHION & ACCESSORIES
Map p232 (☎21 3496-1230; www.wollner.com.br; Av Afrânio de Melo Franco 290, Shopping Leblon; ⏲10am-10pm Mon-Sat, 1-9pm Sun) The great outdoors, and the shirt and shorts you'll need to enjoy it, seem to be the inspiration for Wöllner. Clothes and accessories are ruggedly styled, not unlike Abercrombie and American Eagle. It's located inside the massive Shopping Leblon mall.

SPORTS & ACTIVITIES

SPA MARIA BONITA SPA
Map p228 (☎21 2513-4050; www.ipanema.spamariabonita.com.br; Level P, Prudente de Morais 729, Ipanema) Although better known for its lush spa resort in Friburgo, Maria Bonita does offer a full range of treatments here for those who'd rather not trek out to the countryside. Options include aromatherapy baths, deep-tissue massage, shiatsu and acupuncture. There is also an organic and raw-food restaurant on-site.

MUSEUM OF YOGA YOGA
Map p228 (☎21 98291-0211; www.themuseumofyoga.com; Joana Angélica 116, Ipanema; per class R$50; ⏲Mon-Sat) Near Praça NS da Paz, this peaceful center offers a full schedule of morning, afternoon and evening classes in Vinyasa, Hatha and power yoga. Some instructors speak English.

TETIANA TUCHYK/SHUTTERSTOCK ©

. Copacabana Beach (p92) **2.** *Futevôlei* (volleyball played without ands), Copacabana Beach (p92) **3.** Stand-up paddle boarding, opacabana Beach (p92)

Beach Life

The beaches of Rio are the city's wondrous and carefree backyard. It's where *cariocas* (Rio residents) from all walks of life – rich and poor, young and old, black and white, svelte thin and beer-bellied – come to play and socialize against a backdrop of crashing waves and the ever-present green peaks towering over the city.

The Perfect Crowd

Although the mix is incredibly democratic, *postos* subdivide the beach into different sections, with each subculture drawn to its particular *posto,* whether that be favela kids, volleyballers, well-heeled families or the beauty crowd.

Seaside Sport

Sports are a big seaside draw, and entail surfing, stand-up paddle boarding, jogging, cycling and skating the beachside path, football, volleyball and *futevôlei* – that uniquely Brazilian combination of volleyball played with football-style rules (no hands allowed!). There's also *frescobol,* a simple game where two players with wooden rackets stand 10m apart and pound a rubber ball back and forth.

Sit Back & Relax

Many beachgoers, however, would rather just relax and enjoy the scene. For sun lovers, there's much to take in: the sand, the sea, the food and drink vendors, the passing parade of people.

BEACH ETIQUETTE

- Leave valuables at your hotel. Take only the cash you need for the beach.
- Don't use a towel on the beach – instead, sit on a chair or a *kanga* (sarong); Brazilian men stand or sit on the sand.
- Choose your spot, then find a *barraca* (stall) you like and hire chairs and sunshades from it.
- Don't bother bringing food or drink to the beach; support the local vendors.

Gávea, Jardim Botânico & Lagoa

GÁVEA | JARDIM BOTÂNICO | LAGOA

Neighborhood Top Five

1 Lagoa Rodrigo de Freitas (p80) Hiring a bike and going for a spin around Rio's most picturesque lake.

2 Jardim Botânico (p81) Taking a stroll through this lush and flower-filled exotic garden, complete with towering palms, massive water lilies and an orchid house.

3 Parque Lage (p81) Looking for monkeys on the forested paths of this beautiful park, then lunching in the restaurant while taking in the views of Cristo Redentor (Christ the Redeemer).

4 Palaphita Kitch (p86) Sipping creative cocktails made from exotic Amazonian fruits in an open-air setting while admiring the sundown vistas.

5 Instituto Moreira Salles (p81) Checking out the latest thought-provoking art exhibitions at this top-notch cultural center.

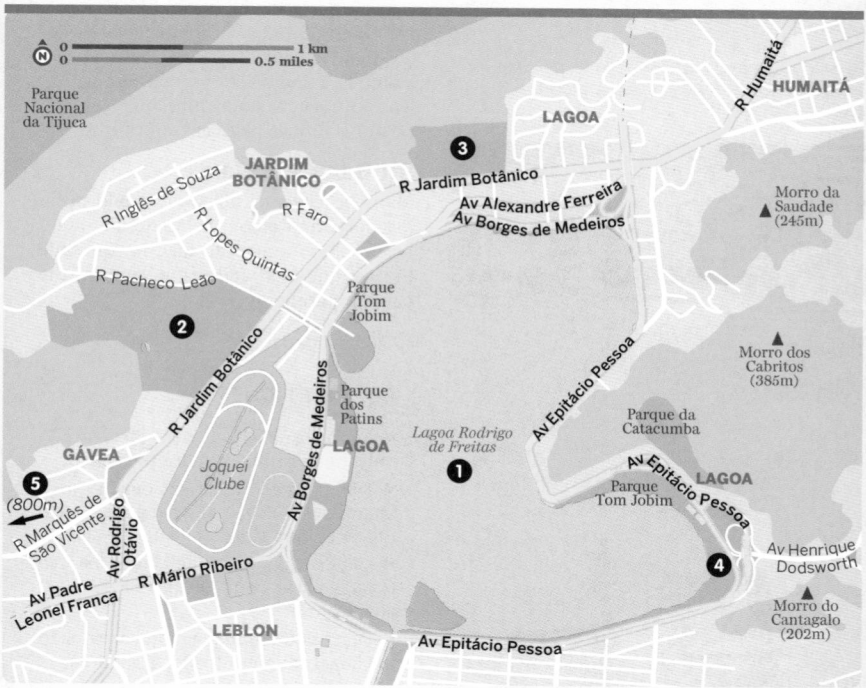

For more detail of this area see Map p234

Explore Gávea, Jardim Botânico & Lagoa

Rio's picturesque lake is the focal point of these well-heeled neighborhoods. Lagoa Rodrigo de Freitas (p80) is actually a saltwater lagoon and is much utilized by *cariocas* (residents of Rio). Joggers and cyclists zip along the shoreline trail by day, while the lakeside restaurants fill with people enjoying a meal and live music in the open air by night. This area includes the north, east and west sides of the lake. The streets on the south side of Lagoa are generally considered part of Ipanema and Leblon.

West of the lake are the botanical gardens for which the neighborhood, Jardim Botânico, is named. Here you'll find stately palms and a variety of flowering plants. South of the gardens is Gávea, home to Rio's premier horse-racing track and a planetarium. Aside from their natural attractions, these neighborhoods also have some excellent restaurants, lively nightlife and one of the Zona Sul's best cultural centers, the Instituto Moreira Salles (p81).

Much of the development of this area is linked to the lake, which is named Rodrigo de Freitas in honor of the Portuguese settler who made his fortune off the sugarcane fields surrounding the lake in the 16th century. Factories blighted the landscape in the 1900s, and it took much of the 20th century for the area to recover. Although the lake is still too polluted for swimming, some wildlife has returned, and visitors might see egrets on the lookout for fish in the lake.

Local Life

Walks For a scenic hike, you can take the uphill trail to Cristo Redentor in Parque Lage (p81). A shorter trail offers great views from Parque da Catacumba (p82).

Markets Praça Santos Dumont hosts an antiques market on Sundays and a fruit market on Fridays.

Nightlife Bars near Praça Santos Dumont attract a young, festive crowd during the week.

Getting There & Away

Bus – Gávea Centro, Flamengo and Catete (170); Ipanema and Copacabana (571, 572 and 574); Leblon (432, 435 and 593).

Bus – Jardim Botânico Centro, Flamengo and Catete (170); Copacabana and Ipanema (162, 570 and 584); Leblon (512, 574 and 584).

Metro na Superfície Metro buses connect Botafogo station with Jardim Botânico.

Lonely Planet's Top Tip

One of Rio's often overlooked attractions, the Instituto Moreira Salles is well worth a visit. It has a picturesque setting and the museum stages first-rate exhibitions. If you have kids in tow, Saturdays are a good time to visit, as there are special (free) activities such as crafts and music and the like.

Best Places to Eat

- Casa Camolese (p83)
- Prana Vegetariano (p83)
- Plage Café (p83)
- Olympe (p85)
- Jarbô (p83)
- Lagoon (p84)

For reviews, see p83

Best Places to Drink

- Palaphita Kitch (p86)
- Hipódromo (p85)
- Palaphita Gávea (p85)

For reviews, see p85

Best Places to Shop

- Dona Coisa (p87)
- Gabinete (p87)
- O Sol (p87)
- Shopping da Gávea (p86)

For reviews, see p86

TOP SIGHT
LAGOA RODRIGO DE FREITAS

Rio is blessed with mountains, beaches and rainforest, so it's perhaps a little unfair that it would also have a picturesque lake – surrounded by highly desirable neighborhoods, no less. *Cariocas*, however, take it in their stride and make ample use of the watery expanse by running the lakeside path, dining near the water's edge or simply admiring the view from almost any vantage point.

Lake Activities

No matter the time of year, you'll always find runners and cyclists making good use of the 7.2km path that encircles the lake. If you'd like to join them, there are various places to hire bikes, including the Parque dos Patins on the west side.

For an even better view over the lake, book a seat on a scenic helicopter flight that departs from a **heliport** (Av Borges de Medeiros) on the west side of the lake. A much cheaper way to admire the view is to hike to the top of Parque da Catacumba.

Another way to experience the lake is to get out on the surface. Pollution makes swimming a bad idea, but you can hire pedal boats from the eastern side near the Parque do Cantagalo.

One of the major events in the city's calendar is the lighting of the floating Christmas tree on the lake each year. If you're around in December, don't miss a visit by night.

Lagoa by Night

For those who prefer caipirinhas to plastic swan boats, there are two worthwhile kiosks (Palaphita Kitch and Arab da Lagoa) anchoring either side of the lake that make memorable settings to kick off the evening. There's also the lakeside complex Lagoon (p84), which houses indoor restaurants with views, a few food trucks with outdoor seating, a cinema and a live-music venue.

DON'T MISS

- Cycling around the lake
- Skimming over the surface on a pedal boat
- Drinks and live music at a lakeside kiosk

PRACTICALITIES

- Map p234, E4

LAZYLLAMA/SHUTTERSTOCK ©

SIGHTS

This lakeside district has some wonderful green spaces. The Jardim Botânico is not to be missed, followed by the lush Parque Lage. Both have fine cafes that should also figure into your itinerary. When the rain arrives, there are a few galleries where you can take in Rio's art scene, including the Instituto Moreira Salles, OM.art and Carpintaria. Those with young kids in tow should also check out the Planetário.

Gávea

★INSTITUTO MOREIRA SALLES CULTURAL CENTER

(IMS; ☎21 3284-7400; www.ims.com.br; Marquês de São Vicente 476; ⏲11am-8pm Tue-Sun) FREE This beautiful cultural center hosts impressive exhibitions, often showcasing the works of some of Brazil's best photographers and artists. The gardens, complete with artificial lake and flowing river, were designed by Brazilian landscape architect Roberto Burle Marx. There's also a craft shop, and an excellent cafe that serves breakfast all day as well as lunch and afternoon tea.

On display there's usually at least one Rio-focused exhibition, which taps into the extensive archive here: the IMS has more than 80,000 photographs, many portraying the old streets of Rio as well as the urban development of other Brazilian cities over the last two centuries. Check the website to see what's on when you're town.

PARQUE DA CIDADE PARK

(☎21 2512-2353; www.rio.rj.gov.br/cultura; Estrada de Santa Marinha 505; ⏲8am-5pm Tue-Sun) On the outer reaches of Gávea, this lush park of native Mata Atlântica rainforest and replanted secondary forest provides a refreshing escape from the heavy traffic on nearby Rua Marques de São Vicente. Local residents come to jog here, to go for long walks with their dogs and to let their kids run about at the large playground.

A hiking trail connects the park with Solar da Imperatriz, an 18th-century colonial building that is today part of a school for horticultural studies, near Jardim Botânico; it's best to go with a local who knows the way, as the path isn't well marked, and the danger of assault is an unlikely but serious consideration. The trail starts near the small waterfall. The park also has a small chapel, and a 19th-century colonial mansion and museum that remain closed for renovations.

PLANETÁRIO PLANETARIUM

Map p234 (☎21 2088-0536; www.planetariodorio.com.br; Av Padre Leonel Franca 240; adult/child R$13/6.50, incl cúpula session R$26/13; ⏲9am-5pm Tue-Fri, 2:30-8pm Sat, 2-6pm Sun) Gávea's stellar attraction, the Planetário features a museum, a *praça dos telescópios* (telescopes' square) and a couple of state-of-the-art operating *cúpulas* (domes), each capable of projecting more than 6000 stars onto its walls. Forty-minute sessions in the domes take place on weekends and holidays. Visitors can also take a peek at the night sky through the telescopes on Wednesdays and Saturdays from 7:30pm to 8:30pm (6:30pm to 7:30pm from June to August).

The modern Museu do Universo (Universe Museum) houses sundials, a Foucault's Pendulum and other permanent exhibitions, plus temporary displays.

Jardim Botânico

★JARDIM BOTÂNICO GARDENS

Map p234 (☎21 3874-1808; www.jbrj.gov.br; Jardim Botânico 920; R$15; ⏲noon-6pm Mon, 8am-6pm Tue-Sun) This exotic 137-hectare garden, with more than 8000 plant species, was designed by order of the Prince Regent Dom João (later to become Dom João VI) in 1808. The garden is quiet and serene on weekdays and blossoms with families on weekends. Highlights of a visit here include the row of palms (planted when the garden first opened), the Amazonas section, the lake containing the huge Vitória Régia water lilies and the enclosed **orquidário**, home to 600 species of orchids.

There's an outdoor snack bar on the grounds (near a playground) and an appealing cafe just outside the main entrance. The new visitor center shows films (in English and Portuguese) that give the history of the gardens, and has a gift shop selling unique crafts and souvenirs, such as shirts made of bamboo and bowls with pre-Columbian designs made from banana fibers.

PARQUE LAGE PARK

Map p234 (☎21 2334-4088; www.eavparquelage.rj.gov.br; Jardim Botânico 414; ⏲8am-5pm

CATACUMBA

Lagoa is one of the few neighborhoods in Rio that doesn't have a neighboring favela (slum, informal community). This wasn't always the case: the Parque da Catacumba was once the site of a favela, and home to more than 10,000 residents at its height in the 1960s. According to the historical records, the area was part of an estate belonging to a wealthy landowner in the 19th century. Upon her death, she left the lands to her slaves, though the first constructions didn't begin to appear until the 1930s. According to some former favela residents, the name Catacumba predates the favela, and refers to an indigenous burial ground – although no remains were ever found on the site.

Under the strong-armed government of Francisco Negrão de Lima, the *favelados* were removed in 1970 and their houses razed, in large part owing to the commercial value of the occupied lands. The expelled residents went on to form the Complexo da Maré, a favela near the airport that later became known as the 'Gaza Strip' because of its high murder rate.

Catacumba was subsequently reforested and turned into a public park. You can still see a few vestiges of the old favela on a hike to the Mirante do Sacopã lookout.

Apr-Nov, to 6pm Dec-Mar) FREE This beautiful park lies at the base of the Floresta da Tijuca, about 1km from Jardim Botânico. It has English-style gardens, little lakes, and a mansion that houses the **Escola de Artes Visuais** (School of Visual Arts), which hosts free art exhibitions and occasional performances. The park is a tranquil place and the cafe here offers a fine setting for a coffee or a meal.

Native Atlantic rainforest surrounds Parque Lage, and you can sometimes see monkeys and toucans among the foliage. This is the starting point for challenging hikes up Corcovado (don't attempt a hike without checking the latest security situation, as robberies on the trail have occurred).

OM.ART GALLERY

Map p234 (☎21 2239-9019; www.om.art.br; Jardim Botânico 997; ⏲10am-7pm Tue-Fri, to 6pm Sat) In the Jockey Club, this avant-garde gallery opened to much acclaim in 2018. Expect challenging multimedia shows and big installations that often incorporate interactive components. Film, music, sculpture and photography have all featured in past exhibitions. OM.art was founded by artist and designer Oskar Metsavaht, the creator of the well known Osklen brand.

CARPINTARIA GALLERY

Map p234 (☎21 3875-5554; www.fdag.com.br/carpintaria; Jardim Botânico 971, Jockey Club; ⏲10am-7pm Tue-Fri, to 6pm Sat) One of several new galleries in the Jockey Club, Carpintaria stages exhibitions by both Brazilian and foreign artists. It's a great place to see sculpture, painting and mixed media by up-and-coming stars on the art circuit.

Lagoa

LAGOA RODRIGO DE FREITAS LAKE

See p80.

PARQUE DA CATACUMBA PARK

Map p234 (☎21 2247-9949; Av Epitácio Pessoa; ⏲8am-5pm Tue-Sun) FREE On the edge of Lagoa Rodrigo de Freitas, across a busy road, this park and sculptural garden has a short but steep trail to the **Mirante do Sacopã** (Map p234; Av Epitácio Pessoa). It's a 15-minute walk along a 600m forest-lined path to the lookout, which has memorable views from its perch 130m above the lake. For a bit more excitement, you can scale a rock-climbing wall, go rappelling (abseiling) or take a treetop walk offered by Lagoa Aventuras (p87).

FUNDAÇÃO EVA KLABIN MUSEUM

Map p234 (☎21 3202-8551; www.evaklabin.org.br; Av Epitácio Pessoa 2480; adult/child R$10/free, Sat & Sun free; ⏲2-6pm Tue-Sun) An old mansion full of antiques, the former residence of Eva Klabin houses the works of art she collected for 60 years. Reflecting Eva's diverse interests, the collection has 1100 pieces from ancient Egypt, Greece and China, including paintings, sculptures, silver, furniture and carpets.

EATING

The open-air restaurants around the peaceful Lagoa Rodrigo de Freitas are big draws. Gávea has a few dining and drinking spots around Praça Santos Dumont, while Jardim Botânico's densest concentration of eateries are on Rua JJ Seabra and Rua Pacheco Leão.

Gávea

BRASEIRO DA GÁVEA BRAZILIAN **$$**

Map p234 (☎21 2239-7494; www.braseiroda gavea.com.br; Praça Santos Dumont 116; sandwiches around R$24, mains for 2 people R$60-120; ⏲11:30am-1am Sun-Thu, to 3am Fri & Sat) This family-style place serves large portions of its popular *linguiça* (garlicky pork sausage) appetizers, *picanha* (rump steak) and *galetos* (grilled chicken). On weekends the open-air spot fills with the din of conversation and the aroma of freshly poured *chope* (draft beer). As the evening wanes, a younger crowd takes over, drinking late into the night.

GUIMAS BRAZILIAN **$$$**

Map p234 (☎21 2259-7996; www.restaurante guimas.com.br; José Roberto Macedo Soares 5; mains R$64-86; ⏲noon-1am) An upscale *carioca boteco* (small open-air bar) with a creative flair, Guimas has been going strong since 1981. Winning dishes include the *bacalhau à brás* (codfish mixed with potatoes, eggs and onions), shrimp risotto and the juicy *picanha wessel* (grilled rump steak). There's outdoor seating in front.

Jardim Botânico

★CASA CAMOLESE BRAZILIAN **$$**

Map p234 (☎21 3514-8200; www.casacamolese.com.br; Jardim Botânico 983; mains R$42-70; ⏲noon-midnight Mon-Sat, to 11pm Sun;) One of the most talked about openings in recent years is this beautifully designed eating, drinking and entertainment space overlooking the Jockey Club Brasileiro. Camolese is home to a microbrewery, a cafe, a live-music spot and a spacious restaurant, with soaring ceilings, glass walls and an elegant plant-trimmed terrace – the best place to be on clear nights.

Start off with classic appetizers, like codfish balls or paprika-dusted octopus, then tuck into seafood pasta in white-wine sauce, grilled Angus steaks or veg-friendly options like creamy polenta with mushrooms.

The restaurant is accessed via a small lane opposite the main entrance to the botanical gardens.

PRANA VEGETARIANO VEGETARIAN **$$**

Map p234 (☎21 2245-7643; www.pranavegetariano.com; Lopes Quintas 37; mains around R$40; ⏲noon-4pm Mon-Sat;) A short stroll from the Jardim Botânico's north exit, this very friendly vegetarian restaurant has garnered quite a following for its deliciously healthy meat-free plates. The small menu changes daily (check the website to see what's cooking), and features creative and filling lunch combinations, as well as great juices and smoothies, and decadent desserts.

PLAGE CAFÉ CAFE **$$**

Map p234 (☎21 2535-7336; www.plagecafe.com.br; off Jardim Botânico 414; mains R$32-54; ⏲9am-6pm Mon-Fri, to 5pm Sat & Sun;) Inside the lush Parque Lage, this beautifully located cafe serves an expansive array of dishes, including eggs Benedict and roasted eggplant lasagna, as well as sandwiches and lighter fare such as yogurt with house-made granola or salad Niçoise. It's an ideal spot for taking in Rio's tropical verdure, with views of Cristo Redentor.

JARBÔ FRENCH **$$**

Map p234 (☎21 2259-2924; www.jarbocafe.com; Jardim Botânico 1008; mains R$38-67; ⏲noon-6:30pm Mon, 8am-6:30pm Tue-Sun;) Just outside the entrance to the Jardim Botânico (but inside the gates off the busy roadway), Jarbô is a great anytime favorite, with a wide-ranging menu encompassing tartines (open-faced sandwiches), eggs Benedict, Gorgonzola-topped salads or fancier fare like beet and goat cheese ravioli or duck confit.

It's set in a lovely colonial building and has outdoor seating on a peaceful veranda.

BRÁZ PIZZA **$$**

Map p234 (☎21 3563-4670; www.brazpizzaria.com.br; Maria Angélica 129; pizzas R$54-88; ⏲6:30pm-midnight) The much-touted pizzeria from São Paulo has had a huge following with *cariocas* since opening in the city in 2007. Perfect crusts and superfresh ingredients are two of the components that make Bráz one of the best pizza spots in town. This is no secret, however, so arrive early and plan on having a few quiet *chopes* on the front patio before scoring a table.

ELLA PIZZARIA PIZZA **$$**
Map p234 (☎21-3559-0102; www.ellapizzaria.com.br; Pacheco Leão 102; pizzas R$39-54; ⏲noon-5pm & 6pm-midnight) Located in a prime spot next to the Jardim Botânico, this upmarket pizzeria offers Neapolitan-style pizzas with elaborate toppings such as crispy octopus, smoked pancetta and wild arugula. Drinks are taken as seriously as the pizzas, with staff behind a sunken bar serving excellent cocktails (try the Negroni). The exposed brick walls and subdued lighting lend a stylish, romantic ambience.

The word *pizzaria* in the restaurant's name is not a spelling mistake – that's the Portuguese spelling.

TAJ MAHAL INDIAN **$$**
Map p234 (☎21 2148-1049; www.tajmahalrio.com; JJ Seabra 19; mains R$62-72; ⏲noon-4pm & 5pm-midnight Tue-Sun) Hands down Rio's best Indian restaurant, Taj Mahal serves pure decadence from its extensive menu: plates of lamb masala, creamy palak paneer and piping hot naan bread fresh from the oven. The setting is elegant, with white tablecloths and large, brightly saturated photographs of India that bring the subcontinent to life.

LA BICYCLETTE CAFE **$$**
Map p234 (☎21 3256-9052; www.labicyclette.com.br; Pacheco Leão 320; sandwiches R$19-42; ⏲8:30am-9pm Mon-Fri, to 8pm Sat & Sun; 📶) La Bicyclette whips up creative sandwiches (named after Parisian neighborhoods), hearty quiches, salads and desserts. Vegetarians can opt for the Olympia, with goat cheese, olives, capers and cherry tomatoes. Bakery items are superb, and there's ample outdoor seating for a coffee break. It's located across from the headquarters of media giant Globo. There's a second location in Leblon.

JOJÖ CAFE **$$**
Map p234 (☎21 3565-9007; www.jojocafe.com.br; Pacheco Leão 812; mains R$39-65; ⏲6pm-2am Tue-Fri, 1pm-1am Sat, 1-8pm Sun) This small, charming neighborhood cafe and bistro on a peaceful corner in Jardim Botânico serves delectable salads, pastas, appetizers and creative seafood dishes such as Thai-style seafood rice with shrimp. There are a handful of sidewalk tables. Oyster lovers should come on Thursdays during happy hour, when oysters arrive fresh from Santa Catarina.

PURO BRAZILIAN **$$$**
Map p234 (☎21 3284-5377; www.purorestaurante.com.br; Visconde de Carandaí 43; mains R$62-86, multicourse lunch menu R$49; ⏲noon-5pm & 7pm-midnight Mon-Fri, 12:30-5pm & 7pm-1am Sat, 12:30-10pm Sun) Puro offers consistently excellent food and service in the upmarket Jardim Botânico neighborhood. Chef Pedro Siqueira's menu features traditional Brazilian dishes that have been given modern updates. Head to the top floor for open-air views over the botanical gardens – it's a fine setting for dishes such as roasted lamb with rice, octopus and smoked pork belly, or oven-baked fish of the day.

In 2016 Siqueira opened his second restaurant, Massa (p67), which specializes in pasta and gnocchi. Both restaurants are marked out by an attention to detail and commitment to high-quality ingredients that is rare outside Rio's most expensive fine-dining establishments.

Lagoa

LAGOON BRAZILIAN **$$**
Map p234 (☎21 2529-5300; www.lagoon.com.br; Av Borges de Medeiros 1424; mains R$35-75; ⏲noon-2am) This lakefront eating and entertainment complex houses a handful of restaurants, plus a cinema, a bar and a live-music venue. The best tables are on the 2nd floor, and offer photogenic views over Lagoa Rodrigo de Freitas. Italian, seafood, bistro fare and traditional Brazilian cooking are among the options. No matter where you sit, you can order from any of the menus.

The back of the complex, by the lake, usually has food trucks (burgers, snacks and microbrews), plus reclaimed wood loungers and tables where you can take in the relaxing views.

ARAB DA LAGOA MIDDLE EASTERN **$$**
Map p234 (☎21 2540-0747; www.restaurantearab.com.br; Av Borges de Medeiros, Parque dos Patins; mains R$42-75; ⏲10am-11pm) This is one of Lagoa Rodrigo de Freitas' most popular outdoor restaurants. It serves traditional Middle Eastern specialties such as hummus, baba ghanoush, tabbouleh, kibbe and tasty thin-crust pizzas. The large platters for two or more are good for sampling a flavorsome variety.

During the day it's a peaceful refuge from the city, while at night you can hear live samba, *choro* (romantic, intimate samba) or jazz (from 9pm on weekdays and 7pm on Saturdays and Sundays).

LA CARIOCA CEVICHERIA PERUVIAN **$$**
Map p234 (☎21 2226-8821; Maria Angélica 113; sharing plates R$35-51; ⏲noon-midnight) On a peaceful tree-lined street, La Carioca is an excellent spot for ceviche and other Peruvian hits. It has another, equally charming branch in Ipanema (p63).

OLYMPE FUSION **$$$**
Map p234 (☎21 2539-4542; Custódio Serrão 62; 5-/7-course tasting menu R$390/450; ⏲7:30-11pm Mon-Thu & Sat, noon-4pm & 7:30-11pm Fri) Thomas Troisgros, one of Rio's top chefs, dazzles guests with unforgettable meals at this award-winning restaurant set in a peaceful villa on a quiet, tree-lined street. Originally from France, Troisgros mixes the Old World with the New in dishes such as scallops with *tucupí* (a manioc root from the Amazon) or *açaí*-crusted lamb loin, followed perhaps by caramelized passion-fruit soufflé.

Vegetarians can also opt for a five-course tasting menu (R$390). Wine pairings are available.

DRINKING & NIGHTLIFE

Gávea has one of Rio's liveliest drinking spots for the collegiate crowd: Baixo Gávea, near Praça Santos Dumont. The bars here are usually packed, with imbibers spilling onto the plaza most nights. Jardim Botânico has a few enticing spots, though it's generally a low-key affair. Meanwhile, the lakeside kiosks offer an equally sedate experience, with couples gathering at drinking spots to the backdrop of Lagoa and Cristo Redentor. If you're up for something livelier, Palaphita Gávea is the obvious choice.

Gávea

PALAPHITA GÁVEA BAR
Map p234 (☎21 3114-0853; www.palaphitakitch.com.br; Bartolomeu Mitre 1314; ⏲6pm-1am Mon, 8pm-4am Thu, 9pm-4am Fri & Sat, 5pm-1am Sun) Overlooking the Jockey Club Brasileiro (p86), this sprawling open-air bar and party space is a wonderful mess of rustic wooden structures, thatch-roofed bars and scattered-about handmade furniture. It draws a young, animated crowd most nights and is a great place at which to end the night. On racing days, you can even place bets here and watch the horses thunder past.

From Thursday through Saturday (11pm to 5am), DJs spinning at the attached nightclub Palaphita Privê draw dance-loving crowds from across the Zona Sul.

HIPÓDROMO BAR
Map p234 (☎21 2274-9720; Praça Santos Dumont 108; ⏲noon-1am) In an area commonly referred to as Baixo Gávea, Hipódromo is one of several bar-eateries responsible for the local residents' chronic lack of sleep. Most nights you'll find a college-age and twenty-something crowd celebrating here, with patrons spilling onto the facing Praça Santos Dumont.

Jardim Botânico

BASTARDA CAFE
Map p234 (☎21 3577-8142; www.instagram.com/bastarda.cafe; Von Martius 325; ⏲7:30am-7pm Tue-Sat, 7:30am-2pm Sun) Lovers of good coffee and cycling unite at this artfully designed space tucked away in Jardim Botânico. The roasted beans are prepared as you prefer (AeroPress, Chemex, Siphon etc) and served in pretty ceramic cups with saucers. You can browse the bike jerseys and coffee-table books (or ogle the wall-mounted road bikes) while you wait.

There's outdoor seating and ample snack options: ciabatta sandwiches (R$27 to R$32), eggs with avocado toast and yogurt with granola. Great for some post-ride nourishment.

BAR DO HORTO BAR
Map p234 (☎21 3114-8439; Pacheco Leão 780; ⏲noon-2am Tue-Sun) This colorful bar is one of Jardim Botânico's most charming. The decor is festive and kitsch: walls covered with shimmering fabric and an interior that's festooned with brightly hued paper lanterns, butterfly appliqués, bottle-cap curtains and other recycled ephemera. At night the sidewalk tables gather a festive crowd that comes for cocktails and good cheer.

Lagoa

★PALAPHITA KITCH LOUNGE

Map p234 (☎21 2227-0837; www.palaphitakitch.com.br; Av Epitácio Pessoa s/n; ⏲6pm-midnight Mon-Fri, from 10am Sat & Sun) A great spot for a sundowner, Palaphita Kitch is an open-air, thatched-roof wonderland with rustic bamboo furniture, flickering tiki torches and a peaceful setting on the edge of Lagoa Rodrigo de Freitas. It's a popular spot with couples, who come for the view and the creative (but pricey) cocktails: the caipirinhas, made from unusual fruits from the Northeast and Amazonia, are a hit.

BAR LAGOA BOTECO

Map p234 (☎21 2523-1135; Av Epitácio Pessoa 1674; ⏲noon-midnight) With a view of Lagoa Rodrigo de Freitas across a busy road, Bar Lagoa is one of the neighborhood's classic haunts. Founded in 1935, this open-air spot hasn't changed all that much since then: the bar still has surly waiters serving excellent beer to ever-crowded tables and, in spite of its years, a youthful air pervades.

ENTERTAINMENT

CLUBE MANOUCHE LIVE MUSIC

Map p234 (www.casacamolese.com.br; Jardim Botânico 983; R$60-90) Downstairs from the main restaurant in Casa Camolese (p83), Clube Manouche is an intimate music bar designed in the tradition of West Village clubs in New York City. Sight lines are excellent no matter where you sit, and you can order drinks throughout the show. The club lines up some top-notch jazz artists, as well as eclectic sounds from Brazil and beyond.

There are shows three or four nights per week (typically starting around 9pm). Check the website to see what's on. Advance reservations are essential.

BLUE NOTE RIO LIVE MUSIC

Map p234 (☎21 3799-2500; www.bluenoterio.com.br; Av Borges de Medeiros 1424; cover R$70-150) In 2017 the famed NYC jazz club opened this Rio outpost (Blue Note's first venture into South America) in an entertainment complex on the edge of Lagoa Rodrigo de Freitas. True to form, it's a classy venue with excellent acoustics that hosts a quality lineup of performers (roughly 75% from Brazil, and the other 25% international performers). Concerts typically happen Wednesday through Saturday.

Ticket prices are steep, but music aside, the service is top-notch, and there's good food (and two bars) on hand. It's located inside the Lagoon (p84) complex.

JOCKEY CLUB BRASILEIRO HORSE RACING

Map p234 (Hipódromo da Gávea; ☎21 3534-9001; www.jcb.com.br; Jardim Botânico 1003, Gávea; ⏲6-11pm Mon & Tue, 2-8pm Sat & Sun) One of the country's loveliest racetracks, with a great view of the mountains and Corcovado, the Joquei Clube (Jockey Club) seats 35,000. It lies on the Gávea side of Lagoa Rodrigo de Freitas, opposite Praça Santos Dumont. Local race fans are part of the attraction – it's a different slice of Rio life.

Tourists are welcome in the members' area, which has a bar overlooking the track. Races are held on Mondays, Tuesdays, Saturdays and Sundays. The big event is the Brazilian Grand Prix (Grande Prêmio Brasil), usually held on the first or second Sunday in June.

SHOPPING

The best street for shopping is along Lopes Quintas in Jardim Botânico. You'll find a few fashion boutiques, a bakery and several eye-catching home-furnishings stores. On Sundays, antique-hunters descend on the small market that takes over Praça Santos Dumont.

Gávea

PRAÇA SANTOS DUMONT ANTIQUE FAIR MARKET

Map p234 (Feira de Antiguidades da Gávea; Praça Santos Dumont; ⏲9am-5pm Sun) Gávea's 80-stall antique fair features ceramics, artwork, jewelry, records, watches, books and other odds and ends.

SHOPPING DA GÁVEA SHOPPING CENTER

Map p234 (☎21 2294-1096; www.shoppingdagavea.com.br; Marquês de São Vicente 52; ⏲10am-10pm Mon-Sat, 2-9pm Sun) Shopping da Gávea touts itself as the preferred mall of artists and intellectuals, which may or may not matter to you when you're laying down serious cash for those sneakers. It's home to 200 stores, a five-screen cinema, several theaters and numerous restaurants, including La Pastaciutta, which serves tasty pastas and appetizers.

PARCERIA CARIOCA FASHION & ACCESSORIES
Map p234 (☎21 2511-8023; www.facebook.com/parceria.carioca.7; Marquês de São Vicente 52; ⏲10am-10pm Mon-Fri) Parceria Carioca stocks clothes, jewelry, accessories and an assortment of ornaments from up-and-coming local designers (especially those from Rio's poorer communities). There's an emphasis on fair pay for the designers and fair prices for the customers, including some bargains to be had. Items are generally bright and colorful and feature contemporary design that will appeal to younger shoppers.

As well as this store in Gávea, there are also branches in Jardim Botânico and Museu do Amanhã.

Jardim Botânico

DONA COISA FASHION & ACCESSORIES
Map p234 (☎21 2249-2336; www.donacoisa.com.br; Lopes Quintas 153; ⏲10am-8:30pm Mon-Fri, to 6pm Sat) One of Rio's top boutiques, Dona Coisa sells top labels by Brazilian and international designers, including one-of-a-kind pieces you won't find elsewhere. Head upstairs to browse original objects for the home (including delicate ceramics by Heloisa Galvão) as well as skincare products by Phebo, and beautifully designed stationery by Nina Write.

The small, well-lit cafe out back serves ciabatta sandwiches, espresso drinks and decadent desserts.

GABINETE HOMEWARES
Map p234 (☎21 3173-8828; Lopes Quintas 87, Jardim Botânico; ⏲11am-8pm Mon-Sat) On a street with a growing number of shops and cafes, Gabinete is a fun place to browse for unusual items – geometric jewelry made of volcanic rock, delicately fluted vases and glassware, illuminated teapot lamps, wind-up circus miniatures and earth-toned pottery – that line the artfully lit display shelves of this intriguing curiosity cabinet.

O SOL ARTS & CRAFTS
Map p234 (☎21 2294-5149; www.osolartesanato.org.br; Corcovado 213, Jardim Botânico; ⏲9am-6pm Mon-Fri, to 1pm Sat) O Sol is run by Leste-Um, a nonprofit social-welfare organization. This delightful store displays the works of regional artists and sells Brazilian folk art made from clay, wood and porcelain. Aside from handicrafts, the store also stocks baskets, hammocks, pottery and woven rugs.

VENDA EM GARAGEM ANTIQUES
Map p234 (JJ Seabra 6; ⏲10:30am-6pm Mon & Tue, to 7:30pm Wed-Sun) You never know what you'll unearth at this rambling little antique shop two blocks from Lagoa Rodrigo de Freitas. Recent finds have included a porcelain espresso cup with Rio imagery, a small surfboard, landscape paintings of Brazil, craft items, oversized jewelry and various other bric-a-brac.

CASA SOMA FASHION & ACCESSORIES
Map p234 (☎21 3442-4943; www.facebook.com/casasoma; Lopes Quintas 147; ⏲11am-7pm Mon-Fri, to 3pm Sat) On Jardim Botânico's liveliest shopping strip, Casa Soma is a designer space that hosts a rotating selection of up-and-coming Brazilian fashion brands. Upstairs is the Os/On showroom with its eye-catching swimwear, stylish dresses, summer tops and jewelry.

SPORTS & ACTIVITIES

LAGOA AVENTURAS ADVENTURE SPORTS
Map p234 (☎21 4105-0079; www.lagoaaventuras.com.br; Av Epitácio Pessoa 3000; zip line R$20, climbing wall R$25, treetop walk R$35, rappelling R$130; ⏲9:30am-4:30pm Tue-Sun; 👪) Located in Parque da Catacumba (p82), across from Lagoa Rodrigo de Freitas, this is a fine place to come for outdoor adventures. You can get a workout scaling a 7m rock-climbing wall, take a zip-line ride, rappel (abseil) down a rock face or take a canopy walk through the treetops. Kids aged four years and up are welcome.

VITORMARIGO/SHUTTERSTOCK ©

1. Cristo Redentor (p114) rising over Parque Nacional da Tijuca (p158) **2.** Jardim Botânico (p81) **3.** Parque do Flamengo (p116) **4.** Sítio Burle Marx (p157)

GUSTAVOMELLOSSA/SHUTTERSTOCK ©

Green Spaces

No matter where you are in the city, you won't have to travel far to get a dose of nature. Rio has abundant parks and green spaces, some quite small and manicured (Parque do Catete), and others veritable wildernesses (Floresta da Tijuca).

Parque do Flamengo

The landfill-turned-green-space (p116) is best on Sunday, when through streets close to traffic, and runners and cyclists claim the long, curving paths skirting the bay.

Jardim Botânico

These stately botanic gardens (p81) make for a fine break from the beach. Here you can take in rare orchids, see massive Vitória Régia lilies and other Amazonian flora, and admire the palms planted when the Portuguese royals ruled from Rio.

Parque do Catete

Behind the former presidential palace, this small but elegant park (p116) is complete with a swan-filled pond and a gallery (and cinema) adjoining the green space.

Sítio Burle Marx

Far west of town, but worth the trip, the gardens (p157) of Rio's famous landscape architect bloom with thousands of plant species. The lush estate is full of history, which you'll discover on a guided tour.

Floresta da Tijuca

Rio's wide, rainforest-covered expanse (p158) is teeming with plant and animal life. You can take scenic or challenging walks, including rewarding scrambles up its 900m-high peaks.

Copacabana & Leme

COPACABANA

Neighborhood Top Five

1 Copacabana Beach (p92) Soaking up the sunshine, followed by some snacks and drinks at an oceanfront kiosk.

2 Forte de Copacabana (p93) Learning about Brazil's colonial history and taking in the view across the beach.

3 Forte Duque de Caxias (p93) Walking to mountaintop heights along a forested trail inside this military base open to the public.

4 Stand-up paddle boarding (p100) Going for an early morning paddle off the southern end of the beach with a rental board from places such as Universo Paddle Surf.

5 Bip Bip (p99) Joining Rio's samba lovers over evening jam sessions at one of the city's favorite live *roda de samba* spots.

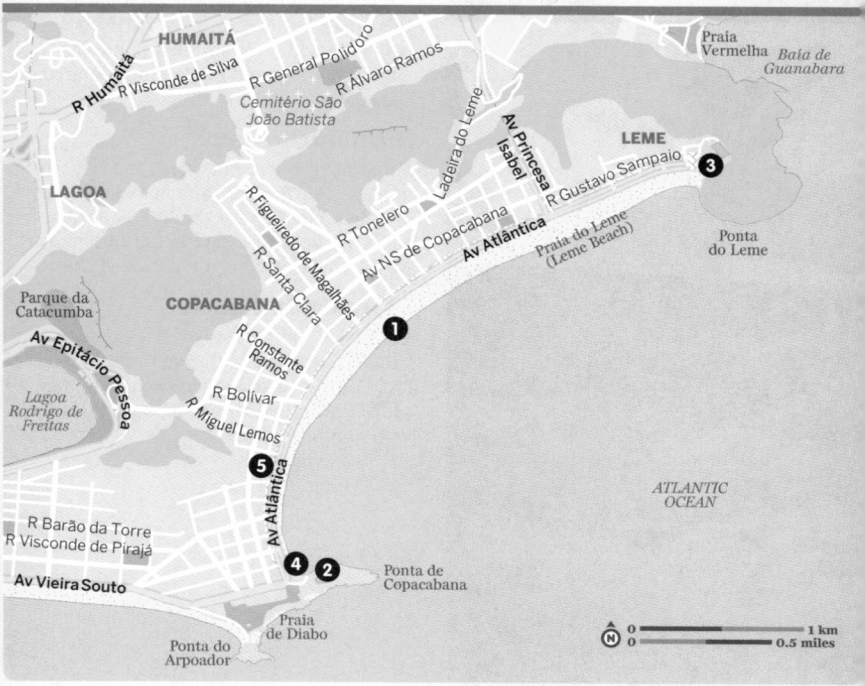

For more detail of this area see Map p236 and p240

Explore Copacabana & Leme

With the construction of the neoclassical Copacabana Palace hotel in 1923, Copacabana – and Rio – became South America's most elegant destination, one frequented by international celebrities. Copacabana remained Rio's untarnished gem until the 1970s, when the area fell into decline. Today's Copa is a chaotic mix of discount stores and noisy traffic-filled avenues, with a humming red-light district and slightly edgy streets. While paradise it clearly is not, the beach remains beautiful. Framed by mountains and deep blue sea, the magnificent curve of shoreline stretches more than 4km.

Packing the beach are sun-worshippers of every age and background, from favela (slum, informal community) kids to aging socialites, from tourists to families from the Zona Norte. Copacabana's democratic mix, old-school *botecos* (small open-air bars), eclectic restaurants and nightclubs, myriad shops and, of course, the handsome shoreline still entrance many visitors. While the cool kids cling to Ipanema and Leblon, Copacabana seems poised on the edge of a renaissance. Its glassy kiosks have brought class to the neighborhood, while Baixo Copa has become a nightlife destination.

The small neighborhood of Leme, just northeast of Copacabana (Av Princesa Isabel divides the two), has a village feel, with its mix of old-timers, upper-middle-class families and favela residents. The lack of major roads through Leme creates a more peaceful vibe, and the oceanfront restaurants make for a more relaxing setting for a drink than the buzzing Copacabana strip.

Local Life

Markets Copacabana has a handful of weekly produce markets held at various locales. Our favorite happens in peaceful Bairro Peixoto (p93).

Hangouts One of Copacabana's liveliest areas for a drink is Baixo Copa, a bar- and restaurant-lined strip just back from Av Atlântica around Rua Domingos Ferreira and Barão de Ipanema.

Arts Little frequented by tourists, Espaço SESC (p99) often hosts an excellent lineup of dance and theater performances.

Getting There & Away

Bus Ipanema (161 and 573), Leblon (161, 511 and 583), Gávea (161 and 583), Jardim Botânico (161, 573 and 583) and Centro (121, 123 and 124).

Metro Cardeal Arcoverde, Siqueira Campos, Cantagalo and Ipanema/General Osório.

Lonely Planet's Top Tip

The restaurant strip along Av Atlântica has fine views of the seaside, but generally unexceptional food. Leme is a notable exception, with a few quality establishments right across from the crashing waves.

Best Places to Eat

- Churrascaria Palace (p96)
- Salomé (p97)
- El Born (p94)
- Azumi (p96)
- Adega Pérola (p95)
- Santa Satisfação (p95)

For reviews, see p93

Best Places to Drink

- Cafe 18 do Forte (p98)
- Escondido (p98)
- Boteco Belmonte (p98)
- Bodega (p98)
- Ponto da Bossa Nova (p98)

For reviews, see p97

Best Places to Shop

- Gilson Martins (p99)
- Loja Fla (p100)
- Osklen Surfing (p100)

For reviews, see p99

TOP SIGHT
COPACABANA BEACH

A magnificent confluence of land and sea, the long, scalloped beach of Copacabana extends for some 4km, with a flurry of activity along its length: over-amped soccer players singing their team's anthem; *cariocas* (Rio residents) and tourists lining up for caipirinhas at kiosks; favela kids showing off their football skills; and beach vendors shouting out their wares among the tanned beach bodies.

Each group stakes out its stretch of sand. The area between the Copacabana Palace hotel and Rua Fernando Mendes is the gay and cross-dresser section, known as the Stock or Stock Market – easily recognized by the rainbow flag. Young football and *futevôlei* (soccer volleyball) players hold court near Rua Santa Clara. *Postos* 5 and 6 are a mix of favela kids and *carioca* retirees, while the spot next to Forte de Copacabana is the *colônia dos pescadores* (fishers' colony). As Copacabana Beach curves north you get into the quieter sands of Leme (Av Princesa Isabel forms the demarcation between the two neighborhoods). Here you'll find a mix of older Leme residents as well as kids from the nearby favelas of Babilônia and Chapeu Mangueira.

Aside from frolicking in the waves and people-watching, the main attraction for visitors to the beach is running or cycling the beach path; the beachside lane closes to traffic on Sundays. Early risers can greet the sunrise while exercising. Another way to get physical is to have a go on a stand-up paddle board, which you can hire from the south end of the beach. Hire outfits also offer lessons if you need a bit of a primer.

By afternoon and nightfall, the beach kiosks are a great place to relax, rehydrate over *agua de côco* (coconut water), snack and have a few libations before the night begins. On weekends there's also live music. Things get decidedly lively when football games are screened, with kiosks setting up TVs, and passers-by and beach-goers joining the celebratory crowds over ever-flowing drinks.

DON'T MISS

- Stand-up paddle boarding across the sea
- Evening drinks at a beachfront kiosk
- A Sunday run, walk or bike ride along the beach boulevard

PRACTICALITIES

- Map p236, E4
- Av Atlântica

CATARINA BELOVA/SHUTTERSTOCK ©

SIGHTS

Aside from the beach, which hogs all the attention, there are a few other notable attractions in the neighborhood, including a fort with a historic museum (and several well-placed open-air eating spots) at the southern end of Copacabana. The north (Leme) end has a hilltop fort offering sweeping views over the district.

COPACABANA BEACH — BEACH

See p92.

BAIRRO PEIXOTO — AREA

Map p236 (Anita Garibaldi) A world away from the bustle of Copacabana's busy avenues, the Bairro Peixoto is a peaceful enclave centered on the leafy Praça Edmundo Bittencourt. Here you'll find a playground, park benches and tables where folks play dominoes and read the paper, all of which seems to lend the setting more of a village-like air than that of a big-city neighborhood. You might even see a few marmosets up in the trees.

Wednesday's a good day to visit, when the weekly fruit market takes place.

FORTE DE COPACABANA — FORT

Map p236 (☎21 2521-1032; Av Atlântica & Rua Francisco Otaviano; adult/child R$6/free, Tue free; ⏲10am-7:30pm Tue-Sun) Built in 1914 on the promontory of the old Our Lady of Copacabana chapel, the fort of Copacabana was one of Rio's premier defenses against attack. You can still see its original features, including walls that are up to 12m thick, defended by Krupp cannons. Inside is a museum with several floors of exhibits tracing the early days of the Portuguese colony through to the mid-19th century. The views out across the full length of Copacabana are striking.

There are several cafes here with fine vantage points, including Cafe Colombo.

COLÔNIA DOS PESCADORES — MARKET

Map p236 (Av Atlântica, near Francisco Otaviano; ⏲market 7:30am-1pm) At the southern end of Copacabana Beach you'll see fishing folk at work, if you go early enough, mending lines and hauling in the catch. There's a small fish market here open to the public, and usually one vendor who sells and cooks up whole fresh fish on a small charcoal grill – a great deal at about R$25 for a decent-sized fish.

PRAIA DE DIABO — BEACH

Map p236 (off Av Francisco Bering) This tiny hidden beach is located between Copacabana and Ipanema. Reach it by heading to the rocky outcropping of Arpoador and turning left. You'll see it just beyond the palm trees.

FORTE DUQUE DE CAXIAS — FORT

Map p240 (Forte do Leme; ☎21 3223-5076; www.cep.eb.mil.br/visitacao; Praça Almirante Júlio de Noronha; adult/child R$4/free; ⏲9:30am-4:30pm Tue-Sun) More commonly known as Forte do Leme, this military base is open to the public. Visitors can walk to the top of Morro do Leme (Leme Mountain) along a steep 800m trail that passes through Atlantic rainforest. At the top stands an 18th-century fort affording magnificent views of Pão de Açúcar (Sugarloaf Mountain) and the Cagarras Islands.

MUSEU DA IMAGEM E DO SOM — MUSEUM

Map p236 (www.mis.rj.gov.br; Av Atlântica, near Miguel Lemos) If work on this new museum is ever complete, Copacabana will finally have an outstanding rainy-day attraction. The building, designed by celebrated New York firm Diller Scofidio + Renfro (who also designed NYC's High Line), will feature high-tech interactive galleries devoted to the great Brazilian music and film that has played such a pivotal role in the nation's culture. Performance halls and an open-air rooftop amphitheater (for outdoor films) will be other highlights.

EATING

Rio's most visited neighborhood has an enormous variety of restaurants, from award-winning dining rooms to charming old bistros from the 1950s, as well as creperies, *churrascarias* (traditional barbecue restaurants), sushi bars and other ethnic haunts. In general, you will encounter less experimentation, but if you're looking for excellent traditional cuisine – both Brazilian and international – you will find plenty of delectable options in Copacabana, as well as in neighboring Leme.

Copacabana

BROTA VEGETARIAN $

Map p236 (☎21 3269-8736; Francisco Otaviano 67; snacks R$12-25; ⏲10am-midnight; ❄) Rio's vegetarian scene has improved dramatically in recent years, with places like this inviting snack bar inside the ultra-hip Void store. Amazing falafel sandwiches, pea and tamarind samosas, vegan nachos and lentil and mushroom bowls are among the hits. Get it to go (and take it to the beach!) or scramble for one of the few tables out on the sidewalk.

MOMO ICE CREAM $

Map p236 (Av Atlântica 1702; small/large ice cream R$16/22; ⏲noon-11pm) A few steps from the entrance to the Copacabana Palace, Momo is a cheery gelateria serving the neighborhood's best ice cream. All the classics are on hand, as well as tropical flavors such as mango and *maracujá* (passion fruit). Grab an outdoor table in front to take in the passing people parade.

ANTÔNIA CASA E CAFÉ BRAZILIAN $

Map p236 (Dias da Rocha 9; sandwiches R$19-27; ⏲7am-10pm; 📶) Though it's just a short stroll from Copacabana's busiest thoroughfare, this little cafe (which shares space with a home-design store) maintains a peaceful air, particularly if you sit at one of the tables on the small plaza out front. Stop in for sandwiches, *empanadas* (heart of palm, chicken, or shrimp-filled pasties), desserts, juices and coffee.

GALETO SAT'S BRAZILIAN $

Map p236 (☎21 2275-6197; Barata Ribeiro 7; mains R$30-76, lunch specials R$34; ⏲11am-5am) One of Rio's best roast-chicken spots, laid-back Galeto Sat's has earned many fans since it opened back in 1962. Grab a seat along the mirrored, tiled wall, order a *chope* (draft beer) and enjoy the scent of grilled spit-roasted birds before tucking into a filling meal. Price-wise you can't beat the *galeto completo,* a R$55 chicken feast for two.

CERVANTES BRAZILIAN $

Map p236 (☎21 2275-6147; www.restaurantecervantes.com.br; Barata Ribeiro 7; sandwiches R$25-42; ⏲noon-4am Tue-Thu, to 6am Fri & Sat, to 2am Sun) A Copacabana institution, the late-night Cervantes attracts *cariocas* who come to feast on the trademark filet mignon and pineapple sandwiches. This popular branch on busy Barata Ribeiro brings a mostly standing-room-only crowd. For the sit-down restaurant, head a few steps around the corner to Av Prado Junior 335.

VEZPA PIZZA $

Map p236 (www.vezpa.com.br; Djalma Ulrich 91; pizza slice R$13; ⏲11:30am-midnight Sun-Tue, to 2am Wed-Sat) Serving up the city's best pizza by the slice, Vezpa has taken Rio by storm. It has dozens of locations around town, including this one, well-placed for a snack after the beach or an evening out.

BIBI SUCOS BRAZILIAN $

Map p236 (☎21 2513-6000; Miguel Lemos 31; mains R$26-40; ⏲8:30am-midnight Sun-Thu, to 1am Fri & Sat) Offering much the same recipe for success as its Leblon branch (p73), Bibi serves dozens of juices, along with savory and sweet crepes, sandwiches, burgers, pastas, quiches and build-your-own salads. It has outdoor tables and a bustling vibe. Go early or late to beat the lunchtime crowds.

KONI STORE JAPANESE $

Map p236 (☎21 3208-8815; Constante Ramos 44; hand rolls R$18-24; ⏲11am-1am Mon-Sat, noon-1am Sun) This popular spot serves tasty *temaki,* seaweed hand rolls filled with tuna, salmon and other bites. It stays open late, making it ideal for a post-bar snack.

RESTAURANTE NATURALEVE VEGETARIAN $

Map p236 (Travessa Cristiano Lacorte; food per kg R$55; ⏲11am-4pm Mon-Sat; ❄❄) Set just off Rua Miguel Lemos, this tidy health-conscious restaurant cooks up a reasonably priced lunch buffet, with vegetarian black beans, *moqueca* (Bahian fish stew) with salmon, grilled tofu, various baked dishes and fresh salads.

★EL BORN SPANISH $$

Map p236 (☎21 3496-1780; www.barelborn.com.br; Bolívar 17; tapas R$13-57, sandwiches R$25-31; ⏲5pm-2am Mon-Fri, from 4pm Sat & Sun) Named after Barcelona's hippest, foodie-loving neighborhood, El Born fires up some of Rio's best tapas plates, such as Galician-style octopus, spicy prawns and tender Iberian ham. The setting channels a bit of old-world Spain, with rustic stone and brick walls, outdoor tables on the sidewalk, and ample bar seating, which is a fine spot for watching the dexterous bartenders in action.

ADEGA PÉROLA TAPAS $$

Map p236 (☎21 2255-9425; www.facebook.com/adegaperolariodejaneiro; Siqueira Campos 138; sharing plates R$24-46; ⏲11am-1am Mon-Thu, to 2am Fri & Sat) Going strong since 1957, this atmospheric bottle-lined eating and drinking den serves outstanding Spanish and Portuguese small plates, including marinated octopus, whole sardines, stuffed olives, codfish balls, fried squid and marinated shrimp. Just step inside and check out the culinary bounty on the long front counter.

SANTA SATISFAÇÃO BRAZILIAN $$

Map p236 (☎21 2255-9349; www.santasatisfacao.com; Santa Clara 36C; mains R$41-62; ⏲10am-11pm Mon-Sat) Oozing farmhouse charm, this always-packed bistro is worth forking out a bit extra for its outstanding daily lunch specials (R$37) of upscale Brazilian comfort food and sophisticated sandwiches. Among the favorites: pasta with Gorgonzola and sliced filet mignon, caprese salad, and open-faced ham and Brie sandwiches.

LA TRATTORIA ITALIAN $$

Map p236 (☎21 2255-3319; Fernando Mendes 7A; mains R$47-80; ⏲noon-11pm) Set with checkered tablecloths, exposed brick and decorations from the Old World, La Trattoria has been a neighborhood favorite since 1976. Shrimp dishes are the Italian family's specialty: many diners have been won over by the *camarões com spaghetti ao funghi tartufado* (shrimp with spaghetti and truffles).

LF CAFÉ & BISTRO CAFE $$

Map p236 (☎21 2275-7449; www.lfcafe.com.br; Duvivier 12; mains R$22-45; ⏲8am-midnight) This neighborhood favorite exudes charm with its wooden tables and chairs, bottle-lined shelves and warmly lit exposed brick. Stop by for coffees and breakfast fare (waffles, omelets), lunchtime specials (pastas, stuffed potatoes, sandwiches) or snacks throughout the day. There's a good craft-beer selection, including Noi and other Rio brewers.

BARRACA DA CHIQUITA BRAZILIAN $$

Map p236 (☎21 2548-9144; www.barracadachiquita.com.br; Santa Clara 33; mains for 2 R$68-120; ⏲11:30am-1am) If you can't make it to up to Brazil's Nordeste (Northeast), this convivial, rather whimsically decorated restaurant is your next best option. Here you can sample traditional meaty fare like sun-dried *picanha* (rump steak) with fried yucca, Bahian-style polenta with pork offal, or oxtail stew with rice and beans.

EMPÓRIO GRÃO-PARÁ AMAZONIAN $$

Map p236 (☎21 3489-0262; Barão de Ipanema 94; mains R$25-50; ⏲9am-9pm Sun-Thu, to 10pm Fri & Sat) A creative addition to the Copacabana food scene, this small snack bar serves delicacies from the north, including pure *açaí* (a berry-like fruit), *casquinha de caranguejo* (crabmeat served in its shell), *pato no tucupí* (duck in a spicy manioc sauce) and the wild-tasting *tacacá,* a dish with lip-numbing jambu leaves, manioc and shrimp.

PORTO DAS CARNES STEAK $$

Map p236 (☎21 3518-6066; www.restauranteportodascarnes.com.br; Joaquim Nabuco 14; mains R$35-88; ⏲noon-11pm; 📶) Around the corner from the beach, Porto das Carnes serves excellent cuts of meat that are chargrilled to juicy perfection. Stop in for the good-value R$54 lunch specials, which include two sides and dessert. Antique wagon wheels and rustic kitchen items adorn the wood-paneled walls of the small dining room.

ARAB MIDDLE EASTERN $$

Map p236 (☎21 2235-6698; www.restaurantearab.com.br; Av Atlântica 1936; mains R$53-97; ⏲5pm-midnight Mon, 8am-midnight Tue-Sun) On Copacabana's oceanfront road, Arab is a laid-back spot where you can linger at an outdoor table over delicious platters of tabbouleh, hummus, baba ghanoush, falafel, shawarma and other treats. There's also a lunch buffet.

TT BURGER BURGERS $$

Map p236 (☎21 96458-8674; www.ttburger.com.br; Francisco Otaviano 67; burgers R$42-48; ⏲noon-midnight Sun-Thu, to 2am Fri & Sat; ✎) The son of famed local chef Claude Troisgros runs this high-end Brooklyn-style burger outpost, and has gained a strong following for his delicious burgers (the guava ketchup is outstanding), sweet potato fries, milkshakes and craft beers. It's a charming spot, with subway tiles, framed photos, wood floors and a small front deck. TT also fires up a respectable veggie burger.

PRINCIPE DE MÔNACO SEAFOOD $$

Map p236 (☎21 2521-0195; Miguel Lemos 18; mains R$35-45, seafood for 2 R$90-170; ⏲11am-1am) The casual Principe de Mônaco is the neighborhood destination for sizzling plates of grilled squid, fresh *cherne* (grouper), shrimp and a mean bowl of *Leão Veloso* (a rich seafood soup). Sidewalk tables provide a relaxing spot for a meal or a drink on a fairly untrafficked street.

BAKERS CAFE **$$**

Map p236 (☎21 3209-1212; www.thebakers.com.br; Santa Clara 86; desserts R$9-15, sandwiches R$29-40, mains R$47-64; ⏲9am-8pm; 📶) The Bakers is a fine spot for flaky croissants, banana Danishes, apple strudels and other treats. There are also waffles, omelets, salads, gourmet sandwiches (such as prosciutto and mozzarella on ciabatta), quiches (including ricotta with sun-dried tomatoes), pastas, and heartier fare such as filet mignon with Gorgonzola sauce or grilled salmon with risotto and passion-fruit sauce.

AMIR MIDDLE EASTERN **$$**

Map p236 (☎21 2275-5596; Ronald de Carvalho 55C; mains R$48-62, sandwiches R$23-39; ⏲noon-midnight Mon-Sat, to 11pm Sun) At Amir you'll enter a world of delicate aromas amid a brightly painted interior complete with Middle Eastern decorative touches. Daytime crowds come for good-value set menus (around R$29), while at night the à la carte menu features all the favorites, including delicious platters of hummus, *kaftas* (spiced meat patty), falafel, kibbe and salads.

SKYLAB INTERNATIONAL **$$**

Map p236 (☎21 2106-1666; www.restaurantesklab.com.br; Av Atlântica 3264; mains R$75-120; ⏲noon-3pm & 7pm-11:30pm Fri-Wed, noon-3pm Thu) On the 30th floor of the Rio Othon Palace, the Skylab serves decent steaks, pastas and seafood, but it's the view that steals the show. Most tables are inside, though there are a few outdoor seats near the pool.

DEVASSA BRAZILIAN **$$**

Map p236 (☎21 2236-0667; Bolívar 8; mains R$28-40; ⏲11am-2am) This upscale *boteco* is well known for its excellent beers (like the refreshing Loura, perfect for a hot day, or the IPA-style Índia, for something with a bit more body). Devassa also serves tasty pub fare, including juicy burgers, veggie quesadillas, seafood pastas and the usual bar food. The open-sided restaurant enjoys a good location on the edge of Av Atlântica.

ARATACA AMAZONIAN **$$**

Map p236 (☎21 2548-6624; Domingos Ferreira 41D; mains R$53-85; ⏲10am-9pm) The casual, no-nonsense Arataca serves cuisine of the Amazon. There's *moqueca* made with *pirarucu* (a freshwater fish), *pato no tucupi* (roast duck flavored with garlic) or *vatapá* (a seafood dish with a thick sauce of manioc paste and coconut), all of which go nicely with real guaraná juice or first-rate *açaí* (order it 'natural,' without added sugar).

The classic hole-in-the-wall has a few tables in front, or you can belly up to the counter for your meal.

CAPRICCIOSA PIZZA **$$**

Map p236 (☎21 2255-2598; www.capricciosa.com.br; Domingos Ferreira 187; pizzas R$56-92; ⏲noon-4pm & 6pm-midnight Mon-Fri, noon-midnight Sat & Sun) Like its better-known version in Ipanema (p64), Capricciosa serves excellent thin-crust pizzas.

★CHURRASCARIA PALACE CHURRASCARIA **$$$**

Map p236 (☎21 2541-5898; www.churrascariapalace.com.br; Rodolfo Dantas 16; all you can eat R$140; ⏲noon-midnight; ❄) This elegantly set dining room is one of the best *churrascarias* (traditional barbecue restaurants) in town. Aside from juicy, high-quality cuts of meat, the included buffet nearly steals the show with fresh oysters, grilled heart of palm, sushi and sashimi, rice with wild mushrooms and goji berries, codfish casseroles, smoked fish, grilled prawns and octopus and amazing salads.

Waiters make frequent rounds with the goods; don't be shy about saying no, otherwise you'll end up with more than you could possibly eat.

AZUMI JAPANESE **$$$**

Map p236 (☎21 2295-1098; Ministro Viveiros de Castro 127; meals R$90-220, lunch specials from R$50; ⏲noon-3pm & 7pm-midnight) Hands down, Azumi serves some of the best traditional Japanese cuisine in Rio. This laid-back sushi bar certainly has its fans – both in the *nisei* community and from abroad. Azumi's *sushiman* (sushi chef) masterfully prepares delectable sushi and sashimi, and the tempuras and soups are also excellent. Be sure to ask what's in season.

DON CAMILLO ITALIAN **$$$**

Map p236 (☎21 2549-9958; Av Atlântica 3056; pastas R$44-75, mains R$46-88; ⏲noon-1am) This handsomely appointed Italian restaurant has flavorful pastas and lasagnas, as well as some excellent seafood dishes.

KIOSKS OF COPACABANA

The *quiosque* (kiosk) has long been a presence on the beachfront of Rio. It's where cold drinks and snacks are doled out to *cariocas* (residents of Rio) on the move, and where plastic tables and chairs provide a fine vantage point for contemplating the watery horizon. In recent years Copacabana Beach has seen a new crop of flashy kiosks replacing the old-fashioned wooden ones. Now it's possible to get a decent meal (the kitchens are cleverly concealed underground), an ice-cold draft beer or gourmet snacks without ever leaving the sand.

The new kiosks are sprinkled all along Copacabana Beach, with most options roughly between Rua Siqueira Campos and the Copacabana Palace hotel.

Antique tile floors, distressed wood beams and black-and-white photos make for a nice setting, though it's hard to top the outdoor tables facing the beach. For pure decadence, try the linguine with lobster, crayfish and cherry tomatoes.

Leme

ESPETTO CARIOCA SNACKS $

Map p240 (☎21 3514-2111; off Av Atlântica, near Praça Almirante Júlio de Noronha; snacks R$16-32; ⏲9am-midnight) At the northeast end of Leme, elevated over the beach, this peacefully set kiosk serves *espettos* (kebabs or skewers) of vegetables, meats and cheeses, which go nicely with drinks. Nearby, you can watch fearless *carioca* kids diving off the seawall. There's usually live music on weekends.

SALOMÉ BISTRO $$

Map p240 (☎21 2541-2416; www.facebook.com/salomebistro; Av Atlântica 994; mains R$48-65; ⏲6:30pm-midnight Tue-Thu, noon-midnight Fri-Sun; ✎) Run by the same people behind Ipanema's enormously popular Canastra (p69), Salomé brings a dash of style to the Leme beachfront. The easy-going open-sided bistro has vintage mirrors and curious wall hangings, potted palms and atmospheric lighting – though on fine days, the outdoor tables are the best place to enjoy high-quality small plates, grilled meats and seafood, and wines by the glass.

JOAQUINA BRAZILIAN $$

Map p240 (☎21 2275-8569; Av Atlântica 974; mains R$40-58; ⏲11:30am-midnight; 📶✎) Joaquina has much to recommend it: a great ocean-facing location with outdoor seating, excellent caipirinhas that don't stint on the fresh fruit, and tasty Brazilian fare at fair prices. On Sundays Joaquina serves *feijoada* (bean-and-meat stew; R$50); on Saturdays it's oxtail rice (also R$40). Arrive early before it runs out. Other hits: *moqueca* for one, shrimp risotto and vegetarian *feijoada*.

LA FIORENTINA ITALIAN $$$

Map p240 (☎21 2543-8395; Av Atlântica 458A; mains R$52-120, pizzas R$38-52; ⏲noon-midnight) One of Leme's classic Italian restaurants, La Fiorentina attracted Rio's glitterati in the 1960s. Today its beach-facing outdoor tables draw a loyal, mostly neighborhood crowd, who come to feast on mussels, seafood risottos and thin-crust pizzas.

SHIRLEY SPANISH $$$

Map p240 (☎21 2275-1398; www.facebook.com/restauranteshirley; Gustavo Sampaio 610; mains for 2 R$120-175; ⏲noon-1am) The aroma of succulent paella hangs in the air as waiters hurry to and from the kitchen bearing platefuls of fresh seafood. Shirley, opened in 1954, was one of the first Spanish restaurants in town, and attracts a local following in its small Leme dining room.

DRINKING & NIGHTLIFE

Ocean-fronting kiosks make great spots for a late-afternoon drink. Just inland, the area known as Baixo Copa (Lower Copa), has half a dozen or so lively bars and restaurants sprinkled along a quiet area just back from Av Atlântica. To explore here, head along Rua Aires de Saldanha and Rua Domingos Ferreira, between Rua Almirante Gonçalves and Rua Constante Ramos.

CAFE 18 DO FORTE
CAFE

Map p236 (☎21 2523-0171; www.cafe18doforte.com.br; Av Atlântica & Francisco Otaviano, Copacabana; ⏲10am-8pm Tue-Sun) The best place for a coffee or a microbrew in the Forte de Copacabana (p93), this outdoor cafe serves a fine array of craft beers from Rio (Hocus Pocus, Three Monkeys, Três Cariocas), including Praya on draft (R$18). The burgers, pastas and hearty Brazilian fare (mains R$42 to R$70) go nicely with the views from the red-umbrella-shaded tables.

BODEGA
BAR

Map p236 (☎21 2542-8963; www.facebook.com/bodegabebidaseantepastos; Rua Ministro Viveiros de Castro 102, Copacabana; ⏲5-11pm Tue-Sun) A hip little spot with furniture and fixtures made of recycled products, Bodega stocks an impressive array of craft beer from near and far (including Rio labels like Hocus Pocus and world-class Chimay from Belgium). There are also three rotating beers on tap. Match these brews with cheese platters, codfish balls, foie gras and eggplant dip, among other temptations (appetizers R$15 to R$30).

SOFÁ CAFÉ
COFFEE

Map p236 (☎21 2543-9107; www.sofacafe.com.br; Av NS de Copacabana 300, Copacabana; ⏲8am-8pm Mon-Sat) You'll find Copacabana's best coffee inside this roomy and atmospheric coffeehouse – part of a chain. You select your beans and your preferred method of preparation (Siphon, Chemex, French press, AeroPress etc), and there are plenty of iced options for those hot and steamy days.

PAVÃO AZUL
BAR

Map p236 (☎21 2236-2381; Hilário de Gouveia 71, Copacabana; ⏲noon-midnight Mon-Sat, to 8pm Sun) A Copacabana classic, Pavão Azul is a simple open-sided bar where huge crowds gather on the sidewalk out front to drink ice-cold *chope* (draft beer) and chat late into the night. It's been so successful in fact that the owners have opened a similar *boteco,* Pavãzinho, across the street. Don't miss the fantastically good, inexpensive *pataniscas* (codfish balls).

AS MELHORES CERVEJAS DO MUNDO
BAR

Map p236 (☎21 3497-3808; www.melhorescervejasdomundo.com.br; Ronald de Carvalho 154, Copacabana; ⏲4pm-midnight Wed-Sat) More bottle shop than bar, this friendly space is nevertheless a must-visit spot for any self-respecting beer lover. You'll find an impressive selection of brews from around the globe (including Belgian Trappist ales like Chimay and Rochefort), as well as a dozen or so local microbrews on tap. There's occasional live music and screenings of big football matches.

ESCONDIDO
BAR

Map p236 (☎21 2522-9800; Aires de Saldanha 98, Copacabana; ⏲6pm-1am Tue-Sun) One of the top beer bars in Copacabana, Escondido has a rotating selection of microbrews such as American pale ales (IPAs), stouts and ciders, including about two dozen on draft at any one time. It's a laid-back spot to head to with friends to sample a few brews and nibble on pub grub (including huge burgers).

MUD BUG
BAR

Map p236 (☎21 2543-5052; www.mudbug.com.br; Rudolfo Dantas 16, Copacabana; ⏲4pm-1am Tue & Wed, to 3am Thu-Sat, to midnight Sun) Mud Bug is a buzzing, warmly lit sports bar that has a rustic, all-wood interior where *cariocas* and foreigners mingle over football games, bar bites and a broad beer selection. There's also live music – typically classic rock – on weekends, and a jukebox at other times.

BOTECO BELMONTE
BAR

Map p240 (☎21 2239-1649; www.facebook.com/botecobelmonte; Av Atlântica 514, Leme; ⏲11:30am-2am Mon-Wed, to 3:30am Thu-Sat, to 5pm Sun) With a peaceful beachfront location, this casual, breezy bar is a relaxing and largely local spot to enjoy a draft or a filling meal. Like the other Belmontes in town, there's a huge selection of appetizers, grilled meats, sandwiches and seafood plates to go with those perfectly frothy brews.

PONTO DA BOSSA NOVA
BAR

Map p236 (☎21 2235-4616; Domingos Ferreira 215, Copacabana; ⏲5pm-1am Tue-Thu, noon-1am Fri-Sun) On a lively street sprinkled with bars, this boxy, wood-lined space has a tiny outdoor patio that makes a peaceful spot for sampling appetizers such as *carne seca com aipim* (jerked beef with fried cassava) and well-made caipirinhas. True to its name, there's live bossa nova – and Música Popular Brasileira (MPB) – from time to time.

BAR SURFSHOP BAR
Map p236 (Francisco Otaviano 67, Copacabana; ⏲10:30am-1am) A hole-in-the-wall drinkery that has a winning combination of burgers (R$28 to R$33) and beers, the Bar Surfshop draws a lively crowd on sunny days. As the name suggests, you can also take care of your surfing needs here. Surfboard hire runs R$50 for two hours (R$100 for the day).

TV BAR GAY, BAR
Map p236 (www.bartvbar.com.br; Av NS de Copacabana 1417, Shopping Cassino Atlântico, Copacabana; ⏲11pm-5am Thu-Sat, to 3am Sun) The trendy favorite in town, with DJs spinning amid an audiovisual assault in the space of a former TV station. The cover charge is R$15 to R$50.

FOSFOBOX CLUB
Map p236 (☎21 2548-7498; www.fosfobox.com.br; Siqueira Campos 143, Copacabana; ⏲11:30pm-6am Wed-Sat) This subterranean club is hidden under a shopping center near the metro station. Good DJs spin everything from funk to glam rock, and the crowd here is one of the more eclectic in the club scene. Admission R$20 to R$60.

ENTERTAINMENT

★BIP BIP LIVE MUSIC
Map p236 (☎21 2267-9696; www.facebook.com/barbipbip; Almirante Gonçalves 50, Copacabana; ⏲7pm-midnight Sun-Fri) For years Bip Bip has been one of the city's favorite spots to catch a live *roda de samba* (informal samba played around a table), despite it being just a storefront with a few battered tables. As the evening progresses the tree-lined neighborhood becomes the backdrop to serious jam sessions, with music and revelers spilling into the street.

The musical lineup features samba on Thursdays, Fridays and Sundays, *choro* (short for *chorinho;* a romantic, intimate samba) on Mondays and Tuesdays, and bossa nova on Wednesdays. Music kicks off around 8pm.

BECO DAS GARRAFAS LIVE MUSIC
Map p236 (☎21 2543-2962; www.becodasgarrafas.mus.br; Duvivier 37, Copacabana; entry R$30-40; ⏲shows daily from 8pm) Come to this club to connect to a small part of Brazilian history – and a big part of musical lore. It was on this lane where Tom Jobim and other innovators first unveiled bossa nova in the 1960s. Shuttered for years, the bar was brought back to life in 2014 and today hosts an excellent lineup of bossa and MPB singers.

CINE JOIA CINEMA
Map p236 (☎21 2236-5624; www.facebook.com/cinejoiacopa; Av NS de Copacabana 680, Copacabana) Hidden in the lower level of a shopping complex, this small, charming cinema screens a mix of Brazilian and independent fare, as well as the odd Hollywood movie. There are a few cafes in the same complex.

SALA MUNICIPAL BADEN POWELL PERFORMING ARTS
Map p236 (☎21 2548-0421; www.facebook.com/salabadenpowell; Av NS de Copacabana 360, Copacabana; entry R$20-80) One of the few music halls in the Zona Sul, the 500-seat Sala Municipal Baden Powell hosts a broad range of concerts throughout the year, with MPB and jazz figuring prominently.

ESPAÇO SESC PERFORMING ARTS
Map p236 (☎21 2548-1088; www.sescrj.org.br; Domingos Ferreira 160, Copacabana) Hosting an excellent assortment of theater and dance performances, Espaço SESC is a bulwark of the Copacabana arts scene. The repertoire tends toward the experimental and avant-garde, particularly during annual dance and theater festivals.

SHOPPING

Copacabana's shops, just like its local residents, are a diverse bunch, with everything from *cachaça* (sugarcane alcohol) to football jerseys on hand, as well as shoe stores, surf shops and record stores thrown in the mix. Fashion hunters will find more lower-tier labels than in neighboring Ipanema, along with lower prices to match. Between Copa and Ipanema is the Galeria River, a low-rise shopping mall lined with surf and swimwear shops.

GILSON MARTINS FASHION & ACCESSORIES
Map p236 (☎21 2235-5701; http://shop.gilsonmartins.com.br; Av Atlântica 1998, Copacabana; ⏲9am-8pm Mon-Sat, 10am-4pm Sun) Like its flagship store in Ipanema (p73), this

colorful shop sells well-crafted wallets, messenger bags, purses, key chains and other items with images of Cristo Redentor (Christ the Redeemer), the Brazilian flag and other iconic designs. Products are durable and use recycled and sustainable materials – and are not available outside Rio.

LOJA FLA FASHION & ACCESSORIES

Map p236 (☎21 2295-5057; www.lojafla.com.br; Av NS de Copacabana 219, Copacabana; ⏲9am-7pm Mon-Fri, 10am-4pm Sat) With more than 30 million fans worldwide, Flamengo is one of the most-watched football (soccer) teams in all of Brazil. This shop sells all the Flamengo merchandise, including jerseys, logo-emblazoned soccer balls, posters, bean bags, smartphone covers, clocks, flip-flops (thongs), socks, mugs, pens, pacifiers, baby bottles and heaps of other items.

OSKLEN SURFING CLOTHING

Map p236 (☎21 2513-0369; Francisco Otaviano 67, Arpoador; ⏲9am-8pm Mon-Fri, 10am-8pm Sat, 11am-5pm Sun) The famous Brazilian beachwear brand sells its well-made board shorts, T-shirts, *sungas* (Speedo-sized male swimsuits) and a few bikinis from this attractive store in Arpoador. You can even buy a very beautiful Kronig design surfboard here, if you have a spare R$1700.

HAVAIANAS SHOES

Map p236 (☎21 2267-2418; Xavier da Silveira 19, Copacabana; ⏲9am-8pm Mon-Fri, to 6pm Sat, 10am-6pm Sun) If you're out of ideas for gifts to take home, head to this sizable Havaianas shop, where the ubiquitous Brazilian rubber sandal comes in all different styles, sporting the flags of Brazil, Argentina, Portugal, England, Australia and Spain. There are snazzy designs for women, and even logo-bearing bags, key chains and beach towels.

GALERIA RIVER SHOPPING CENTER

Map p236 (www.galeriariver.com.br; Francisco Otaviano 67, Arpoador; ⏲9am-8pm Mon-Sat, 10am-7pm Sun) Surf shops, skateboard outlets, and shops selling beachwear and fashions for young people fill this shopping gallery in Arpoador. Shorts, bikinis, swim trunks, outdoor-adventure gear and party attire are here in abundance. You can also rent surfboards (though for short rentals it's easier hiring on the beach).

AV ATLÂNTICA FAIR MARKET

Map p236 (Av Atlântica, near Rua Djalma Ulrich, Copacabana; ⏲6pm-midnight Mon-Sat) Paintings, drawings, jewelry, clothing and a fair bit of tourist junk make up this Copacabana market. It's located on the median along Av Atlântica.

PRAÇA DO LIDO MARKET MARKET

Map p236 (Praça do Lido, Copacabana; ⏲8am-6pm Sat & Sun) Copacabana's response to Ipanema's widely popular Hippie Fair (p73), this smaller weekend market features handicrafts and souvenirs, soccer jerseys, jewelry stands and, from time to time, a man selling amazing slices of chocolate cake.

SHOPPING CIDADE COPACABANA SHOPPING CENTER

Map p236 (☎21 2549-0650; Siqueira Campos 143, Copacabana; ⏲10am-9pm Mon-Fri, to 6pm Sat, to 4pm Sun) One of Rio's first malls, this quirky shopping gallery packs in an intriguing mix of stores in a no-nonsense parking-garage-like interior. Scattered across several floors are antique shops, used-book and record stores, art galleries and other surprising finds.

SPORTS & ACTIVITIES

UNIVERSO PADDLE SURF WATER SPORTS

Map p236 (Posto 6, Copacabana Beach; per hour R$60; ⏲8am-6pm) Near the southern end of Copacabana, Universo is one of several places on the beach where you can hire stand-up paddle boards (SUPs). The view is fantastic across the length of Copacabana Beach, and the waters here are generally calmer than mid-beach, so it's not a bad place to try it out if you've never done it before.

RIO ELECTRIC CYCLING

Map p236 (☎21 3496-9969; www.rioelectric.com.br/lojas.php; Ronaldo de Carvalho 21, Copacabana; bike/electric bike/longboard hire per hour R$25/80/25; ⏲9am-7pm) Rio Electric is a one-stop shop for hiring bikes, tandems, longboards, inline skates and hoverboards. If you want some extra power when you're going uphill, opt for an electric bike. It's in a handy location just across the street from the beach (and more importantly the bike path).

Botafogo, Humaitá & Urca

BOTAFOGO & HUMAITÁ | URCA

Neighborhood Top Five

1 Pão de Açúcar (p103) Gliding up to the top of this peak by cable car for the awe-inspiring view of Rio at your feet.

2 Praia Vermelha (p104) Basking on the sands at one of Rio's prettiest little beaches, taking in great vistas of the rocky coastline.

3 Pista Cláudio Coutinho (p109) Walking between forest and sea, keeping an eye out for monkeys, on this peaceful, winding trail.

4 Sailing cruise (p203) Taking in the beauty of Rio's mountainous landscape from Baía de Guanabara on an afternoon cruise with Sail in Rio.

5 Drinking and dining scene (p107) Joining the cool kids over creative cocktails and market-fresh fare at places such as CoLAB.

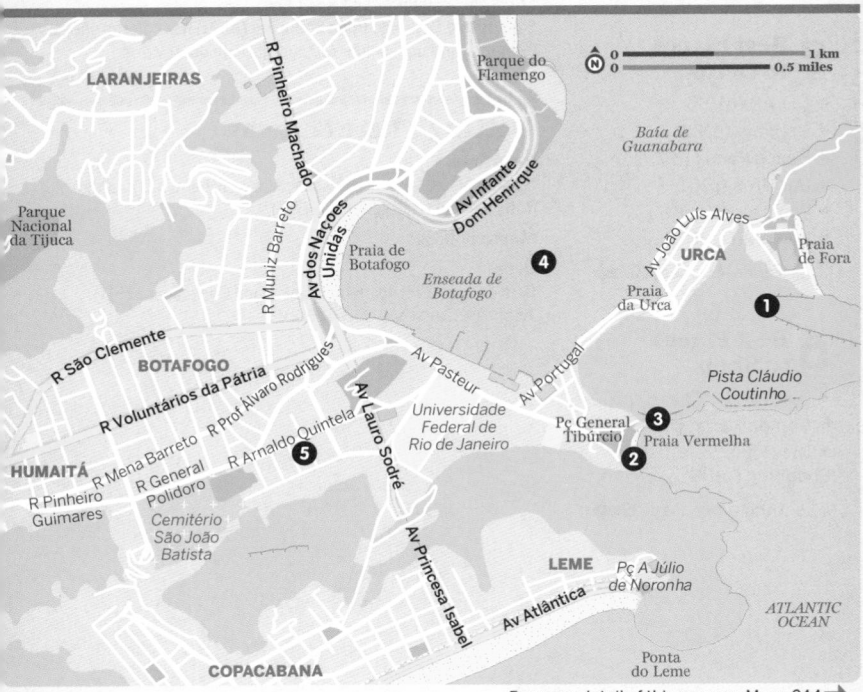

For more detail of this area see Map p244

Lonely Planet's Top Tip

Although Urca is home to one of Rio's top attractions, few visitors venture into the neighborhood beyond Pão de Açúcar. The quiet tree-lined streets (like Rua Otávio Correia) make for some intriguing exploring, and there are picturesque views from the bayside roads (such as Av João Luís Alves).

Best Places to Eat

- Lasai (p106)
- Oteque (p106)
- Marchezinho (p104)
- Meza Bar (p106)
- South Ferro (p106)
- Bar Urca (p107)

For reviews, see p104

Best Places to Drink

- CoLAB (p107)
- Comuna (p107)
- Hocus Pocus (p107)
- Bar Urca (p108)
- WineHouse (p107)
- Bar 1928 (p107)

For reviews, see p107

Best Places to Shop

- Baratos de Ribeiro (p109)
- Comparsaria (p109)
- Botafogo Praia Shopping (p109)

For reviews, see p109

Explore Botafogo, Humaitá & Urca

The traditional, middle-class neighborhood of Botafogo, and neighboring Humaitá, may not have the beaches of their neighbors to the south, but they don't lack for much else, with intriguing museums, movie theaters, quaint bookshops, a shopping center, and festive, open-air bars on tree-lined backstreets. There are also a few nightclubs and a boulevard dotted with old mansions.

To the east, Urca is even more idyllic, with shaded, quiet streets. Its eclectic architecture includes art deco and modernist houses backed by manicured gardens. Along the seawall, which forms the northwestern perimeter of Pão de Açúcar, fishermen cast for dinner as couples lounge beneath palm trees, taking in views of Baía de Guanabara (Guanabara Bay) and Cristo Redentor (Christ the Redeemer). Tiny Praia Vermelha in the south marks the beginning of a pleasant walking trail and has one of Rio's finest beach views.

Local Life

Hangouts At Bar Urca (p108), locals sip beers and munch on appetizers along the seawall across the street, while taking in the pretty views.

Markets Browse the produce stands of Cobal do Humaitá (p37) by day and sample the bars by night.

Shopping Botafogo Praia Shopping (p109) has colorful shops, a cinema, and upper-floor restaurants with great views.

Getting There & Away

Botafogo

Bus Ipanema, Leblon and Copacabana (161 and 573), Jardim Botânico and Gávea (170, 176, 592).

Metro Botafogo.

Urca

Bus Centro (107), Ipanema, Leblon and Copacabana (511), Jardim Botânico and Gávea (512).

RAPHAEL KOERICH/500PX ©

TOP SIGHT
PÃO DE AÇÚCAR

One of Rio's dazzling icons, Pão de Açúcar (Sugarloaf Mountain) offers a vision of Rio at its most disarming. Following a steep ascent to the mountain, you'll be rewarded with superb views of Rio's gorgeous shoreline, and the city planted among the green peaks. From the summit, 395m above Rio and the Baía de Guanabara, it's quite clear why Rio is called the Cidade Maravilhosa (Marvelous City).

The most traditional way to reach the top is to board the two-stage cable car (pictured) that departs from Urca every 20 minutes or so. The glass-and-steel cars are good fun in themselves, and ascend 215m to Morro da Urca. From here, you can see Baía de Guanabara and along the winding coastline; on the ocean side of the mountain is Praia Vermelha, in a small, calm bay. Aside from the traditional visit, you can also arrange for a guided tour that delves into the history of the sight; there's also a backstage tour that allows a behind-the-scenes look at the cable-car engine rooms.

Morro da Urca has a restaurant, souvenir shops, outdoor theater and a helipad. In the summer, concerts are sometimes staged in the amphitheater. The second cable car continues up to Pão de Açúcar.

At the top, the city unfolds beneath you, with Corcovado mountain and Cristo Redentor off to the west, the twinkling lights of Niteroi across the bay to the east, and the long curve of Copacabana Beach to the south. If the breathtaking heights unsteady you, there's a stylish restaurant and bar on hand serving caipirinhas and snacks. For prime views of the Cidade Maravilhosa, go around sunset on a clear day.

Those who'd rather take the long way to the top should sign up with one of the granite-hugging climbing tours offered by various outfits in Rio, including Crux Eco (p52). Morro da Urca is much easier to climb, and you can do it on your own. The short but steep path takes about 30 minutes to climb. You'll find the unmarked trail along the Pista Cláudio Coutinho.

DON'T MISS

- The view of planes landing beneath you
- The walking trail up Morro da Urca
- A behind-the-scenes history tour

PRACTICALITIES

- Sugarloaf Mountain
- Map p244, G2
- ☎21 2546-8400
- www.bondinho.com.br
- Av Pasteur 520, Urca
- adult/child R$85/42
- ⏲8am-8pm

SIGHTS

Botafogo has relatively few traditional sights. Most of the action here happens after sunset, when its top-notch restaurants, buzzing microbrew bars and lounges draw *cariocas* (Rio residents) of all stripes. Over in Urca, the grand attraction is Pão de Açúcar, which is best visited by day (or at sunset). You can also tack on a stroll through Urca's serene streets or a lounge on Praia Vermelha.

Botafogo & Humaitá

MUSEU DO ÍNDIO MUSEUM

Map p244 (☎21 3214-8700; www.museudoindio.gov.br; Rua das Palmeiras 55, Botafogo; ⏲9am-5:30pm Tue-Fri, 1-5pm Sat & Sun) FREE Though closed for renovations at the time of research, the small Museu do Índio features multimedia exhibitions on Brazil's northern tribes and provides an excellent introduction to the economic, religious and social life of the country's indigenous people. Next to native food and medicinal plants, the four life-size dwellings in the courtyard were actually built by four different tribes.

MUSEU CASA DE RUI BARBOSA MUSEUM

Map p244 (☎21 3289-4600; www.casaruibarbosa.gov.br; São Clemente 134, Botafogo; ⏲10am-5:30pm Tue-Fri, 2-6pm Sat & Sun) FREE The former mansion of famous Brazilian journalist and diplomat Rui Barbosa is now a museum housing his library and personal belongings. Barbosa played a pivotal role in shaping the country's socioeconomic development in the early 20th century.

Urca

PÃO DE AÇÚCAR MOUNTAIN

See p103.

PRAIA VERMELHA BEACH

Map p244 (Praça General Tibúrcio) Beneath Morro da Urca, narrow Praia Vermelha has superb views of the rocky coastline from the shore. Its coarse sand gives the beach the name *vermelha* (red). Because the beach is protected by the headland, the water is usually calm.

EATING

The dining scene has exploded here recently, with some of Rio's most creative restaurants opening up on the tree-lined backstreets of Botafogo and Humaitá. A great street for browsing is Rua Nelson Mandela (right next to the Botafogo metro station), which is lined with casual open-air eating and drinking spots. For higher-end dining, Rua Conde de Irajá, 12 blocks west in Humaitá, has excellent restaurants. Urca, largely residential, has only a few choices.

Botafogo & Humaitá

CEVICHE RJ CEVICHE $

Map p244 (☎21 3549-7077; www.facebook.com/cevicherj; Arnaldo Quintela 66B, Botafogo; ceviche around R$35; ⏲noon-4pm & 6pm-midnight Wed-Fri, 1pm-midnight Sat, 1-11pm Sun) This simple Peruvian-run restaurant serves arguably the best ceviche in Rio. Although there is some seating inside the restaurant, most diners sit outside in what is essentially a car park. The sublime ceviche is the compulsory order, but a few other classic Peruvian dishes are available, alongside a selection of decent craft beers and a handful of wines.

MARCHEZINHO CAFE $$

Map p244 (www.facebook.com/marchezinho; Voluntários da Pátria 46, Botafogo; sandwiches R$28-38; ⏲9am-1am Mon-Wed, to 2am Thu & Fri, 10am-2am Sat) This multipurpose space operates as a cafe, bar and minimarket. The owner's French roots show through on the menu and store shelves, with the excellent cheese, bread and coffee. The carefully selected ingredients and produce are exclusively Brazilian, however, with most coming from small local producers. Come for creative tapas, delectable sandwiches, craft beers and first-rate cocktails.

SLOW BAKERY BAKERY $$

Map p244 (☎21 3563-8638; www.theslowbakery.com.br; São João Batista 93, Botafogo; sandwiches R$24-29; ⏲9am-7pm Tue-Fri, 9am-3pm Sat;) The sourdough revolution has yet to take hold in Rio, so this modern bakery is something of a pioneer. A range of superb sourdough loaves are baked on-site and available both for takeaway purchase and as chunky sandwiches that can be enjoyed

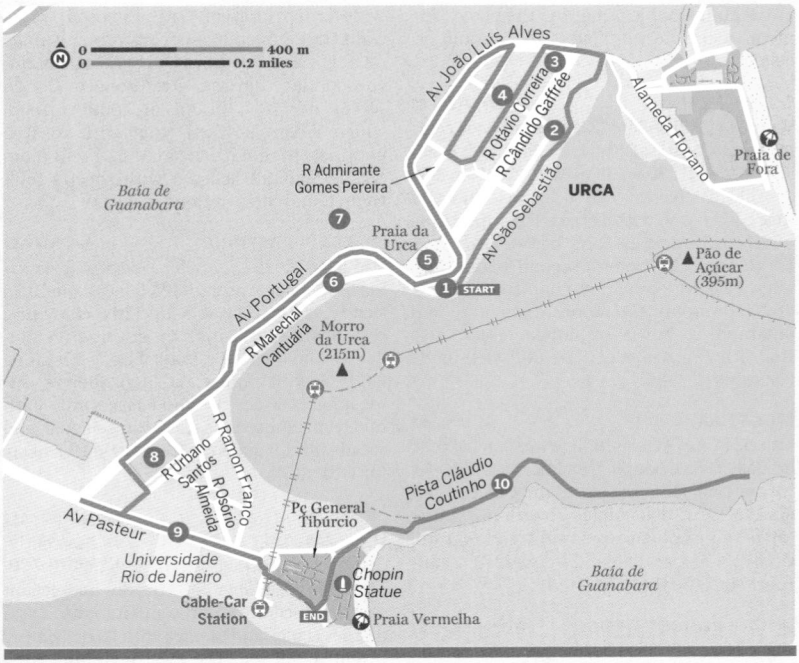

Neighborhood Walk
Urca, the Village by the Sea

START RUA MARECHAL CANTUÁRIA
END PRAIA VERMELHA
LENGTH 5KM; THREE HOURS

One of Rio's most charming neighborhoods is also one of its least explored. This walk begins where Rua Marechal Cantuária meets Av São Sebastião. On your left, you'll see the former 1 **Cassino da Urca**, a once-popular gambling and nightspot, where Carmen Miranda and Josephine Baker both performed.

Veer right along Av São Sebastião, following the road uphill. You'll pass 2 **Carmen Miranda's former residence** at No 131 and soon reach the wall that separates the military fort from the neighborhood.

At the end of the street, take the steps down to Av João Luís Alves. Stop at much-loved neighborhood bar/restaurant 3 **Bar Urca** (p108), where you can enjoy cold drinks, appetizers and admire the fine views.

Head down 4 **Rua Otávio Correira** to explore the tree-lined backstreets. Loop back along Rua Admirante Gomes Pereira.

Cut back to Av João Luís Alves and follow it to 5 **Praia da Urca**, a tiny beach with more fine views of the bay, popular with neighborhood kids who gather here to play football.

Stay on the bay side as the road forks. Peek inside 6 **Igreja de Nossa Senhora do Brasil** (the chapel is on the ground floor; the church is upstairs), noting the small Brazilian flag on the Madonna's cloak.

Facing the church is the floating 7 **statue of São Pedro no Mar**. On June 29, St Peter's feast day, the fishermen process across the bay, past the statue, scattering flowers across the water.

Go along what is now Av Portugal to a bridge. On the left is 8 **Quadrado da Urca**, a harbor.

Follow 9 **Av Pasteur** southeast past majestic buildings like Companhia de Pesquisa de Recursos Minerais (Av Pasteur 404), guarded by a lion and a winged creature.

Follow 10 **Pista Cláudio Coutinho** (p109), a paved 1.2km trail winding along the southern contour of Morro da Urca, out and back to Praia Vermelha.

at the simple tables that line the place. The menu also includes salads, pastries and excellent coffee.

SOUTH FERRO ASIAN, PIZZA **$$**

Map p244 (☎21 3986-4323; www.facebook.com/southferro; Arnaldo Quintela 23, Botafogo; mains R$41-62; ⏲11:30am-3pm Mon, 11:30am-3pm & 6:30-11pm Tue-Sat;) Chef Sei Shiroma made his name with Ferro e Farinha (p118), widely regarded as Rio's best pizza place. South Ferro, Shiroma's second restaurant, adds a healthy pinch of Asian spice in vegetable dumplings, tempura, fish curry and outstanding bowls of ramen. You'll also find a few pizza selections and well-made cocktails (R$32).

MEZA BAR TAPAS **$$**

Map p244 (☎21 3239-1951; www.mezabar.com.br; Capitão Salomão 69, Humaitá; tapas R$16-42; ⏲6pm-1am) Humaitá's see-and-be-seen hot spot serves delectable, Brazilian-slanted tapas to a sophisticated and trendy crowd. Creative cocktails and delightful staff round out the fun.

VOID – HOUSE OF FOOD INTERNATIONAL **$$**

Map p244 (☎21 3593-3326; www.avoid.com.br; Voluntários da Pátria 31, Botafogo; snacks R$18-36; ⏲noon-midnight;) This venue has two halves: on one side is Void, a store and cafe/bar selling sneakers, T-shirts, baseball caps, brownies and drinks. On the other side of the divide is House of Food, a 'guest kitchen' hosting chefs, cooks and general food enthusiasts on daily rotation. The menus are heavy on international street food and food-truck classics.

LE DEPANNEUR CAFE **$$**

Map p244 (☎21 2537-5250; www.ledep.com.br; Voluntários da Pátria 86, Botafogo; sandwiches R$27-36; ⏲8am-10pm Sun-Thu, to 11pm Fri & Sat;) This buzzing cafe and deli serves juices, waffles, crepes, salads, antipasti plates and specialty sandwiches. On weekends the large plant-trimmed front patio fills with brunching locals and makes a good people-watching perch. There's also a self-serve bakery with croissants and other goodies, and plenty of other provisions for picnickers.

MIAM MIAM BRAZILIAN **$$**

Map p244 (☎21 2244-0125; www.miammiam.com.br; General Goés Monteiro 34, Botafogo; mains R$62-82; ⏲noon-3:30pm & 7pm-midnight Mon-Fri, 1pm-midnight Sat) Exposed brick walls and a mishmash of retro furnishings set the scene for dining in style at Botafogo's culinary darling. Chef Roberta Ciasca serves her own brand of comfort food, which means smoked trout with roasted potatoes, pork with basmati rice and pineapple, eggplant lasagna with sheep's milk yogurt, and other unique dishes.

LIVRARIA PREFÁCIO BRAZILIAN **$$**

Map p244 (☎21 2527-5699; Voluntários da Pátria 39, Botafogo; mains R$28-56; ⏲10am-10pm Mon-Fri, 2-10pm Sat & Sun) This charming restaurant scores high on novelty: it's hidden in the back of a bookshop, with stone walls, low-lit lamps and bookshelves. Atmosphere aside, the food is decent, with nicely presented pastas, sandwiches and salads, and it's also a great little hideaway for a drink.

★LASAI GASTRONOMY **$$$**

Map p244 (☎21 3449-1834; www.lasai.com.br; Conde de Irajá 191, Humaitá; prix fixe R$350; ⏲7:30-10pm Tue-Fri, 1-10pm Sat) Inside an elegant early-20th-century house in Humaitá, Lasai dazzles critics and foodies with its deliciously inventive cuisine. The award-winning *carioca* chef Rafa Costa e Silva earned his chops in some of the world's best dining rooms (including Mugaritz in Spain), and he puts his skills to brilliant use here. Reservations are essential.

OTEQUE GASTRONOMY **$$$**

Map p244 (☎21 3486-5758; www.oteque.com; Conde de Irajá 581, Humaitá; 8-course tasting menu R$250; ⏲7:30-11:30pm Tue-Sat) Much to the delight of *cariocas,* celebrated São Paulo chef Alberto Landgraf recently moved to Rio and opened this small, beautifully designed restaurant, complete with a theatrically lit open kitchen. The menu changes daily but features exquisite seafood (grilled octopus, scallops, monkfish, oysters) artfully prepared with Brazilian accents like hearts of palm and *tucupi* (a sauce made from wild manioc).

Urca

JULIUS BRASSERIE EUROPEAN **$$**

Map p244 (☎21 3518-7117; Av Portugal 986; mains R$67-85; ⏲noon-midnight Tue-Sat, noon-6pm Sun) This elegant Dutch-Brazilian-run restaurant in Urca turns out a creative mix of grilled meats (rack of lamb, duck breast), seafood (shrimp curry with black rice), pastas and risottos in a quiet location on the edge of Praia da Urca. It makes a great lunch or dinner spot, followed by a stroll around the neighborhood.

GAROTA DA URCA BRAZILIAN **$$**

Map p244 (☎21 2541-8585; Av João Luís Alves 56; mains R$42-82; ⏲noon-1am Sun-Thu, to 2:30am Fri & Sat) Overlooking small Praia da Urca, this neighborhood restaurant serves good-value weekday lunch specials, and you can enjoy views over the bay from the open-air veranda. By night, a more garrulous crowd converges for steak and *chope* (draft beer).

BAR URCA BRAZILIAN **$$$**

Map p244 (☎21 2295-8744; Cândido Gaffrée 205; mains R$57-170; ⏲noon-3pm & 7-11pm Mon-Sat, noon-8pm Sun) Upstairs from Bar Urca's popular snack stand, you'll find an elegantly set dining room with memorable views across the bay. The seafood is first rate, with scrumptious *caldeirada* (seafood stew), *moqueca* (Bahian fish stew) and grilled octopus on the menu. Bar Urca's most famous dish is *camarão na moranga:* shrimp cooked in creamy sauce and served in a pumpkin (R$219 for two people).

DRINKING & NIGHTLIFE

Botafogo has become the hot destination of the moment, with microbrew pubs, creative cocktail spaces and even a wine bar. This is the place to go for lively, authentic *carioca* bars, with fun, mixed crowds and little of the pretense you might encounter in bars further south. Over in Urca, the action largely consists of grabbing drinks at casual snack bars and drinking along the seawall.

Botafogo & Humaitá

HOCUS POCUS BAR

Map p244 (☎21 4107-3107; www.facebook.com/hocuspocusdna; Dezenove de Fevereiro 186, Botafogo; ⏲6pm-midnight Mon-Wed, to 2am Thu-Sat) Helping to lead Rio's craft-beer revolution, Hocus Pocus opened this beer hall in 2016 to provide its fans with easy access to its brews. There are over a dozen drafts here – including HP's finest (try the Magic Trap, a Belgian-style golden ale) as well as a few beers from other microbrewers. The buzzing barn-like setting is a great place to while away the evening.

BAR 1928 COCKTAIL BAR

Map p244 (☎21 3586-2511; contato@bar1928.com.br; Álvaro Ramos 170, Botafogo; ⏲6:30pm-12:30am Tue-Fri, noon-1am Sat, noon-11pm Sun) Tucked away on an otherwise quiet backstreet, Bar 1928 specializes in cocktails and superior bar food. The street-side veranda gets packed early on weekends but more seating is available in a side alley and dining room. Traditional Brazilian dishes have been given a modern twist (sharing plates around R$34), and the excellent cocktails are not to be missed.

COLAB BAR

Map p244 (☎21 3592-0470; www.colab-rio.com; Fernandes Guimarães 66, Botafogo; ⏲10am-1am Tue-Sat) CoLAB is one of Botafogo's increasing number of lively bar/restaurants attracting a predominantly young crowd with a combination of international cuisine, cocktails and craft beers. The menu boasts curries (both Indian and Thai) as well as samosas, falafel sandwiches, burgers and other temptations. Calm by day, CoLAB picks up in the evenings – with DJs and the occasional band keeping things lively.

WINEHOUSE WINE BAR

Map p244 (☎21 3264-4101; www.winehouserio.com; Paulo Barreto 25, Botafogo; ⏲5pm-midnight Mon-Wed, to 1am Thu-Sat) WineHouse is a stylish yet unpretentious wine bar – a welcome break from Rio's traditionally expensive and starchy wine-drinking scene. A blackboard lists a dozen or so wines available by the glass and always includes a few Brazilian wines. The menu features light bites and an excellent selection of charcuterie. Arrive before 8pm on weekdays for happy-hour prices.

COMUNA BAR

Map p244 (☎21 3579-6175; www.facebook.com/comunacc; Sorocaba 585, Botafogo; ⏲noon-1am Tue-Fri, 6:30pm-1:30am Sat, 6:30pm-midnight Sun) This creative space is equal parts bar, art gallery and independent bookseller (and indie publishing house). There's always something afoot in the delightfully off-the-beaten-path locale, with workshops, music sessions, readings, exhibitions and fashion shows. It's also just a great spot for a local microbrew and a bite (try one of the award-winning burgers).

FUSKA 2.0 BAR

Map p244 (☎21 2266-3621; www.facebook.com/fuskabar2.0; Capitão Salomão 52, Humaitá; ⏲8am-3am Tue-Sun) When you need a break from upmarket drinking and dining, head to Fuska 2.0, a hole-in-the-wall gathering space where a fun crowd gathers at tables on the front sidewalk. There's always something going on, and you can catch live music from Thursday to Sunday nights.

CAVERNA BAR

Map p244 (☎21 3507-5600; www.espacocaverna.com; Assis Bueno 26, Botafogo; ⏲6pm-midnight Mon-Thu, to 2am Fri, 7pm-2am Sat) Yet another reason why Botafogo may be surpassing Ipanema in the cool factor these days, this always buzzing rock-and-roll-loving bar and bistro serves microbrews and juicy burgers amid a fun and festive atmosphere (though the music rocks a little loud some nights).

BAR BUKOWSKI CLUB

Map p244 (☎21 2244-7303; Álvaro Ramos 270, Botafogo; ⏲9pm-6am Fri & Sat) Paying homage to the eponymous bohemian American writer, this club has a downstairs dance floor and bar, and an upstairs level for live bands playing rock, pop and blues. It's a great scene, and usually attracts a fun crowd. There's also a pool table and darts, and you can have a go at one of the water pipes. The cover charge is R$55.

ALICE BAR BAR

Map p244 (☎21 3079-6484; www.facebook.com/alicebar.botafogo; Sorocaba 594, Humaitá; ⏲6pm-3am Tue-Sun) Hordes of young drinkers spill out onto the sidewalks around Alice Bar, merging with the crowds from nearby bars to make this one of the liveliest spots in the city. The upbeat vibe continues inside with color-shifting, Wonderland-inspired graffiti and tightly packed tables. Barman Walter Garin, a renowned mixologist, is responsible for the cocktail menu.

CHAMPANHARIA OVELHA NEGRA BAR

Map p244 (☎21 2226-1064; www.champanhariaovelhanegra.com.br; Bambina 120, Botafogo; ⏲6pm-midnight Mon-Fri) One of Rio's top happy-hour scenes, Ovelha Negra draws a mostly local crowd who come for the lively conversation and the 40 varieties of champagne and prosecco – the specialties of the house.

Urca

BAR URCA BAR

Map p244 (☎21 2295-8744; Cândido Gaffrée 205; ⏲6:30am-11pm Mon-Sat, 8am-8pm Sun) This much-loved neighborhood bar and restaurant has a marvelous setting near Urca's bayside waterfront. At night, young and old crowd along the seaside wall to enjoy cold drinks, appetizers and fine views.

CLÁSSICO BEACH CLUB LOUNGE

Map p244 (☎21 2542-8966; www.classicobeachclub.com/urca; Av Pasteur 520; ⏲9am-9pm) Atop Pão de Açúcar (p103), the handsomely designed Clássico Beach Club serves excellent cocktails, which go down nicely with the satisfying appetizers (ceviche, panko-crusted squid, codfish balls), not to mention the fabulous views at your feet.

URCA GRILL BAR

Map p244 (Marechal Cantuária 10; ⏲9am-midnight) *Cariocas* have found creative ways to spend a summer evening while the economic crisis still grips the city – namely stopping by well-positioned snack bars like this one, picking up ice-cold beers and appetizers, and enjoying them along Urca's lovely seawall. The views (of Cristo Redentor and the bay) are magical.

ENTERTAINMENT

TERRA BRASILIS LIVE MUSIC

Map p244 (☎21 2275-4651; www.restaurante terrabrasilis.com.br; Praça General Tibúrcio; ⏲noon-midnight) Just beside Praia Vermelha, Terra Brasilis has gorgeous views of Pão de Açúcar looming overhead. Jazzy Música Popular Brasileira (MPB) bands play from about 8pm on weeknights (and at 1pm on weekends), making for a delightful open-air setting. It's located in the building marked Circulo Militar da Praia Vermelha.

ESPAÇO ITAÚ CINEMA

Map p244 (www.itaucinemas.com.br; Praia de Botafogo 316, Botafogo) A high-quality six-screen cinema that shows a wide variety of fare. You can linger before or after the film at the cafe, bookstore or snack counters.

OLHO DA RUA LIVE MUSIC

Map p244 (☎21 3178-6601; www.facebook.com/olhodarua06; Bambina 6; ⏲6pm-midnight Tue-Sat) This multifunctional space hosts a wide range of live music, theatrical performances, DJ sets and other cultural and community events such as art exhibitions and yoga classes. In addition to the event space, there is a store selling clothes, jewelry and accessories, a selection of artworks, and a cafe and bar with pizzas, sandwiches and locally brewed beers.

ESTAÇÃO NET RIO CINEMA

Map p244 (☎21 2226-1986; www.grupoestacao.com.br; Voluntários da Pátria 35, Botafogo) This two-screen cinema in Botafogo shows a range of films – Brazilian, foreign, independent and the occasional Hollywood offering. It has a cafe inside, as well as a shop selling used records and books, with a number of works focusing on the film arts.

SHOPPING

Shopping in Botafogo usually means heading to the high-rise mall overlooking the bay. There are, however, other options, including a few bookshops, a good record store and a footwear shop.

BARATOS DA RIBEIRO MUSIC

Map p244 (☎21 3547-2220; www.baratosdaribeiro.com.br; Paulino Fernandes 15, Botafogo; ⏲10am-8pm Mon-Fri, 11am-8pm Sat) Vinyl fans and bookworms flock to this cabinet of musical and literary curiosities with its extensive collection of unusual albums combined with secondhand art books, novels and other intriguing publications – including titles in English (spotted when last we passed through: the cowboy novel *Wyatt Earp* and an autobiography of Katharine Hepburn).

COMPARSARIA SHOES

Map p244 (☎21 3178-2114; www.facebook.com/comparsaria; Voluntários da Pátria 45, Botafogo; ⏲10am-8pm Mon-Wed, to 9pm Thu & Fri, 10am-7pm Sat) This small attractive boutique stocks handsomely crafted shoes and sandals, leather bags and satchels, hats, wallets and other accessories. Production runs are limited and styles veer between timeless and classic versus avant-garde and utterly unwearable.

LIVRARIA DA TRAVESSA BOOKS

Map p244 (☎21 3195-0200; www.travessa.com.br; Voluntários da Pátria 97, Botafogo; ⏲10am-10pm) Rio's best-loved bookstore chain now has a Botafogo branch. With an appealing cafe, a music section (CDs, vinyl reprints) and a small but decent foreign-language section (English, French, Spanish), it's a fine place to while away a rainy day.

RIO SUL SHOPPING SHOPPING CENTER

Map p244 (☎21 3723-9500; www.riosul.com.br; Lauro Müller 116, Botafogo; ⏲10am-10pm Mon-Sat, 3-9pm Sun) The biggest shopping center you can reach without heading to Barra da Tijuca, Rio Sul has more than 400 shops, featuring both the prominent and the obscure, plus cinemas and restaurants.

BOTAFOGO PRAIA SHOPPING SHOPPING CENTER

Map p244 (☎21 3171-9872; www.botafogopraiashopping.com.br; Praia de Botafogo 400, Botafogo; ⏲10am-10pm Mon-Sat, 2-9pm Sun; 📶) Botafogo's large shopping center has dozens of stores, featuring Brazilian and international designers to suit every style – and clothe every part of the body. The 3rd floor's the best for top designers: check out stores such as Maria Filó, Reserva and Hope. The mall also has a cinema and several 5th-floor restaurants with panoramic views.

SPORTS & ACTIVITIES

PISTA CLÁUDIO COUTINHO WALKING

Map p244 (off Praça General Tibúrcio, Urca; ⏲6am-sunset) This paved 1.2km trail winds along the southern contour of Morro da Urca. It's a lush area, with the craggy mountain rising on one side, and waves crashing on rocks below. To get here, walk 100m north along the edge of Praia Vermelha (with your back to the cable-car station) and you'll see the entrance to the path straight ahead, just past the beach.

VITORMARIGO/SHUTTERSTOCK ©

1. Hiking, Parque Nacional da Tijuca (p158) 2. Surfing, Ipanema Beach (p60) 3. Hang gliding off Pedra Bonita (p52) 4. Rock climbing (p52)

FRED S. PINHEIRO/SHUTTERSTOCK ©

Outdoor Adventures

Blessed with tropical rainforest, towering peaks and sparkling seaside, the Cidade Maravilhosa (Marvelous City) offers some captivating ways to spend a sun-drenched afternoon. You can go hang gliding, surfing, biking, hiking, running and rock climbing amid spectacular scenery without leaving the city limits.

Hang Gliding

Although it will cost you a fair bit, hang gliding off Pedra Bonita (p52) is an unforgettable experience: just the pilot and you, soaring high over treetops and landing near the sea.

Rock Climbing

Sure, you can take the aerial tram to the top of Pão de Açúcar (Sugarloaf Mountain), but for an adrenaline rush and mesmerizing scenery, sign up for a rock-climbing trip (p52) to the top. The view will be all the sweeter.

Surfing

There are superb waves (p52) all around Rio. For a quick fix, you can join the locals off Arpoador. More serious surfers should get a ride on the surf bus and head west to Macumba or Prainha.

Hiking

Rio's tropical rainforest makes a fine setting for a hike (p51). Head to the Floresta da Tijuca for hikes through lush forest followed by a dip in a waterfall.

Cycling

The beachside bike path is great any time for cycling (p51), and you can plot a route from Leblon up through Flamengo, riding waterside for most of the journey. You can also take a scenic spin around Lagoa.

Flamengo & Around

FLAMENGO | COSME VELHO | CATETE & GLÓRIA | LARANJEIRAS | LARANJEIRAS

Neighborhood Top Five

❶ **Cristo Redentor** (p114) Taking the steep cog train up Corcovado for a panoramic view beneath Rio's open-armed Christ the Redeemer.

❷ **Museu da República** (p116) Exploring Rio's past days of demagogues and political intrigue in this wonderfully restored museum.

❸ **Marina da Glória** (p117) Enjoying the fine views over the bay while dining at an open-air waterfront restaurant in this beautifully located marina.

❹ **Igreja de Nossa Senhora da Glória do Outeiro** (p117) Making the short but steep climb up to this 18th-century church atop Ladeira da Glória to enjoy the great views.

❺ **Parque do Flamengo** (p116) Working up a sweat on a bike ride through this expansive urban park.

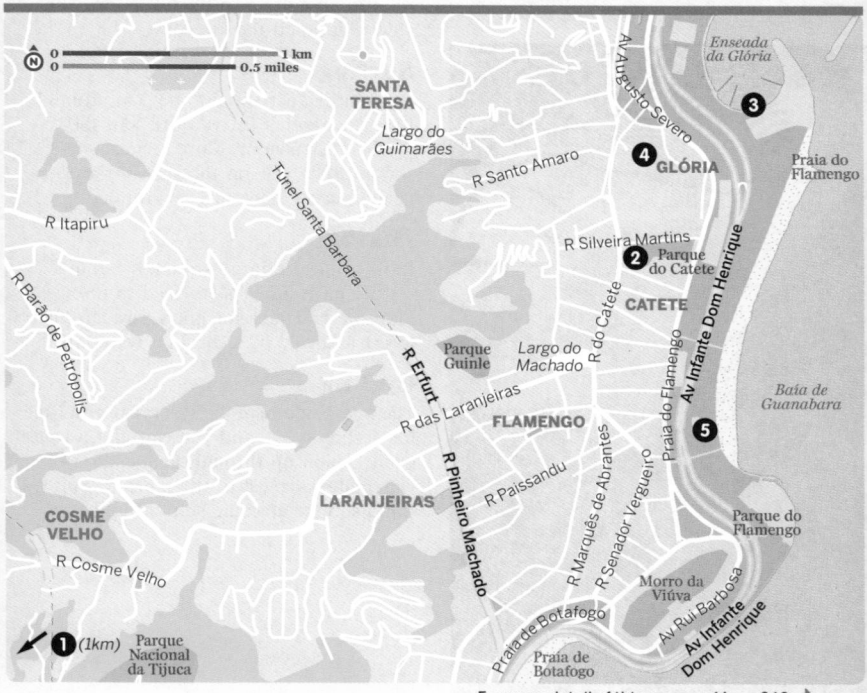

For more detail of this area see Map p242

Explore Flamengo & Around

Running west from the bay out to Corcovado are the residential neighborhoods of Flamengo, Laranjeiras, Catete, Glória and Cosme Velho. The Parque do Flamengo dominates the region. Also known as the *aterro* (landfill), this beach-fronting green space is one of the world's largest urban parks, and includes a nationally recognized art museum, biking and running trails, sports fields, and thousands of trees and flowering plants. Inland from the park, the shaded streets of Flamengo are sprinkled with a few cafes, historic *botecos* (small open-air bars) and gossip-filled juice bars.

West of Flamengo, Laranjeiras is a tightly woven community with a small-town feel. Charming plazas such as the Praça São Salvador are great spots for taking in the neighborhood. Cosme Velho lies beyond Laranjeiras and is the key access point for those heading up to the statue of Cristo Redentor by cog train.

The aging buildings of bustling Catete and Glória have seen better days. These twin districts flourished in the mid-19th century when their locations on the city outskirts made them desirable places to live. Nobles and merchants built homes in this district, including the Barão de Novo Friburgo, who built the stately Palácio do Catete. By the end of that century, however, the wealthy began moving further out as the inner city expanded.

Local Life

Outdoors Parque do Flamengo (p116) draws locals, especially on Sundays, when the main road through the park closes to traffic. Parque Guinle (p117) and Parque do Catete (p116) are peaceful escapes from the bustling city.

Folk art The Museu de Folclore Edison Carneiro (p116) has beautiful pieces from around Brazil. One-of-a-kind works of art make fine gifts at Pé de Boi (p120).

Hangouts Centro Cultural Oi Futuro (p116) often hosts cutting-edge exhibits, and stages plays and concerts.

Getting There & Away

Flamengo

Bus Leblon, Ipanema and Copacabana (571 and 573).

Metro Flamengo, Largo do Machado, Catete and Glória.

Laranjeiras & Cosme Velho

Bus Leblon (570 and 583), Ipanema and Copacabana (569 and 583).

Express bus 580 from Largo do Machado metro station.

Lonely Planet's Top Tip

On Sundays, the motorway through the Parque do Flamengo closes to traffic, making it an excellent time to go for a bike ride. Afterwards, you can treat yourself to a meal in the Marina da Glória.

Best Places to Eat

- Ferro e Farinha (p118)
- Corrientes 348 (p119)
- Brou (p117)
- Tacacá do Norte (p117)
- Sírio Libaneza (p118)
- Luigi's (p118)

For reviews, see p117

Best Places to Drink

- Brou (p117)
- Bar do Zé (p119)
- Adega Portugália (p119)
- Belmonte (p119)
- Herr Brauer (p119)
- Café Secreto (p119)

For reviews, see p119

Best Places to Shop

- Pé de Boi (p120)
- Maracatu Brasil (p120)
- Praça São Salvador (p120)

For reviews, see p120

TOP SIGHT
CRISTO REDENTOR

One of Rio's most identifiable landmarks, the magnificent 38m-high Cristo Redentor (Christ the Redeemer) looms large atop the granite mountain of Corcovado. The statue has stunning views over Rio, which probably explains the contented expression on his face. The traditional way up here is via a steep cog train that ascends through tropical forest, adding a touch of excitement to the experience.

The Views

Corcovado, which means 'hunchback,' rises straight up from the city to a height of 710m, and at night the brightly lit statue is visible from nearly every part of the city. When you reach the top, you'll notice the Redeemer's gaze directed at Pão de Açúcar (Sugarloaf Mountain), with his left arm pointing toward the Zona Norte; Maracanã football stadium crowds the foreground. You can also see the international airport on Ilha do Governador just beyond and the Serra dos Órgãos mountain range in the far distance. Beneath Christ's right arm you can see Lagoa Rodrigo de Freitas, Hipódromo de Gávea, Jardim Botânico, and over to Ipanema and Leblon.

Historical Background

Named one of the world's Seven New Wonders in 2007, Cristo Redentor is Brazil's largest and most recognized monument. The Redeemer, which opened in 1931, is considered to be the world's largest art deco statue. It's not a gift from the French, as is popularly believed. However, chief sculptor Paul Landowski was of French-Polish origin and carried out much of the construction in France. He collaborated with the Rio architect-engineer Heitor Silva Costa

DON'T MISS

- The hike up Corcovado from Parque Lage
- The splendid views along the way (sit on the right side of the train for the best scenery)
- Other nearby sites in Cosme Velho

PRACTICALITIES

- Christ the Redeemer
- Map p242, A4
- ☎21 2558-1329
- www.tremdocorcovado.rio
- cog train station, Cosme Velho 513
- adult/child R$75/49
- ⏲8am-7pm

MICHAEL HEFFERNAN/LONELY PLANET ©

(1873–1947). Many organizations helped make the statue a reality, including several individuals who went door-to-door asking for contributions.

The idea of the statue originated in 1921 when a group called Círculo Carioca held a competition for a religious monument to commemorate Brazil's upcoming 100 years of independence. Heitor's winning project, which took 10 years to build, was considered particularly ambitious at the time – naysayers doubted whether it could be accomplished at all. Heitor's original idea depicted Christ as a vertical form with a long cross held against his side but the committee wanted something recognizable from a great distance, so the crosslike outstretched arms were chosen instead. Today it's one of Brazil's most frequented attractions, welcoming more than one million visitors a year.

Cog Train

The most popular way up to the statue is to take the red narrow-gauge train that departs every 30 minutes from the cog station. Note that you must buy your cog train tickets in advance (either online or at various sale points in town). It takes approximately 20 minutes to get to the top. To reach the cog station, take any 'Cosme Velho' bus; from Copacabana, Ipanema or Leblon bus 583 will get you here.

When to Go

Avoid going on weekends when the crowds are thickest. Obviously, keep an eye on the sky and don't bother going on cloudy or overcast days. Your best bet for beating the crowds is to go first thing in the morning.

CRISTO ON FILM

The benign savior has played a supporting role in a few Hollywood films. It has appeared in *Now, Voyager* (1942) starring Bette Davis, and in Alfred Hitchcock's *Notorious* (1946), with Cary Grant and Ingrid Bergman. More recently the disaster film *2012*, which depicted the end of the world in vivid, unadulterated glory, showed Cristo crumbling as a giant tidal wave destroyed the city of Rio. As an aside, the archdiocese of Brazil didn't take kindly to the depiction and sued Columbia Pictures for copyright infringement (for using the image without permission).

While touristy, the restaurant just below the statue serves decent Brazilian food, and the views from the terrace are fabulous.

LARGO DO BOTICÁRIO

If you visit the statue by cog train, you can take a stroll west to visit the **Largo do Boticário** (Map p242; Cosme Velho 822). This beautiful plaza looks like something straight out of the 1800s.

SIGHTS

The main attraction here is the iconic hilltop statue of Cristo Redentor. If you're taking the van from Largo do Machado to the top, you can easily tack this on with a visit to the Museu da República – a must for history buffs. Further east of there, the Parque do Flamengo is one of several pretty parks in this area.

Flamengo

PARQUE DO FLAMENGO — PARK

Map p242 (Av Infante Dom Henrique) Officially called Parque Brigadeiro Eduardo Gomes, Parque do Flamengo was the result of a landfill project that leveled the São Antônio hill in 1965. It now spreads all the way from downtown Rio through Glória, Catete and Flamengo, and on around to Botafogo. The 1.2 sq km of land reclaimed from the sea now sees every manner of outdoor activity by *cariocas* (residents of Rio).

Cyclists and rollerbladers glide along the myriad paths, while the park's many football fields and sports courts are framed against the sea. On Sundays and holidays, the avenues through the park are closed to vehicle traffic from 7am to 6pm.

Designed by famous Brazilian landscaper Burle Marx (who also landscaped Brasília), the park features some 170,000 trees of 300 different species. There are two indoor attractions in the park: the **Museu de Arte Moderna** and the **Monumento Nacional aos Mortos da II Guerra Mundial**.

CENTRO CULTURAL OI FUTURO — ARTS CENTER

Map p242 (☎21 3235-5815; www.oifuturo.org.br; Dois de Dezembro 63; ⏲11am-5pm Tue-Sun) FREE One of the city's most visually exciting additions is this futuristic space right on the edge of Flamengo. Within 2000 sq meters of exhibition area spread across six floors, the center features temporary multimedia installations that run the gamut from architecture and urban design to pop art, photo-journalism and eye-catching video art.

There's also a permanent exhibition on the history of telecommunications in Brazil. The top floor houses an auditorium, where visitors can attend concerts and plays or catch a documentary.

Cosme Velho

CRISTO REDENTOR — MONUMENT

See p114.

Catete & Glória

MUSEU DA REPÚBLICA — MUSEUM

Map p241 (☎21 2127-0324; http://museudarepublica.museus.gov.br; Rua do Catete 153, Catete; R$6, Wed & Sun free; ⏲10am-5pm Tue-Fri, 11am-6pm Sat & Sun) The Museu da República, located in the Palácio do Catete, has been wonderfully restored. Built between 1858 and 1866, and easily distinguished by the bronze condors on its eaves, the palace was home to the president of Brazil from 1896 until 1954, when President Getúlio Vargas committed suicide here. The museum has a good collection of art and artifacts from the Republican period, and also houses a small cafe, an art-house cinema and a bookstore.

Vargas made powerful enemies in the armed forces and the political right wing, and was attacked in the press as a communist for his attempts to raise the minimum wage and increase taxes on the middle and upper classes. Tensions reached a critical level when one of Vargas' bodyguards fired shots at a journalist. Although the journalist was unharmed, an air-force officer guarding him was killed, giving the armed forces the pretext they needed to demand the resignation of Vargas. In response, Vargas committed suicide; the 3rd-floor bedroom in which the suicide occurred is eerily preserved.

MUSEU DE FOLCLORE EDISON CARNEIRO — MUSEUM

Map p241 (☎21 3826-4434; www.cnfcp.gov.br; Rua do Catete 179, Catete; ⏲11am-6pm Tue-Fri, 3-6pm Sat & Sun) FREE Created in 1968, this museum is an excellent introduction to Brazilian folk art, particularly that from the Northeast. Its permanent collection comprises 1400 pieces, and includes Candomblé costumes, ceramic figurines and religious costumes used in festivals. The museum also features a folklore library and a small shop that sells handicrafts, books and folk music. The museum is located next door to the Palácio do Catete.

PARQUE DO CATETE — PARK

Map p241 (⏲8am-6pm) This small landscaped park on the grounds of the Palácio do Catete provides a quiet refuge from the city. Its pond and shade-covered walks are popular with neighborhood strollers and children. Special performances in the park include concerts and plays.

MARINA DA GLÓRIA MARINA
Map p241 (☎21 2555-2200; www.marinadagloria.com.br; Av Infante Dom Henrique s/n, Glória) Rio's beautifully sited marina saw a makeover in preparation for the 2016 Olympics – where it served as the venue for sailing events. Half a dozen midrange restaurants with outdoor seating provide prime views of the waterfront. The marina also hosts big concerts from time to time.

IGREJA DE NOSSA SENHORA DA GLÓRIA DO OUTEIRO CHURCH
Map p241 (☎21 2225-2869; www.outeirodagloria.org.br; Praça NS da Glória 26, Glória; ⏲9am-noon & 1-4pm Mon-Fri, to noon Sat & Sun) This tiny church atop Ladeira da Glória commands great views out over Parque do Flamengo and the bay. Considered one of the finest examples of religious colonial architecture in Brazil, the church dates from 1739 and became the favorite of the royal family upon their arrival in 1808.

Laranjeiras

PARQUE GUINLE PARK
Map p241 (Paulo Cesar de Andrade 407, Laranjeiras) This handsomely landscaped park is a pleasant escape from busy Rua das Laranjeiras outside its sphinx-guarded gates. It has a small wooded area and a tiny lake with ducks, and there are always a few *cariocas* lounging on the grass.

Designed by French landscape architect Gochet (with later flourishes by Roberto Burle Marx), the park is also home to the dramatic **Palácio das Laranjeiras** (Map p241), the state governor's residence (not open to the public). The palace overlooks the west side of the park and is partially hidden by a thicket of trees.

EATING

Flamengo has a mix of longtime local favorites and stylish newcomers. Catete is dotted with inexpensive juice bars and lunch counters, as well as a few culinary surprises, like the deliciously hip Ferro e Farinha (p118). In the Marina da Glória, you'll find a row of sparkling new restaurants with well-placed outdoor seating. Laranjeiras doesn't have much of a restaurant scene, but the neighborhood has several charming options for those wanting to get off the beaten path.

Flamengo

FRESH COMIDA SAUDÁVEL HEALTH FOOD $
Map p242 (☎21 2226-4396; www.facebook.com/healthsalads; 3rd fl, Rua do Catete 347; mains from R$15; ⏲10am-5pm Mon-Sat; ✎) Hidden away on the 3rd floor of a shopping/office complex, this casual place serves deliciously healthy fare at rock-bottom prices. The changing menu features creative salads, grilled fish with coconut curry, stuffed chicken, mini quiches and the like, and there's dining on a small terrace.

TACACÁ DO NORTE AMAZONIAN $
Map p242 (☎21 2205-7545; Barão do Flamengo 35; tacacá R$27; ⏲9am-11pm Mon-Sat) In the Amazonian state of Pará, people order their *tacacá* late in the afternoon from their favorite street vendor. In Rio, you don't have to wait until the sun is setting. The fragrant soup of manioc paste, lip-numbing leaves of *jambú* (a Brazilian vegetable), and fresh and dried shrimp isn't for everyone. But then again, neither is the Amazon.

This simple lunch counter also serves savory bowls of *açaí* (berry-like fruit), which is how folks in the Amazon eat it; it's quite different from the sweet juice versions served everywhere else in Rio.

INTIHUASI PERUVIAN $$
Map p242 (☎21 2225-7653; Barão do Flamengo 35D; mains R$63-85; ⏲noon-3pm & 7-11pm Tue-Sat, 12:30-5pm Sun) Colorfully decorated with Andean tapestries and artwork, this tiny Peruvian restaurant serves mouthwatering ceviches, *papas rellenas* (meat-filled potatoes), seafood soups and other classic dishes from the Andes. For a break from caipirinhas, try a pisco sour or a nonalcoholic *chicha morada* (a sweet concoction made from purple corn).

BROU BRAZILIAN $$
Map p242 (☎21 2556-0618; www.facebook.com/casa.brou; Senador Vergueiro 2; mains lunch R$18-30, dinner R$32-56; ⏲11:30am-3pm &

6pm-midnight) A brilliant new addition to Flamengo, this bright and attractive eating and drinking spot features a daytime menu of creative salads topped with grilled veggies, salmon or roast meat, as well as quiches and soups. By night, crowds come for nicely prepared prime rib, grilled octopus and thin-crust pizzas fired up in a wood-burning oven.

True to its name, Brou is a brew-lover's paradise, with more than 20 brews on tap. You'll get a card when you come in, which you can then use to pour your own drafts. This clever new incarnation of pay by weight allows you to sample a wide range of local and Brazilian microbrews.

MAJORICA STEAK **$$$**

Map p242 (☎21 2205-6820; www.majoricario.com.br; Senador Vergueiro 11/15; mains R$62-120; ⏲noon-midnight Mon-Thu, to 1am Fri & Sat, 11:30am-11:30pm Sun) Established in 1963, Majorica is regarded as an institution among Rio's discerning carnivores. Although the all-you-can-eat option is not offered, we prefer Majorica's quality over quantity approach. Customers choose from a mouthwatering display of monster-sized steaks, which are then expertly grilled to order. This old-school steakhouse makes a welcome alternative to the overcrowded *churrascarias* of Ipanema and Copacabana.

The waiters provide excellent service but don't speak any English, so brush up on those Portuguese terms for your preferred doneness – *mal passado* for rare, *ao ponto* for medium and *bem passado* for well done.

Laranjeiras

LUIGI'S ITALIAN **$$**

Map p242 (☎21 2205-5331; Senador Corrêia 10, Laranjeiras; mains R$45-68; ⏲noon-midnight Tue-Sun) Well off the beaten path, Luigi's is a casual Italian restaurant set in an old villa in Laranjeiras. Join neighborhood regulars for a drink in the small covered courtyard or head inside to blessed air-conditioning for homemade pastas, authentic pizzas (available after 6pm) fired in the wood-burning oven and creamy tiramisu.

BOTERO BRAZILIAN **$$**

Map p242 (☎21 3235-6314; www.facebook.com/BoteroBar; Travessa Euricles de Matos 46, Laranjeiras; sandwiches R$29-34; ⏲noon-midnight Tue-Thu, to 1am Fri & Sat, to 8pm Sun) Chef Bruno Magalhães and his partners have created a consistently excellent eating and drinking option in the somewhat sparse neighborhood of Laranjeiras. This bar-restaurant offers a menu full of well-executed comfort food, craft beers and excellent cocktails. During busy times the acoustics in the small rooms make it difficult to hold a conversation though, leading many to take their drinks outside.

Catete & Glória

SÍRIO LIBANEZA MIDDLE EASTERN **$**

Map p242 (Largo do Machado 29, Loja 16-19; snacks R$6-28; ⏲8am-11pm Mon-Sat; 📶) Always packed, this bustling place serves tasty and cheap Syrian-Lebanese cuisine and great juices. Try the hearty *kibe de forno* (an oven-baked ground-beef dish with spices), a hummus platter or *kafta* (spiced meat patty), followed by baklava and other sweets. It's inside the Galleria Condor on Largo do Machado.

★FERRO E FARINHA PIZZA **$$**

Map p241 (Andrade Pertence 42, Glória; pizzas R$40-50; ⏲7-11:30pm Tue-Sat, from 6:30pm Sun) Sei Shiroma, an expat from NYC, and a dexterous team of dough handlers serve Rio's best pizza at this atmospheric and delightfully ramshackle spot in Catete. Seats are few, with just a handful of bar stools crowding around the pizza makers and oven at center stage, plus a few outdoor tables, so go early to try to beat the crowds.

MAZE INN INDIAN **$$**

Map p241 (☎21 97967-8270; www.themazerio.com/en/hoje-tem-curry; Casa 66, Tavares Bastos 414, Catete; buffet R$59; ⏲12:30-3:30pm Sun) For an alternative taste of Rio, head up to Tavares Bastos for an amazing feast of Indian cuisine. Chef Bruno Dantas Nadkarni learned from his Indian relatives how to make outstanding samosas, pork vindaloo and *bhingan bharta* (made with roasted eggplant), among other dishes. Come on Sundays for a full spread of delicacies from the subcontinent.

CARIOCANDO BRAZILIAN **$$**

Map p241 (☎21 2557-3646; www.barcariocando.com.br; Silveira Martins 139, Catete; lunch specials R$24; ⏲noon-3pm & 7pm-midnight Mon-Sat) This atmospheric restaurant serves a good selection of classic Brazilian dishes by day, and transforms to a live-music spot with a menu of mostly drinks and appetizers by night (cover charge around R$20).

Saturday afternoons, which feature *feijoada* (a bean-and-meat stew served with rice) and live samba or *choro* (a romantic, improvised samba-related music), are a great time to stop in (per person R$65).

CARMELO
ITALIAN **$$**

Map p241 (☎21 2225-1890; www.carmelorestaurante.com.br; Corrêa Dutra 75, Catete; mains R$45-70; ⏲11:30am-4pm & 6-11:30pm Mon-Sat, to 10:30pm Sun; ✎) Catete's best restaurant is this understated Italian gem, with its aromas of herb-roasted vegetables wafting from the kitchen. The stars of the menu are the superb pastas and risottos (try the San Felice with flambéed shrimp, fresh mushrooms and summer squash), though there are also grilled meat and fish dishes, and decadent tiramisu for dessert.

CORRIENTES 348
STEAK **$$**

Map p241 (☎21 2557-4027; www.corrientes348.com.br; Av Infante Dom Henrique, Marina da Glória, Glória; mains R$65-98; ⏲noon-11pm) The makeover of the Marina da Glória has seen the arrival of a handful of upscale eating establishments facing the waterfront, including this classy Argentine steakhouse. Juicy steaks are grilled up to perfection and there's a decent selection of salads and vegetable dishes (plus grilled salmon) for noncarnivores. The outdoor tables are the place to be on a clear day.

TABERNA DA GLÓRIA
BRAZILIAN **$$**

Map p241 (☎21 2265-7835; Rua do Russel 32, Glória; mains R$45-81; ⏲noon-1am) On a small plaza in the heart of Glória, this large outdoor eatery serves decent Brazilian staples in abundance; most dishes here serve two. Along with the roast-chicken restaurant next door, this is a fine spot to enjoy an ice-cold *chope* (draft beer) and the open-air ambience.

DRINKING & NIGHTLIFE

Few tourists visit the bars in Flamengo, which are mostly low-key neighborhood hangouts popular around happy hour. Rua Marquês de Abrantes is the best street to take in the scene. This area also has several good options for beer-lovers.

CAFÉ SECRETO
CAFE

Map p241 (☎21 2084-9020; www.facebook.com/cafesecretorj; Casa 8, Gago Coutinho 6, Flamengo; ⏲9am-6pm Mon-Fri) This excellent little coffee shop, hidden down an alleyway off bustling Largo do Machado, is well worth searching out. The expert staff – including a veteran from São Paulo's legendary Coffee Lab – offers a range of coffee beans and extraction methods, including espresso, AeroPress and Hario V60 drippers. Don't miss out on the fantastic cheese breads.

ADEGA PORTUGÁLIA
BAR

Map p241 (Largo do Machado 30, Catete; ⏲11am-midnight) Overlooking leafy Largo do Machado, Adega Portugália has an ideal location for enjoying a bit of open-air drinking and eating in an untouristy corner of Rio. In addition to a garrulous crowd and ice-cold *chope* (draft beer), you'll fine classic bar snacks such as *bolinhos de bacalhau* (codfish croquettes) and Portuguese-style sardines.

BAR DO ZÉ
BAR

Map p241 (Barão de Guaratiba 59, Catete; ⏲6pm-midnight Mon-Sat) Hidden down a narrow cobblestone side street off Rua do Catete, Bar do Zé has bohemian charm and remains little known to most *cariocas* (Rio residents). You'll find just a few tables inside among the old bottle-lined shelves, low-playing samba on the radio and groups of friends gathered on the street out front.

BELMONTE
BOTECO

Map p242 (☎21 2552-3349; Praia do Flamengo 300, Flamengo; ⏲10am-2am) One of the classic *botecos* in Rio, Belmonte is a vision of Rio from the '50s. Globe lights hang overhead as patrons down ice-cold drafts from the narrow bar. Meanwhile, hurried waiters make their way across the tile floors, carrying plates of *pasteis de camarão* (shrimp pasties) or steak sandwiches. The hugely successful chain, born here, is now widespread across Rio.

HERR BRAUER
BAR

Map p242 (☎21 2225-4359; Barão do Flamengo 35, Flamengo; ⏲5pm-1am Mon-Sat) Dedicated to the great beers of the world, this cozy drinking den serves some 80 labels: Belgian beers, such as Duvel and Deus; German labels, including Erdinger and Warsteiner; English brews Abbot Ale and Newcastle; plus Guinness, Brazilian microbrews and dozens of other offerings. Stop in for happy hour from 6pm to 8pm, when you can get a first-rate pint for R$19.

ARMAZÉM DO CHOPP BAR

Map p242 (☎21 2225-1796; Marquês de Abrantes 66, Flamengo; ⏲11am-midnight) On a bar-sprinkled stretch of Flamengo, this wooden, barn-like bar has outdoor seating on the raised veranda in front, and cooler (air-conditioned) seating inside. It's a lively local meeting spot, particularly in the early evenings, and there's a good-value selection of dishes including appetizers and grilled meats to accompany the cold beers.

ENTERTAINMENT

MAZE INN LIVE MUSIC

Map p241 (☎21 2558-5547; www.jazzrio.info; Casa 66, Tavares Bastos 414, Catete; R$50; ⏲10pm-4am 1st Fri of month) Also known as the 'Casa do Bob' after owner Bob Nadkarni, the once-a-month event here is well worth attending. It's set in the guesthouse (p168) of the same name high up in Tavares Bastos (one of Rio's safest favelas). There's a fun mix of *cariocas* and expats, with live jazz and fantastic city views.

SEVERYNA DE LARANJEIRAS LIVE MUSIC

Map p242 (☎21 2556-9398; www.severyna.com.br; Ipiranga 54, Laranjeiras; cover R$15-25; ⏲11:30am-1am) At night this broad, rustically decorated dining hall forms the backdrop to Brazilian rhythms, and there's a broad menu of Northeastern fare. Groups perform *forró,* a popular music of the Northeast (Thursdays from 7:30pm); samba (Fridays from 9pm); and rock (Saturdays from 9pm).

CINE MUSEU DA REPÚBLICA CINEMA

Map p241 (☎21 98482-7785; Museu da República, Rua do Catete 153, Catete) The screening room located behind the dramatic Museu da República shows contemporary and vintage films of indie and world cinema. Entrance is via the Parque do Catete.

SHOPPING

While this is not a traditional shopping destination, the area is still well worth exploring, particularly at the excellent art gallery/handicrafts emporium known as Pé de Boi in Laranjeiras.

PÉ DE BOI ARTS & CRAFTS

Map p242 (☎21 2285-4395; www.pedeboi.com.br; Ipiranga 55, Laranjeiras; ⏲10am-7pm Mon-Fri, to 1pm Sat) Although everything is for sale here, Pé de Boi feels more like an art gallery than a handicrafts shop, owing to the high quality of the wood and ceramic works, and the tapestries, sculptures and weavings. This is perhaps Rio's best place to see one-of-a-kind pieces by artists from Bahia, Amazonia, Minas Gerais and other parts of Brazil.

Don't miss the upstairs area, which has photos of some of the artists whose work is on sale.

PRAÇA SÃO SALVADOR MARKET

Map p242 (Praça São Salvador, Laranjeiras; ⏲8am-5pm Sun) On Sunday mornings this otherwise sleepy square comes alive with one of the city's finest markets. Stalls sell art, jewelry, crafted goods and home-cooked food, and a *chorinho* (romantic, improvised samba) band plays under the bandstand from 10am until early afternoon. Luizinho's drinks stall sells caipirinhas strong enough to sustain the party long after the band have packed up and gone home.

MARACATU BRASIL MUSIC

Map p242 (☎21 2557-4754; www.maracatubrasil.com.br; Ipiranga 49, Laranjeiras; ⏲11am-8pm Mon-Sat) You can't miss the lime-green building that houses this small percussion store and workshop. Inside, you can buy an *afoxê* (a gourd shaker with beads strung around it), conga and bongo drums, tambourines and other Brazilian percussion instruments. Upstairs there's a drum clinic (p205), where you can study with local instructors.

SPORTS & ACTIVITIES

MAR DO RIO DIVING

Map p241 (☎21 2225-7508; www.mardorio.com.br; Shop 17A, Marina da Glória, Av Infante Dom Henrique, Glória) One of several dive operators in the Marina da Glória, Mar do Rio offers two-tank dives for around R$220 (gear hire costs extra) on Saturdays and Sundays, departing at 8:30am and returning at 2pm. It also offers night dives twice a month. Less experienced divers can opt for one of the courses, including a five-day PADI-certified basic course.

Centro & Praça Mauá

CINELÂNDIA & AROUND | PRAÇA TIRADENTES & AROUND | PRAÇA XV & AROUND | PRAÇA MAUÁ & AROUND

Neighborhood Top Five

1 Boulevard Olímpico (p128) Making your way along this tranquil promenade and checking out the city's best street art en route.

2 Museu de Arte do Rio (p127) Taking in first-rate installations and rooftop views at the MAR, one of Rio's finest art museums.

3 Museu do Amanhã (p128) Pondering life and the future while browsing interactive exhibits in this architecturally stunning science museum that's strategically perched overlooking the bay.

4 Museu Histórico Nacional (p123) Checking out gilded carriages and learning about the Portuguese royals in Brazil at Rio's best history museum.

5 Theatro Municipal (p124) Taking a behind-the-scenes tour or watching a show inside the lavish home of Rio's opera, orchestra and ballet.

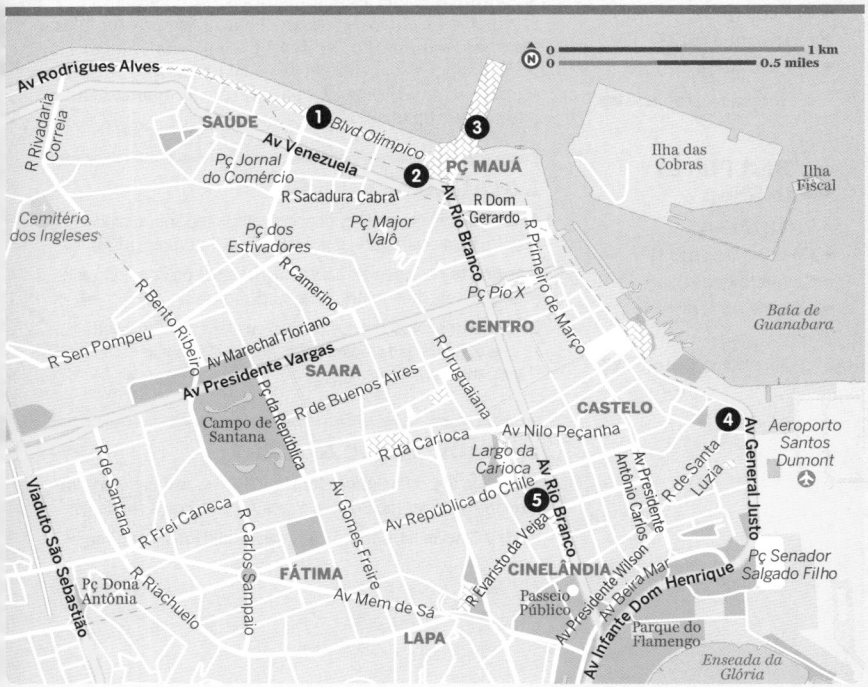

For more detail of this area see Map p246

Lonely Planet's Top Tip

Plan your sightseeing days carefully. Tuesday offers free admission to two of the big museums here: the Museu de Arte do Rio and the Museu do Amanhã.

Best Places to Eat

- Xian (p130)
- L'Atelier du Cuisinier (p131)
- Ancoramar (p131)
- Cais do Oriente (p131)
- Govardhana Harí (p130)
- Belga (p131)

For reviews, see p130

Best Places to Drink

- Xian (p130)
- Bar Léo (p132)
- Amarelinho (p132)
- Curto Cafe (p132)

For reviews, see p132

Best Places to Shop

- CRAB (p134)
- Casa Naara (p134)
- Granado (p134)
- Livraria da Travessa (p134)

For reviews, see p133

Explore Centro & Praça Mauá

Rio's downtown is a wild architectural medley of old and new, with striking baroque churches and narrow colonial streets juxtaposed against looming office towers and wide, traffic-filled boulevards. During the week it's all fuss and hurry as Rio's lawyers, secretaries and clerks jostle among the crowded streets. Despite the pace, it's well worth joining the fray. Centro has some of the city's best museums and its most intriguing historical sights, including avant-garde art galleries and 18th-century cathedrals.

The southern focal point of downtown is Cinelândia, which has a wide plaza framed with grand buildings, a historic theater, an old cinema and several outdoor cafes. Near the waterfront, Praça XV (Quinze) do Novembro is another pivotal sight, home to a former royal residence turned into a museum and some cafes. A short stroll from there leads to the Travessa do Comércio, one of the oldest intact parts of Rio. Lined with colonial architecture, the narrow cobblestone streets here buzz with life on weekday evenings, as *cariocas* (residents of Rio) pack the outdoor bars and cafes.

Many pedestrian-only areas crisscross Centro, and for the urban wanderer, there's no better destination in Rio. In addition to Praça XV and Cinelândia, it's worth exploring the streets around picturesque Praça Tiradentes. A handful of galleries and historic sites lie nearby.

North of Centro is Praça Mauá, a waterfront plaza that has become the symbol of Rio's renaissance. The once derelict streets here have been revitalized with museums, an aquarium and a picturesque promenade lined with massive murals.

Local Life

Arts There are several key concert halls in the area, including Theatro Municipal (p124) and Teatro Rival Petrobras (p133).

Hangouts The open-air bars along Travessa do Comércio and nearby streets draw festive after-work crowds.

Shopping strips Browse the narrow, pedestrian-packed streets of Saara and stop for refreshment at Lebanese snack stands and restaurants.

Getting There & Away

Bus From the Zona Sul look for the following destinations printed in the window: 'Rio Branco,' 'Praça XV' and 'Praça Tiradentes.'

Metro Cinelândia, Carioca, Uruguaiana and Presidente Vargas.

ANDREW HOLT/GETTY IMAGES ©

TOP SIGHT
MUSEU HISTÓRICO NACIONAL

Home to one of the most important collections in Brazil, the National History Museum has a treasure trove of artifacts dating back to the early days of the Portuguese presence in the New World. The extensive collection, containing more than 250,000 items, is set inside a sprawling 18th-century complex that was once part of the Forte de Santiago, a strategic point for the city's defense.

The Exhibitions

The collection begins with a survey of Brazil's pre-Columbian cultures in the hall titled 'Oreretama,' meaning 'Our Land' in Tupi. From there, it continues to the Portuguese maritime empire of the 15th century, with exquisite porcelain and objects from trading in the Far East, and moves on to the colonization of Brazil. Exhibits depict early life through models, such as the curious mechanized model of a sugar mill, and don't shy away from the horrors of slavery.

There are also some fine pieces documenting the presence of the Portuguese royal family (from when the entire court packed up and sailed to Rio ahead of Napoleon's invasion); displays from the bloody war of the Triple Alliance; and a fascinating collection of imperial carriages. One of the museum's most photogenic rooms is a reconstruction of a working pharmacy that functioned on Rua Gonçalves Dias in Centro from 1847 to 1983. The 20th century receives less attention, and for an understanding of the Vargas period, you'll have to pay a visit to the former presidential palace of President Getúlio Vargas, the Museu da República (p116), in Catete.

DON'T MISS

- Pre-Columbian exhibits portraying indigenous culture, myths and everyday tools
- The full-size re-creation of a 19th-century pharmacy
- The gilded imperial carriages

PRACTICALITIES

- Map p246, G4
- ☎21 3299-0324
- http://mhn.museus.gov.br
- off General Justo, near Praça Marechal Âncora
- adult/child R$10/5, Sun free
- ⏲10am-5:30pm Tue-Fri, 1-5pm Sat & Sun

SIGHTS

Centro is packed with sights and you could easily spend a few days just trying to fit them all in. While walkable, Centro covers a large area, so it's best to focus on one or two areas, and take the metro or the VLT (light rail) to break up longer walks.

Cinelândia & Around

MUSEU DE ARTE MODERNA — MUSEUM

Map p246 (MAM; ☎21 3883-5600; www.mamrio.org.br; Av Infante Dom Henrique 85, Parque do Flamengo; adult/child R$14/free; ⏲noon-6pm Tue-Fri, 11am-6pm Sat & Sun) At the northern end of Parque do Flamengo, the Museu de Arte Moderna is immediately recognizable by its striking postmodern edifice designed by Affonso Eduardo Reidy. The landscaping of Burle Marx is no less impressive. Inside, the design feels a bit dated, but it's still worth a visit for the superb collection of Brazilian artists, which includes works by Bruno Giorgi, Di Cavalcanti and Maria Martins.

THEATRO MUNICIPAL — THEATER

Map p246 (☎21 2332-9220; www.theatromunicipal.rj.gov.br; Av 13 de Maio, Praça Floriano; tours R$20) Built in 1905 in the style of the Paris Opera, the magnificent Municipal Theater is the home of Rio's opera, orchestra and ballet. Its lavish interior contains many beautiful details – including the stage curtain painted by Italian artist Eliseu Visconti that contains portraits of 75 major figures from the arts, such as Carlos Gomes, Wagner and Rembrandt.

Guided multilingual tours lasting 45 minutes are offered from Tuesday to Friday (at noon, 2:30pm and 4pm) and on Saturday (at 11am, noon, 1pm and 4pm). Call ahead to confirm availability of an English-speaking guide. It's also well worth coming here for a performance.

BIBLIOTECA NACIONAL — HISTORIC BUILDING

Map p246 (☎21 2220-9484; Av Rio Branco 219; ⏲10am-5pm Mon-Fri) FREE Inaugurated in 1910, Rio's neoclassical national library is the largest in Latin America. It's home to more than nine million volumes, including many rare books and manuscripts. Among the treasure trove are original letters written by Princess Isabel, the first newspapers printed in the country and two copies of the precious Mainz Psalter Bible, printed in 1492. Free guided tours in English are available by advance notice (contact visiguia@bn.gov.br).

MUSEU NACIONAL DE BELAS ARTES — MUSEUM

Map p246 (☎21 3299-0600; www.mnba.gov.br; Rio Branco 199; adult/student R$8/4, Sun free; ⏲10am-6pm Tue-Fri, 1-5pm Sat & Sun) Rio's fine-arts museum houses more than 18,000 original paintings and sculptures, some of which date back to works brought over from Portugal by Dom João VI in 1808. One of its most important galleries is the **Galeria de Arte Brasileira**, which includes 20th-century classics, such as Cândido Portinari's *Café*. Other galleries display Brazilian folk art, African art and furniture, as well as contemporary exhibits. Audio guides are available (R$8).

CENTRO CULTURAL JUSTIÇA FEDERAL — CULTURAL CENTER

Map p246 (☎21 3261-2550; Av Rio Branco 241; ⏲noon-7pm Tue-Sun) FREE The stately building overlooking the Praça Floriano served as the headquarters of the Supremo Tribunal Federal (Supreme Court) from 1909 to 1960. Following a restoration project completed in 2001 it opened as a cultural center. It features exhibitions on photography and Brazilian art, and some fascinating shows from abroad periodically make their way here.

BONDE STATION — CABLE CAR

Map p246 (Lélio Gama 65) From this station you can take the Bonde tram (p138) to Santa Teresa. It's a marvelous ride on a quaint yellow streetcar over the Lapa Arches to the hilltop neighborhood. However, the lines can be long, so allow yourself plenty of time.

PASSEIO PÚBLICO — PARK

Map p246 (www.passeiopublico.com; Rua do Passeio; ⏲9am-5pm) The oldest park in Rio, the Passeio Público was built in 1783 by Mestre Valentim, a famous Brazilian sculptor, who designed it after Lisbon's botanical gardens. In 1860 the park was remodeled by French landscaper Glaziou. The park features some large trees, a pond with islands and an interesting crocodile-shaped fountain. The entrance gate was built by Valentim. Before neighboring Parque do Flamengo was created from landfill, the sea came right up to the edge of this park.

PRAÇA FLORIANO PLAZA

Map p246 (Rio Branco) The heart of modern Rio, the Praça Floriano (known to *cariocas* simply as Cinelândia) comes to life at lunchtime and after work when its outdoor cafes fill with a beer-swilling office crowd. The square is also Rio's political marketplace and is a major meeting point for protestors.

Praça Tiradentes & Around

CRAB CULTURAL CENTER

Map p246 (Centro Sebrae de Referência do Artesanato Brasileiro; ☎21 3380-1850; www.crab.sebrae.com.br; Praça Tiradentes 69; ⏲10am-5pm Tue-Sat) FREE Inside a beautifully restored mansion overlooking Praça Tiradentes, this exhibition hall is dedicated to Brazilian crafts from across the country. Several small exhibitions are staged here, and there's also a ground-floor restaurant and an airy upstairs cafe. The real reason to come, however, is to browse the exceptional handicrafts for sale in the shop (p134).

CENTRO DE ARTE HÉLIO OITICICA MUSEUM

Map p246 (☎21 2242-1012; Luis de Camões 68; ⏲noon-6pm Mon-Sat) FREE This avant-garde museum is set in a 19th-century neoclassical building that originally housed the Conservatory of Music and Dramatic Arts. Today the center displays permanent works by the artist, theoretician and poet Hélio Oiticica, as well as bold contemporary art exhibitions, well-tuned to Oiticica's forward-leaning aesthetics.

REAL GABINETE PORTUGUÊS DE LEITURA HISTORIC BUILDING

Map p246 (☎21 2221-3138; www.realgabinete.com.br; Luís de Camões 30; ⏲9am-6pm Mon-Fri) FREE Built in the Portuguese Manueline style in 1837, the gorgeous Portuguese Reading Room houses more than 350,000 works, many dating from the 16th, 17th and 18th centuries. It also has a small collection of paintings, sculptures and ancient coins.

IGREJA DE NOSSA SENHORA DO ROSÁRIO E SÃO BENEDITO CHURCH

Map p246 (Uruguaiana 77; ⏲7am-5pm Mon-Fri, to 1pm Sat) Dedicated to Our Lady of the Rosary as well as the black St Benedict, this church has been an important icon for Afro-Brazilians, serving a congregation of mostly black and biracial Catholics over the years. Sadly, a fire in 1967 destroyed much of the elaborate interior of this historic church, leaving only the unadorned walls that date back to the early 1700s.

VLT: A NEW DOWNTOWN RAIL LINE

Rio's new light rail – the **VLT** (www.vltcarioca.com.br; one way R$3.80; ⏲6am-midnight) – is part of a massive urban-renewal project helping to revitalize Centro. Launched in 2016, the VLT has 26 stations in Rio, running on two different routes through downtown. For visitors, handy access is at Cinelândia (outside the metro) to Praça Mauá (to the stop labelled Parada dos Museus). To reach Praça XV (Quinze) de Novembro or Praça Tiradentes, take the Praia Formosa line, which you can access on Rua Sete de Setembro, just west of Rio Branco. The VLT also goes to Aeroporto Santos Dumont and Rodoviária Novo Rio bus station. For maps, schedules and other info, download the free **VLT Carioca** app.

IGREJA SÃO FRANCISCO DA PENITÊNCIA & CONVENTO DE SANTO ANTÔNIO CHURCH

Map p246 (☎21 2262-0129; www.conventosantoantonio.org.br; Largo da Carioca 5; ⏲church 8am-6pm Mon-Fri, 8-11am Sat) Overlooking the Largo da Carioca is the baroque Igreja São Francisco da Penitência, dating from 1726. Restored to its former glory, the church's sacristy, which dates from 1745, has blue Portuguese tiles and an elaborately carved altar made out of jacaranda wood. It also has a roof panel by José Oliveira Rosa depicting St Francis receiving the stigmata.

Next door, the Convento de Santo Antônio was built between 1608 and 1615. It contains the chapel of Nossa Senhora das Dores da Imaculada Conceição.

CAMPO DE SANTANA PARK

Map p246 (Praça da República & Frei Caneca) Campo de Santana is a pleasant green space that, on September 7, 1822, was the scene of the proclamation of Brazil's independence from Portugal by Emperor Dom Pedro I of Portugal. The landscaped park, with swans and an artificial lake, is a fine

WORTH A DETOUR

NITERÓI

A short ferry ride across the bay from Rio, Niterói is a mid-sized city (population around 500,000) with some impressive modern architecture near the bay front and pretty beaches further out.

Niterói's principal attraction is the famous **Museu do Arte Contemporânea** (MAC; ☎21 2620-2481; www.macniteroi.com.br; Mirante da Boa Viagem, Niterói; adult/child R$10/5; ⏲10am-6pm Tue-Sun). Designed by Brazil's most famous architect, Oscar Niemeyer, the MAC has a wild curvilinear design that blooms like a flower (or more prosaically, a flying saucer) against sweeping bay views. Unfortunately the exhibits inside the museum are less inspiring. It's about 1.5km from the Niterói ferry terminal. To get here, turn right as you leave the terminal and walk about 50m across to the bus stop in the middle of the road; a 47B minibus will drop you at the museum door.

A handful of other Niemeyer-designed buildings are also located bayside in Niterói; they're part of the so-called 'Caminho de Niemeyer' (Niemeyer Way). A good starting point is the **Teatro Popular** (☎21 2621-5104; www.teatropopularoscarniemeyer.art.br; Av Jornalista Rogério Coelho Neto, Niterói), located just a short stroll north of the ferry terminal.

The **Ponte Rio-Niterói** (Ponte Pres Costa e Silva) offers spectacular views of Baía de Guanabara (Guanabara Bay). The bridge is 15.5km long, 60m high and 26.6m wide, with two three-lane roads. It has a tollbooth 3km from Niterói city center.

The **ferry to Niterói** (Map p246; ☎0800-721-1012; www.grupoccr.com.br/barcas; one way R$6.10; ⏲6am-11:30pm Mon-Fri, to 11pm Sat, to 10:30pm Sun) leaves from Praça XV (Quinze) de Novembro in Centro every 10 to 60 minutes; it's usually packed with commuters. When you reach the dock in Niterói, there isn't much to see in the immediate area. From here, catch a bus to the MAC or to one of the beaches – or just turn around and return by ferry.

The cruise back across the bay, however, is perhaps just as valid a reason for leaving Rio. Out on the water, you'll have impressive views of downtown, Pão de Açúcar (p103) and the other green mountains rising up out of the city; you'll also see planes (quite close) landing and taking off at Aeroporto Santos Dumont. Try to be on the water at sunset when Centro glows with golden light.

place for a respite from the chaotic streets, and you're likely to see a few wild agoutis (hamster-like rodents native to Brazil) scuttling about.

Praça XV & Around

MUSEU HISTÓRICO NACIONAL — MUSEUM

See p123.

IGREJA DE NOSSA SENHORA DO CARMO DA ANTIGA SÉ — CHURCH

Map p246 (www.antigase.com.br; Sete de Setembro 14; ⏲8am-4pm Mon-Fri) This beautifully restored church and former cathedral dates back to the 1770s, and it played an important role in the imperial days of Rio. The elaborately gilded rococo-style interior witnessed royal baptisms, weddings and funereal rites. Several kings were crowned here (including Pedro I in 1822 and his son Pedro II in 1841); it is the only place in the New World where this occurred. The royal family used to sit in the balcony boxes overlooking the altar.

PALÁCIO TIRADENTES — HISTORIC BUILDING

Map p246 (☎21 2588-1251; Primeiro de Março; ⏲10am-5pm Mon-Sat) FREE The stately Tiradentes Palace houses the seat of the legislative assembly. Exhibits on the 1st and 2nd floors relate the events that have taken place here since 1926. One of its darkest hours was when the National Assembly was shut down in 1937 under the Vargas dictatorship; it later served as the Department of Press and Propaganda.

PAÇO IMPERIAL — HISTORIC BUILDING

Map p246 (☎21 2215-2093; www.amigosdopacoimperial.org.br; Praça XV/Quinze de Novembro 48; ⏲noon-7pm Tue-Sun) FREE The former imperial palace was originally built in 1743 as a governor's residence. Later it became the home of Dom João and his family when the Portuguese throne transferred the royal seat of power to the colony. In 1888 Princesa Isabel proclaimed the Freedom from Slavery Act from the palace's steps. The building was neglected for many years but has been restored and now hosts excellent changing exhibitions and concerts. There's also a good cafe and a restaurant here.

ILHA FISCAL — HISTORIC BUILDING

Map p246 (☎21 2233-9165; tours R$30; ⏲tours 12:30pm, 2pm & 3:30pm Thu-Sun) This eye-catching lime-green neo-Gothic palace sitting in Baía de Guanabara looks like something out of a child's fairy-tale book. It was designed by engineer Adolfo del Vecchio and completed in 1889. Originally used to supervise port operations, the palace is famous as the location of the last Imperial Ball on November 9, 1889. Today it's open for guided tours, which leave from the dock near Praça XV (Quinze) de Novembro. Purchase tickets from the Espaço Cultural da Marinha.

ESPAÇO CULTURAL DA MARINHA — MUSEUM

Map p246 (☎21 2532-5992; Blvd Olímpico; adult/child R$10/5, Tue free; ⏲11am-5pm Tue-Sun) Naval enthusiasts shouldn't miss this waterfront museum, a short stroll from Praça XV. It contains the *Riachuelo* submarine, which you can wander through, the *Bauru* (a WWII torpedo boat) and the royal family's large rowboat. Boat tours going to Ilha Fiscal palace as well as around the bay leave from the docks here.

CENTRO CULTURAL BANCO DO BRASIL — CULTURAL CENTER

Map p246 (CCBB; ☎21 3808-2020; www.culturabancodobrasil.com.br; Primeiro de Março 66; ⏲9am-9pm Wed-Mon) FREE Housed in a beautifully restored 1906 building, the Centro Cultural Banco do Brasil hosts some of Rio's top exhibitions. Facilities include a cinema, two theaters and a permanent display of the evolution of currency in Brazil. There is always something going on, from exhibitions and lunchtime and evening concerts to film screenings, so look up details in *O Globo's* entertainment listings or the 'Veja Rio' insert in *Veja* magazine before you go.

CENTRO CULTURAL CORREIOS — CULTURAL CENTER

Map p246 (☎21 2253-1580; Visconde de Itaboraí 20; ⏲noon-7pm Tue-Sun) FREE In a grand edifice dating from the 1920s, this cultural center houses three spacious floors that host a creative lineup of changing exhibitions, mostly focusing on Brazilian artists, writers and architects. Take the old-fashioned elevator to the top floor and work your way down.

IGREJA DE NOSSA SENHORA DE CANDELÁRIA — CHURCH

Map p246 (☎21 2233-2324; Praça Pio X; ⏲8am-4pm Mon-Fri, 9am-noon Sat, to 1pm Sun) Built between 1775 and 1894, NS de Candelária was the largest and wealthiest church of imperial Brazil. The interior is a combination of baroque and Renaissance styles. The ceiling above the nave reveals the origin of the church. The cupola, fabricated entirely from limestone shipped from Lisbon, is one of its most striking features. Mass is held at 12:15pm on weekdays and at 10:30am and noon on Sundays. Be sure to watch out for traffic as you cross to the church.

MUSEU NAVAL — MUSEUM

Map p246 (☎21 2104-5506; Dom Manuel 15; ⏲noon-5pm Tue-Sun) FREE Chronicling the history of the Brazilian navy from the 16th century to the present, this museum also has exhibitions of model warships, maps and navigational instruments.

PRAÇA XV (QUINZE) DE NOVEMBRO — HISTORIC SITE

Map p246 (near Primeiro de Março) The first residents on this historic site were Carmelite fathers who built a convent here in 1590. It later came under the property of the Portuguese crown and became Largo do Paço, which surrounded Paço Imperial, the royal palace. The square was later renamed Praça XV (Quinze) de Novembro after Brazil declared itself a republic on November 15, 1822.

Praça Mauá & Around

★MUSEU DE ARTE DO RIO — MUSEUM

Map p246 (MAR; ☎21 3031-2741; www.museudeartedorio.org.br; Praça Mauá 5; adult/child R$20/10, Tue free; ⏲10am-5pm Tue-Sun) Looming large over Praça Mauá, the MAR is an icon for the rebirth of Rio's once derelict port. The huge museum hosts wide-ranging exhibitions that focus on Rio in all its complexity – its people, landscapes, beauty, challenges and conflicts. Start off by taking the elevator to the top (6th) floor, and absorbing the view over the bay. There's also an excellent restaurant here. Then work your way down through the galleries, taking in a mix of international and only-in-Rio exhibitions.

BOULEVARD OLÍMPICO AREA

Map p246 Rio's formerly derelict port district has been reborn as a wide promenade lined with massive street art. A handful of renowned artists have painted spectacular murals on the old warehouses, though Brazilian artist Eduardo Kobra (www.eduardokobra.com) deserves special mention for his jaw-dropping work entitled *Etnias* (Ethnicities). The massive mural stretches for 190m and features photogenic portraits of indigenous people from around the globe.

The boulevard stretches from Praça Mauá to AquaRio, and the tracks for the VLT run down the center, so watch your step. Near the east end of the promenade, you'll find a few food trucks selling sandwiches, craft beer and ice cream, with shaded tables out front. Further west along the boulevard, there are benches where you can take in the street art as well as lookouts that provide glimpses over the bay.

AQUARIO AQUARIUM

Map p253 (☎21 3613-0700; www.aquariomarinhodorio.com.br; Av Rodrigues Alves 379; adult/child R$100/50; ⏲10am-6pm) The largest aquarium in South America is Rio's newest major downtown attraction. You can get an up-close look at some 350 different species (there are more than 8000 animals in all), spread among two dozen different tanks. The highlight is a 3.5-million-liter aquarium with a tunnel through the middle that gives fine views of sharks, rays and shimmering schools of fish gliding past.

To get here, you can take the VLT (which has stops at the metro stations of Cinelândia and Carioca) to the Utopia Aquario stop. There's also a Bike Rio stand out front.

MUSEU DO AMANHÃ MUSEUM

Map p246 (www.museudoamanha.org.br; Rodrigues Alves 1; adult/child R$20/free, Tue free; ⏲10am-6pm Tue-Sun) Designed by famed Spanish architect Santiago Calatrava, this thoughtfully conceived science museum has interactive exhibitions on outer space, the earth and its biodiversity, humans (and our impact on the world), and the major global trends and challenges that lie in the future. In all the museum takes a somewhat pessimistic view of the human species and its long-ranging impact on everything around it.

MOSTEIRO DE SÃO BENTO CHURCH

Map p246 (☎21 2206-8100; www.mosteirodesaobentorio.org.br; Dom Gerardo 68; ⏲6:30am-6:30pm) This is one of the finest colonial churches in Brazil. Built between 1617 and 1641 on Morro de São Bento, the monastery has an excellent view over the city. The simple facade hides a baroque interior richly decorated in gold. Among its historic treasures are wood carvings designed by Frei Domingos da Conceição and made by Alexandre Machado, and paintings by José de Oliveira Rosa.

CAIS DO VALONGO ARCHAEOLOGICAL SITE

Map p246 (Barão de Tefé) Unearthed in 2011, the Valongo Wharf was the first arrival point for an estimated 900,000 enslaved peoples brought to Brazil after long, harrowing voyages from Africa. Those who survived the journey were sold in markets, while those who didn't were buried without ceremony in mass graves nearby. The heartbreaking tragedy of the Atlantic slave trade remained a topic little broached for many years, and this newly designated archaeological site is an important reference for coming to grips with this aspect of the nation's history.

INSTITUTO DE PESQUISA E MEMÓRIA PRESTO NOVOS MUSEUM

Map p253 (☎21 96465-9983; www.pretosnovos.com.br; Pedro Ernesto 32; ⏲1-6pm Tue-Fri, 11am-2pm Sat) **FREE** When Mercedes Guimarães was doing construction work on her house in 1996, workers uncovered huge quantities of human fragments. After discussions with a historian, she learned the site had been the burial place of enslaved Africans, halted work and turned her house into this small museum, cultural center and memorial to all the captive people brought to Brazil. The displays are quite powerful and provide a context for what life was like for newly arrived Africans in the 18th and 19th centuries.

MORRO DA CONCEIÇÃO HISTORIC SITE

Map p246 One of Rio's oldest neighborhoods, this pretty area feels like a tiny slice of Portugal, with its old shuttered houses, quiet cobblestone streets and twittering birds. While there isn't a lot to do here (it's really just one long winding street), there are a few galleries open to visitors (look for 'atelier'

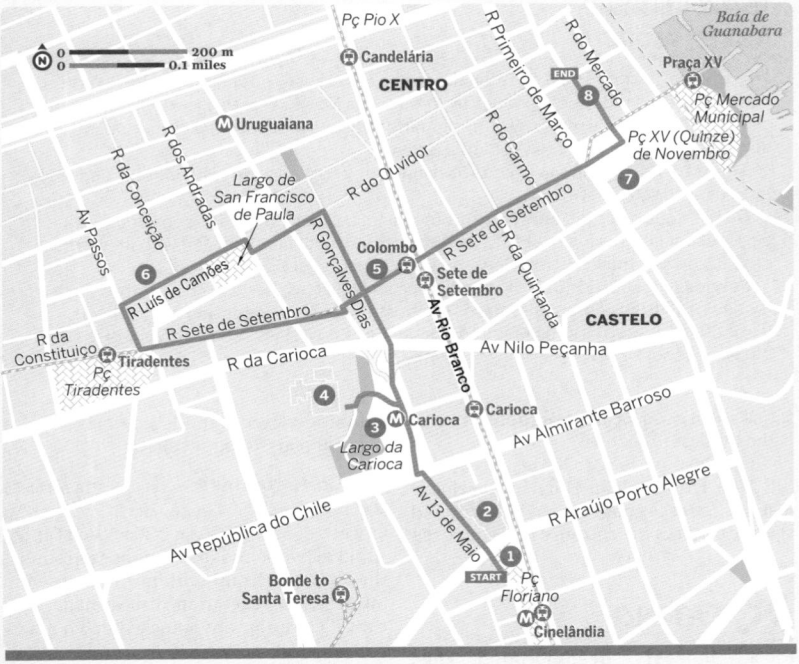

Neighborhood Walk
Historic Centro

START PRAÇA FLORIANO
END TRAVESSA DO COMÉRCIO
LENGTH 3KM; FOUR HOURS

A mélange of historic buildings and skyscrapers, Centro is a fine place to experience the city away from its beaches and mountains. Do this tour during the week, as the area's deserted (and unsafe) on weekends.

Start at the **1 Praça Floriano** (p125), known to *cariocas* simply as Cinelândia, a scenic plaza set with several outdoor cafes. The square is also Rio's political marketplace and is a major meeting point for protestors. On the north side, the neoclassical **2 Theatro Municipal** (p124) is one of the city's finest buildings, particularly after its recent R$65 million renovation. Home of Rio's opera, orchestra and ballet, it has a lavish interior containing beautiful details. Time your visit to take one of the guided tours.

Stroll north along Av 13 de Maio. You'll pass through the **3 Largo da Carioca**, a bustling area with a market. On the hill is **4 Igreja São Francisco da Penitência** (p125), an 18th-century church with a jaw-dropping gilded interior. Reach the church via stairs or elevator near Carioca metro station.

After taking in the views, walk to narrow Rua Gonçalves Dias to reach **5 Confeitaria Colombo** (p130) for caffeine, pastries and art nouveau surroundings.

From Rua Gonçalves Dias, turn left on Rua do Ouvidor, following it to Largo de San Francisco de Paula. One block further is the **6 Real Gabinete Português de Leitura** (p125), a historic reading room that seems straight out of 19th-century Portugal.

Turn right when exiting and pass Praça Tiradentes, before heading left over to Rua Sete de Setembro. Follow it until it ends near the **7 Paço Imperial** (p126). Once the seat of the Portuguese rulers in Brazil, the building ow houses cafes and art exhibitions.

Leaving the Paço, cross Praça XV (Quinze) de Novembro and take the narrow lane beneath the arch. You'll walk along one of Centro's oldest lanes, **8 Travessa do Comércio**, full of open-air restaurants and bars. It's a fitting ending to a day's wander.

WORTH A DETOUR

ILHA DE PAQUETÁ

This tropical island in Baía de Guanabara was once a very popular tourist spot and is now frequented mostly by families from the Zona Norte. There's a certain decadent charm to the colonial buildings, unassuming beaches and businesses catering to local tourism. The place gets crowded on weekends.

There are no cars on the island. Transport is by foot, bicycle (with literally hundreds for rent) or horse-drawn cart.

Go to Paquetá for the boat ride through Rio's famous bay and to see *cariocas* at play – especially during the Festa de São Roque, which is celebrated with fireworks, a procession and music on the weekend following August 16.

Ferries (☎0800-721-1012; www.grupoccr.com.br/barcas) leave from near the Praça XV (Quinze) de Novembro in Centro. The boat takes 70 minutes and will cost you R$12.20 for a return trip. There are 12 departures daily, leaving roughly every 90 minutes from about 7am.

signs) and a good local restaurant. Saturday is the liveliest time to visit.

To get here on foot, take the narrow uphill lane Ladeira João Homem, reachable just off Praça Mauá. The mosaic-covered staircase marks the entrance to the quarter.

EATING

Rio's busiest neighborhood has everything from greasy lunch counters to French bistros. Most restaurants open only for lunch on weekdays. Many pedestrian-only areas throughout Centro (such as Rua do Rosário) are full of restaurants, some spilling onto the sidewalk, others hidden on upstairs floors. Restaurant hunting here is something of an art.

Cinelândia & Around

★XIAN ASIAN **$$**

(☎21 2303-7080; www.xianrio.com.br; top fl, Almirante Silvio de Noronha 365, Bossa Nova Mall; mains R$65-90; ⏲noon-11pm Mon-Thu, to midnight Fri & Sat, noon-10pm Sun; 📶) One of Rio's loveliest new additions is this spacious, theatrically decorated dining room, open-air cocktail bar and nightclub, all set rather dramatically on the edge of the bay. Come for mouthwatering seafood and tender meats with Asian accents, such as fresh oysters with ponzu sauce, salmon truffle tartar or marinated pork ribs with miso.

Dishes are great for sharing, and go nicely with the brilliant cocktail menu. The stunning views over the bay make this a magical place to be at sunset.

GOVARDHANA HARÍ VEGETARIAN **$$**

Map p246 (☎21 2544-2636; 2nd fl, Rodrigo Silva 6; lunch R$35; ⏲11:30am-3:30pm Mon-Fri; ✍) Amid artwork and decorations from India, the always-welcoming Hare Krishnas whip up delicious vegetarian dishes made with care. The restaurant is tucked down a narrow lane just off Rua São José and is always packed, so arrive early to get a seat.

Praça Tiradentes & Around

CONFEITARIA COLOMBO BRAZILIAN **$**

Map p246 (☎21 2505-1500; www.confeitariacolombo.com.br; Gonçalves Dias 34; pastries R$11-16, sandwiches R$22-46; ⏲9am-7pm Mon-Fri, to 5pm Sat) Stained-glass windows, brocaded mirrors and marble countertops create a lavish setting for coffee or a meal here. Dating from the late 1800s, the Confeitaria Colombo serves desserts – including a good *pastel de nata* (custard tart) – befitting its elegant decor.

The restaurant above, **Cristóvão** (Map p246; buffet per person R$100; ⏲11:30am-4pm), spreads an extensive buffet of Brazilian dishes for those wanting to further soak up the splendor.

CASA PALADINO BRAZILIAN **$**

Map p246 (Uruguaiana 224; mains R$16-30; ⏲7am-8:30pm Mon-Fri, 8am-noon Sat) Going strong since 1906, this frozen-in-time delicatessen is lined with bottles, canned goods and other preserves. The attached restaurant serves

Paladino's famed sandwiches, like the *triplo* (pastrami, egg and melted cheese), and fluffy omelets with ingredients including cod, squid and octopus. It all goes nicely with an ice-cold draft beer.

BELGA BELGIAN **$$**

Map p246 (www.belgahotel.com.br; Rua dos Andradas 129; mains R$48-64; ⏲6:30am-10pm Mon-Fri, 7am-3pm Sat;) Belgian chef Alexandre Binard heads this delightful brasserie a few blocks west of Av Rio Branco. Stop by in the morning for coffees, muffins and quiches. Later in the day, there are lunch specials, happy-hour tapas and, of course, Belgian waffles. You can also enjoy one of the delectable beers on tap (including Straffe Hendrik Tripel from Bruges).

BAR LUIZ GERMAN **$$**

Map p246 (☎21 2262-6900; Rua da Carioca 39; mains R$35-64; ⏲11am-4pm Mon & Sat, to 9pm Tue-Fri) Bar Luiz first opened in 1887, making it one of the city's oldest *cervejarias* (pubs). A festive air fills the old saloon as diners get their fill of traditional German cooking (potato salad and smoked meats), along with ice-cold drafts – including dark beer – on tap.

Praça XV & Around

BISTRÔ DO PAÇO CAFE **$**

Map p246 (☎21 2262-3613; www.bistro.com.br; Praça XV/Quinze de Novembro 48, Paço Imperial; mains R$22-45; ⏲noon-7pm) On the ground floor of the Paço Imperial, this informal restaurant offers a tasty assortment of quiches, salads, soups and other light fare. Save room for the delicious pies and cakes.

L'ATELIER DU CUISINIER FRENCH **$$**

Map p246 (☎21 3179-0024; www.latelierducuisinier.com.br; Teófilo Otoni 97; mains R$45-60, multicourse lunch R$86-120; ⏲noon-2pm Mon-Fri) Set in a 19th-century building just off busy Av Rio Branco, this small 24-seat place serves some of the best cuisine in Centro. The menu is tiny (just a few options each day), but beautifully executed, with French chef David Jobert creating recipes with fresh-from-the-market Brazilian ingredients.

RANCHO INN INTERNATIONAL **$$**

Map p246 (☎21 2233-6144; www.ranchoinn.com.br; 2nd fl, Rua do Rosário 74, Centro; mains R$36-54; ⏲11:30am-3:30pm Mon-Fri) Exposed brick and tall windows lend a vaguely Parisian air to this charming upstairs lunchtime spot. The menu changes daily and features specials like lasagna, risotto with duck and shiitake mushrooms, and farfalle with smoked salmon. If you're particularly hungry, you may want to opt for the less fancy, fixed-price lunch buffet (from R$35).

CAFÉ ARLEQUIM CAFE **$$**

Map p246 (☎21 2220-8471; www.arlequim.com.br; Praça XV/Quinze de Novembro 48, Paço Imperial; mains R$32-48; ⏲10am-8pm Mon-Fri, to 6pm Sat;) In the middle of a shop selling books and CDs, this small, lively, pleasantly air-conditioned cafe is a fine spot to refuel, with Italian (Illy) coffee, sandwiches, salads, quiches, lasagna and desserts.

CAIS DO ORIENTE BRAZILIAN **$$$**

Map p246 (☎21 2203-0178; www.caisdooriente-rj.com.br; Visconde de Itaboraí 8; mains R$55-75; ⏲11am-10pm Mon-Sat, to 5pm Sun) Brick walls lined with tapestries stretch high to the ceiling in this almost-cinematic 1870s mansion. Set on a brick-lined street, hidden from the masses, it blends elements of Brazilian and Mediterranean cooking in dishes such as duck breast with Brazil-nut *farofa* (garnish of manioc flour sautéed with butter) and *açaí* sauce.

ANCORAMAR SEAFOOD **$$$**

Map p246 (☎21 2240-8378; www.ancoramar.com.br; Praça Marechal Âncora 186; mains R$72-140; ⏲11:30am-5pm Mon-Fri) Ancoramar (previously known as Albamar) has long been one of Rio's best lunchtime seafood destinations. Its top picks are fresh oysters, grilled seafood with vegetables and *moqueca* (seafood stew cooked in coconut milk) dishes. The old-fashioned green gazebo-like structure offers excellent views of Baía de Guanabara and the area of Niterói across the bay.

Praça Mauá & Around

MIRONGA BRAZILIAN **$$**

Map p246 (☎21 2518-7727; www.mironga.com.br; Av Rio Branco 19; mains R$28-40; ⏲noon-3:30pm Mon, 11:30am-10pm Tue-Fri, noon-5:30pm Sat & Sun;) With its tall ceilings, exposed Edison bulbs, lounge-like music and chunky wooden tables, Mironga channels a Brooklyn vibe, which is unsurprising given the owner has deep NYC connections. Aesthetics aside, the food is excellent, with a wide-ranging menu of Moroccan-style couscous salads, mushroom and filet mignon risotto, grilled dishes (*picanha,* salmon and chicken breast), pastas and quiches.

ASA AÇAÍ AMAZONIAN **$$**

Map p246 (☎21 2263-9094; www.facebook.com/asaacai; Sacadura Cabral 79; mains R$29-46; ⏲11:30am-6pm Mon-Fri) This small, handsomely designed snack spot has colorfully painted walls to match the vitamin-rich berry that it serves to perfection. The *açaí* here (from R$13 to R$21) is outstanding; order it with house-made granola for an energizing midday snack. ASA also serves juices made from other Amazonian super fruits (like *cupuaçú* and *taperaba*), plus craft beers and filling lunch specials.

IMACULADA BRAZILIAN **$$**

Map p246 (☎21 2253-3999; Ladeira do João Homem 7; mains R$32-50; ⏲11am-4pm Mon, to 10pm Tue-Sat; 📶) Located in the old neighborhood of Morro da Conceição, Imaculada is a Rio classic. The walls are adorned with artwork and the cooking doesn't disappoint. Come for daily lunch specials – *bobó de camarão* (manioc paste with dried shrimp, coconut milk and cashew nuts) on Thursdays or *feijoada* (bean-and-meat stew) on Fridays and Saturdays – and beer and appetizers at day's end.

BOTEQUIM BODEGA DO SAL BRAZILIAN **$$**

Map p246 (☎21 2516-4548; www.botequimbodegadosal.com.br; Argemiro Bulção 33; mains R$36-76; ⏲11am-10pm Tue-Thu, to midnight Mon, Fri & Sat) Near Pedra do Sal (a major destination for samba lovers on Mondays and Fridays), this classic eating and drinking spot serves a fine variety of deliciously unhealthy appetizers (fried sardines, chicken wings, codfish balls) to go with the beers and cocktails. You'll also find sandwiches and a few heartier plates of steak, grilled chicken, salmon and tilapia.

DRINKING & NIGHTLIFE

Rio's workers have some fine choices when it comes to joining the happy-hour fray. One of the liveliest settings for a sundowner is along the historic Travessa do Comércio. The sidewalk tables on this narrow, cobbled lane are packed on weekday nights, particularly as the weekend nears – Thursday is always a good bet. Places see a bit of action during the day on Saturdays, but close the rest of the weekend. Just east of Centro (and reachable by VLT), Xian (p130) can't be beaten for sunset cocktails over the bay.

CURTO CAFE CAFE

Map p246 (☎21 98176-2582; www.facebook.com/curtocafe; 2nd fl, Av Erasmo Braga 278, Centro; ⏲8am-8pm Mon-Thu, to 11pm Fri; 📶) Though it's tricky to find, and it has all the charm of a department store, Curto Cafe shouldn't be missed if you're a coffee fan. Staff prepare excellent espresso drinks and there are plenty of snacks (pizza, brownies) on hand. The price? You decide. It's a pay-what-you-wish system, though suggested prices are posted on most products.

BAR LÉO BAR

Map p246 (☎21 2509-5725; www.facebook.com/barleoouvidor; Rua do Ouvidor 18, Centro; ⏲11am-11pm Mon-Sat) A great place to retire after a day of exploring, Bar Léo serves ice-cold brews with just the right amount of froth. The setting on a pretty cobblestone lane makes for great people-watching, particularly in the evening when the neighboring bars spring to life.

CINE BOTEQUIM BAR

Map p246 (☎21 2253-1414; www.cinebotequim.com.br; Conselheiro Saraiva 39; ⏲11am-11pm Mon-Fri) Vintage film posters and the odd Star Wars figurine adorn the old stone walls at this atmospherically lit space at the north end of Centro. The after-work crowd comes for Rio craft beers, an extensive appetizer menu, and screenings of big football games. DJs occasionally add to the good cheer.

WEEK GAY

Map p246 (☎21 2253-1020; www.theweek.com.br; Sacadura Cabral 135, Centro; ⏲11:45pm-7am Sat) Rio's best gay dance club has a spacious dance floor, excellent DJs and lots of go-go dancers. Saturday nights are when the big parties are held. On other nights, there might not be anything on, so check online before heading out.

AMARELINHO BOTECO

Map p246 (☎21 3549-8434; Praça Floriano 55, Cinelândia; ⏲10am-1am) Easy to spot by its bright *amarelo* (yellow) awning, Amarelinho has a splendid setting on the Praça Floriano, with the Theatro Municipal in the background. Waiters serve plenty of *chope* (draft beer) here as they wander among the crowded tables. Amarelinho is a popular lunch spot but packs in even bigger crowds for that ever-important after-work brew.

BAR MERCADORES BAR

Map p246 (Rua do Ouvidor 21, Centro; ⏲3pm-midnight Tue-Fri, noon-6pm Sat) Hidden in a narrow lane leading off Praça XV (Quinze) de Novembro, this place is one of many popular open-sided drinking spots tucked into Rio's old colonial center. The narrow pedestrian lane is a popular meeting spot, and a festive air arrives at workday's end as *cariocas* fill the tables spilling onto the pedestrian lane.

ENTERTAINMENT

PEDRA DO SAL SAMBA

Map p246 (Largo João da Baiana, Gamboa; ⏲8pm-midnight Mon & Fri) The Monday- and Friday-night street parties here are major draws for lovers of samba, whether they're Brazilian or foreign, rich or poor. The lively *samba da mesa* features a handful of changing players who belt out well-known songs to swaying, joyful crowds surrounding the tiny plaza.

TEATRO RIACHUELO CONCERT VENUE

Map p246 (☎21 2533-8799; www.teatroriachuelorio.com.br; Rua do Passeio 38; entry from R$25; ⏲box office noon-8pm Tue-Sat, to 7pm Sun) Opened in 2016, the beautifully designed Riachuelo hosts a high-quality repertoire of concerts and dance performances. Come for a show, but be sure to return by day to check out the gorgeous facade — the neo-Moorish building dates from 1890 and has gone through many incarnations over the years (Brazil's first sound film was screened here back in 1929).

THEATRO MUNICIPAL THEATER

Map p246 (☎21 2332-9191; www.theatromunicipal.rj.gov.br; Manuel de Carvalho, Centro) This gorgeous art nouveau theater provides the setting for Rio's best opera, ballet and symphonic concerts. The theater seats 2400, and sight lines are generally quite good.

TRAPICHE GAMBOA SAMBA

Map p246 (☎21 2516-0868; Sacadura Cabral 155, Gamboa; entry R$25-35; ⏲6:30pm-1am Thu, 7:30pm-3am Fri, 8:30pm-3am Sat) A charming live-samba joint, Trapiche Gamboa is set in a multistory colonial edifice in Gamboa (just north of Centro) and has a friendly, mixed crowd and decent appetizers. It's a casual affair, with samba musicians gathering around a table on the ground floor, and dancers spilling out in front of them.

CINE ODEON CINEMA

Map p246 (Centro Cultural Luiz Severiano Ribeiro; www.cineodeon.com.br; Praça Floriano 7, Cinelândia; ⏲1:30-9pm Tue-Sun) Rio de Janeiro's landmark cinema is a remnant of the once flourishing movie-house scene that gave rise to the name Cinelândia. Following a restoration before the 2016 Olympics, this 1926 film palace was converted into a multifunction venue. Aside from screenings of the latest Hollywood fare, the Odeon stages occasional concerts, plays and dance performances.

TEATRO RIVAL PETROBRAS LIVE MUSIC

Map p246 (☎21 2240-4469; www.rivalpetrobras.com.br; Álvaro Alvim 33, Cinelândia; entry R$30-80; ⏲box office 3-9pm Mon-Fri, 4-9pm Sat) Going strong since 1934, Teatro Rival stages Música Popular Brasileira (MPB), samba, *chorinho* (informal instrumental music) and *forró* (Northeast popular music) groups – with both up-and-comers as well as veteran musicians such as Tânia Alves and Mart'nália. The setup is dinner-theater style, and you can order drinks and snacks throughout the show.

SHOPPING

For a break from the chrome and glass of the Zona Sul, check out the old-school shops of historic Centro. Bargains abound in the narrow pedestrian streets around Saara, where shops peddle everything from clothes and cosmetics to toys, jerseys and all the fabric, feathers and sequins you'd ever need to make your own Carnaval costume. Nearby streets offer a little of everything, including discounted record stores, secondhand bookshops and percussion stores, often set behind century-old shop fronts.

★CRAB ARTS & CRAFTS

Map p246 (☎21 3380-1850; www.facebook.com/crabsebrae; Praça Tiradentes 69, Centro; ⏲10am-5pm Tue-Sat) One of Rio's best new handicraft stores stocks an exquisite collection of pieces from every corner of Brazil. You'll find ceramics with pre-Columbian imagery found in the Serra da Capivara, lovely eco-jewelry made of seeds and nuts from indigenous groups and brightly painted folk art from the Northeast, as well as sustainably made animal-free bags, vegetable-fiber woven textiles and all-rubber footwear.

CASA NAARA ARTS & CRAFTS

Map p246 (☎21 97399-0642; www.casanaara.com.br; 2nd fl, Teófilo Otoni 134, Centro; ⏲11am-8pm Mon-Fri) This upstairs shop has loads of character, with original paintings, carved wooden folk art, artfully bound blank books, coffee from small producers and other curiosities for sale. There's a small cafe on-site, and Casa Naara hosts yoga sessions, photo courses, round-table discussions and other cultural fare (in Portuguese of course).

GRANADO COSMETICS

Map p246 (☎21 2252-4136; Primeiro de Março 14, Centro; ⏲8am-7pm Mon-Fri, 10am-2pm Sat) A classic-looking apothecary with a name that's been around since 1870, Granado incorporates Brazilian ingredients in its all-natural products. Favorites include the Castanha do Brasil line of moisturizers, shampoos and conditioners (made from chestnuts from the Amazon).

LIVRARIA DA TRAVESSA BOOKS, MUSIC

Map p246 (☎21 3231-8015; Sete de Setembro 54, Centro; ⏲9am-8pm Mon-Fri, to 2pm Sat) Livraria da Travessa offers a peaceful refuge from the people-packed sidewalks. There are some books in English, and an array of colorful (but pricey) coffee-table books. There's also a small in-store cafe-restaurant where you can order drinks and creatively topped focaccia sandwiches.

PLEIDISCO MUSIC

Map p246 (☎21 2507-2905; Rua da Carioca 50, Centro; ⏲9am-7pm Mon-Fri, to 1pm Sat) One of several excellent music shops on Rua da Carioca, Pleidisco sells all the pieces that make up the rhythm section of Carnaval *baterias* (percussion sections). Unique souvenirs for the musically minded include *cavaquinhos* (ukulele-sized guitars), which start at around R$250, and *pandeiros* (tambourines), starting at R$60.

NOVA LIVRARIA LEONARDO DA VINCI BOOKS

Map p246 (☎21 2533-2237; www.leonardodavinci.com.br; Rio Branco 185, Edifício Marquês de Herval, Centro; ⏲10am-7pm Mon-Fri, to 1:30pm Sat) Boasting one of Rio's best foreign-language book collections, da Vinci also has a wide range of art and photography books, as well as coffee-table books covering Rio's history and architecture. It's one floor down; follow the spiral ramp. There's a decent coffee shop nearby too.

SPORTS & ACTIVITIES

PASSEIO MARÍTIMO BOATING

Map p246 (Boat Tour; ☎21 2532-5992; adult/child R$30/15; ⏲tours 1:15pm & 3pm Thu-Sun) In addition to visits of Ilha Fiscal, the Espaço Cultural da Marinha (p127) runs 80-minute boat tours around the bay touching on Rio's history and development over the years (in Portuguese only). Even it you can't speak the language, the views of the city and its mountainous landmarks are stunning, and make it well worth going.

Santa Teresa & Lapa

SANTA TERESA | LAPA

Neighborhood Top Five

1 **Escadaria Selarón** (p137) Photographing the mosaic-covered staircase by Chilean-born Jorge Selarón, who made this moving creation his life's work.

2 **Bonde** (p138) Riding the tram over the Arcos do Lapa and up to village-like Santa Teresa.

3 **Catedral Metropolitana** (p139) Watching sunlight play through the cathedral's dazzling stained-glass windows.

4 **Museu Chácara do Céu** (p138) Surveying the museum's exquisite modern-art collection.

5 **Parque das Ruínas** (p138) Taking in the fine views over Rio and Baía de Guanabara (Guanabara Bay).

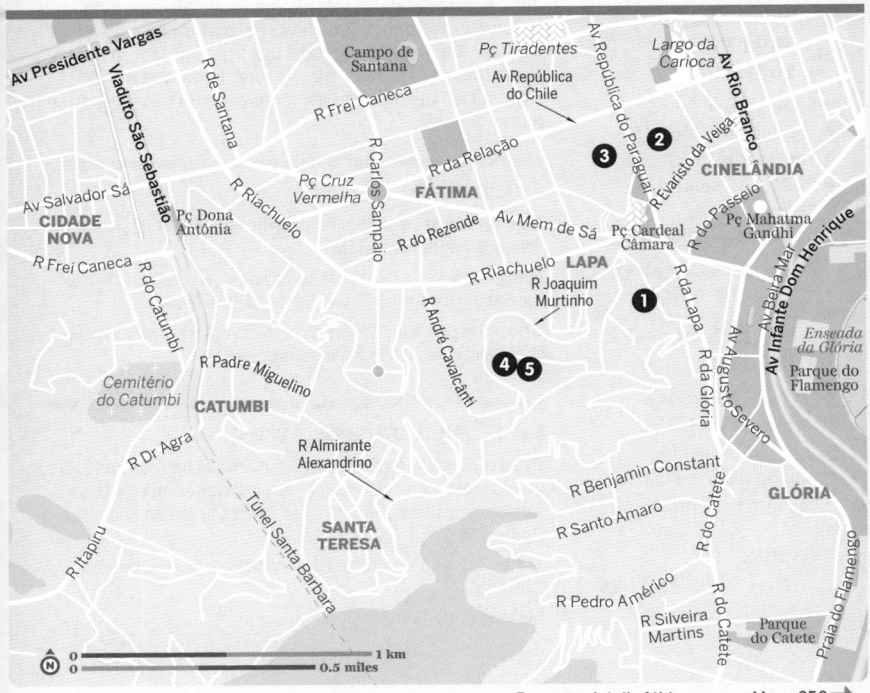

For more detail of this area see Map p250

Lonely Planet's Top Tip

The best time to explore Santa Teresa is on Saturday or Sunday, when the neighborhood is at its liveliest. That's when you'll find all the cultural centers, galleries and restaurants open, as well as street artists selling their wares between Largo do Guimarães and Bar do Gomes (follow the *bonde* tracks).

Best Places to Eat

- Espírito Santa (p140)
- Casa Momus (p141)
- Lilia (p140)
- Aprazível (p140)
- Térèze (p140)
- Refeitório (p141)

For reviews, see p139

Best Places to Drink

- Explorer Bar (p142)
- Rio Scenarium (p143)
- TribOz (p143)
- Clube dos Democráticos (p144)
- Carioca da Gema (p143)

For reviews, see p141

Best Places to Shop

- Favela Hype (p144)
- La Vereda (p145)
- Loja Pence (p145)
- Galeria Bazá (p145)
- Feira do Rio Antigo (p145)
- Tucum (p145)

For reviews, see p144

Explore Santa Teresa & Lapa

Icons of bohemian Rio, Santa Teresa and Lapa are two rough-and-tumble neighborhoods that have contributed considerably to the city's artistic and musical heritage. On a hill overlooking the city, Santa Teresa has an impressive collection of 19th-century mansions set along winding lanes. Many beautiful colonial homes stretch skyward, their manicured gardens hidden behind gabled fences.

Today Santa Teresa is the byword for a vibrant arts scene. Throughout the year the sounds of impromptu festivals and street parties fill the air, ranging from Afro-Brazilian *maracatu* drumming along Rua Joaquim Murtinho to live jazz at the Parque das Ruínas, and the annual Portas Abertas event that sees dozens of artists open their studios and cover the streets with living installations. The neighborhood makes for a great day of browsing craft stores and galleries, stopping for views at the Parque das Ruínas (p138), followed by dinner and drinks at one of the unique spaces overlooking the city.

The streets of Lapa lie south of Cinelândia. Formerly a wealthy residential neighborhood, Lapa became a red-light district in the 1930s. Although it's still gritty, it's also one of the music capitals of Brazil. The music scene has brought some gentrification to the area, including new restaurants, hostels and even a luxury hotel. Nighttime is the best time to visit Lapa, when you can catch live samba at bars, clubs and eateries all across the neighborhood.

Lapa's landmark aqueduct, Arcos da Lapa (p139), is one of the neighborhood's most prominent features. Coursing over the 64m-high structure are narrow tracks that carry the photogenic *bonde* (tram) to and from Santa Teresa.

Local Life

Markets Lapa's excellent Feira do Rio Antigo (p145) features antiques, crafts, food and live music.

Hangouts Santa Teresa has some fine local haunts, including the Bar do Gomes (p142) and Bar do Mineiro (p140).

Shopping strips The Rua do Lavradio is dotted with antique shops and cafes, plus samba clubs by night.

Getting There & Away

Bus For Santa Teresa, take buses marked Centro (206 and 214) from Carioca metro station; for Lapa, take buses marked Leblon, Ipanema and Copacabana (161) or Gávea and Jardim Botânico (158 and 161).

Tram For Santa Teresa, take the *bonde* from Centro (on Lélio Gama 65).

Metro Lapa's metro stop is Cinelândia.

PINTAI SUCHACHASRI/GETTY IMAGES ©

TOP SIGHT
ESCADARIA SELARÓN

Created by Chilean-born artist Jorge Selarón, the staircase bearing his name boasts colorful mosaics that cover the 215 steps leading into the hilltop enclave of Santa Teresa. Situated in the heart of Rio's vibrant samba district, the *escadaria* has come to symbolize Lapa's creative and bohemian spirit, and its rebirth from a worn and battered former red-light district to a musical powerhouse.

Sadly, Selarón died at the age of 65 in early 2013 – his body was found on the same steps to which he'd devoted the last 20 years of his life. Selarón was a well-known figure in the neighborhood, having moved to Rio in 1983 and settled in a house right off the stairway. What started out as a whim in 1990 evolved into an obsession; he was often spotted at work in Lapa and rarely left the neighborhood.

The mosaics started out as a homage to the Brazilian people by utilizing green, yellow and blue, the colors of the flag. Later, the artist added mirrors and unusual colors and patterns to illustrious effect. As the media began to cover his unusual contribution to the urban landscape, Selarón's fame spread, and soon travelers began arriving with ceramics from their own countries to donate, which he later incorporated into his ever-evolving installation. The stairs' tiles hail from more than 60 countries. After he completed the stairs, he began covering other surfaces in need of cosmetic attention; the mosaics near the Arcos da Lapa are also his work.

The stairs have been named a city landmark, and have been featured in numerous magazines, and photo and film shoots. The music video for Snoop Dogg's 'Beautiful' features the steps, as does that for U2's 'Walk On.' Rio's stirring bid for the 2016 Olympics, 'Passion Unites Us,' also showcased the steps.

DON'T MISS

- The plaque describing Selarón's work
- Mosaics of pregnant women, including one with Selarón's own face!
- Depictions of the steps in music videos

PRACTICALITIES

- Map p250, F4
- btwn Joaquim Silva & Pinto Martins, Lapa

SIGHTS

There's much to see in these two neighborhoods. You can start the day by taking in the brilliant stained-glass windows of Catedral Metropolitana and the Arcos da Lapa. Then stroll over to the *bonde* station and head up to Santa Teresa by tram. Once there, you can take in the great views over downtown from the Parque das Ruinas, then go next door for art gazing at the Museu Chácara do Céu.

Santa Teresa

BONDE
CABLE CAR

Map p250 (return ticket R$20; ⏲9am-5pm Mon-Fri, 10am-5.30pm Sat, 11am-4.30pm Sun; Ⓜ Carioca) The *bonde* is the last of the historic streetcars that once crisscrossed the city. Its romantic clatter through the cobbled streets is the archetypal sound of bohemian Santa Teresa. Currently the *bonde* travels every 15 to 20 minutes from the cable-car station in Centro (p124) over the scenic Arcos da Lapa and as far as Largo do Guimarães in the heart of Santa Teresa.

MUSEU CHÁCARA DO CÉU
MUSEUM

Map p250 (☎21 3970-1093; www.museuscastromaya.com.br; Murtinho Nobre 93; adult/child R$6/free, Wed free; ⏲noon-5pm Wed-Mon) The former mansion of art patron and industrialist Raymundo Ottoni de Castro Maya contains a small but diverse array of modern art, formerly Ottoni's private collection, which he bequeathed to the nation. In addition to works by Portinari, Di Cavalcanti and Lygia Clark, the museum displays furniture and Brazilian maps dating from the 17th and 18th centuries, and hosts temporary exhibitions.

PARQUE DAS RUÍNAS
VIEWPOINT

Map p250 (☎21 2215-0621; www.facebook.com/parquedasruinas; Murtinho Nobre 169; ⏲8am-6pm Tue-Sun) FREE This park contains the ruins – exterior brick walls and a newly built staircase – of the mansion belonging to Brazilian heiress Laurinda Santos Lobo. Her house was a meeting point for Rio's artists and intellectuals for many years until her death in 1946. There's a small gallery on the ground floor, but the real reason to come is the excellent panorama from the viewing platform up top.

There's also a small outdoor cafe-kiosk (11am to 6pm) and terrace where open-air concerts and theater performances are sometimes held. Go online for the latest schedule.

LARGO DAS NEVES
SQUARE

Map p250 A slice of village life in the city, this small plaza is one of Santa Teresa's most picturesque little squares. While Largo das Neves is empty by day, on weekend nights the bars surrounding it come alive, with revelers crowding the walkways. At times Música Popular Brasileira (MPB) bands perform to a young crowd.

LARGO DO GUIMARÃES
SQUARE

Map p250 (Almirante Alexandrino) The plaza named after Joaquim Fonseca Guimarães (a local resident whose house became Hotel Santa Teresa, just up the road) now forms the center of bohemian Santa Teresa. A festive Carnaval street party originates here, and a number of restaurants, handicrafts and thrift shops lie within a short distance.

CENTRO CULTURAL LAURINDA SANTOS LOBO
CULTURAL CENTER

Map p250 (☎21 2215-0618; Monte Alegre 306; ⏲10am-7pm Tue-Fri, noon-8pm Sat & Sun) FREE Built in 1907, this large mansion once served as a salon for artists from Brazil and abroad and as the location of parties hosted by socialite Laurinda Santos Lobo. Guests included Brazilian composer Heitor Villa-Lobos and American dancer Isadora Duncan. Today, as a cultural center, the building still plays an active role in the neighborhood by hosting exhibitions and open-air concerts throughout the year.

RETRATO ESPAÇO CULTURAL
CULTURAL CENTER

Map p250 (☎21 2232-1377; Santa Cristina 6) Opened by a photographer in 2017, this new cultural space features a dynamic lineup of still-image and videography exhibitions, film screenings, discussions and photography workshops, and the occasional concert. It lies downhill from most of Santa Teresa on the edge of Glória.

CASA DE BENJAMIN CONSTANT
HISTORIC BUILDING

Map p250 (☎21 3970-1177; Monte Alegre 255) This tranquil estate served as the residence of one of Brazil's most influential politicians in the founding of the young republic. Benjamin Constant (1837–91) was an engineer, military officer and professor before taking an active role in the provisional government. He is also remembered for founding a school for blind children. Painstakingly preserved, his house provides a window into his life and times.

MUSEU DE ARTE SACRA MUSEUM

Map p250 (Museum of Sacred Art; Catedral Metropolitana, Av República do Chile 245, Fátima; R$5; ⏲9am-4pm Tue-Fri, to noon Sat & Sun) This small museum in the basement of the **Catedral Metropolitana** (Map p250; ☎21 2240-2669; www.catedral.com.br; ⏲7am-5pm) contains some exquisite carvings by Mestre Valentim and a number of historical items. Don't miss the baptismal font used at the christening of royal princes and the throne of Dom Pedro II.

Lapa

ESCADARIA SELARÓN LANDMARK

See p137.

ARCOS DA LAPA LANDMARK

Map p250 A much-photographed symbol of Lapa, the arches date back to the mid-1700s, when the structure served as an aqueduct to carry water from the Carioca River to downtown Rio. In a style reminiscent of ancient Rome, the 42 arches stand 64m high. Today the arches carry the bonde on its way between Centro and Santa Teresa. Located near Av Mem de Sá.

FUNDIÇÃO PROGRESSO ARTS CENTER

Map p250 (☎21 3212-0800; www.fundicaoprogresso.com.br; Rua dos Arcos 24; ⏲11am-8pm Mon-Fri, noon-11pm Sat) Once a foundry for the manufacturing of safes and ovens, Fundição Progresso today hosts avant-garde exhibitions, concerts and samba performances throughout the year. There's also a cafe, a bar and a shop selling locally made apparel and accessories. The building is one of the few in the area that survived the 1950s neighborhood redistricting project to widen Av República do Paraguai.

EATING

Great views, a diverse crowd and a scenic atmosphere among late 19th-century buildings set the stage for a great night out in bohemian Santa Teresa. Most restaurants are within a short stroll of Largo do Guimarães. Although Lapa is better known for its samba than for its cuisine, more and more restaurants are opening in the area, catering to the young crowds heading to the dance halls.

Santa Teresa

GALERIA BAZÁ VEGETARIAN $

Map p250 (☎21 2533-0686; www.facebook.com/galeriabaza; Rua do Oriente 414; mains R$18-25; ⏲noon-11pm Tue-Sun;) One of Santa Teresa's most creative spaces, Bazá is equal parts vegetarian cafe, handicraft gallery and live-music venue. Stop in for tasty lentil or tabbouleh salads, curry rice, black-bean burgers and veggie *moqueca* (stew). Throughout the month you can catch live samba as well as more diverse Brazilian sounds (like *carimbó* from the Amazon).

ALDA MARIA DOCES PORTUGUESES BAKERY $

Map p250 (☎21 2232-1320; www.aldamaria.com.br; Almirante Alexandrino 1116; small cakes R$9-16; ⏲2-7pm Fri-Sun; 🚌006/007) This charming family-run bakery and cafe is one of the secret spots that make Santa Teresa so popular with locals and visitors alike. The beautiful little house is both the family home and a bakery specializing in classic Portuguese sweets and pastries, such as *pasteis de nata* (Portuguese custard tarts), *bem casados* ('happily married' cookies) and *toucinho de ceu* (both bite-size cakes).

At weekends Alda Maria opens her living room to the public. The living room doubles as a museum, featuring antique bakery equipment used by Alda Maria's ancestors and old family photos. From Lapa the 006 and 007 buses will get you close; otherwise, take a taxi.

ALQUIMIA CRÊPES $

Map p250 (☎21 99500-1330; Largo das Neves 11; crepes R$15-28; ⏲5pm-midnight Wed-Sun) Beautifully set on tranquil Largo das Neves, Alquimia is a friendly Franco-Brazilian-run creperie that fires up delicious crepes, and it's also a charming spot to come for a drink in the evening. There's live music, and occasional art exhibitions are held here.

CAFE DO ALTO BRAZILIAN $$

Map p250 (☎21 2507-3172; Paschoal Carlos Magno 143; mains R$25-48; ⏲noon-9pm Mon, Tue, Thu & Fri, 9am-9pm Sat & Sun;) Located a few steps from Largo do Guimarães (Santa Teresa's epicenter), Cafe do Alto whips up filling Northeastern dishes. The wide-ranging menu features *tapiocas* (crepes made from manioc flour), *casquinha de siri* (pulled crab), *xinxim de galinha* (chicken and dried shrimp with coconut, ginger and spices over rice) and other regional fare, plus lighter options, such as sandwiches.

BAR DO MINEIRO BRAZILIAN **$$**

Map p250 (☎21 2221-9227; Paschoal Carlos Magno 99; mains R$65-125, weekday lunch special R$22-35; ⏲noon-2am Tue-Sat, to midnight Sun) Black-and-white photographs of legendary singers cover the walls of this old-school *boteco* (small open-air bar) in the heart of Santa Teresa. Lively crowds have been filling this spot for years to enjoy traditional Minas Gerais dishes. The *feijoada* (bean-and-meat stew served with rice) is tops, and served every day, along with appetizers, including *pasteis* (savory pastries).

★APRAZÍVEL BRAZILIAN **$$$**

Map p250 (☎21 2508-9174; Aprazível 62; mains R$90-130; ⏲noon-11pm Thu-Sat, 11am-6pm Sun; 📶✎) Hidden on a winding road high in Santa Teresa, Aprazível offers beautiful views and a lush garden setting. Grilled fish and roasted dishes showcase the country's culinary highlights from land and sea. Start with grilled heart of palms before moving on to standout main courses like delectable *moquequinha* (seafood stew), roast pork with pineapple chutney and polenta, or house-made vegetarian ravioli.

★ESPÍRITO SANTA AMAZONIAN **$$$**

Map p250 (☎21 2507-4840; Almirante Alexandrino 264; mains R$55-98; ⏲noon-11pm) At this beautifully restored mansion, you can sit on the back terrace with its sweeping views or in the charming, airy dining room, and feast on rich, expertly prepared meat and seafood dishes from the Amazon and Northeast. Top picks include the *moqueca* (fish stew), made with pintado (a delicious river fish), and the slow-roasted pork ribs served with sweet potato.

TÉRÈZE FUSION **$$$**

Map p250 (☎21 3380-0220; Hotel Santa Teresa, Rua Almirante Alexandrino 660; mains R$80-140; ⏲noon-3:30pm & 7:30-11pm) Under the command of chef Esteban Mateu, Térèze provides a memorable dining experience. All the elements are there, from the decadent menu to the suggested wine pairings and the superb views over the city. Choose from the likes of creamy codfish risotto with lobster bisque, suckling pig with mashed sweet potatoes and truffles, and eggplant gnocchi with cashew pesto.

SOBRENATURAL SEAFOOD **$$$**

Map p250 (☎21 2224-1003; Almirante Alexandrino 432; mains for 2 R$80-155; ⏲noon-11pm Thu-Tue) The old hardwood ceiling and exposed brick set the stage for feasting on *frutas do mar* (seafood). Lines gather at weekends for crabmeat appetizers, fresh grilled fish and flavorful platters of *moqueca* (fish stew). During the week, stop by for tasty lunchtime specials. There's live music most nights.

Lapa

VEZPA PIZZA **$**

Map p250 (www.vezpa.com.br; Rua do Lavradio 198; pizza slices R$11-13; ⏲noon-midnight Mon & Tue, to 2am Wed & Thu, to 5am Fri, 3pm-5am Sat, 3pm-1am Sun) With over a dozen locations around Rio, this New York–style pizza-by-the-slice shop has taken the city by storm. This branch is the perfect pre- or post-party snack spot, with satisfyingly crispy crusted slices sprinkled with creative toppings (if you wish) and served up in a hurry.

RANGO VEGGIE VEGETARIAN **$**

Map p250 (☎21 97561-0141; Joaquim Silva 123; burgers R$12-18; ⏲10am-6pm Mon-Thu, 11am-11pm Fri, 11am-7pm Sat; ✎) Tucked in the back of the Loja Pence boutique (p145), this place cooks up tasty veggie burgers made of pea, lentil, black bean or falafel. Appetizers like *esfihas* (broccoli- or eggplant-filled triangles), desserts and hibiscus tea round out the menu.

★LILIA BRAZILIAN **$$**

Map p250 (☎21 3852-5423; www.facebook.com/lilia.restaurante; Rua do Senado 45; set menu R$50; ⏲11.30am-3pm Mon-Fri, noon-4pm Sat; 📶✎; Ⓜ Cinelândia) You could easily miss the low-key entrance to this tranquil lunch spot. Covering the top two floors of a 19th-century building, the restaurant has an airy, creative design, with white brick walls, shelves of plants, and decorative balconies overlooking the street. The three-course menu changes daily, focusing on simple but beautifully prepared dishes; it always includes a vegetarian option.

★CASA MOMUS MEDITERRANEAN $$

Map p250 (☎21 3852-8250; www.casamomus.com.br; Rua do Lavradio 11; mains R$42-58; ⏲11:30am-5pm Mon, to midnight Tue & Wed, to 2am Thu-Sat) One of the best and loveliest restaurants in Lapa, Casa Momus has a small but well-executed menu of Mediterranean-influenced dishes. Start with prawn croquettes, fried polenta with spicy Gorgonzola or a Moroccan lamb *kafta* (spiced meat patty) with tabbouleh and yogurt sauce, then feast on oxtail risotto with watercress, seared tuna with couscous, grilled beef tenderloin, and other rich main courses.

REFEITÓRIO BRAZILIAN $$

Map p250 (☎21 2252-2257; www.facebook.com/refeitoriorj; Gomes Freire 226; 3-course lunch special R$48; ⏲11:30am-3pm; ✎) One of the neighborhood's best restaurants, Refeitório serves only set lunches. Diners choose from a small selection of beautifully prepared dishes and there's always one vegetarian option. Look for the cleaver over the unsigned entrance to the low-lit space.

SANTO SCENARIUM BRAZILIAN $$

Map p250 (☎21 3147-9007; www.santoscenarium.com.br; Rua do Lavradio 36; mains R$35-50; ⏲11:30am-4pm Tue-Thu, to 5pm Fri) Angels, saints and other sacred images adorn the exposed brick walls of the marvelously atmospheric Santo Scenarium restaurant on Lapa's antique row. Grilled meats and other Brazilian staples are on offer at lunchtime, as well as decadent appetizers (baby back ribs with beer sauce), sandwiches (such as the popular filet mignon with mozzarella and sliced pineapple) and an extensive drinks menu.

CORTIÇO CARIOCA BRAZILIAN $$

Map p250 (☎21 2210-0663; www.corticocarioca.com.br; Joaquim Silva 105; mains R$32-53; ⏲noon-midnight Tue-Sat, to 6pm Sun; ✎) A standout among the dining options of Lapa, Cortiço Carioca serves carefully prepared *'mexidos.'* filling plates of roast pork, codfish or roast vegetables served with rice and other sides. There are also satisfying burgers and snacks, such as ceviche and guacamole – all fine options before a night exploring the neighborhood's samba clubs.

GOHAN JAPANESE $$

Map p250 (☎21 2232-0479; www.gohanrio.com.br; Joaquim Silva 127; mains R$33-78; ⏲11am-9pm Mon-Wed, to 11:45pm Thu-Sat, noon-5pm Sun) Lapa may not seem the most obvious choice for a sushi dinner, but that hasn't dented the popularity of this inviting spot near the Arcos da Lapa (p139). Gohan has an ample selection of sushi and sashimi combo platters, as well as grilled fare (salmon, tuna, chicken, squid), tempura and noodle dishes.

ESPAÇO LAPA CAFE BRAZILIAN $$

Map p250 (☎21 3971-6812; www.espacolapacafe.com.br; Gomes Freire 457; mains R$25-54; ⏲10am-6pm Mon & Tue, to 11pm Wed-Fri) This creative eating, drinking and live-music space serves up good three-course lunch specials, plus sandwiches, snacks and a huge beer selection from across the globe (more than 600 varieties, though not all are always available). Regular events on the small stage in the back include live bands playing rock, pop and salsa. There are also beer-tasting nights.

MANGUE SECO CACHAÇARIA BAHIAN $$

Map p250 (☎21 3852-1947; www.mangueseco cachacaria.com.br; Rua do Lavradio 23; mains R$43-79; ⏲11am-3pm Mon, to midnight Tue-Thu, to 2am Fri & Sat) Part of the Rio Scenarium nightspot empire, Mangue Seco serves a mix of seafood and Bahian fare, with hearty *moquecas* and *caldeirada de frutos do mar* (both seafood stews). Upstairs is a bar with more than 100 types of *cachaça* (sugarcane alcohol), and there's live music (often samba) on Friday night.

NOVA CAPELA PORTUGUESE $$

Map p250 (☎21 2552-6228; Av Mem de Sá 96; mains R$38-68; ⏲11am-4pm Mon, to midnight Tue-Sun) This classic, old-time eating and drinking spot opened in 1967 and is a well-known draw for neighborhood bohemians: a noisy mix of artists, musicians and party kids fill the place till early morning. Efficient waiters in ties and white coats serve up big plates of traditional Portuguese cuisine.

DRINKING & NIGHTLIFE

Santa Teresa and Lapa are two of Rio's most atmospheric neighborhoods, but they're still rough around the edges, so take care when visiting. Lapa is at its wildest during the weekends, when

***cariocas* (residents of Rio) from all over the city head to the neighborhood's samba clubs. Santa Teresa's bar scene is sprinkled along the main street near Largo do Guimarães, though Largo das Neves, with its tiny plaza and open-sided bars, is also a draw. Take a taxi when visiting these neighborhoods at night.**

Santa Teresa

EXPLORER BAR COCKTAIL BAR

Map p250 (☎21 3264-9665; www.explorerbar.com; Almirante Alexandrino 399; ⏲5pm-midnight Tue-Fri, from 2pm Sat & Sun) A gorgeous multilevel garden with fairy lights is the centerpiece of this charming cocktail bar. Its beautifully conceived cocktails (around R$30) showcase exotic flavors in elixirs like TLV, with orange, tamarind, ginger foam and grated nutmeg. The first-rate food menu features an eclectic mix of Sicilian seafood pasta, *sabich* (a roasted eggplant and hummus sandwich) and other globally inspired dishes (mains R$32 to R$56).

BAR DOS DESCASADOS LOUNGE

Map p250 (☎21 3380-0200; Almirante Alexandrino 660, Hotel Santa Teresa; ⏲6pm-1am Fri & Sat, 5pm-11pm Sun) This stylish bar with outdoor seating has lovely views over the city (looking north). You can enjoy decadent cocktails (including a caipirinha made with tangerines grown on the property) and savory snacks, such as salmon tartare, while pondering the A-list crowd.

BAR DO GOMES BOTECO

Map p250 (☎21 2232-0822; www.armazemsaothiago.com.br; Áurea 26; ⏲noon-1am Mon-Sat, to 10pm Sun) Although the sign says 'Armazém do São Thiago,' everyone calls this place Bar do Gomes. Regardless, this atmospheric drinking den with its old photographs and bottle-lined cabinets is a favorite meeting spot for ice-cold *chope* (draft beer) and such delicious *petiscos* (snacks) as *bolinhos de abóbora con carne seca* (pumpkin and jerked beef surrounded by deep-fried breading).

GOYA-BEIRA BAR

Map p250 (☎21 2232-5751; Largo das Neves 13; ⏲6pm-midnight Sun-Thu, to 2am Fri & Sat) Small but charming Goya-Beira is one of Santa Teresa's treasures, and has a peaceful view onto Largo das Neves. Owner Rose Guerra prepares intriguing *cachaça* (high-proof sugarcane alcohol) infusions as well as pizzas and appetizers. Things are liveliest at weekends.

Lapa

FAZENDA PARADISO CAFÉ CAFE

Map p250 (☎21 3852-3082; www.facebook.com/fazendaparadisocafe; Rua dos Inválidos 126; ⏲8am-7pm Mon-Fri) This excellent family-run cafe provides true 'farm to cup' service. Several kinds of coffee (all grown on the family farm in Minas Gerais) are roasted on-site and available to purchase. Choose from preparation methods including AeroPress, Chemex and Siphon, and team with cakes, wraps, quiches and more substantial lunch dishes.

VACA ATOLADA BAR

Map p250 (☎21 2221-0515; Gomes Freire 533; ⏲9pm-3am Tue-Sat) For an authentic samba experience, head to this simple, brightly lit, tile-covered eating and drinking den. You'll find a *samba de roda* (table with samba-playing musicians) and a local crowd that squeezes up and joins in with the songs and dance (when space allows). This is old-school Lapa: friendly, ungentrified and full of life.

BOOZE BAR BAR

Map p250 (www.facebook.com/boozebarrj; Av Mem de Sá 63; ⏲5pm-midnight Mon-Wed, to 2am Thu, to 3am Fri & Sat) Though unimaginatively named, the Booze Bar deserves high marks for bringing quality beer to Lapa. You'll find nearly a dozen intriguing microbrews on draft, as well as the bar's own signature easy-drinking pilsen. The attractive high-ceilinged space is a fine spot for a bite, offering *coxinhas* (croquettes), burgers, fish and chips, rice balls and other pub fare (mains R$22 to R$40).

ARMAZÉM SENADO BAR

Map p250 (☎21 2509-7201; Av Gomes Freire 256; ⏲8am-8pm Mon-Fri, to 9pm Sat; Ⓜ Carioca) Armazém Senado is an ancient rough diamond of a bar tucked away on a backstreet. Floor-to-ceiling shelves are crammed with dusty old bottles of *cachaça* and wine – the history is almost palpable. Every Saturday the bar comes alive with excellent, rootsy samba sessions.

SARAU BAR

Map p250 (www.facebook.com/sarauriolapa; Av Mem de Sá 64; ⏲6pm-4am Wed-Sun) Just past the Arcos da Lapa (p139) and tucked inside a building covered with an enormous mural, this place is a hard one to miss. There's live music – samba and *forró* (popular music of the Northeast) – from 8pm. It's also a wonderful spot to have a few drinks at one of the many outdoor tables on the plaza in front and take in the vertiginous street scene.

LEVIANO BAR BAR

Map p250 (☎21 99580-6462; www.levianobar.com.br; Av Mem de Sá 49; ⏲6pm-late) Near the entrance to Mem de Sá, the Leviano Bar is part of a new crop of slightly more upscale drinking and dance spots. Watch the passing people parade – and take in the great view of the Arcos da Lapa (p139) – from the outdoor area before heading to the upstairs dance floor, where DJs mix house, electro-samba, soul and reggae.

BURACO DA LACRAIA GAY

Map p250 (☎21 2242-0446; www.facebook.com/buracodalacraia; André Cavalcante 58; R$25-55; ⏲10pm-5:30am Fri & Sat) Going strong since the 1980s, Buraco da Lacraia always makes for a riotous night out. You'll find glamorous and trashy visitors, bizarre drag shows, karaoke, a dark room and other amusements. Don't be deterred by the high price tag: pricier admission typically includes free drinks – beer and certain well drinks – all night long.

BAR DA NALVA BAR

Map p250 (☎21 2509-4717; www.facebook.com/bardanalva; Silvio Romero 8; ⏲10am-9pm Mon-Thu, to 11pm Fri & Sat) Tucked down a lane a few blocks from the mayhem of Lapa, unpretentious Bar da Nalva is a low-key meeting spot by day (with good-value set lunches) and a lively drinking den by night. It's best on Friday night when live samba draws the crowds.

ANTÔNIO'S BOTECO

Map p250 (☎21 2224-4197; Av Mem de Sá 88; ⏲4pm-3am Mon-Fri, from noon Sat & Sun) Antônio's has lots of old-school charm with its hanging lamps, wrought-iron trim and simple wooden tables. There are a few seats on the sidewalk for taking in the pulsing street scene.

★ ENTERTAINMENT

TRIBOZ JAZZ

Map p250 (☎21 2210-0366; www.triboz-rio.com; Conde de Lages 19, Lapa; R$15-30; ⏲6-8pm & 9pm-1am Thu-Sat) Not for lazy ears, this avant-garde jazz house known to the sonic cognoscenti is unique in Rio for its serious approach to performances. Run by an Australian ethnomusicologist, it sits in a shadier part of old Lapa in a signless mansion, which transforms into a beautiful showcase space.

RIO SCENARIUM SAMBA

Map p250 (☎21 3147-9000; www.rioscenarium.art.br; Rua do Lavradio 20, Lapa; R$35-60; ⏲7pm-4am Tue-Sat) One of the city's most photogenic nightspots, Rio Scenarium has three floors, each lavishly decorated with antiques. Balconies overlook the stage on the 1st floor, where dancers keep time to the jazz-infused samba, *choro* (romantic, improvised, samba-related music) or *pagode* (popular samba music) filling the air. Rio Scenarium receives much press outside Brazil, and attracts about twice as many foreigners as locals. Bring ID.

CARIOCA DA GEMA SAMBA

Map p250 (☎21 2221-0043; www.barcariocadagema.com.br; Av Mem de Sá 79, Lapa; R$20-40; ⏲7:30pm-1:30am Sun-Tue & Thu, to 3am Fri, from 9pm Sat) Although it's now surrounded by clubs, Carioca da Gema was one of Lapa's pioneers when it opened in 2000. This small, warmly lit club still attracts some of the city's best samba bands, and you'll find a festive mixed crowd filling the dance floor most nights.

FAVELA HYPE LIVE MUSIC

Map p250 (www.facebook.com/favelahype; Paschoal Carlos Magno 103, Santa Teresa; ⏲10am-11pm Tue-Sun) Santa Teresa's best-loved clothing shop (p144) transforms into a neighborhood party space with live music several times a week. Come on Friday (8pm) for samba and other Brazilian sounds. On Saturday (also 8pm) you can catch salsa, featuring musicians from across Latin America. On Sunday there's a jazz jam session (from 4pm).

FUNDIÇÃO PROGRESSO CONCERT VENUE

Map p250 (☎21 3212-0800; www.fundicaoprogresso.com.br; Rua dos Arcos 24, Lapa; R$50-120) This former foundry hides one of Rio's top music and theater spaces. A diverse range of shows is staged here: big-name acts, such as Manu Chao and Caetano Veloso, plus theater, video arts and ballet.

BECO DO RATO LIVE MUSIC

Map p250 (☎21 96984-5797; www.becodorato.com.br; Joaquim Silva 11, Lapa; ⏲7pm-2am Tue-Sat, from 5pm Sun) One of Lapa's classic bohemian spots, this tiny bar in a battered part of the neighborhood has excellent live groups playing to a samba-loving crowd. The outdoor seating and informal setting are an unbeatable mix. Friendly owner Márcio Pacheco hails from Minas Gerais; to get the night started, ask him for a fiery *cachaça* from his home state.

CLUBE DOS DEMOCRÁTICOS SAMBA

Map p250 (☎21 2252-4611; Rua do Riachuelo 93, Lapa; R$30-50; ⏲8pm-3am Wed, 10pm-4am Fri & Sat, 8pm-midnight Sun) Murals line the foyer of this 1867 mansion and rhythms filter down from above. Follow the sound up the marble staircase and out to a large table-filled hall, an enormous dance floor and a long stage covered with musicians. A wide range of *cariocas* gathers here to dance, revel in the music and soak up the splendor of the samba-infused setting.

LAPA 40 GRAUS LIVE MUSIC

Map p250 (☎21 3970-1338; www.lapa40graus.com.br; Rua do Riachuelo 97, Lapa; R$20-50; ⏲8pm-4am Thu-Sat) This impressive multi-story music venue and pool hall has tables for lounging on the 1st floor, more than a dozen pool tables on the 2nd floor, and a small stage and dancing couples on the top floor. There are usually two shows nightly. Pop, rock, samba and *choro* typically kick off around 9pm.

CIRCO VOADOR CONCERT VENUE

Map p250 (☎21 2533-0354; www.circovoador.com.br; Rua dos Arcos, Lapa; R$60-120; ⏲box office noon-7pm Tue-Thu, to midnight Fri, 2pm-midnight Sat) In a curvilinear building behind the Arcos da Lapa (p139), Circo Voador hosts big-name Brazilian and international artists. The acoustics here are excellent, and after a show you'll find plenty of other musical options in the area. Check the website to see what's on. You can also take classes in capoeira, dance, percussion and yoga.

SACRILÉGIO SAMBA

Map p250 (☎21 3970-1461; www.sacrilegio.com.br; Av Mem de Sá 81, Lapa; R$20-40; ⏲7pm-2am Tue-Thu, to 6am Fri, 8pm-6am Sat) A short stroll past the Arcos da Lapa (p139) you'll find Sacrilégio, a key spot for catching live samba bands in an intimate setting. The garden makes a fine spot for imbibing a few cold *chopes* while the music filters through the windows. In addition to samba, Sacrilégio hosts *choro, forró* and MPB bands.

TEATRO ODISSÉIA SAMBA

Map p250 (☎21 2224-6367; www.facebook.com/teatroodisseia; Av Mem de Sá 66, Lapa; R$25-50; ⏲7:30pm-2am Wed-Fri, to 6am Sat, 2pm-midnight Sun) This spacious three-story club features live-music shows and DJs, with a relaxed area upstairs when you need a break from the sounds. There's also a terrace with views of the Arcos da Lapa (p139). You'll find plenty of samba, and MPB and rock make an occasional appearance.

SALA CECÍLIA MEIRELES PERFORMING ARTS

Map p250 (☎21 2332-9223; www.salacecilia meireles.com.br; Largo da Lapa 47, Lapa; ⏲box office 1-6pm Mon-Fri, 1pm-showtime Sat) Lapa's splendidly restored early 20th-century gem hosts orchestral concerts throughout the year. Lately the repertoire has included contemporary groups, playing both *choro* and classical music.

SHOPPING

The stomping ground for Rio's bohemian crowd, Santa Teresa has a growing number of handicraft shops and vintage stores. In Lapa you'll find Rua do Lavradio, the city's best antiques street. It's at its liveliest on the first Saturday of the month.

FAVELA HYPE FASHION & ACCESSORIES

Map p250 (www.facebook.com/favelahype; Paschoal Carlos Magno 103, Santa Teresa; ⏲10am-11pm Tue-Sun) This ultra-hip but very friendly gathering spot is part fashion boutique, part restaurant and (at certain times) all party space (p143). The art-filled shop sells swimwear, dresses, jewelry, sunglasses, eco-friendly flip-flops, floral-print button-downs (for the guys) and original artworks. Most products are made by local designers. Favela Hype also serves creative Brazilian fare, including an excellent *feijoada*.

LA VEREDA ARTS & CRAFTS

Map p250 (☎21 2507-0317; www.lavereda.art.br; Almirante Alexandrino 428, Santa Teresa;

⏲10am-8pm) La Vereda stocks a colorful selection of handicrafts from local artists and artisans in a spot near Largo do Guimarães. Handpainted clay figurines by Pernambuco artists, heavy Minas ceramics, delicate sterling-silver jewelry and loosely woven tapestries cover the interior of the old store.

FEIRA DO RIO ANTIGO MARKET
Map p250 (Rua do Lavradio, Lapa; ⏲10am-6pm 1st Sat of month) Don't miss the Rio Antiques Fair if it's on while you're in town. The colonial buildings become a living installation as the whole street fills with antiques, clothing and craft vendors, and food stalls, with samba bands adding to the festive atmosphere.

GALERIA BAZÁ ARTS & CRAFTS
Map p250 (www.facebook.com/galeriabaza; Rua do Oriente 414, Santa Teresa; ⏲noon-11pm Tue-Sun) This vegan restaurant and creative cultural venue also sells Brazilian folk art, eye-catching jewelry and graphic T-shirts, with many pieces made by local artisans.

LOJA PENCE FASHION & ACCESSORIES
Map p250 (www.instagram.com/lojapence; Joaquim Silva 123, Lapa; ⏲10am-6pm Mon-Thu, to 11pm Fri, 11am-7pm Sat) Loja Pence is Lapa's most creative boutique and captures the bohemian spirit of the neighborhood in a wide range of clothing and accessories, all created by local designers. Check out geometric necklaces and bracelets by Linguagem Primativo, bath products by Vanzinga, swimwear by Rota do Sul, dresses by Fios e Atavios, eco-*joias* (sustainably made jewelry) by Raquel Duarte and printed shirts (for men) by Geração.

Other finds include lovely wooden cutting boards by Raiz and notebooks and satchels covered in brightly printed fabrics. There's also veg-friendly cafe Rango Veggie (p140) on-site.

ATELIÊ BONIFÁCIO FASHION & ACCESSORIES
Map p250 (☎21 97135-2510; Rua do Senado 49, Lapa; ⏲10am-6pm Mon-Sat) A creative, bohemian space that sells artwork, mosaic-adorned mirrors, vases, fabric-covered sketch-books, handbags, soaps and skincare products, and cleverly crocheted jewelry – all crafted by local artisans. From the tiny cafe you can order good-quality loose-leaf teas and other refreshments.

There's a strong social component, and owner Juliana Bonifácio hosts Friday-afternoon happy hours (from 2pm) and creative three-course evening meals (reserve ahead).

BAOBÁ BRASIL CLOTHING
Map p250 (☎21 98660-2406; www.baobabrasil.iluria.com; Paschoal Carlos Magno 92, Santa Teresa; ⏲10am-8pm) This neat little clothing store draws strongly on Brazil's African roots. The primary influence comes from Mozambique in the form of bold, colorful printed fabrics used to create beautiful shirts (from R$100), blouses and full-length dresses (R$250).

TUCUM ARTS & CRAFTS
Map p250 (☎21 3197-2957; Paschoal Carlos Magno 100, Santa Teresa; ⏲noon-7pm Tue-Sun) This small but welcoming shop specializes in crafts and artwork from the Amazon. You'll find woven baskets, organic jewelry made from Amazonian seeds and fibers, hammocks, small woodcarvings, pottery, wall hangings and more.

VELHA LAPA ANTIQUES
Map p250 (☎21 2508-8836; Rua do Lavradio 160, Lapa; ⏲9am-5:30pm Mon-Fri, to 3pm Sat) This old colonial edifice hides an intriguing selection of antiques, from tables and chairs to chandeliers, glassware, ceramics and oil paintings. Although many of the objects for sale won't fit in your suitcase, it's still a fun place to browse.

SPORTS & ACTIVITIES

FUNDIÇÃO PROGRESSO DANCING
Map p250 (☎21 3212-0800; www.fundicaoprogresso.com.br; Rua dos Arcos 24, Lapa) This cultural center offers a wide range of courses, including dancing lessons in African styles and samba. Those seeking something different can sign up for classes in percussion, acrobatics (run by the respected dance-theater-circus outfit Intrépida Trupe) or capoeira. Percussion and circus-arts courses typically cost R$210 for twice-weekly classes for a month. Capoeira costs R$120 for a month.

You can also take a drop-in yoga class (R$30), currently held on Tuesday and Thursday at 12:30pm and Wednesday at 12:45pm.

1

2

MICHAEL HEFFERNAN/LONELY PLANET ©

1. Outdoor bars, Lapa (p142) 2. Alfresco dining, Copacabana Beach (p92) 3. Dancing, Rio Scenarium (p143), Lapa

Nightlife

By night, the energy on Rio's streets is electric. All-night street parties in Lapa, old-school samba *gafieiras* (dance halls), impromptu jam sessions at outdoor bars, riotous dance floors presided over by celebrated DJs – Rio's nightlife is all this and much more. The only thing you have to do is show up.

Lapa

Epicenter of Rio's samba scene, this atmospheric neighborhood on the edge of Centro always has something afoot. At weekends the party takes over and the streets are closed to traffic.

Nightclubs

Lapa aside, some of the best spots for dancing are in the Zona Sul, with trendy places like Barzin (p203) bringing in the party people.

Botecos

A much-loved institution in Rio, the *boteco* is a casual open-sided bar where *cariocas* (Rio residents) gather over ice-cold *chopes* (draft beer) and snacks. Eating is an essential part of Rio's drinking culture.

Lagoa

The pretty lagoon (p80) behind Ipanema and Leblon is a favorite spot for couples at night. Lakeside kiosks serve up cocktails and live music (as well as food) in tranquil open-air settings.

Alfresco

Cariocas make good use of the warm nights, with open-air drinking spots all around town. Try the Travessa do Comércio in Centro for colonial flavor, Bar Urca (p108) for great views, or the Copacabana kiosks for afternoon cocktails on the beachfront.

Zona Norte

Neighborhood Top Five

❶ **Maracanã Football Stadium** (p150) Hearing the roar of the crowds as some of the world's best players take to the field inside this hallowed arena.

❷ **Feira Nordestina** (p152) Browsing handicrafts, snacking on Northeastern dishes and partner-dancing to live *forró* inside this enormous, sprawling fair.

❸ **CADEG** (p152) Enjoying a tasty lunch at one of a number of good restaurants at this market.

❹ **Quinta da Boa Vista** (p152) Taking a stroll amid the greenery of this former estate of the Portuguese imperial family.

❺ **Salgueiro** (p154) Joining in the pre-Carnaval revelry for a big Saturday-night party at one of Rio's best-loved samba schools.

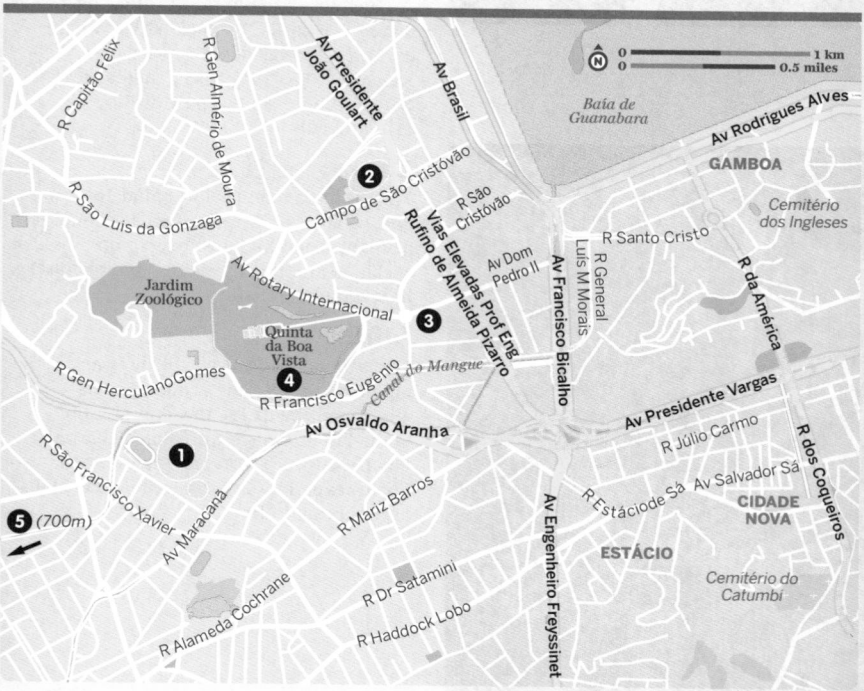

For more detail of this area see Map p253

Explore Zona Norte

Vast Zona Norte sprawls many kilometers toward the Baixada Fluminense. It boasts fewer attractions than the Zona Sul and Centro, but there are still excellent reasons to visit, including soccer rowdiness at Maracanã, great views from little-visited landmarks and historical intrigue at former palaces.

The Zona Norte is home to many distinct neighborhoods and favelas (slums, informal communitites), including several with pivotal roles in the competitive Carnaval parade. Rehearsals at samba schools are a worthwhile draw and attract huge crowds as Carnaval approaches each year.

In the 19th century the Zona Norte was the home of the nobility, including Dom João VI. The area saw dramatic transformation as mangrove swamps were cleared to make way for stately homes. In the 20th century the wealthy moved out and exploding urbanism transformed the landscape into a gritty, heavily populated, working-class suburb. A visit is recommended for those who want to see how the rest of Rio lives. You'll escape the tourist crowds and experience an authentic slice of Rio far removed from the picture-postcard sights of the Zona Sul.

Although the area is spread out, several sites are fairly close together and are easily reached by metro, lying just west of Centro. Other places are best reached by taxi.

Local Life

Nightlife Dusting off your dance shoes and joining *forró*-loving crowds for a long night of live music and dancing in the Feira Nordestina (p152).

Markets CADEG (p152) is Rio's largest market and a fine place to browse the endless rows of produce, meats and fish; it's also home to great-value restaurants, with a festive air (and live music) on weekends.

Eating & Drinking A handful of new bars and eating spots, like Bar Kalango (p152), have opened just south of Praça da Bandeira, drawing food-minded crowds from all across town.

Getting There & Away

Bus – Maracanã From Copacabana, Ipanema and Leblon (464); to Copacabana and Ipanema (456 and 457), to Leblon (464).

Metro – Maracanã Maracanã.

Bus – Quinta da Boa Vista Copacabana, Ipanema and Leblon (474).

Metro – Quinta da Boa Vista São Cristóvão (for Museu Nacional and Jardim Zoológico).

Lonely Planet's Top Tip

The best time to visit this area is at the weekend, when you'll find the markets, parks and other attractions at their liveliest.

Best Places to Eat

- Aconchego Carioca (p152)
- Barsa (p153)
- Da Gema (p153)
- Bar Kalango (p152)

For reviews, see p152

Best Places to Drink

- Salgueiro (p154)
- Noo Cachaçaria (p153)
- Hop Lab (p154)

For reviews, see p153

Best Live Music

- Renascença Clube (p154)
- Feira Nordestina (p152)

For reviews, see p152

TOP SIGHT
MARACANÃ FOOTBALL STADIUM

Rio's Maracanã stadium is hallowed ground among football lovers. The massive arena has been the site of legendary victories and crushing defeats. Maracanã played a starring role in the 2014 World Cup and hosted the opening and closing ceremonies of the 2016 Summer Olympics. No matter who takes the field, the 78,800-seat open-air arena comes to life in spectacular fashion on game days.

DON'T MISS

- A match between any of Rio's hometown rivals
- Peering behind the scenes on a stadium tour

PRACTICALITIES

- Map p253, A3
- 21 2334-1705
- www.suderj.rj.gov.br/maracana.asp
- Av Maracanã, São Cristóvão

The Spectacle

A game at Maracanã is a must-see. Matches here rate among the most exciting in the world, and the fans among the most colorful. The devoted pound huge samba drums, spread vast flags across great swaths of the stadium, dance in the aisles, and detonate smoke bombs in team colors. You'll hear – and feel – the deafening roar when the home team takes the field, and a wall of sound and palpable air of near hysteria will hit you when a player pounds the ball into the back of the net. Things are only slightly calmer since alcohol was banned inside the stadium back in 2003 – though with pressure from FIFA, an exception to the law was put in place for the 2014 World Cup.

Going to a Game

Games take place year-round and generally happen on Saturday or Sunday (starting at 4pm or 6pm) or on Wednesday and Thursday (around 8:30pm). Seating at the stadium is by sector, A through F. The north (E and F) and south (C and B) seats are behind the goals and are generally the cheapest and liveliest sections. East (D) and West (A) sectors have better sight lines and are pricier; these have numbered seats and are not as rowdy as the goal seats. Maracanã Mais is part of the west sector, with buffet service included

CP DC PRESS/SHUTTERSTOCK ©

with your ticket. The ticket price is R$40 to R$80 for most games.

Renovations & Olympic Highs & Lows

Maracanã remains Brazil's largest sports arena, seating nearly 79,000 fans (78,838 to be exact) – which is not as many as in years past. It underwent a massive R$1 billion renovation before the 2014 World Cup. During renovations, all seats were replaced in the arena, the lower level was demolished to improve visibility, access ramps were expanded and the stadium added a new roof, which now covers all seats. It's also sustainably designed – complete with a rainwater collection system. The facade, which is a protected landmark under the National Institute of Historical & Artistic Heritage, has remain unchanged.

In 2016 the stadium took the spotlight once again as the setting for the opening and closing ceremonies of the Summer Olympics and Paralympic Games. After the Olympics, Maracanã fell into disrepair during Rio's economic crisis, and sat vacant for nearly a year. The lights, however, have turned back on, and the stadium continues to be the staging post for matches between Rio's league teams – Flamengo, Fluminense, Vasco da Gama and Botafogo.

Maracanã Tour

For a behind-the-scenes look at the stadium, take a tour. A must for football fans, the tour takes you through the press box, the grandstand, into the locker rooms and then through the tunnel out onto the field. You'll also visit a room that pays tribute to Brazilian legends who made history here, like Pelé and Garrincha. Tours (R$60) take place from 9am to 4pm; on game days the last tour starts four hours before kick-off.

GAME-DAY TOURS

If you prefer to go in a group, a number of English-speaking tour operators organize game-day outings, including round-trip transportation. Leading big-group tours are **Brazil Expedition** (www.brazilexpedition.com) and **Be A Local** (www.bealocal.com). For something more personalized, independent guide **Sergio Manhães** (www.futebolnomaracana.blogspot.com) takes small groups (usually via metro) on game days. Tours cost from R$100 per person.

The first time Brazil hosted the World Cup was in 1950, when the final was played inside Maracanã stadium, which had been built in preparation for the tournament. Brazil made it to the finals, and more than 170,000 fans packed the stadium to watch the match against Uruguay. With the match tied at 1–1, Uruguay scored a goal with just 11 minutes left to play. The victory stunned the crowd and left a deep scar on the nation's psyche – this crippling defeat on home soil is still in parlance today and referred to as the *maracanaço*, roughly translated as 'that God-awful thing that happened in Maracanã!'

SIGHTS

The Zona Norte sprawls for many miles north and west of the city center. The main attractions for visitors, however, are within easy reach by metro. These are the Maracanã Football Stadium (Brazil's most famous sporting arena) and the Quinta da Boa Vista (the former Portuguese royal estate). Further out, you'll find the Feira Nordestina – a market and food and entertainment complex that's quite lively on weekends.

MARACANÃ FOOTBALL STADIUM — STADIUM

See p150.

FEIRA NORDESTINA — MARKET

Map p253 (Northeastern Fair; ☎21 2580-5335; www.facebook.com/feiradesaocristovaoofficial; Campo de São Cristóvão; R$5, Tue-Thu free; ⏲10am-6pm Tue-Sat, to 8pm Sun) This enormous fair (32,000 sq meters, with over 600 stalls) is not to be missed. It showcases the culture of the Northeast of Brazil, with *barracas* (food stalls) selling Bahian dishes as well as beer and *cachaça* (sugarcane alcohol), which flows in great abundance here. The best time to go is at the weekend, when you can catch live bands playing *forró,* plus samba groups and comedy troupes, Música Popular Brasileira (MPB) and *rodas de capoeira* (capoeira circles).

In addition to food and drink, you can browse music CDs (*forró,* of course), hammocks and a wide assortment of handicrafts.

SAMBÓDROMO — STADIUM

Map p253 (www.sambadrome.com; Marques do Sapuçai) The epicenter of Rio's Carnaval, the Sambódromo was designed by Oscar Niemeyer and completed in 1984. During the big parades, come here for the fantastic views from the stands of the elaborate floats, whirling dancers and pounding drum corps. The open-air arena received a makeover for the 2016 Olympics, with improved sight lines and a more symmetrical design in keeping with Niemeyer's original vision.

QUINTA DA BOA VISTA — PARK

Map p253 (☎21 3938-6900; ⏲8am-6pm) Quinta da Boa Vista was the estate of the Portuguese imperial family until the Republic was proclaimed. Today it's a large and busy park with gardens and lakes. On weekends it's crowded with football games and families from the Zona Norte.

CADEG — MARKET

Map p253 (Centro de Abastecimento do Estado da Guanabara, Supply Center of Guanabara State; www.cadeg.com.br; Capitão Félix 110, Benfica; ⏲1am-5pm Mon-Sat, to 2pm Sun) While CADEG doesn't have quite the same ring to it as 'Ipanema Beach,' this voluminous market packs a treasure trove of fruits, vegetables, meats, fish, cheeses, flowers and spices. And while the 350-plus shops are mostly a wholesale affair (hence the 1am opening time), the real reason to come here is for lunch, with a number of good and decidedly unfussy restaurants spread around the four-story building.

EATING

Formally a culinary desert, the district has seen much new life with the opening of restaurants and bars near Praça da Bandeira. These casual spots make a great setting for a snack and pub crawl. For a foodie excursion, sign up with Eat Rio Food Tours (p204).

ACONCHEGO CARIOCA — BRAZILIAN $$

Map p253 (☎21 2273-1035; Barão de Iguatemi 245, Praça da Bandeira; mains for 2 people R$80-120; ⏲noon-11pm Tue-Sat, to 5pm Sun) Aconchego Carioca consistently ranks as one of the best places in town to eat traditional Brazilian cuisine. The setting, cozy and welcoming, has a casual neighborhood vibe, but attracts diners from across the city who come for *bobó de camarão* (shrimp and coconut milk stew), pork ribs with guava sauce, and a *cachaça*-tinged flan for dessert.

BAR KALANGO — BRAZILIAN $$

Map p253 (☎21 2504-0088; www.facebook.com/barkalango; Joaquim Palhares 513, Praça da Bandeira; lunch special R$35, appetizers from R$15; ⏲noon-6pm Tue, Wed, Sat & Sun, to 10pm Thu & Fri) This small, colorful bar is yet another in the growing number of watering holes and restaurants that pepper the neighborhood of Praça da Bandeira. The menu features hearty dishes from Northeast Brazil along with superior versions of traditional bar snacks. The drinks list is short, but includes the mandatory caipirinha and a range of juices.

MUSEU NACIONAL

The Museu Nacional in the Quinta da Boa Vista was once among the great treasures of Brazil. The 200-year-old former palace housed the Portuguese royal family and subsequently the Brazilian imperial family until 1892 when it was transformed into a museum. Over the years, its collection grew to some 20 million objects. It housed one of the nation's most important natural history and archaeological collections, complete with dinosaur fossils, saber-toothed tiger skeletons, pre-Columbian ceramics from the littoral and high plains of Peru, a huge meteorite and an 11,500-year-old skull — one of the oldest human remains in the Americas.

Sadly, the entire collection went up in flames in a devastating fire in 2018. The loss, estimated at 90% of the collection, was of such significance that the fire made headlines around the world. Critics said the tragedy could have been prevented: the building was deeply underfunded and curators had been constantly lobbying, to no avail, for more financial support, including for infrastructure and fireproofing improvements.

DA GEMA — BRAZILIAN $$

(☎21 3549-1480; Barão de Mesquita 615, Tijuca; snacks R$8-32; ⏲6pm-midnight Tue-Fri, from 1pm Sat, 1-6pm Sun) Well off the beaten path, this humble-looking *botequim* (bar with table service) serves mouthwatering *petiscos* (appetizers). It was started by three culinary graduates, who have elevated simple bar ingredients into high art with dishes like *pastel de feijao-preto* (black-bean pasties), house-made *linguiça* (sausage) and *fondue da gema* (polenta with crunchy pork rinds and sweet peppers, served with pork ribs and sausage).

Its location near Salgueiro (p154), 400m away, makes it a good pre-party spot on Saturday nights.

RESTAURANTE QUINTA DA BOA VISTA — PORTUGUESE $$

Map p253 (☎21 2589-4279; www.restaurantequintaboavista.com.br; Quinta da Boa Vista, São Cristóvão; mains R$52-85; ⏲10am-6pm) Inside the former 1822 chapel of the former royal palace, this place serves excellent *bacalhau ao forno* (oven-baked codfish), *caldeirada de frutos de mar* (seafood stew) and other Portuguese classics. The *picanha* (rump steak) is also top-notch. The servers, dressed in period costume, add a whimsical touch to proceedings.

BARSA — PORTUGUESE $$$

Map p253 (☎21 2585-3743; 4th fl, Capitão Félix 110, Benfica; mains R$75-180; ⏲noon-4pm Mon-Thu, to 5pm Fri-Sun) Inside the massive CADEG market, Barsa serves mouthwatering dishes made with the freshest ingredients imaginable (not surprising, since Rio's largest produce market surrounds the place). The most famous dish is its roast suckling pig with all the fixings, which serves four and costs about R$300 – though half servings are also available. On Sunday there's live *chorinho* (a kind of instrumental music).

DRINKING & NIGHTLIFE

Samba and Carnaval fans shouldn't miss a night out at one of Rio's famed *escolas de samba* (samba schools or clubs) – such as Salgueiro (p154). There's also samba excitement twice weekly at Renascença Clube (p154). The gritty hood of Praça da Bandeira has experienced a renaissance of late, with new drinking spots, including a microbrew bar and an inviting *cachaçaria* (place serving sugarcane alcohol).

NOO CACHAÇARIA — BAR

Map p253 (☎021 3689-4388; www.facebook.com/noocachacaria; Barão de Iguatemi 358; ⏲5-10pm Tue-Fri, noon-11pm Sat) This cozy little bar is one of the highlights of the growing oasis of drinking dens in the otherwise drab neighborhood of Praça da Bandeira. While the impressive list of *cachaça* options will appeal to connoisseurs of Brazil's national spirit, the main draw for everyone else will be the inventive snacks, sharing plates and *cachaça*-based cocktails.

The standout drink is the Aditivada, a caipirinha made with the addition of a sweet molasses-like cane syrup. The fruit

WORTH A DETOUR

BEACHES EAST OF RIO

A number of beaches lie just east of Niterói. The ones closest to town are too polluted for swimming, but as you continue out you'll reach some pristine beaches – **Piratininga**, **Camboinhas**, **Itaipu** and finally **Itacoatiara**, the most fabulous of the bunch. Framed by two looming hills on either side of the shore and backed by vegetation, the white sands of Itacoatiara seem a world away from the urban beaches of Rio. *Barracas* (food stalls) sell scrumptious plates of fish, and there are also food stands overlooking the beach. The surf is strong here – evidenced by the many surfers jockeying for position – so swim with caution. To get here, you can take bus 38 or any bus labeled 'Itacoatiara' from the ferry terminal (R$5, 50 minutes). If you're traveling in a group, you can negotiate a return fare with a taxi driver.

shot *batidas* are also not to be missed. On Thursdays there are oysters, shipped up fresh from the southern Brazilian coast, and from time to time (check the Facebook page to confirm), it offers an all-you-can-eat selection of traditional Brazilian comfort-food dishes.

HOP LAB — BEER HALL

Map p253 (☎21 3217-1146; www.facebook.com/hoplab; Barão de Iguatemi 292; ⏲5pm-midnight Tue-Thu, to 2am Fri & Sat, 3-10pm Sun) This beer-lover's paradise offers 30 draft beers on rotation – more than any other bar in Rio – many of which are locally brewed. The English-speaking waiters are certified beer sommeliers, ready to provide guidance and recommendations to curious or indecisive customers. Hearty staples such as burgers and croquettes should keep the hungry drinker satisfied.

Hop Lab is located on Rua Barão de Iguatemi, home to enough quality eating and drinking options to easily justify the taxi/metro ride from Zona Sul.

☆ ENTERTAINMENT

RENASCENÇA CLUBE — SAMBA

(☎213253-2322; www.facebook.com/renascencaclube; Rua Barão de São Francisco 54, Andaraí; ⏲5-10pm Mon & Sat) For an authentic slice of Rio, head to one of the massive open-air samba parties that happen several times a week in Andaraí. The setup is simple: a handful of musicians around a table play samba, while huge dance-loving crowds gather around. Monday nights (*samba do trabalhador* or 'samba for the worker'), which are lead by maestro Moacyr Luz, are excellent.

If you like samba, don't mind big crowds and are up for a bit of adventure, then this place is for you – it's well off the tourist circuit.

MANGUEIRA — SAMBA

Map p253 (☎21 2567-3419; www.mangueira.com.br; Visconde de Niterói 1072, Mangueira; ⏲10pm Sat) One of Rio's most famous samba schools, Mangueira has many followers all across the city. They come out en masse in their green and pink (Mangueira's colors), when the school parades on Carnaval weekend.

SALGUEIRO — SAMBA

(☎21 2238-9226; www.salgueiro.com.br; Silva Teles 104, Andaraí; ⏲10pm Sat) One of the best samba schools for foreigners to visit, Salgueiro hosts big Saturday-night parties from late August until Carnaval. Expect live music, ever-flowing caipirinhas and lots of fiery footwork.

Barra da Tijuca & Western Rio

Neighborhood Top Five

❶ **Parque Nacional da Tijuca** (p158) Hiking through tropical rainforest, enjoying memorable views from rocky lookouts and recovering beneath cool waterfalls.

❷ **Praia da Barra da Tijuca** (p157) Spending the day basking on the wide golden sands of one of Rio's loveliest (and longest) beaches.

❸ **Sítio Burle Marx** (p157) Exploring the lushly decadent gardens while learning about the eponymous legendary landscape architect.

❹ **Casa do Pontal** (p157) Delving into Brazil's rich folk-art traditions at this impressive museum, home to an astonishing array of finely crafted pieces from across the country.

❺ **Parque Ecológico Chico Mendes** (p157) Looking for capybaras and other wildlife on the peaceful trails of this park in Barra's western end.

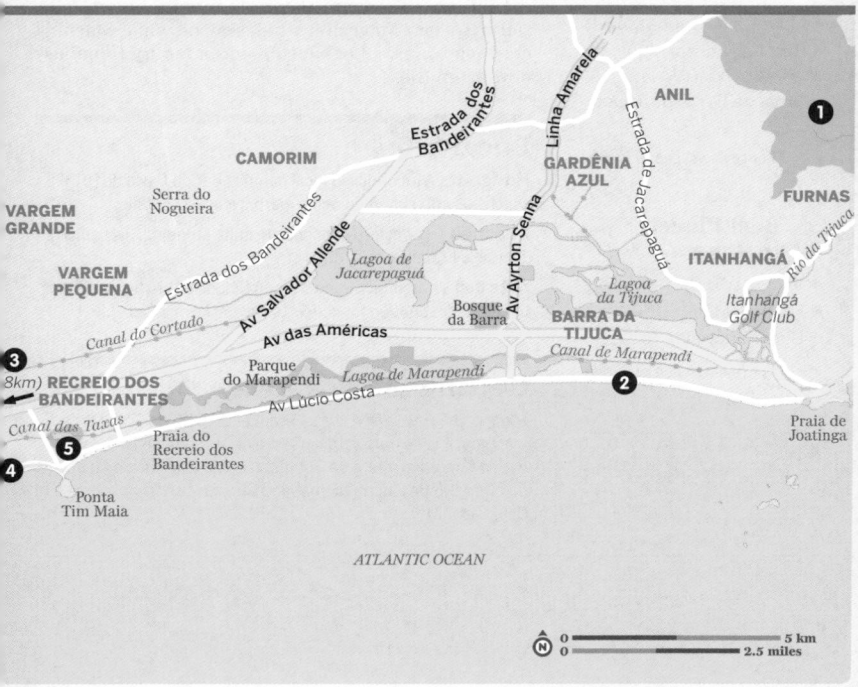

For more detail of this area see Map p254

Lonely Planet's Top Tip

You can go for a spin on the beachfront using Bike Rio (p201), the city's extensive bike-sharing network. If you don't want to make the return trip, you can drop your bike at a kiosk (like the one found at the western end of Av Lúcio Costa, near Pedra do Pontal) and take a ride-sharing service back.

Best Places to Eat

- Laguna Restaurante (p158)
- Don Pascual (p158)
- Bira (p159)

For reviews, see p157

Best Places to Walk

- Floresta da Tijuca (p158)
- Parque Natural Municipal de Marapendi (p157)
- Praia da Barra da Tijuca (p157)

For reviews, see p157

Best Places to Shop

- Village (p159)
- Fashion Mall (p159)
- Barra Shopping (p159)

For reviews, see p159

Explore Barra da Tijuca & Western Rio

The Miami of Rio, Barra da Tijuca is a sprawling suburb with huge malls and entertainment complexes, long traffic corridors and very little pedestrian movement. Barra – as it's known locally – is also where much of the 2016 Summer Olympic Games were held (sadly the stadiums were largely abandoned afterwards and aren't open to the public). The beach here is the real attraction, a wide and lovely 15km-long stretch of shoreline.

The commercial area feels quite different from other parts of Rio, as Barra's development happened relatively recently. The middle class first began moving here in the 1970s, when *cariocas* (residents of Rio) fled crowded, crime-ridden streets to live on an unpopulated stretch of beachfront. Today, the influx of new residents has created crowded, problematic conditions once again.

While first-time visitors to Rio don't always make it to Barra da Tijuca, there are some intriguing sights here, aside from the beach. The Sítio Burle Marx (p157) contains some of the city's most picturesque gardens, while the Casa do Pontal (p157) houses a fascinating collection of folk art.

Once you get beyond the development of Barra, the region gets less and less urban, and you'll soon feel like you're deep in the tropics. Some of Rio's best beaches lie out this way. There are also great restaurants in idyllic settings where you can feast on seafood while watching crashing waves, all of which seems a far cry from busy downtown Rio.

Local Life

Hangouts A much-loved local haunt is Bar do Oswaldo (p159), which has good bar food and superb tropical cocktails.

Beaches The western beaches are quite stunning, particularly Joatinga, Prainha and Grumari.

Arts Barra's architecturally striking Cidade das Artes (p159) is the go-to destination for concerts and performances.

Getting There & Away

Metro The new *linha* 4 (line 4) connects Barra da Tijuca to Ipanema. It runs from Jardim Oceânico station (eastern Barra) to São Conrado, Antero de Quental (Leblon), Jardim de Alah (Leblon), NS da Paz (Ipanema) and General Osório (Ipanema and Copacabana).

SIGHTS

Barra da Tijuca doesn't have a dense concentration of sights. Those that are here are sprinkled far and wide, and you'll need a car to reach most areas. Travelers usually come here on organized trips (or with their own hire car) to visit the Sítio Burle Marx, the Casa do Pontal and the western beaches.

SÍTIO BURLE MARX — GARDENS

(☎21 2410-1412; visitas.srbm@iphan.gov.br; Estrada Roberto Burle Marx 2019, Guaratiba; R$10; ⏲tours 9:30am & 1:30pm Tue-Sat) This 35-hectare estate was once the home of Brazil's most famous landscape architect, Roberto Burle Marx. The estate's lush vegetation includes thousands of plant species, some of which are rare varieties from different corners of the globe. A 17th-century **Benedictine chapel** also lies on the estate, along with Burle Marx's original farmhouse and studio, where you can see displays of paintings, furniture and sculptures by the talented designer. Tours are by advance appointment only.

On the downside, it's a very long drive to get out here (either take a costly taxi or go by private vehicle, making sure you have a good map or GPS). Also, you're not allowed to wander on your own and there's no food at the museum.

PRAINHA — BEACH

One of the most picturesque beaches near Rio, Prainha is backed by cliffs and thick forest. The sea can be rough, but it's a favorite among surfers. It feels secluded during the week, but gets crowded on weekends (go early to beat the crowds).

You'll need to take a taxi or a ride share to get to this beach, which is roughly 22km west of the Jardim Oceânico metro station in Barra da Tijuca.

PRAIA DA BARRA DA TIJUCA — BEACH

Map p254 (Av Sernambetiba, Recreio dos Bandeirantes) The best thing about Barra is the beach. It stretches for 18km, with the blue sea lapping at the shore. The first few kilometers of its eastern end are filled with bars and seafood restaurants.

PARQUE NATURAL MUNICIPAL DE MARAPENDI — PARK

Map p254 (Av Alfredo Balthazar da Silveira, Recreio dos Bandeirantes; ⏲8am-5pm Tue-Sun) FREE Near Barra da Tijuca's coastal strip, this155-hectare biological reserve has photogenic views over the Marapendi lagoon dotted with mangroves, towering jacarandas and other tropical tree species. There are lots of bird species (keep an eye out for rarities like the black-billed toucan), a few caiman and marmosets. There's also a small education center with info on the flora and fauna of the area.

CASA DO PONTAL — MUSEUM

Map p254 (☎21 2490-4013; www.museucasadopontal.com.br; Estrada do Pontal 3295, Recreio dos Bandeirantes; permanent collection/temporary exhibits R$12/4; ⏲9:30am-5pm Tue-Sun) Owned by French designer Jacques Van de Beuque, this impressive museum containing some 4500 pieces has one of the best folk-art collections in Brazil. The assorted artifacts are grouped according to theme, including rural life, popular festivals, religion and erotic art. The grounds of the museum are surrounded by lush vegetation.

PARQUE ECOLÓGICO CHICO MENDES — PARK

Map p254 (☎21 2437-6400; Km 17, Av Jarbas de Carvalho 679, Recreio dos Bandeirantes; ⏲8am-5pm Tue-Sun) This 40-hectare park was created in 1989 and named after the Brazilian ecological activist who was murdered for his work. The park protects the remaining sand-spit vegetation from real-estate speculators. The facilities include a visitor center and ecological trails that lead to a small lake.

Enter on the north side of the park.

BOSQUE DA BARRA — PARK

Map p254 (Av das Américas 6000, at Av Ayrton Senna, Barra da Tijuca; ⏲7am-5pm Tue-Sun) FREE Covering 50 hectares of salt-marsh vegetation, this park is a refuge and breeding area for many small birds and animals, and you might spy capybaras, agouti or marmosets (and caiman gliding through the waters). The woods have a jogging track and cycle path but not much infrastructure (there are no park benches, picnic tables etc).

EATING

Far from the bustling streets of central Rio, some of the city's more rustic dining experiences can be found, such

WORTH A DETOUR

FLORESTA DA TIJUCA – PARQUE NACIONAL DA TIJUCA

The **Parque Nacional da Tijuca** (☎21 2492-2250; www.parquedatijuca.com.br; Estrada da Cascatinha 850, Alto da Boa Vista; ⏲8am-5pm) FREE is all that's left of the Atlantic rainforest that once surrounded Rio de Janeiro. This 39-sq-km tropical-jungle preserve is an exuberant green, with beautiful trees, creeks and waterfalls, mountainous terrain and high peaks. It has an excellent, well-marked trail system. Candomblistas (practitioners of the Afro-Brazilian religion of Candomblé) leave offerings by the roadside, families have picnics and serious hikers climb the 1012m to the summit of Pico da Tijuca.

The heart of the forest is the **Alto da Boa Vista** area in the **Floresta (Forest) da Tijuca**, which has many natural and human-made features. Among the highlights of this beautiful park are several waterfalls (**Cascatinha de Taunay**, **Cascata Gabriela** and **Cascata Diamantina**), a 19th-century chapel (**Capela Mayrink**) and numerous caves (**Gruta Luís Fernandes**, **Gruta Belmiro** and **Gruta Paulo e Virgínia**). Also in the park is a great picnic spot (**Bom Retiro**) and two restaurants – the elegant **Restaurante Os Esquilos** (Map p254; ☎21 2492-2197; www.osesquilos.com.br; Estrada da Cascatinha; mains R$60-95; ⏲noon-5pm Wed-Sun) and **Restaurante a Floresta** near the ruins of Major Archer's house (**Ruínas do Archer**).

The park is home to many different bird and animal species, including iguanas and monkeys, which you might encounter on one of the excellent day hikes you can make here (the trails are well signed). Good free trail maps are given out at the park entrance.

The entire park closes at sunset. It's best to go by car, though if you don't have a vehicle numerous outfits lead hiking tours, including Jungle Me (p51), Rio Adventures (p51) and Rio Natural (p51).

The best route by car is to take Rua Jardim Botânico two blocks past the Jardim Botânico (heading east from Gávea). Turn left on Rua Lopes Quintas and then follow the Tijuca or Corcovado signs for two quick left turns until you reach the back of the Jardim Botânico, where you turn right. Then follow the signs for a quick ascent into the forest and past the picturesque lookout points of Vista Chinesa and Mesa do Imperador. As soon as you seem to come out of the forest, turn right onto the main road and you'll see the stone columns to the entrance of Alto da Boa Vista on your left after a couple of kilometers. You can also drive up to Alto da Boa Vista by heading out to São Conrado and turning right up the hill at the Parque Nacional da Tijuca signs. Coming from Barra da Tijuca, take Estrada da Barra da Tijuca north, which eventually turns into Rua da Boa Vista, from which there are entrances into the park.

as open-air spots with beautiful views complemented by fresh seafood. The liveliest dining strip is along Av Olegário Maciel, about 900m east of the Jardim Oceânico metro stop.

LAGUNA RESTAURANTE — BRAZILIAN $$$

Map p254 (☎21 2495-1229; www.restaurantelaguna.com.br; Ilha da Gigóia 34, Barra da Tijuca; mains R$50-80, seafood mains for 2 people R$180-250; ⏲6pm-midnight Thu & Fri, 1-11pm Sat, 1-8pm Sun; ❄) Located on an island near the eastern section of Barra, this charming spot serves excellent seafood dishes meant for sharing. Start off with *casquinha de siri* (pulled crab), then move to a platter of grilled seafood or a rich *moqueca* (Bahian fish stew). The setting – open-air tables with lake and mountain views – is a big part of the allure. Reserve ahead.

If you're coming by metro, follow the signs to the Lagoa exit and walk to the Unimed e Posto Shell fuel station. Behind this, you can board a small ferry that makes the short trip to the island of Ilha da Gigóia.

DON PASCUAL — BRAZILIAN $$$

Map p254 (☎21 2428-6237; www.donpascual.com.br; Estrada do Sacarrão 867, Vargem Grande; mains R$64-86; ⏲noon-1am) Don Pascual has undeniable charm. Amid lush scenery you'll dine on open-sided wooden decks, listening to birdsong. Not surprisingly, by night it's all couples at the candlelit tables. The food is good – juicy *picanha* (beef rump), *moquequinha de frutas do mar* (seafood and coconut stew) and *ravioli de cordeiro* (lamb ravioli) – but not quite as dazzling as the ambience.

The only problem is that it's hard to get to; call ahead for specific directions. You can also spend the night, while day use (including access to pool, sauna and Jacuzzi) costs R$196, generally available Monday to Thursday only.

BIRA SEAFOOD **$$$**

(☎21 2410-8304; Estrada da Vendinha 68A, Barra de Guaratiba; mains for 3 people R$250-320; ⏲noon-5pm Thu-Sun) Splendid views await diners who make the trek to Bira. On a breezy wooden deck, you can partake in flavorful, rich seafood served in huge portions – big enough for three. It's located about 35km west of Rio in the marvelous seaside setting of Barra de Guaratiba, 45 to 80 minutes from the city, depending on traffic. Cash only.

DRINKING & NIGHTLIFE

The nightlife scene in Barra is a mostly local affair, and it's a good place to mingle with Brazilians. The best place to go bar-hopping is along Av Olegário Maciel, about 900m east of the Jardim Oceânico metro stop. On weekend nights, the open-sided bars and eating establishments are packed.

BAR DO OSWALDO BAR

Map p254 (www.facebook.com/bardooswaldo; Estrada do Joá 3896, Barra da Tijuca; ⏲noon-1am) Going strong since 1946, this Barra classic serves some of Rio's best *batidas* (icy cocktails of *cachaça* and fruit juice). On weekends there's often live music, and there's an easy-going vibe at all times, with plenty of outdoor seating and a huge menu of Brazilian favorites.

ENTERTAINMENT

CIDADE DAS ARTES PERFORMING ARTS

Map p254 (☎21 3325-0102; www.cidadedasartes.org; Av das Américas 5300, Barra da Tijuca) Barra's grandest arts complex is an R$500-million venture that houses an 1800-seat concert hall, as well as theaters, a chamber music hall, a cinema and a restaurant. It's home to the Brazilian Symphony Orchestra, and features a wide-ranging repertoire, including contemporary dance, puppet shows, jazz, musicals, choral recitals and experimental ensembles.

UCI – NEW YORK CITY CENTER CINEMA

Map p254 (☎21 2461-1818; www.ucicinemas.com.br; Av das Américas 5000, Barra da Tijuca) UCI – New York City Center is Brazil's largest megaplex, featuring 18 different screening rooms complete with large, comfortable chairs and stadium seating.

SHOPPING

VILLAGE MALL

Map p254 (☎21 3003-4177; www.shoppingvillagemall.com.br; Av das Américas 3900, Barra da Tijuca; ⏲10:30am-10:30pm Mon-Sat, 2-8pm Sun) This shopping behemoth is Rio's most extravagant mall, with high-end retailers such as Prada, Cartier, Tiffany & Co, Miu Miu, Dolce & Gabbana and Burberry, as well as an Apple store. For more local flavor, check out shops like Lenny, Osklen and Maria Filó.

BARRA SHOPPING MALL

Map p254 (☎21 4003-4131; www.barrashopping.com.br; Av das Américas 4666, Barra da Tijuca; ⏲10am-10pm Mon-Sat, 1-9pm Sun) Rio's largest mall (and one of the biggest on the continent) is an easy place to shop away a few hours – or days – as do 30 million shoppers each year. More than 500 stores clutter this 4km-long stretch, along with five movie screens, a kids' parkland and a wealth of dining options.

FASHION MALL MALL

(☎21 2111-4444; www.fashionmall.com.br; Estrada da Gávea 899, São Conrado; ⏲10am-10pm Mon-Sat, 3-9pm Sun) One of the city's most beautiful malls features plenty of luxe retailers – Fred Perry, L'Occitane and others – plus all of Brazil's most recognizable brands. It's located in the upper-class neighborhood of São Conrado.

RIO DESIGN BARRA SHOPPING CENTER

Map p254 (☎21 2430-3024; www.riodesignbarra.com.br; Av das Américas 7777, Barra da Tijuca; ⏲10am-10pm Mon-Sat, 3-9pm Sun) This architecturally rich center features a number of excellent home-furnishing stores

WORTH A DETOUR

BEACHES WEST OF RIO

Although Copacabana and Ipanema are Rio's most famous stretches of sand, there are many inviting beaches to the west, some in spectacular natural settings.

The first major beach you'll reach heading west of Leblon is **Praia do Pepino** in São Conrado. It's near where the hang gliders land, and it's not the cleanest beach around. Further west is the small, lovely but well-concealed **Praia da Joatinga**, reachable by a steep path down a rocky hillside. Be aware of the tides, so you don't get stranded.

Although it gets crowded on weekends, **Praia do Recreio dos Bandeirantes** is almost deserted during the week. The large rock acts as a natural breakwater, creating a calm bay. The 2km-long stretch of sand is popular with families.

The secluded 700m-long **Praia da Prainha** lies just past Recreio. It's one of the best surfing beaches in Rio, so it's always full of surfers. Waves come highly recommended here.

The most isolated and unspoiled beach close to the city, **Praia de Grumari** is quiet during the week and packed on weekends with *cariocas* (residents of Rio) looking to get away from city beaches. It is a gorgeous setting, surrounded by mountains and lush vegetation.

From Grumari, a narrow road climbs over a jungle-covered hillside toward **Praia de Guaratiba**. West of here you'll get a good view of the **Restinga da Marambaia** (the vegetation-rich strip between the beach and the mainland), closed off to the public by a naval base. *Cariocas* enjoy eating lunch at several of the seafood restaurants in the area.

It's very difficult to reach these beaches by public transport. It's best to go by private car or taxi. Traffic can be quite heavy, so allow plenty of time for the trip.

selling designer lamps, vases, decorative pieces and furniture. It also has some very good restaurants, a cinema and a few art galleries.

VIA PARQUE SHOPPING SHOPPING CENTER

Map p254 (☎21 2430-5100; www.shoppingviaparque.com.br; Av Ayrton Senna 3000, Barra da Tijuca; ⏲10am-10pm Mon-Sat, 1-9pm Sun) With 200 stores, a huge multiscreen cinema and an abundance of restaurants, this shopping center is the heart of Rio's thriving consumer culture. The center also houses one of the city's big, busy and diverse concert arenas.

SPORTS & ACTIVITIES

BARRA WATER SHUTTLE BOATING

Map p254 (☎21 99925-2547; www.bws.tur.br; adult/child R$140/110; ⏲tours 10am, 1pm & 4pm) For a different side of Barra, don't miss this fascinating three-hour boat tour that takes you through the lagoons of the region. Amid a lush watery landscape there are excellent wildlife-watching opportunities: many birds, plus the odd caiman and capybara. The English-speaking guide offers a wealth of info on the area. Call ahead to reserve a spot and arrange a departure location.

Sleeping

Rio has a wide range of lodging, including B&Bs, hostels and guesthouses; there are scores of luxury hotels, particularly in Copacabana. Prices are a bit less than what you'd pay in a North American oceanside city such as Miami or LA. An abundance of options keeps rates from going sky high, except during Carnaval and other major events.

Hotels

Rio has a few appealing new boutique and luxury hotels, but apart from the upscale options the selection can be somewhat lackluster. Most hotels are in glass-and-steel high-rises, with marble- and chrome-filled lobbies, and comfortable but uninspiring rooms. The best features will be the view (if there is one) and the door by which to exit the room and explore this fascinating city. Amenities to look for include pools, wi-fi and beach service (towels, chairs and attendants).

Hostels

With more than 100 hostels scattered around the city, Rio does not lack for budget lodging. Hostels are great settings for meeting other travelers, and with more and more Brazilians traveling, your dorm mate is just as likely to be from Porto Alegre as Perth. Rio's hostels vary in price and style. The best options are in Copacabana and Ipanema, though you'll also find some decent crash pads in Botafogo and Lapa.

Apartment Rentals

There are numerous apartment-rental outfits in Ipanema and Copacabana, though you can also go through Airbnb (www.airbnb.com). This site allows you to rent a whole apartment or simply a room in a shared flat, making it a good way to meet *cariocas* (Rio residents).

If you book an apartment through an agency, nightly high-season rates start at around R$200 for a small studio apartment in Copacabana and R$350 for one in Ipanema. Typically, you'll need to pay 30% to 50% up front; some agencies accept credit cards, and others use PayPal. Make sure you ask whether utilities and cleaning fees are included in the price. Reputable outfits include Rio Spot Homes (p166), **Ipanema for Rent** (Map p228; ☎21 99603-2109, 21 2267-5264; www.ipanemaforrentrj.com; Prudente de Morais 1008, Ipanema; apt from R$310) and Blame It on Rio 4 Travel (p166).

Prices & Reservations

Rooms with an ocean view cost about 30% to 50% more than rooms without. During the summer (December through March), hotel rates typically rise by about 30% and many places book up well in advance, so it's wise to reserve ahead. There's no getting around it: prices double or triple for New Year's Eve and Carnaval, and most accommodations, including hostels, will only book in four- or seven-day blocks around these holidays. It's never too early to book for Carnaval, with better places filling up to a year in advance.

Breakfast

Nearly every guesthouse, hostel and hotel serves some form of *café da manha* (breakfast). At cheaper places this may only be a roll and instant coffee; better places serve fresh fruit, juices, strong coffee, yogurt, cheese, cured meats, fresh bread and perhaps cooked eggs. Oddly, Rio's most expensive lodgings often charge for breakfast.

NEED TO KNOW

Price Ranges

The following price ranges refer to a double room with bathroom in high season (December to March). Unless otherwise stated, breakfast is included in the price. Many hotels add 5% to 15% in taxes and service charges, though cheaper places don't generally bother with this.

$	less than R$200
$$	R$200–500
$$$	more than R$500

Ocean Views

You can expect to pay 30% to 50% more for a room with an ocean view.

Lonely Planet's Top Choices

Casa Beleza (p169) Friendly hosts and an enticing pool in a villa guesthouse in Santa Teresa.

Hotel Santa Teresa (p169) Rio's finest boutique hotel, with a great restaurant and bar.

Pouso Verde (p165) Charming guesthouse in a peaceful Jardim Botânico location.

Maze Inn (p168) Unique English-run place with striking views in Tavares Bastos favela.

Belmond Copacabana Palace (p167) Gorgeous, historic hotel with great restaurants and top service.

Hotel Emiliano (p166) Beautifully designed rooms, a jaw-dropping roof deck and a great beachfront location.

Best by Budget

$

Mango Tree (p164) Great social scene and fun crowd in Ipanema.

El Misti (p164) Friendly hostel with a perfect location in Ipanema, plus more party-minded branches in Copacabana.

Cabana Copa (p165) Buzzing hostel in a peaceful location in Copacabana.

$$

Casa Cool Beans (p169) Wonderfully welcoming villa with pool in Santa Teresa.

LSH Lifestyle (p170) Great value for the money at this luxe option in Barra.

Rio Spot Homes (p166) Reliable rental outfit with apartment listings across the Zona Sul.

$$$

Sofitel Rio de Janeiro Ipanema (p165) With a brand-new location facing Ipanema Beach.

Hotel Fasano (p164) Join the celebrity set in this Philippe Starck–designed Ipanema hotel.

Porto Bay Rio Internacional (p167) A beachfront favorite in Copacabana.

Best Unusual Stays

Casa Caminho do Corcovado (p168) Idyllic B&B amid rainforest surroundings.

Rio Surf 'N Stay (p170) Get away from it all (and surf!) at this Recreio hostel.

Don Pascual (p170) Incredible setting amid tropical rainforest, with an enticing pool and restaurant.

Best Boutique Lodging

Vila Galé (p170) Gorgeous new property in Rio's samba epicenter of Lapa.

Yoo2 (p167) Ultra-hip newcomer to Botafogo with artful touches and a panoramic rooftop.

Mama Shelter (p169) Bohemian-chic guest rooms in Santa Teresa, plus a great bar and restaurant.

Best Guesthouses

Marta Rio Guesthouse (p166) Top-floor high-rise B&B in Copacabana with jaw-dropping views.

Margarida's Pousada (p164) Easy-going option in an ideal Ipanema location.

Casa da Gente (p169) Eco-minded guesthouse above Lapa.

Casa Áurea (p169) Laid-back Santa Teresa guesthouse with a hammock-filled garden.

Mama Ruisa (p170) Peaceful villa in Santa Teresa with high-end rooms and a pool.

Where to Stay

NEIGHBORHOOD	FOR	AGAINST
Ipanema & Leblon	Great location near the beach and the lake, with Rio's best restaurants and bars surrounding. Great views possible: ocean, lake or possibly Corcovado.	Pricier than other locations. Fewer options than Copacabana.
Copacabana & Leme	Wealth of lodging possibilities packed into a long, narrow high-rise-lined neighborhood. Proximity to the beach. Good transport connections to other parts of the city. Good restaurants and bars.	Nightlife more limited than Ipanema or Botafogo. Very touristy; some *cariocas* avoid it. Sex tourism in some parts; tourist-trap restaurants along Av Atlântica.
Botafogo & Urca	Good neighborhood with restaurants, bars and nightclubs that attract a local crowd.	Not within walking distance of the beach. Noisy, traffic-clogged avenues. Few attractions.
Flamengo & Around	Better prices than the beachside districts.	Few options, mostly budget. Very few restaurants and bars, and very little nightlife.
Santa Teresa & Lapa	Santa Teresa is a charming bohemian district with great architecture and alternative, art-minded residents. Has a handful of good restaurants and drinking spots. Lapa is the epicenter of Rio's samba-fueled nightlife.	Santa Teresa is far from the beaches; poor transport links. Lapa is unappealing and gritty by day.
Barra da Tijuca & Western Rio	Great beaches with a laid-back vibe.	No neighborhood vibe; most locals use cars to get places.

Ipanema

MANGO TREE HOSTEL $

Map p228 (☎21 3083-5031; www.mangotreehostel.com; Prudente de Morais 594; dm R$40-55, d with/without bathroom R$220/160; ❄📶) In a cheery yellow house in Ipanema, this well-run hostel offers rooms with two-toned wood floors and a welcoming atmosphere. The back terrace with a bar provides open-air space for unwinding, and it's a great spot to meet other travelers. There's a kitchen, surfboard rental and plenty of activities on offer (including boat parties, surf outings and street art tours).

EL MISTI HOSTEL $

Map p228 (☎21 2246-1070; www.elmistihostelipanema.com; Joana Angélica 47; dm/d from R$45/250; ❄📶) An excellent base in Ipanema, the friendly El Misti has simple, well-maintained dorm rooms (sleeping four to 12) as well as a few private rooms (two with balcony). All rooms have bathrooms. There's a pleasant cafe-bar on the ground floor where you can meet other travelers. Great location just a block from the beach, with a Bike Rio kiosk in front.

CHE LAGARTO IPANEMA HOSTEL $

Map p228 (☎21 2512-8076; www.chelagarto.com; Paul Redfern 48; dm R$65-95, d R$360; ❄@📶) Part of a small empire of hostels in South America, Che Lagarto's Ipanema location is a popular spot for those young travelers who want to be close to the beach. It's a five-story hostel, with basic rooms and not much common space, aside from a bar on the ground floor.

IPANEMA BEACH HOUSE HOSTEL $$

Map p228 (☎21 3202-2693; www.beachhouseipanema.com; Barão da Torre 485; dm R$60-85, d with/without bathroom from R$270/220; 📶) The location is fabulous, in a converted two-story house with a beautiful pool and yard, just a short stroll to the beach. The private rooms, while small, are bright and attractively furnished, and the common areas are quite enticing. On the downside, space is tight in the dorms (with three-tiered bunk beds), and the wait for the communal bathrooms can be long.

BONITA HOSTEL $$

Map p228 (☎21 2227-1703; www.bonitaipanema.com; Barão da Torre 107; dm from R$60, d with/without bathroom R$360/230; ❄@📶) This brightly painted, palm-fringed house has history: it's where bossa nova legend Tom Jobim lived from 1962 to 1965 and wrote some of his most famous songs. Rooms are clean but simply furnished, and most open onto a shared deck overlooking a small pool and patio.

MARGARIDA'S POUSADA POUSADA $$

Map p228 (☎21 2239-1840; www.margaridaspousada.com; Barão da Torre 600; d from R$280, apt from R$360; ❄📶) Those seeking something smaller and cozier than a high-rise hotel should try this superbly located Ipanema pousada (guesthouse). You'll find 11 simply furnished rooms scattered about the low-rise building; the best have small verandas. Margarida also rents out several private, fully equipped apartments nearby.

★HOTEL FASANO HOTEL $$$

Map p228 (☎21 3202-4000; www.fasano.com.br; Av Vieira Souto 80; d R$2500-5100; ❄@📶) Designed by Philippe Starck, the Fasano has fabulously designed rooms with hardwood floors, handsome furnishings (including chairs designed by Sergio Rodrigues) and eye-catching flourishes (oversized ear-shaped mirrors pay homage to Salvador Dalí). The best rooms have balconies overlooking the crashing waves of Ipanema Beach. The rooftop pool (open to guests only) is breathtaking, and the seafood-focused restaurant is outstanding.

HOTEL PRAIA IPANEMA HOTEL $$$

Map p228 (☎21 2141-4949; www.praiaipanema.com; Av Vieira Souto 706; d R$550-1200, ste R$950-1600; ❄📶) With a view of Ipanema Beach, this popular 16-story hotel offers trim, comfortable rooms, each with a balcony. The design is sleek and modern, with off-white tile floors, recessed lighting and artwork on the walls. Stretch out on the molded white lounge chairs next to the rooftop pool or enjoy a meal: the penthouse restaurant, Espaço 7zero6 (p65), is excellent.

SOL IPANEMA HOTEL $$$

Map p228 (☎21 2525-2020; www.solipanema.com.br; Av Vieira Souto 320; d R$690-820; ❄@📶) Occupying prime real estate facing Ipanema Beach, the tall, slender Sol Ipanema features contemporary rooms decorated in creams and earth tones, with dark-wood furnishings and good lighting. Pricier rooms have magnificent, unobstructed ocean views but are otherwise identical to the standard rooms.

SOFITEL RIO DE JANEIRO IPANEMA HOTEL **$$$**

Map p228 (☎21 2525-2525; www.accorhotels.com; Av Vieira Souto 460; d R$830-1300, ste from R$1400; ❄@🏊) Popular with business travelers, this well-located beachfront option has sizable rooms with a warm, inviting feel, artwork on the walls, and high-quality furnishings. The best rooms have ocean views.

Leblon

LEMON SPIRIT HOSTEL HOSTEL **$**

Map p232 (☎21 2294-1853; www.lemonspirit.com; Cupertino Durão 56; dm R$50-90; ❄@📶) One of Leblon's only hostels, Lemon Spirit boasts an excellent location one block from the beach. The dorm rooms (four to six beds in each) are clean and simple, without much decor. There's a tiny courtyard in front, and the attractive lobby bar is a good place to meet other travelers over caipirinhas. There's also a guest kitchen.

RITZ LEBLON HOTEL **$$$**

Map p232 (☎21 2540-4940; www.ritzhotel.com.br; Av Ataúlfo de Paiva 1280; r R$580-910, ste from R$1280; ❄📶🏊) In one of Rio's most desirable areas, this stylish low-key hotel has attractive, uniquely designed rooms and common areas that give it a boutique feel. The best rooms have kitchen units and balconies – some offering partial ocean views – and all have artwork, good lighting and spotless bedrooms.

Jardim Botânico

POUSO VERDE GUESTHOUSE **$$**

Map p234 (☎21 2529-2942; www.pousoverde.com; Caminhoá 14; s/d from R$260/300) On a quiet cobblestone street in a charming corner of Jardim Botânico, Pouso Verde has elegant, comfortably furnished rooms, the best of which have views of Cristo Redentor (Christ the Redeemer). The historic house, dating back to the 1890s, is packed with artwork, and the owners go out of their way to make guests feel at home. Excellent breakfasts.

Copacabana & Leme

CABANA COPA HOSTEL **$**

Map p236 (☎21 97154-9473; www.cabanacopa.com.br; Travessa Guimarães Natal 10, Copacabana; dm R$40-60, d R$150-180; ❄@📶) Top hostel honors go to this Greek-Brazilian-run gem in a colonial-style '50s house tucked away in a Copacabana cranny. Four- to 10-bed dorms prevail throughout the home, which is chock-full of original architectural details and a hodgepodge of funky floorings. There's a lively bar and common areas.

EL MISTI HOSTEL **$**

Map p236 (☎21 98485-5138; www.elmistihostelrio.com; Tonelero 197, Copacabana; dm/d R$60/300; 📶) A welcoming, multistory spot in Copacabana, El Misti is a fine choice if you're looking to socialize. The barman whips up first-rate tropical cocktails (mojitos, caipirinhas) and the location across from the metro station is decent. There are several other El Mistis around town, including a branch in Ipanema.

WALK ON THE BEACH HOSTEL HOSTEL **$**

Map p236 (☎21 2545-7500; www.walk-on-the-beach.com; Dias da Rocha 85, Copacabana; dm R$40-70; ❄@📶) Set in a bright red two-story villa on one of Copacabana's quiet backstreets, this nicely designed hostel offers good-value dorm rooms (sleeping three to 12 people in each), though the metal, institutional-looking bed frames and thin mattresses lessen the appeal. It has a lounge and a small bar, and maintains a welcoming, low-key vibe.

CHE LAGARTO HOSTEL **$**

Map p236 (☎21 3209-0348; www.chelagarto.com; Barata Ribeiro 111, Copacabana; dm/d R$60/150; ❄@📶🏊) This popular full-service hostel has a friendly, party atmosphere. The small rooftop pool with adjoining bar is a good place to meet other travelers, and the hostel arranges loads of activities – boat parties, nights out in Lapa, BBQs and more. There are several other Che Lagartos in Copacabana and one in Ipanema.

PURA VIDA HOSTEL **$**

Map p236 (☎21 99028-9691; www.puravidahostel.com.br; Saint Roman 20, Copacabana; dm R$50-80, d from R$170; @📶) Pura Vida occupies a converted castle-like mansion (built in the 1920s) that was once the home of the Polish ambassador. A big draw for socially minded travelers, the hostel has spacious common areas, including an outdoor veranda with bar. Aside from its dorm rooms sleeping four to 12 people there are also brightly painted multistory units that are good options for couples.

JUCATI APARTMENT **$$**
Map p236 (☎21 2547-5422; www.edificiojucati.com.br; Tenente Marones de Gusmão 85, Copacabana; d/q from R$240/300; ❄📶) On a tranquil street overlooking a small park, Jucati has large, simply furnished serviced apartments with tile floors and small but serviceable kitchens. Most apartments have just one bedroom with a double bed, and a living room with either a bunk bed (*beliche*) or pull-out sofa bed. The small covered courtyard is a fine spot to unwind.

HOTEL SANTA CLARA HOTEL **$$**
Map p236 (☎21 2256-2650; www.hotelsantaclara.com.br; Décio Vilares 316, Copacabana; d R$300-400; ❄📶) Along one of Copacabana's most peaceful streets, you'll find this attractive three-story hotel with a white stucco facade and blue shutters. The front-facing upstairs *(luxo)* rooms are best, with wood floors and balconies. The rooms in back are quieter, but also attractively designed with a wallpaper-covered feature wall and oversized hanging paper lanterns.

OLINDA RIO HOTEL **$$**
Map p236 (☎21 2159-9000; www.olindariohotel.com.br; Av Atlântica 2230, Copacabana; d without/with ocean view from R$420/520; ❄📶) Set in a handsome cream-colored building overlooking Copacabana Beach, the Olinda Rio is a classic. Its marble lobby, complete with chandeliers and grand piano, has an old-world charm, although its rooms are modern. The best of the rooms face the ocean and are worth the price.

MARTA RIO GUESTHOUSE B&B **$$**
Map p236 (☎21 2521-8568; www.martarioguesthouse.com; Francisco Sá 5, Copacabana; d R$350-580; ❄📶) Marta, a gracious host with an innate sense of hospitality, opens up her home and rents out six comfortable rooms at this split-level penthouse overlooking the beach. The highlight is undoubtedly the outdoor veranda, which has gorgeous views over Copacabana.

RIO DESIGN HOTEL BOUTIQUE HOTEL **$$**
Map p236 (☎21 3222-8800; www.riodesignhotel.com; Francisco Sá 17, Copacabana; r R$475-590; ❄@📶🏊) This stylish 13-story hotel demonstrates real design smarts. Rooms have tile floors, artful lighting and big windows, and each floor is decorated in a different style. The staff is friendly and there's a small dip pool on the rooftop, as well as a sauna and shoebox-sized fitness center that don't see much action.

MERCURE ARPOADOR HOTEL **$$**
Map p236 (☎21 2113-8600; www.mercure.com; Francisco Otaviano 61, Copacabana; r from R$350; ❄@📶🏊) This dapper all-suites hotel is nicely located in Arpoador, giving easy access to both Ipanema and Copacabana. The suites have sleek leather sofas that open into beds, modern kitchenettes, TV, stereo and DVD player, ambient lighting and comfortable bedrooms. All of the rooms have balconies, although there is no view.

ORLA COPACABANA HOTEL **$$**
Map p236 (☎21 2525-2425; www.orlahotel.com.br; Av Atlântica 4122, Copacabana; d R$400-750; ❄📶🏊) The Spanish-owned Orla Copacabana has some attractive, understated rooms, but the beach-facing location is the real draw. The standard rooms are too cramped, so it's not worth staying here unless you book one of the deluxe rooms, with their unobstructed ocean views.

BLAME IT ON RIO 4 TRAVEL APARTMENT **$$**
Map p236 (☎21 3813-5510; www.blameitonrio4travel.com; Xavier da Silveira 15B, Copacabana; apt from R$275; @) Created by a kind, helpful expat from New York, this professional agency rents many types of apartments. It also has a travel agency, a few computers for internet use and a laundry next door.

RIO SPOT HOMES APARTMENT **$$**
Map p236 (☎21 3988-7613, 21 99474-8689; www.riospothomes.com; Office 215, Prado Junior 48, Copacabana; apt from R$450) This reputable, well-run rental agency has scores of listings around the Zona Sul, with excellent-value apartments in Ipanema, Copacabana and Barra, from inexpensive crash pads to luxurious five-bedroom flats that can accommodate up to 15 people.

★HOTEL EMILIANO LUXURY HOTEL **$$$**
Map p236 (☎21 3503-6600; www.emiliano.com.br; Av Atlântica 3804, Copacabana; d R$1600-2300;

) Rio's loveliest new hotel sits on a prime spot fronting Copacabana's southern shore. The rooms have a modernist aesthetic, with jacaranda wood furniture, artful lighting and tropical photographs by the artist Leonardo Finotti. The small rooftop pool and bar (for guests only) is a fabulous retreat, and the ground-floor restaurant serves outstanding cuisine – including a decadent weekend brunch (R$195 including drinks).

Other thoughtful touches include high-end bath products by Santapele, a free pair of Havaianas, plus fruit and a free cocktail (enjoy it on the roof) upon arrival.

BELMOND COPACABANA PALACE HOTEL **$$$**

Map p236 (21 3500-0292; www.belmond.com; Av Atlântica 1702, Copacabana; d from R$1850;) Rio's most famous hotel has hosted heads of state, rock stars and other prominent personalities – Queen Elizabeth once stayed here, as did the Rolling Stones. The dazzling white facade dates from the 1920s, when it became a symbol of the city. Today accommodations range from deluxe rooms to spacious suites with balconies.

The pool is the loveliest in Rio, and the restaurants are top notch.

PORTO BAY RIO INTERNACIONAL HOTEL **$$$**

Map p236 (21 2546-8000; www.portobay.com.br; Av Atlântica 1500, Copacabana; d from R$790;) One of Copacabana's top beachfront hotels, Porto Bay has stylish rooms with a light and airy feel that are painted in cool tones. Light hardwoods, elegant furnishings and modern bathrooms all complement each other nicely. Big windows let in lots of light, and some rooms have balconies. Great views from the rooftop pool and fitness center.

PESTANA RIO ATLÂNTICA HOTEL **$$$**

Map p236 (21 3816-8500; www.pestana.com; Av Atlântica 2964, Copacabana; r from R$480;) Beautifully located along Copacabana Beach, the Portuguese-owned Pestana has excellent amenities, decent service and a wide range of rooms. The best rooms have wood floors, balconies and a bright, modern design scheme. Rooms at the lower end are rather bland and too small to recommend.

FAIRMONT LUXURY HOTEL **$$$**

Map p236 (www.fairmont.com; Av Atlântica 4240, Copacabana;) Fairmont's first hotel in South America promises to be a stunner when it opens in 2019. Anchoring the southern end of Copacabana, the 400-room hotel will have accommodations with all the latest mod cons, though the real showstopper will be the magnificent view from the best chambers.

Botafogo

★YOO2 BOUTIQUE HOTEL **$$**

Map p244 (21 3445-2000; www.yoo2.com; Praia de Botafogo 242; d from R$350;) Yoo2, which opened in 2016, has taken a generic high-rise and transformed it into a captivating 138-room hotel with an avant-garde style. Glass elevators ascend up an interior adorned with street art, while the rooftop pool and bar offer 360-degree vistas over a jaw-dropping stretch of the city. Rooms are spacious and most have alluring views.

You can hire bikes, and the ground-floor restaurant is a fine place to try local microbrews while dining on creative Brazilian fusion fare (mains R$58 to R$77).

O VELEIRO BED & BREAKFAST GUESTHOUSE **$$**

Map p244 (21 2554-8980; www.oveleiro.com; Mundo Novo 1440; d R$260-395;) Surrounded by Atlantic rainforest, O Veleiro is a delightfully set guesthouse located on a cobblestone road uphill from Botafogo. The rooms are small and adequately furnished but the backyard is the real attraction, with hammocks, a small pool and pretty views (plus the occasional marmoset visitor).

On the downside, it's a bit of a trudge to get down to Botafogo (even more so on the way back uphill), but for a tranquil escape that's still inside central Rio, this is a decent option.

INJOY HOSTEL GUESTHOUSE **$$**

Map p244 (21 3593-6662; www.injoyhostel.com; Estácio de Coimbra 80; dm R$43-59, d R$160-250;) Despite the name, this place feels less like a hostel and more like a small guesthouse. Injoy has a mix of private doubles and cozy dorms set in a lovely house at the end of a tree-lined lane. Rooms are modern, very clean and well maintained, and each is named after a major city, with iconic photos from the destination decorating one wall. Friendly staff.

Urca

HOTELINHO URCA GUESTHOUSE **$$**
Map p244 (☎21 3449-8867; www.hotelinho.com; Marechal Cantuária 10; r R$280-390; ❄📶🏊) One of the few lodging options in Urca, this quiet, low-key guesthouse has a range of clean, well-equipped rooms with attractive wood floors. The sunny veranda has views over the bay and is the best feature; there's also a tiny dip pool. Hotelinho Urca also rents several apartments nearby.

RECANTO DA URCA GUESTHOUSE **$$**
Map p244 (☎2199247-9523; www.recantodaurca.com.br; São Sebastião 272; d R$180; ❄📶) Tucked in a peaceful part of Urca, this place has simply furnished guest rooms, friendly service and a top-floor terrace with magnificent views (it's rather unfinished though, so watch your step).

Flamengo & Around

★**MAZE INN** GUESTHOUSE **$**
Map p241 (☎21 2558-5547; www.jazzrio.com; Casa 66, Tavares Bastos 414, Catete; s/d R$120/140, with panoramic view R$160/180) Set in the Tavares Bastos favela, the Maze Inn is a fantastic place to overnight for those looking for an alternative view of Rio. The rooms are uniquely decorated with original artworks by English owner and Renaissance man Bob Nadkarni, while the veranda offers stunning views of the bay and Pão de Açúcar (Sugarloaf Mountain).

Don't miss the jazz parties held on the first Friday of every month, or the Sunday curry feasts (p118; Bob's son cooks up delicious Indian curries).

DISCOVERY HOSTEL HOSTEL **$**
Map p241 (☎21 3449-0672; www.discoveryhostel.com; Benjamin Constant 26, Catete; dm/d R$54/190; ❄📶) One of Rio's most socially minded hostels, Discovery is a great place to meet other travelers. While it's not on the beach, the attractive converted house is convenient for exploring the nightlife of Lapa, and it's an easy stroll to the metro. In addition to dorm rooms (a minus for the triple bunks), the hostel has a couple of colorful private rooms.

There's a bar, a lounge and a small plant-lined patio. The staff organizes many activities for guests.

SOLAR DO COSME GUESTHOUSE **$$**
Map p242 (☎21 3596-0585; www.solardocosme.com; Ladeira do Ascurra 124, Cosme Velho; d/tr/q/apt R$200/260/320/420; 📶🏊) Nestled at the foothill of Corcovado, this tranquil guesthouse earns high marks from guests for its verdant surroundings as well as the kindhearted hosts, who are happy to share tips on making the most of Rio. The rooms are tidy and well maintained, and the lush grounds add to the value.

On the downside, it's a long way from the beach, though it's a short walk to the railway station leading up to Cristo Redentor.

CASA CAMINHO DO CORCOVADO B&B **$$**
Map p242 (☎21 2265-2124; www.casacaminhodocorcovado.com.br; Filinto de Almeida 283, Cosme Velho; d from R$240; ❄📶) On the Corcovado hillside, this idyllic place is surrounded by tropical rainforest, and feels like a peaceful escape from the city. Friendly, knowledgeable hosts offer just two attractive rooms and one bungalow overlooking the garden; the place is in high demand so book early. There are fine views, and a relaxing air pervades.

Centro

BELGA HOTEL HOTEL **$$**
Map p246 (☎21 2263-9086; www.belgahotel.com.br; Rua dos Andradas 129; d R$130-320) In a beautifully restored building from the 1920s, this classy hotel is helping to breathe new life into an overlooked corner of downtown. The Belgian-owned pioneer has simple but comfortably priced rooms that are excellent value for the money (the best are the 'executive' rooms with French doors opening onto decorative balconies).

The Belgian bistro (p131) on the ground floor is not to be missed.

Santa Teresa

CASA DA GENTE GUESTHOUSE **$**
Map p250 (☎21 99219-9858; www.casadagente.com; Gonçalves Fontes 33; r R$150-170; 📶) 🍃

A short stroll from the top of the Escadaria Selarón (p137), the Casa da Gente is a welcoming French-Brazilian-run guesthouse with a strong interest in sustainability. Rainwater catchment, solar panels, composting and a green roof are all part of the ethos. The rooms themselves are bright, clean and simply furnished.

★CASA BELEZA POUSADA **$$**

Map p250 (☎21 98288-6764; www.casabeleza.com; Laurinda Santos Lobo 311; r R$290-470, villas R$650; ❄📶🏊) This lovely property dates to the 1930s and was once a governor's mansion. Tropical gardens overlook the picturesque pool, and you can sometimes spot toucans and monkeys in the surrounding foliage. It's a small and peaceful operation, with just four guest rooms and one peacefully set villa (complete with rooftop deck offering panoramic views).

The kind multilingual family that runs the *pousada* lives on-site.

MAMA SHELTER BOUTIQUE HOTEL **$$**

Map p250 (☎21 3980-0300; www.mamashelter.com; Paschoal Carlos Magno 5; r R$320-650; ❄📶) Part of a budget-minded boutique-hotel chain, Mama Shelter has 55 colorful rooms, each with whimsical touches and bursting with personality. Lush greenery surrounds the property, and the various terraces make fine places to enjoy the tropical setting. The airy restaurant serves a mix of Brazilian classics and creatively topped pizzas, and the stylish bar is a destination in its own right.

DISCOVERY SUITES GUESTHOUSE **$$**

Map p250 (☎21 3264-9665; www.discoverysuitesrio.com; Almirante Alexandrino 399; r from R$260; ❄📶) Run by the same folks behind the charming Explorer Bar (p142) next door, Discovery Suites has bright, stylish rooms with nicely framed artwork, colorful textiles, vintage furnishings, comfortable beds and sparkling modern bathrooms. The veranda is a fine spot to relax while taking in views over Santa Teresa.

CASA COOL BEANS GUESTHOUSE **$$**

Map p250 (☎21 2262-0552; www.casacoolbeans.com; Laurinda Santos Lobo 136; s/d R$300/350; ❄@📶🏊) Your expectations will easily be exceeded at this discreet 10-room B&B, where the American owner's mantra focuses on personalized service. Each colorful room in the renovated 1930s Spanish-style villa was designed by a different Brazilian artist; book room 9 for the best views. It also has a spacious sundeck and an enticing pool. No children allowed.

CASA BIANCA GUESTHOUSE **$$**

Map p250 (☎21 3233-1563; www.guesthousebianca.com; Murtinho Nobre 35; r R$270-350; ❄📶) This beautiful 1930s-era mansion down the road from Parque das Ruinas (p138) has lovely details: stained-glass windows, tall ceilings, a marble staircase and period furnishings. Rooms are attractively set, with wood floors and antique fixtures; two have excellent views, and one of these has a private veranda. It's a quiet place with just three rooms. The friendly owner lives on-site.

MODERNISTAS HOSPEDAGEM GUESTHOUSE **$$**

Map p250 (☎21 98139-3892; www.facebook.com/modernistashospedagem; Paschoal Carlos Magno 39; d R$270; ❄📶) Attached to an art gallery, Modernistas has five creatively designed rooms, each dedicated to a different Brazilian artist (Di Cavalcanti, Oswald de Andrade etc) and full of eye-catching works. The best room has a small balcony. The hosts provide a warm welcome, there's an ample breakfast, and you can arrange dinners as well as customized 4WD tours.

CASA ÁUREA GUESTHOUSE **$$**

Map p250 (☎21 2242-5830; www.casaaurea.com.br; Áurea 80; d/tr R$340/370, s/d without bathroom R$170/220; ❄📶) Set in one of Santa Teresa's oldest homes (1871), the two-story Casa Áurea has rustic charm, simple but cozy rooms and a large covered garden where you can lounge on hammocks, fire up the barbecue or whip up a meal in the open-air kitchen.

★HOTEL SANTA TERESA BOUTIQUE HOTEL **$$$**

Map p250 (☎21 3380-0200; www.santateresahotelrio.com; Almirante Alexandrino 660; d from R$950; ❄@📶🏊) What is probably the finest boutique hotel in Rio is set in a lavishly restored building that was part of a coffee plantation in the 19th century. It includes artfully designed rooms, an award-winning restaurant (p140), a full-service spa, a stylish bar and a pool with fine views over the city.

The design incorporates a certain tropical elegance, with art and artifacts from across Brazil on display in common areas and in some rooms.

MAMA RUISA HOTEL **$$$**
Map p250 (☎21 2210-0631; www.mamaruisa.com; Santa Cristina 132; r R$650-950; ❄📶🏊) French-owned Mama Ruisa aims for bohemian chic in its seven spacious, uniquely designed guest rooms. Every whim is catered for in this inspiring converted colonial mansion; guests can opt for massages and private tours or simply enjoy the spectacular view over the bay from the swimming pool.

Lapa

BOOKS HOSTEL HOSTEL **$**
Map p250 (☎21 3437-3783; www.bookshostel.com; Francisco Muratori 10; dm R$45-75; ❄@📶) In the heart of Lapa and true to the nature of the neighborhood, this party hostel is the appetizer for your crazy night out. Dorms have eye-catching graffiti art and there's a social bar styled like a barraca (stall) – rooms overlooking it don't allow for much sleep. All bathrooms are shared, and only some rooms have air-conditioning.

DA LAPA DESIGN HOTEL HOTEL **$**
Map p250 (☎21 2252-4237; www.dalapahotel.com.br; Rua do Lavradio 200; dm R$54-75, d R$200; 📶) Set in lively Lapa, this kooky and colorful little hostel will wow you with its arty vibe and communal atrium. Breakfast is complimentary, and there's a seating area in the atrium for all to enjoy. And, of course, party central is right on the doorstep!

HOTEL 55 RIO BOUTIQUE HOTEL **$$**
Map p250 (☎21 3883-2030; www.55rio.com.br; Visconde de Maranguape 9, Centro; d R$200-250, ste R$475) This stylish boutique hotel is located just a few minutes' walk from Escadaria Selarón (p137), the Arcos da Lapa (p139) and the nightlife hot spots of Av Mem de Sá. The hotel's stunning facade was recently restored, and although the original hotel was built more than 100 years ago, today's incarnation (reopened in 2016) features ultramodern design throughout.

VILA GALÉ BOUTIQUE HOTEL **$$$**
Map p250 (☎21 2460-4500; www.vilagale.com; Riachuelo 124; r R$350-740; ❄📶🏊) Breathing new life into ragged Lapa, Vila Galé – a high-end luxury chain from Portugal – invested some €35 million in this beautiful property. The spacious, well-appointed rooms are good value, and the best of them are set in a 19th-century building overlooking a lovely pool. The rooms are quiet despite having the best of Rio's nightlife right outside the door.

Barra da Tijuca & Western Rio

RIO SURF 'N STAY HOSTEL **$**
Map p254 (☎21 3418-1133; www.riosurfnstay.com; Raimundo Veras 1140, Recreio dos Bandeirantes; dm/d from R$65/196; ❄📶) Just a short stroll to the fine surf off Macumba Beach, this converted house, which is owned by a New Zealander and a Brazilian, is the go-to spot for anyone who has come to Rio to learn to surf. The dorm rooms (sleeping four or five people) and private doubles are comfortably furnished, and the hosts make everyone feel at home.

LSH LIFESTYLE HOTEL **$$**
Map p254 (☎21 3609-1140; www.lshhotel.net; Professor Coutinho Fróis 10, Barra da Tijuca; d from R$450; ❄📶🏊) Boasting an excellent location near Praia do Pepê, this lavish 122-room hotel has handsome interiors (designed by notable American architect David Rockwell), good service and excellent amenities. The rooms are strikingly modern, with floor-to-ceiling windows, spacious bathrooms and verandas. The best suites have their own private outdoor Jacuzzis overlooking the beach.

DON PASCUAL GUESTHOUSE **$$**
Map p254 (☎21 3417-0776; www.donpascual.com.br; Casa 12, Estrada do Sacarrão 867, Vargem Grande; r weekday/weekend from R$325/450; ❄📶🏊) Surrounded by lush vegetation, this hidden spot has attractive rooms with a rustic-chic allure. Some of the rooms are split-level and incorporate reclaimed lumber into the cabin-like design. There's an enticing swimming pool and a restaurant (p158) that invites lingering. The downside? It's a long drive from Ipanema, and you'll need a car and excellent directions to get here. Call ahead for specifics.

Understand Rio de Janeiro

RIO DE JANEIRO TODAY 172

The post-Olympic days have been rough, with an economic crisis and rising crime rates gripping the city.

HISTORY 174

Royals, demagogues and socially minded visionaries have all played a role in Rio's complicated past.

THE SOUNDS OF RIO 185

Rio's greatest hits feature bossa nova, *tropicália*, Música Popular Brasileira (MPB) and, above all, samba.

THE BEAUTIFUL GAME 191

When it comes to football, no other place quite compares: a look at Rio's extraordinary sporting legacy.

ARCHITECTURE 195

From baroque churches to postmodern concert halls, Rio has some surprising architectural treasures.

Rio de Janeiro Today

Rio's infrastructure has seen big improvements, notably a new metro line that makes Barra da Tijuca more accessible than it has ever been. Despite these upgrades, the city remains in a deep recession, brought on by an economic and political crisis partly stemming from overspending on the Olympics. Meanwhile, corruption has inspired a growing number of female activists to enter the political arena. Their aim: to bring a new era of social justice to a city grappling with deep-rooted inequalities.

Best on Film

Cidade de Deus (City of God; 2002) Oscar-nominated film showing the coexistence of brutality and hope in a Rio favela.

Orfeu Negro (Black Orpheus; 1959) The Orpheus-and-Eurydice myth retold in the setting of Rio's Carnaval, with a ground-breaking bossa nova soundtrack.

Central do Brasil (Central Station; 1998) Epic journey through unglamorized Brazil, set in Rio and the northeast.

Rio (2011) Animated film that captures the beauty and diversity of the city in its beaches, mountains, favelas and Carnaval celebrations.

Best in Print

Dancing with the Devil in the City of God (Juliana Barbassa; 2015) Portrait of the great changes happening in the city today, plus a look at Rio's complex social challenges.

Rio de Janeiro Reader (Daryle Williams, Amy Chazkel and Paulo Knauss; 2015) Covers 450 years of history, culture and politics.

Brazil on the Rise (Larry Rohter; 2010) A journey through the culture, history and economic transformation of Brazil.

Post-Olympic Crash

One of Rio's most illustrious periods was during the Summer Olympics in 2016. By all accounts the games were a huge success for the city, and *cariocas* (residents of Rio) took pride in the huge projects that transformed the town ahead of the event: the glittering new metro line extending all the way down to Barra, the high-tech light-rail system zipping around the city center, and a rejuvenated port district, complete with grand museums and a pedestrian boulevard lined with magnificent, large-scale street art.

In the weeks following the games, hopes were high for the Olympics to usher in a new era of prosperity and development. Unfortunately, things didn't go as planned. Many new sporting arenas constructed for the games were abandoned, despite government promises to convert them into venues for the community. Further investment in infrastructure and social projects didn't happen, as city coffers ran dry – owing in large part to a huge corruption scandal that involved both state and federal politicians. Rio's governor Sergio Cabral (along with a group of senior government officials and businessmen) siphoned tens of millions of reais from public construction projects. When he was arrested in November 2016, federal prosecutors suspected him of leading an organized-crime ring that diverted over R$200 million in bribes. The following year he was sentenced to 14 years in prison for corruption and money laundering.

Economic Crisis

An estimated US$13 billion was spent on the Olympics, only slightly more than the US$11 billion spent on the 2014 World Cup. Such enormous spending contributed to a recession that crippled the Brazilian economy. Six months after the games the unemployment rate had doubled and GDP had fallen more than 8%. The wages and pensions of public employees had been cut by 30%. Soon the city was in a full-scale economic crisis and declared a state of calamity as its debt reached around US$6 billion: several hospitals had to close their doors owing to lack of funding; local-government employees and teachers were staging constant protests because they weren't getting paid – some for months; and homelessness doubled. With a smaller police presence, violence returned to the favelas (slums, informal communities), and there were frequent gun battles between rival gangs and between gangs and invading police. Some schools in troubled areas had to close due to the constant dangers posed to the students.

Military Intervention

By early 2018, with crime spiraling out of control, the Brazilian president Michel Temer signed a decree ordering the army to take control of Rio's security situation – a step not taken since the fall of the military dictatorship in the 1980s. Despite the military presence, crime continued to be a problem, and critics declared the military intervention to be little more than a publicity stunt. In fact, for residents of the favelas, the military only made their lives worse: coordinated raids led by tanks and thousands of heavily armed soldiers created violent confrontations with drug gangs, and innocent people sometimes got caught in the crossfire.

New Political Voices

Anger over the corruption scandals led to a surge of new voices clamoring for thorough revision of Brazil's failing political system. Formally marginalized groups rose to the fore, powered by grassroots activism and a public increasingly disenchanted with the status quo. Marielle Franco, elected to the city council in 2016, led the charge for change. As a black, lesbian woman who grew up in a favela, Franco spoke for the disenfranchised, and she was a leading light for both the black-rights movement and the LGBT community. Her charisma and bravery in the face of a corrupt regime earned her the admiration of many in Rio – but it also made her many enemies. Sadly, she was assassinated in 2018, and some suspect her political adversaries of being responsible for the crime. Her death sent shockwaves around the country, and tens of thousands turned out to protest her murder and demonstrate that *'Marielle e presente'* ('Marielle is here'). Indeed, far from silencing Franco, her executioners have only inspired others to rise up in her place, with activists such as Mônica Francisco, Thais Ferreira and Renata Souza continuing the fight to bring a better future to Rio de Janeiro.

if Rio were 100 people

50 would be white
36 would be multiracial
11 would be black
3 would be other

belief systems

(% of population)

population per sq km

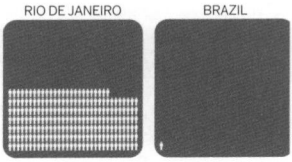

↑ ≈ 25 people

History

Rio was a key settlement in Portugal's empire: magnificent churches and fine colonial-era streets attest to the imperial wealth lavished on the city, though by the late 1800s it was already divided into haves and have-nots. During the 20th century the city saw an influx of immigrants, explosive favela growth, the rise of a military dictatorship, and loss of prestige when Brasília replaced it as the nation's capital. Recent times have brought Olympic glory, followed by bankruptcy and far-reaching corruption.

The Portuguese Arrival

In the 15th century Portugal, ever infatuated with the sea, began the large-scale explorations that would eventually take Portuguese explorers to the coast of Brazil in 1500. A little over a year later Gonçalo Coelho sailed from Portugal, entering a huge bay on the other side of the world in January 1502. It was his chief pilot, Amerigo Vespucci, however, who would name the bay. Mistaking it for a river (or possibly making no mistake at all, since the old Portuguese 'rio' is another word for bay), he dubbed it Rio de Janeiro (River of January).

Brazil is the only country in the Americas that was both the seat of an empire (when the Portuguese king moved his court here) and an independent monarchy (when Dom Pedro I declared independence).

Indigenous Peoples

The indigenous Guarani and Tupinambá (better known as the Tupi) had a large presence all along the Atlantic coast, with as many as a million people living in what is now Brazil. Though little is known of the original inhabitants (save apocryphal accounts by early Portuguese explorers), these indigenous peoples lived in distinct tribes numbering between 400 and 2000 in each settlement. They were semi-nomadic, and had a varied diet from hunting, fishing and gathering as well as farming (with cassava the most important crop).

The Portuguese saw the indigenous people as raw manpower for their empire, and quickly enslaved the region's original inhabitants and set them to work on plantations. Dying in large numbers from introduced diseases, the Tupinambá had died out completely by the 17th

TIMELINE

8000 BC
Descendents of hunter-gatherers who crossed the Bering Strait from East Asia between 10,000 BC and 12,000 BC settle along Baía de Guanabara.

AD 1502
Gonçalo Coelho sails into Baía de Guanabara. His chief pilot, Amerigo Vespucci (after whom 'America' is named), dubs the lovely setting Rio de Janeiro.

1565
After driving off the French and their indigenous allies, the Portuguese found their first permanent colony in the Americas, São Sebastião do Rio de Janeiro.

century. To fulfill their growing labor demands, the Portuguese then turned to Africa.

Africans in Brazil

The Portuguese began forcibly bringing people from Africa into the new colony shortly after its founding. Most were brought from Guinea, Angola and the Congo, and would constitute some three million people brought to Brazil over its three-and-a-half centuries of human trafficking. The port of Rio had the largest number of slaves entering the colony – as many as two million in all. At open-air markets, these new arrivals were sold as local help or shipped to the interior, initially to work on the thriving sugar plantations and later – when gold was discovered in Minas Gerais in 1704 – to undertake back-breaking work in the mines.

In Rio, enslaved people were forced to work mostly in domestic roles as maids and butlers and out on the streets as dock workers, furniture movers, delivery people, boatmen, cobblers, fishermen and carpenters. Among the worst jobs was transporting the barrels of human excrement produced in town and emptying them into the bay.

As Rio's population grew, so too did the number of slaves brought in; labor was also needed for the expanding coffee plantations in the Paraíba Valley. By the early 19th century, African slaves made up two-thirds of Rio's population.

Children born into mixed backgrounds (ie to slave and slave-owner parents) were largely accepted into the social sphere and raised as free citizens. This contributed considerably to creating Brazil's melting pot of racial backgrounds. While escape attempts were fewer in Rio than in the more brutal climate of the Northeast, some attempts were made. Those seeking freedom often set their sights on *quilombos* (communities of runaway slaves). Some of these were quite developed – as was the case with Palmares, which had a population of 20,000 and survived through much of the 17th century before it was wiped out by federal troops.

Abroad, Brazil was under pressure to outlaw slavery, and trafficking in human cargo was eventually banned in 1830. This move, however, did nothing to improve the lives of slaves already in Brazil, who would have to wait another two generations to gain their freedom. Despite the ban, shipment of human cargo continued well into the 1850s, with 500,000 slaves smuggled into Brazil between 1830 and 1850. The British (out of economic self-interest) finally suppressed Brazil's trafficking with naval squadrons.

Pressure from home and abroad reached boiling point toward the end of the 19th century until finally, in 1888, from the steps of the Royal

'Order and Progress,' the slogan on Brazil's flag, comes from the writings of French philosopher Auguste de Comte (1797–1857), whose elevation of reason and scientific knowledge over traditional beliefs was influential on the young Brazilian Republic.

1550–80
The Portuguese bring over 2000 slaves to the new colony. Over the next 300 years more than three million people forcibly taken from Africa will be brought to Brazil.

1763
With gold flowing from Minas Gerais through Rio, the city grows wealthy and swells in population to 50,000; the Portuguese court transfers the capital of Brazil from Salvador to Rio.

1807
Napoleon invades Portugal and the Portuguese prince regent (later known as Dom João VI) and his entire court of 15,000 flee to Brazil. The royal family showers wealth upon Rio.

1822
Left in charge of Brazil after his father, Dom João VI, returns to Portugal, Dom Pedro I declares independence from Portugal and crowns himself 'emperor' of Brazil.

Palace overlooking Praça Quinze de Novembro, slavery was declared to have been abolished. Brazil was the last country in the Americas to end slavery.

Rio's Early Days

In order to get the colony up and running, the Portuguese built a fortified town on Morro do Castelo in 1567 to maximize protection from European invasion by sea and indigenous attack by land. They named their town São Sebastião do Rio de Janeiro, in honor of patron saint Sebastião and his namesake King Sebastião of Portugal. Cobbled together by the 500 founding *cariocas* (residents of Rio), early Rio was a poorly planned town with irregular streets in the medieval Portuguese style. It remained a small settlement through the mid-17th century, surviving on the export of brazilwood and sugarcane. In Rio's first census (in 1600), the population comprised 3000 indigenous, 750 Portuguese and 100 blacks.

In the half-century of gold fever, some 500,000 Portuguese immigrated to Brazil, and one million slaves were brought here. Rio served as the port for people and commerce flowing to and from the goldfields.

With its excellent harbor and good lands for sugarcane, Rio became Brazil's third most important settlement (after Salvador da Bahia and Recife-Olinda) in the 17th century.

The gold rush in Minas Gerais had a profound effect on Rio and caused major demographic shifts on three continents. The rare metal was first discovered by *bandeirantes* (raiders and hired slave-hunters) in the 1690s, and as word spread gold seekers arrived in droves. Over the next half-century an estimated 500,000 Portuguese arrived in Brazil and many thousands of African slaves were brought in. Rio served as the port for the flow of people and commerce to and from the Minas Gerais goldfields.

In the 18th century Rio morphed into a rough-and-tumble place attracting a swarthy brand of European immigrant. Most of the settlement was built near the water, where Praça XV (Quinze) de Novembro stands today, beside rows of warehouses, with noisy taverns sprinkled along the main streets. This was a rough city full of smugglers and thieves, itinerants and assassins. Smuggling was rampant, with ships robbed, sailors murdered, and bribes given to the police. Gold flowing through the city meant that pirates were a constant menace. Adding a note of temperance were the religious orders that came in small bands and built Rio's first churches.

Rio Under Royal Rule

In 1807 Napoleon's army marched on Lisbon. Two days before the French invasion, 40 ships carrying the Portuguese prince regent (later known as Dom João VI) and his entire court of 15,000 set sail for Brazil

1831

Dom Pedro I proves incompetent and abdicates the throne. His son Pedro II takes power and ushers in a long period of growth and stability.

1888

Brazil abolishes slavery, making it the last country in the Americas to do so. The law is signed by Princesa Isabel.

1889

A military coup supported by Brazil's wealthy coffee farmers overthrows Pedro II. The monarchy is abolished and the Brazilian Republic is born.

1900

Mayor Pereira Passos ushers in a period of urbanization, creating grand boulevards, opening up Copacabana (via a tunnel), and improving public health and sanitation.

under the protection of British warships. After the initial landing in Bahia (where their unkempt state was met with bemusement), the royal family moved down to Rio, where they settled.

This had momentous consequences for the city, as the king, missing the high culture of Europe, lavished his attention on his new hometown, envisioning a splendid, European-style city. European artisans flooded in. The British, rewarded for helping the king reach Brazil safely, gained access to the country's ports, and many Anglo traders and merchants set up shop in the town center. Anti-Napoleon French also arrived, as did other Europeans. When the German prince and noted naturalist Alexander Philipp Maximilian arrived in Brazil in 1815, he commented on the many nationalities and ethnicities he encountered.

HISTORICAL SITES

Paço Imperial (p126)	The former imperial palace was home to the Portuguese royal family.
Praça XV (Quinze) de Novembro (p127)	Named after the date Brazil declared itself a republic (November 15, 1822), this plaza has witnessed several key occasions, including the crowning of two emperors and the abolition of slavery.
Travessa do Comércio (p129)	This narrow alley is a window into colonial Rio, with 18th-century buildings converted into bars and restaurants.
Pedra do Sal (p133)	Open-air gathering spot for live music in what was once the epicenter of Afro-Brazilian culture in Rio.
Museu Histórico Nacional (p123)	Set in the 18th-century royal arsenal, this museum houses Rio's best assortment of historical artifacts.
Jardim Botânico (p81)	Prince Regent Dom João VI ordered this verdant garden to be planted in 1808.
Museu da República (p116)	Formerly known as the Palácio do Catete, this mansion was Brazil's presidential residence from 1896 to 1954. Getúlio Vargas, the last president to live here, died by suicide in one of the upstairs rooms.
Praça Floriano (p125)	Centro's picturesque main square has long been the meeting ground for popular demonstrations, including student uprisings against the military dictatorship in the 1960s and victory celebrations following World Cup finals.
Garota de Ipanema (p64)	In this famed spot Tom Jobim and Vinícius de Moraes penned 'The Girl from Ipanema,' whose international success was a major moment in the history of bossa nova.

1917

Samba is officially born, with the first recording of the song 'Pelo Telefone.' This song and others soon get wide radio airplay.

1923

The Copacabana Palace opens its doors. It becomes an icon of Rio's tropical glamour, with international jet-setters flying in during Rio's pre-Depression boom.

1928

Deixa Falar becomes the first *escola de samba* (samba school; called a 'school' because it's located next to a primary school), followed by Mangueira later that year.

1930

Getúlio Vargas comes into power. Inspired by European fascists, Vargas presides over an authoritarian state, playing a major role in Brazilian politics for the next two decades.

Dom João VI fell in love with Rio. A great admirer of nature, he founded the botanical gardens and introduced the notion of sea bathing to Rio's inhabitants. At Caju he had a special pier built with a small tub at the end, in which he would immerse himself fully clothed as the waves rocked gently against it. (His wife, Carlota Joaquina, bathed in the nude.) This was long before Copacabana was opened to the rest of the city, remaining a virgin expanse of white sand framed by rainforest-covered mountains, reachable only by an arduous journey.

With the court came an influx of money and talent that helped build some of the city's lasting monuments, such as the palace at the Quinta da Boa Vista. Within a year of his arrival, Dom João VI also created the School of Medicine, the Bank of Brazil, the Law Courts, the Naval Academy and the Royal Printing Works.

Dom João VI was expected to return to Portugal after Napoleon's Waterloo in 1815, but instead he stayed in Brazil. The following year his mother, mad Queen Dona Maria I, died, and Dom João VI became king. He refused demands to return to Portugal to rule, and declared Rio the capital of the United Kingdom of Portugal, Brazil and the Algarves. Brazil became the only colony of the Americas ever to have a European monarch ruling on its soil.

Five years later Dom João VI finally bowed to political pressure and returned to Portugal, leaving his 23-year-old son Pedro in Brazil as prince regent. In Portugal the king was confronted with the newly formed Côrtes, a legislative assembly attempting to rein in the powers of the monarchy. The Côrtes had many directives, one of which was restoring Brazil to its previous status as a subservient colony. Word was sent to Dom Pedro that his authority had been greatly diminished. According to legend, when Pedro received the directive in 1822, he pulled out his sword and yelled, *'Independência ou morte!'* ('Independence or death!'), putting himself at the country's head as emperor Dom Pedro I.

History Reads

Brazil: Five Centuries of Change (Thomas E Skidmore)

The History of Brazil (Robert M Levine)

The New Brazil (Riordan Roett)

Portugal was too weak to fight its favorite son; meanwhile, the British had the most to gain from Brazilian independence and would have come to the aid of the Brazilians had a conflict ensued. Without spilling blood, Brazil had attained its independence and Dom Pedro I became the head of the Brazilian 'empire' (despite Pedro's claims, Brazil was a regular monarchy, not an empire, since it had no overseas colonies).

Dom Pedro I ruled for only nine years. By all accounts he was a bumbling incompetent who scandalized even the permissive Brazilians by siring numerous illegitimate children. He also strongly resisted any attempts to weaken his power by constitutional means. Following street

1932

Rio holds its first Carnaval parade. Mangueira wins and quickly cements its status as the city's favorite samba school (a sentiment still held by many today).

1937

President Vargas announces a new constitution; he passes minimum-wage laws in 1938, expands the military and centralizes power.

1942

Initially maintaining neutrality, Brazil enters WWII on the Allies' side, providing raw materials, plus 25,000 troops (the only Latin American nation to do so).

1950

Newly constructed Maracanã Stadium plays center stage in the FIFA World Cup. Brazil dominates until the final, when it suffers a stunning loss to Uruguay before 200,000 fans.

demonstrations in Rio in 1831, he surprised everyone by abdicating, leaving power in the hands of his five-year-old, Brazilian-born son.

Brazil then suffered a turbulent period of unrest that finally ended in 1840 when 14-year-old Dom Pedro II took the throne. Despite his youth, his reign stabilized the country and ushered in a long period of peace and relative prosperity. Industrialization began with the introduction of the steamship and the telegraph, and the king encouraged mass immigration from Europe.

Dom Pedro II's shortcomings during his half-century of rule were a bloody war with Paraguay (1864–70) and his slowness in abolishing slavery. He was well liked by his subjects, but eventually they had had enough of the monarchy, and he was pushed from power in 1889.

A true Renaissance man, Dom Pedro II had interests in many subjects – chemistry, philosophy, geology, poetry, anthropology – and he could speak more than a dozen languages (including Arabic and Sanskrit). He corresponded with many great 19th-century figures, including Richard Wagner, Alexander Graham Bell and Louis Pasteur.

The Belle Époque

Rio experienced boom days in the latter half of the 19th century. The spreading wealth of coffee plantations in Rio state (and in São Paulo) revitalized Brazil's economy, just as the city was going through substantial growth and modernization. Regular passenger ships began sailing to London (1845) and Paris (1851), and the local ferry service to Niterói began in 1862. A telegraph system and gas streetlights were installed in 1854. By 1860 Rio had more than 250,000 inhabitants, making it the largest city in South America.

For the wealthy, the goal of creating a modern European capital grew ever closer, as the city embraced all things European – with particular influence from the customs, fashion and even cuisine of Paris. The poor, however, had a miserable lot. In the 1870s and 1880s, as the rich moved to new urban areas by the bay or in the hills, Rio's marginalized lived in tenement houses in the old center of town. There conditions were grim: streets were poorly lit and poorly ventilated, with a stench filling the narrow alleyways.

Rio's flood of immigrants added diversity to the city. On the streets you could hear a symphony of languages – African tongues, Portuguese, English, French – mixing with the sounds of the *bonde* (tram), the clatter of mule-drawn carts, and the cadence of various dances, from maxixes to lundus, polkas and waltzes, interpreted by anonymous performers.

The city went through dramatic changes in the first decade of the 20th century, owing in large part to the work of mayor Pereira Passos. He continued the work of 'Europeanization' by widening Rio's streets and creating grand boulevards, such as Av Central and Mem de Sá. Building the biggest of these boulevards, Av Central (later renamed Rio Branco), required the destruction of 600 buildings; the elegant

1954

Following a political scandal, the military calls for the resignation of President Vargas. He pens a melodramatic letter, then shoots himself at his Rio palace.

1960

President Juscelino Kubitschek moves the capital of Brazil from Rio to the newly constructed Brasília; Rio's political and sociocultural prominence declines.

1963

Brazilian filmmakers create a new movement with Cinema Novo, which tackles Brazil's social problems. Director Glaubo Rocha leads the way with *Black God, White Devil.*

1964

President João Goulart is overthrown by a military coup. Troops arrive in Rio and seize power, and so begins the era of dictatorship, with generals running the show for the next 20 years.

thoroughfare became the Champs-Elysées of Rio, full of sidewalk cafes and promenading *cariocas*.

Passos also connected Botafogo to Copacabana by building a tunnel, paving the way for the development of the southern beaches. Despite his grand vision for Rio, his vision for the poor was one of wide-scale removal from the city center – a short-sighted policy that would dog the Rio (and Brazilian) government for the next 80 years. The *cortiços* (poor, collective lodgings) were breeding grounds for deadly outbreaks of smallpox, yellow fever and typhus. Sighting the widespread health and sanitation problems, the city destroyed thousands of shacks. With

THE ORIGINS OF THE FAVELA

In the Northeast terrible droughts in the 1870s and '80s, coupled with the decline of the sugar industry, brought economic devastation. Offering a vision of hope, Messianic popular movements gained support among Brazil's poor. The most famous was led by Antônio Conselheiro (Antônio the Counselor), an itinerant preacher who had wandered for years through the backlands prophesying the end of the world, defending the poor and antagonizing the authorities. He railed against the new republican government and in 1893 eventually settled with his followers at Canudos, in the interior of northern Bahia. Within 1½ years Canudos had grown to a city of 35,000.

The republican government sensed plots in Canudos to return Brazil to the monarchy. After the first attempts to quiet Canudos failed, the government sent in a federal force of 8000 soldiers – many of whom hailed from Rio – in a war of extermination that nearly wiped out every man, woman and child. The settlement was then burned to the ground to erase it from the nation's memory.

The soldiers and their wives – some of whom were survivors taken from the Canudos massacre – returned to Rio, where they were promised land in exchange for their victory. The government, however, reneged on the promise. The soldiers, who had camped out in front of the Ministry of War, then occupied the nearby hillside of Morro da Providência.

Oddly enough, as the first tenants put up makeshift shelters and settled in, they came across the same hardy shrub they had found in the arid lands surrounding Canudos. Called 'favela,' this plant caused skin irritations in all who came into contact with it – according to some accounts, the shrub even helped repel the army's initial invasions. Over time, hillside residents began calling their new home the Morro da Favela (perhaps in hopes that the plant would protect them from invaders), and the name caught on. Within a generation the word 'favela' was used to describe the ever-increasing number of informal communities appearing around Rio. These communities quickly gathered a mix of former slaves and poverty-stricken inhabitants from the interior, who came to the city seeking a better life.

1968

Caetano Veloso, Gilberto Gil and other musicians release *Tropicália: ou Panis et Circencis*. *Tropicália*, a movement in music and art that takes aim at the military dictatorship, is born.

1968

The government passes the repressive Institutional Act 5, which purges opposition legislators, judges and mayors from public office; most political parties are banned.

1968

The Brazilian economy booms, averaging an incredible 10% growth for the next six years. Rapid income growth continues into the 1970s.

1972

The era of megaprojects and skyrocketing deficits begins with the 5300km Transamazônica highway. It will eventually cost nearly US$1 billion but will never be completed.

no homes, the poor fled to the hills, later creating some of the earliest favelas (slums, informal communities). The city also exterminated rats and mosquitoes and created a modern sewerage system.

By the time Passos' term ended in 1906, Rio was the belle époque capital par excellence of Latin America. Its only possible rival in beauty was Buenos Aires.

Boom Days, Reform & Repression Under Vargas

At the end of the 19th century, the city's population exploded because of both European immigration and internal migration (mostly former slaves from the coffee and sugar regions). By 1900 Rio boasted more than 800,000 inhabitants, a quarter of them foreign born (by contrast, São Paulo's population was 300,000).

Following Passos' radical changes, the period from the early 1920s to the late 1950s was one of Rio's golden ages. With the inauguration of some grand luxury resort hotels (the Glória in 1922 and the Copacabana Palace in 1923), Rio became a romantic destination for Hollywood celebrities and international high society, with Copacabana its headquarters. In some ways Rio's quasi-mythic status as a tropical arcadia spans its entire history, but in the 1940s and '50s its reputation as the urban Eden of Latin America was cemented as the world was introduced to Carmen Miranda, a Rio icon.

This was also when radical changes were happening in the world of music, and when Rio was beginning to celebrate its 'Brazilianness,' namely its mixed heritage and race. Sociologist Gilberto Freyre's influential book *The Masters and the Slaves* (1933) turned things upside down as Brazilians, conditioned to think of their mixed-race past with shame, began to think differently about their heritage – as an asset that set them apart from other nations.

The 1930s was the era of President Vargas, who formed the Estado Novo (New State) in November 1937, making him the first Brazilian president to wield absolute power. Inspired by the fascist governments of Salazar in Portugal and Mussolini in Italy, Vargas banned political parties, imprisoned political opponents, and censored artists and the press.

Despite all this, many liked Vargas. The 'father' of Brazil's workers, he created Brazil's minimum wage in 1938. Each year he introduced new labor laws to coincide with Workers' Day on May 1, to keep Brazil's factory workers sweet. His vision for Brazil was not to increase the country's output but to improve the level of education among all Brazilians.

Outside Rio there are numerous *quilombos* (communities founded by runaway slaves), several of which welcome visitors. The Quilombo do Camorim, about an hour's drive northwest of Barra da Tijuca, offers tours of the community, which sits near the lush Parque Estadual Pedra Branca and hosts cultural events. Contact Rosilane Almeida (www.facebook.com/rosylane.almeyda).

1979–80

The decline of workers' wages leads to nationwide strikes. Unions call for justice, and young workers join with intellectuals and activists to form Brazil's Workers' Party.

1985

After a cautious period of *abertura* (opening), Brazil holds an indirect presidential election. Tancredo Neves wins and millions of Brazilians celebrate the end of military rule.

1985

Neves dies of heart failure before taking office. His vice-presidential candidate, José Sarney, takes power but can't address the inflation and huge debt left by his predecessors.

1994

President Collor de Mello is impeached; Vice-President Itamar Franco takes power. He introduces a new currency, the real, which stabilizes the economy and ushers in an economic boom.

The Military Dictatorship

The world's fascination with Rio was severely curtailed during the rise of the military dictatorship of the 1960s. The era of repression began with press censorship, the silencing of political opponents (sometimes by torture and violence) and an exodus of political activists abroad (including musicians, writers and artists). There were numerous protests during this period (notably in 1968, when some 100,000 people marched upon the Palácio Tiradentes). Even Rio's politicians opposed the military regime, which responded by withholding vital federal funding for certain social programs.

Set in Rio during the military dictatorship, Bruno Barreto's film *Four Days in September* (1997) is based on the 1969 kidnapping of the US ambassador to Brazil by leftist guerrillas.

Despite the repression, the 1960s and '70s witnessed profound changes in the city, with the opening of tunnels and the building of viaducts, parks and landfills. In the realm of public transportation, modernization was on the way. In the 1970s builders connected Rio with Niterói by means of a bay-spanning bridge, while beneath the city the first metro cars began to run.

Meanwhile, the Zona Sul saw skyscrapers rising over the beaches of Copacabana and Leblon, with a shift of the wealthy to places further from neglected downtown Rio. The moving of Brazil's capital to Brasília in 1960 seemed to spell the end for Centro, which became a ghost town after hours and retained none of the energy of its past. By the 1970s its plazas and parks were dangerous places, surrounded by aging office towers.

The center of old Rio remained a bleak place until around 1985, when Brazil held its first direct presidential election in 20 years. With the slow return to civilian rule, *cariocas* turned their attention to sadly abandoned parts of the city, like downtown. Over the next decade citizens, particularly local shop owners, launched a downtown-revitalization campaign, sometimes collecting money by going door to door.

From 1987 to 1997, Brazilians suffered devastating hyperinflation, averaging 2000% annually. This meant that rent doubled every 10 weeks, credit cards charged 25% a month interest, and food and clothing prices went up 40% a month.

By 1995 it was clear that the drive had been a success. Whole blocks in downtown received much-needed facelifts. Handsomely restored buildings attracted new investment, with new shops and cultural centers opening their doors alongside publishers and art galleries. And nightlife returned to Lapa.

Divided City

The latter half of the 20th century was also an era of explosive growth in the favelas, as immigrants poured in from poverty-stricken areas of the Northeast and the interior, swelling the number of urban poor in the city. The Cidade Maravilhosa (Marvelous City) began to lose its gloss as crime and violence increased, and in the 1990s it became known as the Cidade Partida (Divided City), a term that reflected the

2002

Lula da Silva is elected president. The former union leader serves a moderate first term, despite upper-class fears of radical agendas. Meanwhile, Brazil wins its fifth World Cup.

2003

Lula launches the Bolsa Família program of cash payments to 11 million of Brazil's poorest families. The program helps reduce poverty by 27% during Lula's first term.

2006

Despite a corruption scandal in his party, Lula is reelected president. He presides over continued economic growth and receives record approval ratings.

2010

Rio unveils Porto Maravilha, an R$8 billion project that brings museums, parks, bike paths and infrastructure improvements to Rio's waterfront before the 2016 Olympics.

widening chasm between the affluent neighborhoods of the Zona Sul and the slums spreading across the region's hillsides.

As Rio entered the new millennium, crime remained one of the most pervasive problems afflicting the city. Violence continued to take thousands of lives, particularly in the favelas: in 2008, more than 800 people were killed by police during gun battles between law enforcement and drug traffickers (12 police officers were also killed that year). Rio's middle and upper classes seemed mostly resigned to life inside gated and guarded condos, while poverty and violence surged in the nearby slums.

The government's response failed to solve the problem. Crack troops were sent in to take out drug lords, but the heavy-caliber raids often claimed innocent lives. This left many residents with a deep-rooted disdain for the police. Declaring war on the favelas was clearly not working; after the police had left, drug lord in custody (or more likely dead), there was always someone else to take his place.

A New Dawn

As a result of a worsening situation, Brazilian officials began to take a new approach. In 2007 President Lula (full name Luiz Inácio Lula da Silva), who astutely saw the link between poverty and crime, announced that Rio's favelas would receive US$1.7 billion to invest in running water, sanitation, roads and housing. He visited the Cantagalo favela, a first for a Brazilian president. He later told a reporter that such investment – providing adequate services for the people – was the only way to combat drug lords.

Although the first favela appeared on Rio's landscape in 1897, it wasn't until 1994 that the communities were included on maps.

On the local level, police began implementing a new approach to dealing with drug traffickers in the favelas. Led by a new wing called the Pacifier Police Division, they would drive the drug lords out as they had done before, but then some police officers would stay behind in the community. In 2008 the Dona Marta favela became one of the first to be 'pacified,' and millions of reais were invested in the community, repairing or sometimes replacing houses, improving sanitation and adding a new football (soccer) pitch – though the most dramatic improvement was adding a new funicular railroad that saved residents the 788-step slog to the top of the favela. The strategy proved remarkably successful, and was later implemented in about 20 other favelas around Rio, benefiting an estimated 400,000 residents. The success of the pacification program stems in large part from cooperation (and funding) by all three levels of government – municipal, state and federal. Working with President Dilma Rousseff (Lula's successor) was Eduardo Paes, Rio's popular mayor (elected to his second term in 2012), and Sergio Cabral, the state governor. Both were instrumental in carrying out Rio's favela

2010

Rio launches Morar Caricoa, an ambitious R$8 billion favela-improvement scheme to improve infrastructure and living conditions in all 1000 favelas by 2020.

2011

Dilma Rousseff becomes Brazil's first female president. She enjoys widespread popularity for a largely populist agenda in her first term, though she barely wins reelection in 2014.

2014

Rio, along with 11 other Brazilian cities, hosts the 2014 FIFA World Cup. The opener takes place in Maracanã Stadium, which also hosts the opening ceremony of the 2016 Olympics.

2016

In the run-up to the Summer Olympics, Rio opens a new metro line, beautifies its once derelict port district and adds a new light rail to its downtown.

improvements, as well as in developments affecting other facets of the city (notably in infrastructure and civic projects surrounding the 2016 Summer Olympics).

Corruption & Economic Woes

Despite Cabral's successes (the homicide rate also declined substantially while he was governor), his second term ended in disgrace. Street protests erupted in 2013 over rising bus prices and the extravagant funds being lavished on stadiums, while many residents felt that poor services had become the norm. There were also allegations of corruption, and Cabral was later arrested and sentenced to 14 years in prison for his role in a vast bribery scandal.

For insight into the often brutal tactics employed by police to combat drug traffickers, see the semi-fictional film *Tropa Elite* (Elite Squad; 2007). Former police officers and drug traffickers were consulted during research for the film.

Local residents, for the most part, had mixed feelings about Rio's state of progress. While there had been some improvement to social services, formal trash collection and the opening of over 150 new schools, violent crime remained a problem. Unfortunately the problems grew substantially worse in the months following the Olympics. Rio state, on the edge of bankruptcy, cut funding on security, social projects and public works. Joblessness skyrocketed, and violence returned to once peaceful favelas.

On the whole, very few locals benefited from the expensive Olympic preparations. Unsurprisingly, those hit hardest were favela residents. According to the book *SMH 2016: Removals in the Olympic City,* a staggering 67,000 people were evicted from their homes between 2009 and 2013. Amnesty International and other rights organizations have protested the tactics employed: the forcible removal of families, while police disperse the crowd with pepper spray, followed by bulldozers that quickly demolish the buildings.

Following the arrival of the army in Rio in 2018, police and military violence against residents has been a growing concern. Meanwhile, the economic crisis has had some devastating consequences. In 2018, a fast-moving fire destroyed one of the country's most important and best-loved archaeological collections inside the Museu Nacional. Lack of funding to better maintain the site was blamed for the disaster.

2016

Rio hosts the Summer Olympics. It spends an estimated US$13 billion, welcoming over 11,000 athletes from 200 countries, as well as half a million foreign visitors who come to watch the games.

2016

After a widespread corruption scandal is revealed, President Rousseff is impeached. Her vice-president, Michel Temer (also suspected of corruption), assumes power.

2017

Rio's former state governor Sergio Cabral is sentenced to 14 years' imprisonment for corruption and money laundering.

2018

President Temer authorizes the army to take control of security. The military conducts raids on favelas to 'root out' criminals. Human rights organizations decry the violent invasions.

The Sounds of Rio

Rio boasts a rich musical heritage, with live music as deeply connected to Rio culture as its beaches and mountains. Foremost is the city's signature sound of samba, which is heard all across town, particularly in the weeks leading up to Carnaval. Other styles contributing to Rio's lush soundtrack include rock, pop, jazz, Música Popular Brasileira (MPB), hip-hop and *forró* (traditional, fast-paced music from the Northeast) – all opportunities to showcase the city's outstanding pool of musical talent.

Samba

The birth of Brazilian music essentially began with the birth of samba, first heard in the early 20th century in a Rio neighborhood near present-day Praça Onze. Here immigrants from northeastern Brazil (mostly from Bahia) formed a tightly knit community in which traditional African customs thrived – music, dance and the Candomblé religion. Local homes provided the setting for impromptu performances and the exchange of ideas among Rio's first great instrumentalists. Such an atmosphere nurtured the likes of Pixinguinha, one of samba's founding fathers, as well as Donga, one of the composers of 'Pelo Telefone,' the first recorded samba song (in 1917) and an enormous success at the then-fledgling Carnaval.

Samba continued to evolve in the homes and *botequims* (bars with table service) around Rio. The 1930s are known as the golden age of samba. By this point, samba's popularity had spread beyond the working-class neighborhoods of central Rio, and the music evolved at the same time into diverse, less percussive styles of samba. Sophisticated lyricists like Dorival Caymmi, Ary Barroso and Noel Rosa popularized *samba canção* (melody-driven samba). (For insight into Noel Rosa's poetically charged and tragically brief life, check out the 2006 film *Noel: Poeta da Vila.*) Songs in this style featured sentimental lyrics and an emphasis on melody (rather than rhythm), foreshadowing the later advent of cool bossa nova. Carmen Miranda, one of the big radio stars of the 1930s, would become one of the first ambassadors of Brazilian music.

Journalist, author and former dancer Alma Guillermoprieto vividly captures life in the favela of Mangueira and preparations for the big Carnaval parade in her book *Samba*.

The 1930s were also the golden age of samba songwriting for Carnaval. *Escolas de samba* (samba schools), which first emerged in 1928, soon became a vehicle for samba songwriting, and by the 1930s samba and Carnaval would be forever linked. Today's theme songs still borrow from that golden epoch.

Great *sambistas* (samba singers) continued to emerge in Brazil over the next few decades, although other emerging musical styles diluted their popularity. Artists such as Cartola, Nelson Cavaquinho and Clementina de Jesus made substantial contributions to both samba and the styles of music that followed from it.

Traditional samba went through a rebirth over a decade ago with the opening of old-style *gafieiras* (dance halls) in Lapa. Today, Rio is once again awash with great *sambistas*. Classic *sambistas* like Alcione and Beth Carvalho still perform, while singers like Teresa Cristina and Grupo Semente are intimately linked to Lapa's rebirth. Mart'nália, daughter of samba legend Martinho da Vila, is carrying on the tradition of her father. Meanwhile, the talented singer and songwriter Maria Rita, whose voice is remarkably similar to that of her late mother, Elis Regina, continues to create lush, innovative samba-influenced albums.

Bossa Nova

In the 1950s came bossa nova (literally, 'new wave'), sparking a new era of Brazilian music. Bossa nova's founders – songwriter and composer Antônio Carlos (Tom) Jobim and guitarist João Gilberto, in association with lyricist-poet Vinícius de Moraes – slowed down and altered the basic samba rhythm to create a more intimate, harmonic style. This new wave initiated a new style of playing instruments and of singing.

Bossa nova's seductive melodies were very much linked to Rio's Zona Sul, where most bossa musicians lived. Songs such as Jobim's 'Corcovado' and Roberto Meneschal's 'Rio' evoked an almost nostalgic portrait of the city with their quiet lyricism.

By the 1960s bossa nova had become a huge international success. The genre's initial development was greatly influenced by American jazz and blues, and over time the bossa nova style came to influence those musical styles as well. Bossa nova classics were adopted, adapted and recorded by such luminaries as Frank Sinatra, Ella Fitzgerald and Stan Getz, among others.

In addition to the founding members, other great Brazilian bossa nova musicians include Marcos Valle, Luiz Bonfá and Baden Powell. Bands from the 1960s like Sérgio Mendes & Brasil '66 were also influenced by bossa nova, as were other artists who fled the repressive years of military dictatorship to live and play abroad. More recent interpreters of the seductive bossa sound include the Bahian-born Rosa Passos and the *carioca* (Rio resident) Paula Morelenbaum. One band that brilliantly blends bossa nova with electro beats is BossaCucaNova. Their

TIA CIATA: THE MOTHER OF SAMBA

In the early 20th century, one of Rio's most iconic cultural expressions was developing inside the working-class neighborhood of Praça Onze near downtown. In 1915 this was considered 'Africa in miniature' because of the influx of immigrants from Bahia, who had been flocking to the region since the end of slavery in 1888. In Praça Onze, Afro-Brazilian culture – music, dance and religion (Candomblé) – thrived in the homes of old Bahian matriarchs, called *tias* (aunts). At the center of this thriving community was Tia Ciata, something of a self-made woman, who rented out costumes for the Carnaval balls, worked as a healer (she was even consulted by President Venceslau Brás, who had a leg wound that Ciata allegedly healed) and hosted large parties on Candomblé saints' days – all while looking after her 15 children. In time Ciata's house became the meeting point for the city's journalists, bohemians, Bahian expats and musicians. Today's now-legendary names – Pixinguinha, Donga, Heitor dos Prazeres and others – met regularly to play music and experiment with new styles, never imagining that the result, samba, would become one of the world's great musical forms. Coincidentally, this was also around the time that African Americans in New Orleans were playing the music that would later be called jazz.

After the earliest musical creations, the performers gathering at Tia Ciata's went on to make records, and samba's popularity spread like wildfire across the city. The music came first through the working class and, after initial resistance, into the houses of the wealthy. Samba continued to evolve throughout the next few decades as it was adopted for Carnaval, yet the songs developed in those early years would live on (many are still played), and they laid the foundation on which so much Brazilian music is based today.

Sambista (samba singer) Alcione (p185)

latest album, *Our Kind of Bossa* (2014), features veteran singers like Elza Soares and Maria Rita.

Tropicália

One of Brazil's great artistic movements, emerging in the late 1960s, was *tropicália,* a direct response to the repressive military dictatorship that seized power in 1964 (and remained in power until 1984). Bahian singers Caetano Veloso and Gilberto Gil led the movement, making waves with songs of protest against the national regime. In addition to penning defiant lyrics, *tropicalistas* introduced the public to electric instruments, fragmentary melodies and wildly divergent musical styles. In fact, the hero of the *tropicalistas* was poet Oswald de Andrade, whose 1928 *Manifesto Antropofágico* (Cannibalistic Manifesto) supported the idea that anything under the sun could be devoured and recreated in one's music. Hence the movement fused elements of US rock and roll, blues, jazz and British psychedelic styles into bossa nova and samba rhythms. Important figures linked to *tropicália* include Gal Costa, Jorge Ben Jor, Maria Bethânia, Os Mutantes and Tom Zé. Although *tropicália* wasn't initially embraced by the public, who objected to the electric and rock elements (in fact, Veloso was booed off the stage on several occasions), by the 1970s its radical ideas had been absorbed and accepted, and lyrics of protest were ubiquitous in songwriting of the time.

Tropical Truth: A Story of Music and Revolution in Brazil, by Caetano Veloso, describes the great artistic experiment of *tropicália* in 1960s Brazil. Although digressive at times, Veloso's book captures the era's music and politics.

Música Popular Brasileira (MPB)

Música Popular Brasileira is a catchphrase to describe all popular Brazilian music after bossa nova. It includes *tropicália, pagode* (a relaxed and rhythmic form of samba), and Brazilian pop and rock. All Brazilian music has its roots in samba; even in Brazilian rock, heavy metal, disco or pop, the samba sound is often present.

MPB first emerged in the 1970s along with talented musicians such as Edu Lobo, Milton Nascimento, Elis Regina, Djavan and dozens of others, many of whom wrote protest songs not unlike the *tropicalistas*. Chico Buarque is one of the first big names from this epoch, and is easily one of Brazil's greatest songwriters. His musical career began in 1968 and spanned a time during which many of his songs were banned by the military dictatorship – in fact, his music became a symbol of protest during that era. Today the enormously successful *carioca* artist continues to write new albums, though lately he has turned his hand to novel writing.

The Brazilian Sound, by Chris McGowan and Ricardo Pessanha, is a well-illustrated, readable introduction to Brazilian music, with insight into regional styles and musicians (big-name and obscure). The useful discography lists essential albums to add to your collection.

Jorge Ben Jor is another singer whose career, which began in the 1960s, has continued to the present day. Highly addictive rhythms are omnipresent in Benjor's songs, as he incorporates African beats and elements of funk, samba and blues in his eclectic repertoire. The celebratory album *África Brasil* and his debut album, *Samba Esquema Novo* (with recognizable hits like 'Mas, Que Nada!'), are among his best.

Carlinhos Brown continues to make substantial contributions to Brazilian music, particularly in the realm of Afro-Brazilian rhythms. Born in Bahia, Brown has influences that range from *merengue* (fast-paced dance-hall music originating in the Dominican Republic) to Candomblé music to straight-up funk in the style of James Brown (the US artist from whom Carlinhos took his stage name). In addition to creating the popular percussion ensemble Timbalada, he has produced a number of excellent solo albums (notably *Alfagamabetizado*). Involved in many diverse projects, Brown was nominated for an Oscar in 2012 for best original song ('Real in Rio' for the film *Rio*), which he and Sérgio Mendes composed.

The group Da Cruz, headed by the talented Mariana da Cruz, creates lyrically rich songs with infectious disco-charged beats. The album *Disco E Progresso* (2014) features songs about a country divided between the haves and have-nots.

Rock, Pop & Hip-Hop

MPB tends to bleed into other genres, particularly rock and pop. One artist who moves comfortably between genres is Bebel Gilberto (the daughter of João Gilberto), who blends bossa nova with modern beats on jazz-inflected bilingual albums like *All in One* (2009). Another heiress of Brazilian traditions is the Rio-born Marisa Monte, popular at home and abroad for her fine singing and songwriting. Mixing samba, *forró*, pop and rock, Marisa has been part of a number of successful collaborations in the music world. Her brief collaboration with Arnaldo Antunes and Carlinhos Brown resulted in the fine album *Tribalistas* (2003).

Raul Seixas (1945–89) is often called the father of Brazilian rock. Many of his wild rock anthems are well known, and it's not uncommon to hear shouts of *'Toca Raul!'* (Play Raul!) at concerts. Curiously, best-selling author Paulo Coelho cowrote many of his songs.

Other notable young singers who hail from a bossa line include Roberta Sá, whose last album, *Segunda Pele* (2012), features elements of bossa, jazz and even reggae, and Fernanda Porto, whose music is often described as drum 'n' bossa, a blend of electronica and bossa grooves – check out her 2009 album, *Auto-Retrato*. The expat singer-songwriter and performance artist Cibelle incorporates a mix of pop, folk and Brazilian sounds in her lush (mainly English-language) recordings, such as those on *The Shine of Dried Electric Leaves* (2006). Cibelle came to prominence as the main vocalist on Suba's noteworthy album *São Paulo Confessions* (1999). With a host of Grammy nominations to her name, Céu has many fans both at home and internationally. She has recorded three albums over the last seven years, creating dream-like melodies

Brazilian hip-hop artist Marcelo D2

with elements of *tropicália*, samba, reggae and jazz. Her latest, *Caravana Sereia Bloom* (2012), is a colorful work with songs inspired by a road trip across Brazil. Her first album, the self-titled *Céu* (2007), is still considered her best.

Brazilian hip-hop emerged from the favelas (slums, informal communities) of Rio sometime in the 1980s, and has been steadily attracting followers ever since. Big names such as Racionais MC's first emerged out of São Paulo, but Rio has its share of more recent success stories. One of the best on the scene is Marcelo D2 (formerly of Planet Hemp), impressing audiences with albums like *A Procura da Batida Perfeita* (2003) and *A Arte do Barulho* (2008). Better known to international audiences is Seu Jorge, who starred in the film *Cidade de Deus* and performed brilliant Portuguese versions of David Bowie songs on Wes Anderson's film *The Life Aquatic*. His best solo work is *Cru* (2005), an inventive hybrid of hip-hop and ballads, with politically charged beats.

Many top hip-hop artists hail from São Paulo. A few names to look out for include Emicida, a youthful rapper admired for his cutting improvisational rhymes. Check out his funk-laden single 'Triunfo,' one of his early breakthrough songs, or his collaboration with MC Guimê on the antipoverty hit 'País do Futebol.' Yet another Paulista, Rael de Rima is a fast-rapping lyricist with a strong sense of musicality, often performing with guitar and a full back-up band. The MC Criolo tackles themes like urban violence, police brutality and racism, which has made him a hit in the favelas. Following the release of his debut 2011 album, *Nó na Orelha*, he's earned a growing number of admirers. The *carioca* rapper MV Bill is a man with a message. His songs focus on youth facing the ever-present threats of drugs and violence. He's even written a book *(Falcão – Meninos do Tráfico)* and created a network

Music Blogs

The Saudade Project (www.saudadeproject.com)

Slipcue (www.slipcue.com/music/brazil/brazillist.html)

Brazilian Music Day (http://brazilianmusicday.org)

The Brazilian Sound (http://thebraziliansound.blogspot.com)

RIO PLAYLIST

One of the world's great musical cultures, Brazil has an astounding array of talented musicians. The following is a highly subjective pick of 25 songs by 25 different artists.

- 'Canto de Ossanha' – Baden Powell
- 'Soy Loco Por Ti, America' – Caetano Veloso
- 'Alvorado' – Cartola
- 'Samba de Orly' – Chico Buarque and Toquinho
- 'Flor de Lis' – Djavan
- 'Aguas de Março' – Elis Regina (written by Tom Jobim)
- 'Hoje é Dia da Festa' – Elza Soares
- 'Sou Brasileiro' – Fernando Abreu and Mart'nália
- 'Namorinho de Portão' – Gal Costa
- 'Quilombo, O El Dorado Negro' – Gilberto Gil
- 'Desafinado' – João Gilberto
- 'Filho Maravilha' – Jorge Ben Jor
- 'A Procura da Batida Perfeita' – Marcelo D2
- 'Novo Amor' – Maria Rita
- 'Carinhoso' – Marisa Monte (written by Pixinguinha)
- 'Travessia' – Milton Nascimento
- 'Ultimo Desejo' – Noel Rosa
- 'Besta é Tu' – Novos Baianos
- 'Panis et Circenses' – Os Mutantes
- 'Acenda O Farol' – Tim Maia
- 'Garota de Ipanema' (Girl from Ipanema) – Tom Jobim
- 'Aquarela do Brasil' – Toquinho (written by Ary Barroso)
- 'Velha Infância' – Tribalistas
- 'Não Me Deixe Só' – Vanessa da Mata
- 'Felicidade' – Vinicius de Moraes

of youth centers in Rio that offer kids who might otherwise be on the street classes in dancing, music and art. One emerging new artist from Rio is Fabbio Brazza, who blends rap with samba (an unlikely combo) with surprising success in songs like 'Samba de Rap' (on his 2014 album *Filho da Pátria*).

Rock has its promoters, though it enjoys far less airtime than samba. Rio gets its share of mega-rockers on world tours. It also has a few homegrown talents. The group Legião Urbana from Brasília remains one of the all-time greats among rock-lovers. The band (which folded shortly after the death of lead singer Renato Russo in 1996) enjoyed enormous success in the 1980s and early 1990s, and has sold over 15 million records. Raul Seixas, Skank, O Rappa, Os Paralamas do Sucesso and the Rio-based Barão Vermelho are other essential names.

In other genres, indie-rock favorites Los Hermanos were a top band that created catchy albums before breaking up in 2007. Check out *Ventura* (2003) or *Bloco do Eu Souzinho* (2001), one of the seminal pop-rock albums of its time. Vanguart, fitting somewhere in the folk-rock genre, are also a group to watch. Their self-titled debut album (2007) channels samba, blues and classic rock.

The Beautiful Game

Cariocas (Rio residents), like most Brazilians, are football (soccer) mad. No one goes to work on big international game days, with everyone packing into the neighborhood _botecos_ (small, open-air bars) to watch the game. After a big win the whole city celebrates with rowdy nights of partying; should the team lose, the sadness in the air is palpable. Every _carioca_ has a favorite team, and will never pass up the chance to see them play live at Maracanã stadium.

The Football, the Fans

Most of the world generally acknowledges that Brazilians play some of the world's most creative, artistic and thrilling football. They are also generally known as lousy defenders, but no one seems to mind since they make the attack so exciting. The fans, too, are no less fun to watch. Skillful moves and adroit dribbling past an opponent receive a Spanish bullfight-style *'olé!'*, while fans do their best to rev up the action by pounding huge drums (or the backs of the stadium seats), waving giant flags, and launching fireworks and smoke bombs (or sometimes suspicious fluids onto the seats below). Crowds are rambunctious, but they're no more prone to violence than in England, Spain or Italy, for instance.

The Clubs

Rio is home to four major club teams – Flamengo, Fluminense, Vasco da Gama and Botafogo – each with a die-hard local following. Apart from a couple of short breaks for the Christmas and New Year holiday and Carnaval, professional club competitions go on all year. The major event in Rio's sporting calendar is the *classico*, when the four hometown teams play each other. Expect intense and bitter rivalry, matched in excitement only by encounters between Rio and São Paulo clubs.

Futebol, by Alex Bellos (2002), is a fascinating and humorous look at the culture behind Brazil's nationwide obsession, with stories of the legendary players and the way that football has shaped Brazilian society.

Flamengo

The most successful of Rio's big four, Flamengo has an enormous fan base both in Rio and around the world – an estimated 39 million followers, which makes it the most popular football club in Brazil. Flamengo was voted one of the most successful football clubs of the 20th century by FIFA, and it certainly doesn't lack cash flow, with annual revenue of over R$600 million. Famous players who have donned the iconic red-and-black jerseys include Zico, often hailed as the best player never to win a World Cup; Leonidas, leading scorer at the 1938 World Cup; Bebeto, Mario Zagallo and Romario. More recently, Ronaldinho Gaucho, two-time FIFA player of the year, played for Flamengo (2011–12) before making a surprise move to Atlético Mineiro in 2012. He later returned to Rio after signing with Fluminense in 2015.

Flamengo plays its home games at Maracanã; the cheering section is the *setor norte* (north sector, behind the goal). A fan is called a Flamenguista.

Fluminense

Founded by sons of the elite in Laranjeiras back in 1902, Fluminense is a highly successful club that has contributed a number of top players to the national team. It was hailed as the champion of the century, for winning the largest number of Campeonato Carioca titles in the 20th century (28 in all), though its successes have diminished in the current century. Famous players include Didi (1949–56), a superstar midfielder who helped Brazil win the World Cup in both 1958 and 1962, and Roberto Rivellino, who led Fluminense to the state championship in 1975 and 1976 (and was instrumental in Brazil's World Cup victory in 1970). Current stars include Fred (aka Frederico Chaves Guedes), who scored the fastest goal in Brazilian history (finding net 3.17 seconds after the game's start).

Fluminense plays its home games at Maracanã. The cheering section is the *setor sul* (south sector), behind the goal. A fan is known as a Tricolor (a reference to the maroon, green and white uniforms).

The Estádio das Laranjeiras, built for Fluminense in 1905, was the first football stadium constructed in Brazil. It holds 8000 people and still stands today in Laranjeiras, next to the governor's palace.

Vasco da Gama

Founded by Portuguese immigrants near the turn of the 20th century, Vasco remains the favorite club for *cariocas* of Portuguese descent. One of Vasco's all-time greats was Romario (who also played for Flamengo and Fluminense), a powerful striker who scored over 900 goals during his career. Another Vasco legend is Carlos Roberto de Oliveira, nicknamed Roberto Dinamite, who holds the most appearances for the club and is its all-time highest scorer. His passion for Vasco runs deep, and he became president of the club in 2008.

Vasco generally plays its home games at the 25,000-seat Estadio São Januário in the Zona Norte. However, bigger matches (such as the city derbies) are played at Maracanã. At such times, the cheering section is the *setor sul* (south sector), unless the team's playing Fluminense, in which case the cheering section is the *setor norte* (north sector). The uniforms are black with a white diagonal sash. A fan is called a Vascaíno.

The intense interclub rivalry dubbed Fla-Flu (short for Flamengo-Fluminense) began back in 1911, when a group of disgruntled players from Fluminense left the club and went to Flamengo, creating a brand-new team. Games between the clubs attract huge crowds – over 175,000 in 1963, a world record for a club match.

Botafogo

Like other clubs in Rio, Botafogo started out as a rowing club in the late 19th century and quickly embraced football after the game's popularization in the early 1900s. One of Brazil's oldest teams, Botafogo is the only club in Brazilian history to win titles in three different centuries. During the 1950s and '60s, some of Brazil's greatest footballers played for Botafogo, such as Garrincha, who overcame physical disabilities (including legs of uneven length) and became one of the best dribblers of all time. Another legendary player was Nilton Santos, a defender so revered that the club decided to rename their home stadium after him in 2015. Unfortunately, Botafogo's star power diminished significantly in the years after, and in 2002 it was even relegated to the second division after coming last in the Brazilian League (though it quickly returned to the first division the following year).

Botafogo plays its home games at the Estádio Nilton Santos (also known as Engenhão). The stadium was built for the 2007 Pan-Am games, and (under the name Estádio Olímpico) hosted track and field events in the 2016 Summer Olympics. Like Vasco, during big tournaments Botafogo plays in Maracanã. The cheering section is the *setor sul* (south sector), unless the team's playing Fluminense, in which case the cheering section is the *setor norte* (north sector). Botafogo players wear black-and-white striped jerseys; a fan is called a Botafoguense.

PELÉ

One of the world's most famous players – still widely considered to be the greatest ever to have played the game – is Pelé. Not just a legendary footballer, he was also Brazil's first black government minister (for sport, from 1995 to 1998) and he has been knighted by Queen Elizabeth II.

Pelé has come a long way since he was born Edson Arantes do Nascimento in a humble Minas Gerais town on October 23, 1940. Yet despite his stardom, his public image remains impeccable. He's never smoked, has never been photographed with a drink in hand, and has never been involved with drugs.

In a 22-year career, the teams on which Pelé played gained 53 titles, including three World Cups (the first, in Sweden in 1958, when he was just 17 years old) and back-to-back world club championships (with Santos in 1962 and 1963), among many others. Despite lucrative offers to play in Europe, Pelé never did so – in fact, President Janio Quadros had Pelé declared a national treasure in 1971 so that he could not be transferred to a European club.

Pelé retired from the Brazilian team in 1971 and from Santos in 1974. In 1975 the New York Cosmos coaxed him north to the US, where he played until 1977, when the team won the American championship. He finally retired for good at the end of that year, after a game between the Cosmos and Santos in which he played the first half for the Cosmos and the second half with Santos.

In 1366 games (112 for the Brazilian national team), he scored 1282 goals, making him Brazil's all-time highest goal scorer. When he scored his 1000th goal in 1969 in Maracanã stadium, he dedicated it to the children of Brazil.

Pelé, who maintains an oceanfront home in Rio, continues to be a goodwill ambassador for sport, and still commands enormous respect – as evidenced by the roar of the crowd when he made a surprise appearance at the end of the Summer Olympics in London in 2012. In Brazil, Pelé is known simply as 'O Rei' (the king).

Competitions

Apart from the World Cup, which takes place every four years, there are many other tournaments throughout the year. In addition to the key competitions – Campeonato Brasileiro, Copa Libertadores and Campeonato Carioca – other major championships include the Copa do Brasil, the Copa dos Campeões and the Copa América.

Campeonato Brasileiro

The premier competition inside Brazil is the Campeonato Brasileiro (Brazilian Championship). Between about late July and mid-November, 20-odd top clubs play each other once each, then the eight top teams advance to a knockout phase, which culminates in a two-leg final in mid-December to decide the national championship. Since the competition's inception in 1959, São Paulo's top four teams have dominated, followed by Flamengo (five titles), Vasco (four) and Fluminense (four). Underachieving Botafogo has won the championship only twice.

Copa Libertadores

The annual Copa Libertadores is South America's most important football tournament. It's contested by the best-performing clubs from South America and Mexico, and is watched by millions around the world – the event is broadcast in more than 130 countries. It kicks off in February, with the final tournament staged between June and August. Since it was first held in 1960, Argentine teams have won the most titles (24), followed by Brazil (18). Rio's Flamengo and Vasco da Gama have each won the tournament once.

Campeonato Carioca

Each of Brazil's 26 states holds its own championship. Running from January through March, the Campeonato Carioca is the Rio state championship, and one of the oldest held in Brazil – contested since 1906. Although other teams around the state compete, the winner, not surprisingly, is usually one of the big four. Flamengo (34 titles) and Fluminense (31) have dominated, followed by Vasco (24 titles) and Botafogo (21).

Racial Barriers

In 1902, when Oscar Cox, an Anglo-Brazilian, and some of his friends created Rio's first club, Fluminense, it was initially an aristocratic and all-white affair. Black players would not break down the racial barriers until the 1920s, when Vasco da Gama began championing black and multiracial players. By the 1930s Brazil was already gaining fame for its talented players, some of whom were black or biracial and came from poor families, thus inverting the elite-only sport into a sport for the poor and disenfranchised.

Afro-Brazilian player and *carioca* Leonidas da Silva is one of Brazil's early football legends. He played for Vasco, Fluminense and Flamengo, leading each team to the state championship and helping to break down racial barriers. In 1938 he scored the only bicycle-kick goal in World Cup history.

European Vacation

Until recently, most of the best players left Brazil for more lucrative contracts with European clubs. Over the last decade, however, some Brazilian stars have returned home to play for more adoring fans (and not insubstantial contracts). The return of more players to Brazil, coupled with the ongoing growth of new talent in the big clubs, could help transform Brazil into one of the world's footballing giants – at both club and international level.

The World Cup

Bringing the World Cup back to Brazil had long been a dream of the football-crazed nation. In 2007, when Brazil learned that it had won the right to host the 2014 tournament, spontaneous celebrations erupted across town, and tens of thousands took to Copacabana Beach to rejoice in the good news. The South American giant last staged the big sporting event in 1950, when Brazil lost in the dramatic final against Uruguay before some 200,000 fans in Maracanã. This infamous day was later called *'maracanaço'* and the term is still in common use.

Brazil, the most successful football nation in the history of the game (with five World Cup victories), became the fifth country to host the event twice. Aside from Rio, where the opener and final took place, 11 other cities across the country staged games; this, too, was historic, as it was the only time the World Cup was held in more than 10 cities. Brazil spent a staggering R$26 billion in preparation for the event, including stadium construction and upgrades to airports, roads and other infrastructure. Unfortunately, the tournament did not end well for Brazil, which suffered a humiliating 7–1 defeat at the hands of Germany in the semifinals (Brazil subsequently lost the third-place play-off 0–3 against the Netherlands). Germany went on to win the World Cup 1–0 over Argentina.

Architecture

The capital of Brazil for many years, Rio de Janeiro has been the architectural setting for the beautiful, the functional and the avant-garde. Today you can see a sweeping range of styles that span the 17th to the 20th centuries in buildings that often vie for attention alongside one another. The 21st century has brought new eye-catching designs to Rio, with the arrival of several ambitious projects by renowned international architects.

Colonial Rio

Vestiges of the colonial era live on in downtown Rio. Some of the most impressive works are the 17th-century churches built by the Jesuits. The best examples from this, the baroque period, are the Convento de Santo Antônio and the Mosteiro de São Bento. The incredibly ornate interiors, which appear to drip with liquid gold, show little of the restraint that would later typify Brazilian architecture.

The artist mission (a group of artists and architects chosen to bring new life to the city) that arrived from France in the early 19th century introduced a whole new design aesthetic to the budding Brazilian empire. Neoclassicism became the official style and was formally taught in the newly founded Imperial Academy. The works built during this period were grandiose and monumental, dominated by classical features such as elongated columns and wide domes. Among the many fine examples of this period are the Museu Nacional de Belas Artes, the Theatro Municipal and the Casa França-Brasil – considered the most important building from this period. The Casa has a few curious features: its alignment to the cardinal points, the large cross-shaped space inside and its monumental dome.

The end of the 19th century saw the continuation of this trend of returning to earlier forms and featured works such as the Real Gabinete Português de Leitura (Royal Reading Room). Completed in 1887, the room's design was inspired by the much earlier Manueline period (early 1500s), with a Gothic facade and the highlighting of its metallic structure.

Colonial-Era Buildings

Real Gabinete Português de Leitura (p125)

Mosteiro de São Bento (p128)

Igreja de NS do Carmo da Antiga Sé (p126)

Convento de Santo Antônio (p125)

The 20th Century

During the 20th century Rio became the setting for a wide array of architectural styles, including neoclassical, eclectic, art deco and modernist works. During the same period Rio restored some of its colonial-era treasures (others fell to the wrecking ball), becoming one of Latin America's most beautiful cities.

This did not happen by chance. As capital of Brazil, Rio was viewed as a symbol of the glory of the modern republic, and one of Rio's most ambitious mayors, Pereira Passos (in office from 1902 to 1906), lavished European-style neoclassical buildings on the urban streetscape.

Mayor Passos envisioned Rio as the Paris of South America, and he ordered his engineers to lay down grand boulevards and create manicured parks, as some of Rio's most elegant buildings rose overhead. One of the most beautiful buildings constructed during this period was the elegant neoclassical Palaçio Monroe (Monroe Palace; 1906), a recreation of a work built for the 1904 St Louis World's Fair. The Palaçio Monroe sat on the Praça Floriano and housed the Câmara dos Deputados (House of Representatives). Unfortunately, like many of Rio's beautiful buildings, it was destroyed in 1976 in the gross 'reurbanization' craze that swept through the city.

The fruits of this early period were displayed at the International Exposition held in Rio in 1922. This was not only the showcase for neocolonial architecture and urban design; it also introduced Brazil's most modern city to the rest of the world. Another big event of the 1920s was the completion of the Copacabana Palace, the first luxury hotel in South America. Its construction would lead to the rapid development of the beach regions.

Architecture in Print

The Curves of Time, Oscar Niemeyer

When Brazil Was Modern: A Guide to Architecture, 1928–1960, Lauro Cavalcanti

Roberto Burle Marx: The Lyrical Landscape, Marta Iris Montero

Rio's 1930s buildings show the currents of modern European architecture, which greatly impacted upon the city's design. Rio's modernism was born along with the rise of President Vargas, who wanted to leave his mark on federal Rio through the construction of public ministries, official chambers and the residences of government officials. The Ministry of Education & Health, the apotheosis of the modernist movement in Brazil, is one of the city's most significant public buildings, as it's one of the few works designed by French architect Le Corbusier, in conjunction with several young Brazilian architects. (Another Le Corbusier–influenced design is the Aeroporto Santos Dumont, completed in 1937.)

The 1930s was also the era of the art deco movement, which was characterized by highly worked artistic details and an abundance of ornamentation. Good specimens include the central train station and the statue of Cristo Redentor (Christ the Redeemer) on Corcovado.

Oscar Niemeyer

Oscar Niemeyer is one of the giants of 20th-century architecture. Working in the firm of Lúcio Costa, Niemeyer and Costa championed the European avant-garde style in Brazil, making a permanent impact on the next 50 years of Brazilian design. Costa and Niemeyer collaborated on many works, designing some of the most important buildings in Brazil. One of their early successes was their Ministry of Education & Health (built between 1939 and 1943). It was one of Brazil's finest 1930s modernist designs, and a unique collaboration with famed Swiss-French architect Le Corbusier.

In Rio, Niemeyer and Costa broke with the neoclassical style and developed the functional style, with its extensive use of steel and glass,

ARCHITECTURAL ICONS

Belmond Copacabana Palace (p167) The neoclassical gem that came to represent a glitzy new era.

Arcos da Lapa (p139) The 18th-century aqueduct is a widely recognized landmark that also lies at the epicenter of Rio's resurgent music scene in Lapa.

Maracanã Football Stadium (p150) Brazil's temple to football and its largest stadium, freshly made over for the 2014 World Cup.

Museu do Amanhã (p128) Santiago Calatrava's striking building on Praça Mauá is a symbol of Rio's waterfront renaissance.

Theatro Municipal (p124) The flower of the belle époque and the costliest opera house constructed outside Europe.

Arcos da Lapa (p139)

and lack of ornamentation. The Museu de Arte Moderna (inaugurated in 1958) and the Catedral Metropolitana (begun in 1964) are good examples of this style. One of the most fascinating modern buildings close to Rio is the Niemeyer-designed Museu de Arte Contemporânea (MAC) in Niterói. Its fluid form and delicate curves are reminiscent of a flower in bloom (though many simply call it spaceship-like). It showcases its natural setting and offers mesmerizing views of Rio. The MAC is a pivotal part of the Caminho Niemeyer (Niemeyer Way), a collection of seven buildings scattered along the waterfront in Niterói.

Niemeyer, whose designs are known for their elegant curves – the female form was one of his inspirations – became famous for his work designing the nation's capital. He was a longtime Rio resident, and remained passionate about architecture and quite active in the field until his death in 2012 at the age of 104.

A lifelong communist, Niemeyer spent much of the 1960s and '70s in exile due to the military dictatorship. His political affiliations also prevented him from working in the US during the Cold War.

The Petrobras building (Av República do Chile 65, Centro) is often shortlisted by media outlets as one of the world's ugliest buildings. Boxy, gray and uninspiring, the 1970s-era brutalist design looks like a cross between a half-assembled Lego tower and a broken Rubik's Cube.

Recent Projects

The huge amount of investment that poured in for the 2016 Olympic Games led to many new developments around the city.

In 2013 Rio officially inaugurated the Cidade das Artes (City of the Arts) in Barra da Tijuca. The controversial project, originally slated to open in 2008, ran significantly over budget (the projected R$86-million cost eventually ran to over R$500 million). The ultramodern 90,000-sq-meter complex houses a high-tech, 1800-seat concert hall, as well as theaters, a chamber-music hall and a terrace with picturesque views over Barra. Designed by the Pritzker prize–winning French architect

Museu do Amanhã (p128)

Christian de Portzamparc, the building is the new base of the Brazilian Symphony Orchestra.

The revitalization of Rio's derelict port area has also seen a host of new developments. The Rio Museum of Art on Praça Mauá cleverly joins two existing buildings – one a neoclassical early-20th-century mansion, the other a modernist building (and former train station). The unusual juxtaposition serves as an apt metaphor for the mix of classical and contemporary works inside. It opened in 2014. Nearby, the dramatic Santiago Calatrava–designed Museu do Amanhã (Museum of Tomorrow) juts into the water, with a cantilevered roof and a sculptural facade for which Calatrava is so well known. It opened in late 2015.

The cutting-edge Museu da Imagem e do Som (Museum of Image and Sound) will bring a bold new look to Copacabana's boxy, skyscraper-lined waterfront. The design, by New York architectural firm Diller Scofidio + Renfro (the team behind the famous High Line in Manhattan), integrates the building into its dramatic setting – between seafront and hilly backdrop. Public access, outdoor ramps and open-air space (including a rooftop amphitheater) will ensure that the building is accessible to all. It is loosely scheduled to open in late 2020.

Survival Guide

TRANSPORTATION..200

ARRIVING IN RIO DE JANEIRO.....200

Galeão (GIG)..... 200

Santos Dumont (SDU)...200

Rodoviária Novo Rio 201

GETTING AROUND..... 201

Bicycle 201

Boat 201

Bus 201

Car & Motorcycle..... 202

Metro 202

Taxi 202

Train 203

Tram 203

Walking 203

TOURS 203

Bay Cruises..... 203

Bicycle Tours 203

City Tours..... 203

Food Tours..... 204

Favela Tours..... 204

Helicopter Tours..... 204

4WD Tours..... 204

Walking Tours 204

DIRECTORY A–Z....205

Accessible Travel 205

Courses 205

Customs Regulations..... 206

Discount Cards..... 206

Electricity 206

Embassies & Consulates 206

Emergency 207

Health.....207

Internet Access.....207

Legal Matters 208

LGBT+ Travelers..... 208

Medical Services 208

Money..... 208

Opening Hours 209

Post..... 209

Public Holidays..... 209

Telephone 209

Time 210

Toilets.....210

Tourist Information.....210

Visas.....210

LANGUAGE 211

Transportation

ARRIVING IN RIO DE JANEIRO

Flying is the easiest way to get to Rio, with some flights stopping first in São Paulo (one hour away). High-season prices for a return ticket from gateways in North America and Europe typically run from US$900 to US$1400. Long-distance buses arrive in Rio from Chile and Argentina.

Flights, cars and tours can be booked online at www.lonelyplanet.com/bookings.

Galeão (GIG)

Rio's **Galeão international airport** (Aeroporto Internacional Antônio Carlos Jobim; ☎21 3004-6050; www.riogaleao.com; Domestic Arrival Hall, Av Vinte de Janeiro) is 15km north of the city center on Ilha do Governador. It has left-luggage facilities, an internet cafe, ATMs and currency-exchange desks, pharmacies, and a few shops and restaurants.

Airlines flying from Galeão include **Avianca** (AV; ☎21 3398-2529; www.avianca.com), **Azul** (AD; ☎11 4003-3255; www.voeazul.com.br) and **Gol** (G3; ☎0300-115 2121; www.voegol.com.br).

Bus

Premium Auto Ônibus (one way R$16) operates air-con buses along several itineraries. For the Zona Sul, take bus 2018, known locally as the *frescão*. The bus leaves from outside the arrivals floor of Terminal 1 or the ground floor of terminal 2 and runs to Novo Rio bus station, Aeroporto Santos Dumont, south through Glória, Flamengo and Botafogo, and along the beaches of Copacabana, Ipanema and Leblon to Barra da Tijuca (and vice versa) every 30 minutes from 5:30am to 11pm and will stop wherever you ask. The fare is R$16 and the trip takes one to two hours depending on traffic. You can transfer to the metro at Carioca station.

Heading to the airport, you can catch this bus from in front of the major hotels along the main beaches, but you have to look alive and flag it down.

Shuttle

There's a **shuttle** (☎21 2524-7730; www.shuttlerio.com.br; one way R$25; ⏲hourly 8am-7pm) from Terminals 1 and 2 to hotels in Copacabana, Ipanema and Leblon. Reserve ahead.

Many hotels and hostels arrange airport transport, typically charging upwards of R$100.

Taxi

A yellow-and-blue *comum* (common) taxi costs around R$82 to R$100 to Copacabana or Ipanema, depending on traffic (more on Sunday and late at night). A charge of R$2.50 per piece of luggage also applies. Taxis are generally safe, though robberies are occasionally reported.

More expensive, slightly fancier and safer radio taxis charge a set fare of about R$130 to Copacabana or Ipanema. The fare is payable by credit card (or cash) at the counters just before leaving the international arrivals area.

You can use a ride-sharing app (p203) to order a car. Expect to pay around R$60 to Ipanema.

Traffic can lead to long delays on the return journey to the airport; allow up to two hours during peak times (4pm to 7pm).

Santos Dumont (SDU)

Aeroporto Santos Dumont (Map p246; ☎21 3814-7222; www4.infraero.gov.br; Praça Senador Salgado Filho), used by some domestic flights, is by the bay, in the city center, 1km east of Cinelândia metro station. It has ATMs, a few shops and an internet cafe.

Bus

Premium Auto Ônibus service 2018, which departs from Galeão airport, stops at Santos Dumont before

CLIMATE CHANGE & TRAVEL

Every form of transport that relies on carbon-based fuel generates CO_2, the main cause of human-induced climate change. Modern travel is dependent on airplanes, which might use less fuel per kilometer per person than most cars but travel much greater distances. The altitude at which aircraft emit gases (including CO_2) and particles also contributes to their climate change impact. Many websites offer 'carbon calculators' that allow people to estimate the carbon emissions generated by their journey and, for those who wish to do so, to offset the impact of the greenhouse gases emitted with contributions to portfolios of climate-friendly initiatives throughout the world. Lonely Planet offsets the carbon footprint of all staff and author travel.

continuing south to Copacabana and Ipanema.

Light Rail

Rio's new light rail (the VLT), which began operations in 2016, runs from Santos Dumont Airport to the Rodoviária (bus station) via Praça Mauá. This is handy, as you can hop on the metro at the second stop (Cinelândia). The VLT is also useful if you're catching an onward bus, but be mindful of traveling during rush hour if you have luggage as the trams can be quite crowded.

Taxi

Comum taxis cost about R$40 to Copacabana and R$50 to Ipanema. A radio taxi runs R$60 to Copacabana and R$75 to Ipanema.

Rodoviária Novo Rio

Long-distance buses arrive at the sleek **Rodoviária Novo Rio** (Map p253; ☎21 3213-1800; www.novorio.com.br; Av Francisco Bicalho 1), 2km northwest of Centro. There's a Riotur desk here for city info. If you're traveling without much luggage, you can get to/from the bus station using Rio's new light rail, the VLT. If you're headed south, transfer to the metro at Central.

A small booth near the exit at Novo Rio bus station organizes the yellow taxis out the front. Sample fares (with one bag) are about R$50 to the international airport, R$50 to Copacabana and Ipanema, and R$35 to Santa Teresa.

You can consult the schedule and buy tickets online at www.clickbus.com. There's a dedicated pickup booth in the front of the bus terminal. Major bus companies like **Viação 1001** (☎0800-941-3334; www.autoviacao1001.com.br) have frequent departures to São Paulo.

A handful of travel agents, including **Guanatur** (☎21 2548-3275; Dias da Rocha 16A, Copacabana; ⏲9am-6pm Mon-Fri, to noon Sat) and **Dantur** (☎21 2557-7144; www.dantur.com.br; Loja 47, Largo do Machado 29, Flamengo; ⏲9am-6:30pm Mon-Fri, to 1pm Sat), sell bus tickets; the commission is around R$8 per ticket.

GETTING AROUND

Bicycle

Rio has many kilometers of bike paths along the beach, around Lagoa and along Parque do Flamengo. In addition to the public bike-sharing scheme, **Bike Rio** (www.bikeitau.com.br/bikerio), you can rent bikes from stands along the east side of Lagoa Rodrigo de Freitas for around R$20 per hour and at various bike shops along the bike path between Copacabana and Ipanema.

For an excellent guided bike tour, contact **Rio by Bike** (Map p236; ☎21 96871-8933; www.riobybike.com; Av NS de Copacabana 1085, Copacabana; tours R$100-135) or **Bike in Rio** (Map p236; ☎98474-7740; www.bikeinriotours.com; tours US$63-150).

Boat

Rio has several islands in the bay that you can visit by ferry, including Ilha de Paquetá and Ilha Fiscal. Another way to see the city is by taking the commuter ferry to Niterói. Niterói's main attraction is the Museu de Arte Contemporânea, but many visitors board the ferry just for the fine views of downtown and the surrounding landscape. On weekdays the Niterói **ferry** (Map p246; ☎0800-721-1012; www.grupoccr.com.br/barcas; one way R$6.10; ⏲6am-11:30pm Mon-Fri, to 11pm Sat, to 10:30pm Sun) departs every 10 to 20 minutes (departures are half-hourly on Saturday and hourly on Sunday). The boat leaves Praça XV (Quinze) de Novembro in Centro.

Bus

Rio's new BRS (Bus Rapid System) features dedicated public-transportation corridors in Copacabana, Ipanema, Leblon and Barra. Fares on most buses are around R$3.50.

Every bus has its key destination displayed on the illuminated signboard in front. If you see the bus you want, hail it by sticking your arm straight out (drivers won't stop unless flagged down).

Car & Motorcycle

Driving & Parking

In the city itself, driving can be a frustrating experience even if you know your way around. Traffic snarls and parking problems do not make for an enjoyable holiday. Be aware that Rio has extremely strict drink-driving laws (the Lei Seca, or 'dry law'), with a fine of around R$2000 for those with a blood-alcohol content of over 0.06%. Police checkpoints are set up nightly around the city in changing locations.

Rental

Hiring a car is fairly simple as long as you have a driver's license, a credit card and a passport. Most agencies require renters to be at least 25 years old, though some will rent (with an added fee) to younger drivers.

Prices start at around R$100 per day for a car without air-conditioning, but they go down a bit in the low season. If you are quoted prices on the phone, make sure they include insurance, which is compulsory.

Car-rental agencies can be found at both airports and scattered along Av Princesa Isabel in Copacabana.

RENTAL AGENCIES

At the international airport:

Hertz (☎21 2153-2124; www.hertz.com; Av Vinte de Janeiro; ⏲24hr)

Budget (☎21 3398-2350; www.budget.com; Av Vinte de Janeiro)

Unidas (☎21 97697-0407; www.unidas.com.br; Av Vinte de Janeiro; ⏲24hr)

In Copacabana:

Hertz (☎21 2275-3340; Av Princesa Isabel 500; ⏲8am-8pm Mon-Sat, to 2pm Sun)

Unidas (☎21 2543-2067; www.unidas.com.br; Av Princesa Isabel 214; ⏲8am-7:45pm Mon-Fri, to 5:45pm Sat).

Metro

Rio's **metro system** (www.metrorio.com.br; 1 ride R$4.30; ⏲5am-midnight Mon-Sat, 7am-11pm Sun) is an excellent way to get around. Its three lines are air-conditioned, clean and efficient. Line 1 goes from Ipanema-General Osório to Uruguai in the north zone. Line 2, which partly overlaps line 1, travels from Botafogo to Pavuna (passing Maracanã football stadium en route). Line 4 travels between Ipanema-General Osório and the eastern end of Barra da Tijuca at Jardim Oceânico.

You can purchase a *cartão pré-pago* (prepaid card) from a kiosk in any metro station using cash (no change given) with a minimum of R$5. You can then recharge the card at any kiosk. Free subway maps are available from most ticket booths.

During Carnaval the metro operates nonstop from 5am Saturday morning until at least 11pm on Tuesday.

METRO-BUS TICKETS

The **Metrô Na Superfície** (www.metrorio.com.br) subway bus consists of modern, silver buses that make limited stops as they shuttle passengers to and from metro stations. For most destinations, a one-way *metrô na superficie* (surface metro) ticket costs the same as a single metro ride (R$4.30) but includes both the bus and the metro ride.

The most useful option for travelers is the line to Gávea, which passes through Jardim Botânico. It departs from outside Botafogo metro station and stops at Cobal do Humaitá, Rua Maria Angélica, the Hospital da Lagoa, the edge of Jardim Botânico, Praça Santos Dumont, Gávea Trade Center and PUC (Pontifical Catholic University of Rio de Janeiro).

Taxi

Rio's yellow taxis are plentiful, and easy to hail, particularly by using free apps like 99Taxis or Easy Taxi. They're generally a speedy way to zip around and are usually safe. The flat rate is around R$5.50, plus around R$2.50 per kilometer (R$3 per kilometer at night and on Sunday). Radio taxis, which can be ordered in advance, are 30% more expensive than regular taxis. No one tips taxi drivers, but it's common to round up the fare.

Especial Coop Taxi (☎21 3295-9606, WhatsApp 21 99776-5347; www.facebook.com/especialcoop) has vehicles with lifts for wheelchair users. It also has its own app, Especial Coop.

If you prefer to reserve a car, a few reliable radio-taxi operators include **Transcoopass** (☎21 2209-1555; www.transcoopass.com.br), **Coopertramo** (☎21 2209-9292; www.radio-taxi.com.br), **Transcootour** (☎21 2590-2220; www.transcootour.com.br) and **Cootramo** (☎21 3976-9944; www.cootramo.com.br).

In Rocinha and some other favelas (slums, informal communities), mototaxis (basically a lift on the back of a motorcycle) are a handy way to get around, with short rides (usually from the bottom of the favela to the top or vice versa) costing R$3. That said, given the currently unstable security situation, it's unwise to head into a favela on a moto-taxi.

Ride-Sharing Apps

Uber is available in Rio de Janeiro, and service is widespread and generally quite good; it costs about 30% less than a traditional taxi. Lyft is not currently available.

Train

The suburban train station, **Estação Dom Pedro II** (Central do Brasil; ☎0800 726-9494; www.supervia.com.br; Av Presidente Vargas, Praça Cristiano Ottoni, Centro), is one of Brazil's busiest commuter stations, but it's not the safest area to walk around. To get there, take the metro to Central station and head upstairs. This is the train station that was featured in the Academy Award–nominated film *Central do Brasil* (Central Station).

Tram

Rio was once serviced by a multitude of *bondes* (trams), with routes throughout the city. The only remaining line is the *bonde* to Santa Teresa, which reopened 1.7km of its 10km of track in 2015. It runs from the **bonde station** (Lélio Gama 2; per trip R$20; ⏲8am-5pm Mon-Fri, 10am-5pm Sat, 11am-4:30pm Sun) in Centro and travels over the scenic Arcos da Lapa and along Rua Joaquim Murtinho only as far as Largo do Guimarães before turning around.

Walking

Apart from Barra da Tijuca, Rio's neighborhoods are perfect for getting around on foot.

TOURS

Tours in Rio range from historical surveys to strolls through Atlantic rainforest. Aside from providing context for the city's natural beauty and historical treasures, tours can be another fun way to experience the city, whether by sailboat, helicopter, 4WD or bicycle.

Bay Cruises

Sail in Rio (Map p244; ☎21 99998-3709; www.sailinrio.com; Av Pasteur 333, late Clube do Rio de Janeiro; sailing tours from R$250) This recommended outfit offers memorable sailing tours around Rio. When the weather cooperates, there are daily departures (at 11am) from the yacht club in Urca. You can also arrange your own private sailings with up to 10 people; you choose the date and help design the itinerary (private sailings cost R$1500 for three hours, R$1800 for five hours).

Bem Brasil (Map p241; www.bembrasilrio.com; Marina da Glória, Glória; cruises from R$75) Runs popular booze cruises in the bay from a two-story yacht every Monday night at 11pm. Also hosts big, fun parties in Rio venues, including **Barzin** (Map p228; www.facebook.com/barzinriolive; Vinícius de Moraes 75; ⏲noon-1am Sun, Mon, Wed & Thu, noon-4am Tue, Fri & Sat) on a Tuesday night and **Palaphita Gávea** (Map p234; ☎21 3114-0853; www.palaphitakitch.com.br; Bartolomeu Mitre 1314; ⏲6pm-1am Mon, 8pm-4am Thu, 9pm-4am Fri & Sat, 5pm-1am Sun) on a Thursday.

Bicycle Tours

Bike in Rio (Map p236; ☎98474-7740; www.bikeinriotours.com; tours US$63-150) Offers fun half- and full-day bicycle tours around Rio. The four-hour Beach Getaway takes in Copacabana, Parque do Flamengo and the murals and museums of Boulevard Olímpicio. The Carioca Sunset tour goes around Ipanema, Lagoa and Jardim Botânico (and includes a visit to the botanical gardens). A third itinerary travels through the lush scenery of the Parque Nacional da Tijuca.

Rio by Bike (Map p236; ☎21 96871-8933; www.riobybike.com; Av NS de Copacabana 1085, Copacabana; tours R$100-135) Two Dutch journalists operate this biking outfit, and their excellent pedaling tours combine scenery with cultural insight. It's a great way to get an overview of the city, with guides pointing out landmarks and describing key events that have shaped Rio. Tours generally last three to four hours and travel mostly along bike lanes separated from traffic.

City Tours

Brazil Expedition (☎21 99998-2907; www.brazilexpedition.com; all-day city tours R$160) Friendly English-speaking guides run a variety of traditional tours around Rio, including trips to Cristo Redentor, hikes in Parque Nacional da Tijuca, game-day trips to Maracanã football stadium, street-art tours and favela (slum, informal community) tours.

Marcelo Esteves (☎21 99984-7654; marcelo.esteves@hotmail.com; 5/8hr tours US$200/300) A highly experienced multilingual Rio expert offering private tours around the city.

Madson Araújo (☎21 99395-3537; www.tourguiderio.com; 5hr tours from US$300)

Professional English- and French-speaking guide offering custom-made day or night tours around Rio.

Food Tours

Eat Rio Food Tours (www.eatrio.net; tours from US$75) On these highly recommended small-group tours, you'll visit markets, snack bars and other foodie hot spots to taste a wide range of fruits, juices and street food little known outside Brazil. The English-speaking guides are excellent and provide culinary as well as cultural insights. The cost of the tour covers all food, including snacks and a big meal at the end. Tours begin in Lapa or Santa Teresa. Eat Rio also offers a nighttime bar-food tour and an afternoon experience in Santa Teresa where you'll taste Brazilian wines on a terrace with panoramic views.

Fruit Brazil (www.fruitbrazil.com; tours per person R$105) This outfit focuses on the tropical fruits of Brazil, taking small groups on an in-depth, 90-minute tasting tour through a local market in Ipanema. The market varies depending on the day of the week.

Favela Tours

Favela Tour (☎21 3322-2727; www.favelatour.com.br; tours R$95) Marcelo Armstrong's insightful tour pioneered favela tourism. His three-hour excursion in Rocinha provides a fascinating insight into life inside the favela. You'll also stop in a community school, with funding from his tours helping to support various social projects.

Paulo Amendoim (☎21 99747-6860; www.favelatourrio.com; tours R$75) Recommended guide Paulo Amendoim is the former president of Rocinha's residents association. He seems to know everyone in the favela, and leads a warm and personalized three-hour tour that helps visitors see beyond the stereotypes.

Be A Local (☎21 99643-0366; www.bealocal.com; tours from R$100) Offers daily trips into the favela of Rocinha. You'll head up by van and walk back down, with stops along the way. It also organizes a night out at a *baile* (dance) funk party in Castelo das Pedras on Sunday.

Helicopter Tours

Helisight (Map p234; ☎21 2542-7935; www.helisight.com.br; 6/15/30min flight per person R$350/880/1220) Offering helicopter tours since 1991, Helisight has seven itineraries, all giving gorgeous views over the city. There's a three-person minimum. Helipad locations are at the edge of Lagoa and on Morro da Urca, the first cable-car stop up Pão de Açúcar.

4WD Tours

Jeep Tour (☎21 2108-5800; www.jeeptour.com.br; 4hr tours from R$180) Large, open-topped 4WDs go to the Floresta da Tijuca, with a stop at the Vista Chinesa viewpoint, followed by an easy forest hike and a waterfall visit. The price includes hotel pickup and drop-off. Other excursions include trips around the beaches of Búzios.

Walking Tours

Free Walker Tours (Map p246; ☎21 97101-3352; www.freewalkertours.com) This well-organized outfit runs a free walking tour that takes in a bit of history and culture in downtown Rio. You'll visit the Travessa do Comércio, Praça XV (Quinze) do Novembre, Cinelândia, the Arcos da Lapa and the Selarón steps, among other places. Although it's free, the guide asks for tips at the end: R$50 is fair for the insightful three-hour walk. The tour departs at 10:30am Monday through Saturday from Largo da Carioca (exit C out of Carioca metro station). Just show up; reservations aren't necessary. The same outfit also leads pub crawls in Ipanema and Lapa (each R$60), as well as a free Copacabana and Ipanema walking tour.

Lisa Rio Tours (☎21 99894-6867; www.lisariotours.com; tours from US$50) Lisa Schnittger, a German expat who has lived in Rio for many years, leads a wide range of recommended tours. Some of her most popular excursions explore the colonial history of downtown, the bohemian side of Santa Teresa and Afro-Brazilian culture in Rio.

Directory A–Z

Accessible Travel

Rio is probably the most accessible city in Brazil for travelers with disabilities to get around, but that doesn't mean it's always easy. It's convenient to hire cars with driver-guides, but for only one person the expense is quite high compared to the cost of the average bus tour. If there are several people to share the cost, it's definitely worth it. For transportation around the city, make contact with **Especial Coop Taxi** (☎21 3295-9606, WhatsApp 21 99776-5347; www.facebook.com/especialcoop).

The metro system has electronic wheelchair lifts, but it's difficult to know whether they're actually functional. Major sites are only partially accessible – there are about 10 steps to the gondola base of Pão de Açúcar, for instance; and although there's access to the base of Cristo Redentor, there are about two dozen steps to climb before you can reach the statue itself. **Jeep Tour** (☎21 2108-5800; www.jeeptour.com.br; 4hr tours from R$180) offers excursions for mobility-impaired travelers.

The streets and sidewalks along the main beaches have curb cuts and are wheelchair accessible, but most other areas do not have cuts. Most of the newer hotels have wheelchair-accessible rooms, but many restaurants have entrance steps.

The **Centro de Vida Independente** (Map p234; ☎21 2512-1088; www.cvi-rio.org.br; Marquês de São Vicente 225, Gávea; ⏲10am-5pm Mon-Fri) can provide advice about travel in Brazil for visitors with disabilities.

Download Lonely Planet's free Accessible Travel guides from http://lptravel.to/AccessibleTravel.

Courses

Cooking

Cook in Rio (Map p236; ☎21 98894-9857; www.cookinrio.com; 2nd fl, Belfort Roxo 161, Copacabana) Run by Simone Almeida, Cook in Rio is a hands-on one-day course that shows you how to prepare either *moqueca* (seafood stew) or *feijoada* (black bean and pork stew). You'll also learn how to make other sides and drinks including *aipim frito* (fried cassava slices), a perfect pot of rice, dessert and a masterful caipirinha (the secret's in the slicing of the lime). The best part is that you'll get to devour your creations afterwards. Courses cost US$75 per person and include the cost of all food and drinks.

Language

Caminhos Language Centre (Map p228; ☎21 2267-6552; www.caminhoslanguages.com; Farme de Amoedo 135, Ipanema; private class per hour R$90, 4-week 80hr course R$1800) Offers competitively priced Portuguese classes, with intensive group classes – four hours a day for five days for R$450. Profits go toward its social project Mais Caminhis (www.maiscaminhos.org).

Carioca Languages (Map p241; ☎21 98847-0797; www.carioca-languages.com; Sala 6, Rua do Catete 227, Catete; 4-week 60hr course R$1550, online course per hour R$80; ⏲10am-5pm Mon-Fri) A wide range of courses as well as private instruction and online classes.

Instituto Brasil-Estados Unidos (IBEU; Map p236; ☎21 2548-8430; http://portuguese.ibeu.org.br; 5th fl, Av NS de Copacabana 690, Copacabana; intensive 36hr course R$2300) One of the oldest, more respected language institutions in Rio de Janeiro.

Music

Maracatu Brasil (Map p242; ☎21 2557-4754; www.maracatubrasil.com.br; 2nd fl, Ipiranga 49, Laranjeiras;

⏲11am-8pm Mon-Sat) This is the best place in Rio to study percussion, and students have the opportunity to perform in different music events throughout the city. Instructors here offer courses in a number of different drumming styles: Amazonian rhythms, samba, conga drums, Candomblé and much more, plus private lessons in guitar and other instruments. If you plan to stick around in Rio a while, you can sign up for group classes (from R$180 per month) or hire an instructor for private classes. Maracatu also sells instruments on the 1st floor of the building.

Dance

Casa de Dança Carlinhos de Jesus (Map p244; ☎21 2541-6186; www.casadedanca.com; Álvaro Ramos 11, Botafogo; ⏲12:30-11pm Mon-Fri, 10am-6pm Sat) At this respected dance academy in Botafogo, Carlinhos and his instructors offer evening classes in samba, forró (a popular music of the Northeast), salsa and tango. On occasional weekend nights, open dance parties for students and guests are held. One of Botafogo's colorful *bloco* parties, Dois Pra Lá, Dois Pra Cá, begins from here during Carnaval.

Rio Samba Dancer (☎21 98229-2843; www.riosambadancer.com; group/private class US$20/60, private class for 2/3 people US$65/90) English-speaking dance instructor Hélio Ricardo offers private and group dance classes in samba or *forró*. To try out your new dance moves, take a samba class and night tour combo: you'll get a one-hour crash course, then head out to Lapa for a night of dancing in a club (US$60 per person, including guide, transportation and club admissions).

Customs Regulations

Travelers entering Brazil can bring in 2L of alcohol, 400 cigarettes and one personal computer, video camera and still camera. Newly purchased goods worth up to US$500 are permitted duty-free. Fruits, meat, fish and cheese products are not allowed.

Discount Cards

You can save cash at several museums and sights (up to 50% at some places) if you have an international student card (ISIC), available to full-time students. A few tour agencies (such as Urban Adventures) also give small (10%) student discounts. Apply for an ISIC (www.isic.org) well before hitting the road.

Electricity

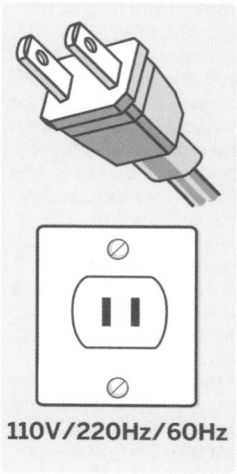

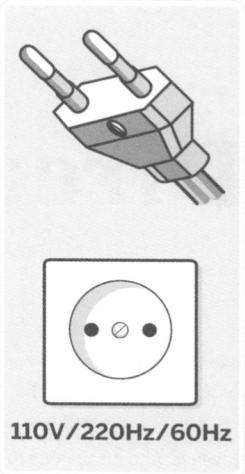

Embassies & Consulates

Many countries have consulates or embassies in Rio. Consulates are listed in Riotur's monthly *Guia do Rio*.

Argentine Consulate (☎21 3850-8150; www.crioj.cancilleria.gov.ar; Sobreloja/1st fl, Praia de Botafogo 228, Botafogo; ⏲10am-3pm Mon-Fri)

Australian Consulate (☎21 3824-4624; www.dfat.gov.au; 23rd fl, Av Presidente Wilson 231, Centro; ⏲10am-4pm Mon-Fri)

Bolivian Consulate (☎21 2552-5490; www.consuladodeboliviaenrio.org.br; No 101, Av Rui Barbosa 664, Flamengo; ⏲9am-2pm Mon-Fri)

Canadian Consulate (☎21 2543-3004; www.brasil.gc.ca; 13th fl, Av Atlântica 1130, Copacabana; ⏲8am-12:30pm & 1:30-5pm Mon-Thu, 8am-12:30pm Fri)

Ecuadorian Consulate (☎21 3738-0380; www.riodejaneiro.consulado.gob.ec; 6th fl, Av Ataúlfo de Paiva 1079, Leblon; ⏲10am-3pm Mon-Fri)

French Consulate (☎21 3974-6699; http://riodejaneiro.ambafrance-br.org; Av Presidente Antônio Carlos 58, Centro; ⏲8:30am-12:30pm Mon-Fri by appointment, 2:30-4pm Tue & Wed)

German Consulate (☎21 3380-3700; www.rio-de-janeiro.diplo.de; Av Presidente Antônio Carlos 58, Centro; ⏲8:30-11:30am Mon, Tue, Thu & Fri, 1-3pm Wed)

Netherlands Consulate (☎21 2157-5400; www.nederlandenu.nl; 6th fl, Av Ataúlfo de Paiva 204, Leblon; ⏲8:30am-4pm Mon-Thu, to noon Fri)

Paraguayan Consulate (☎21 2553-2294; Sala 1009, Praia de Flamengo 66, Flamengo; ⏲8:30am-3:30pm Mon-Fri)

Peruvian Consulate (☎21 2551-9596; www.consuladoperurio.com.br; 2nd fl, Av Rui Barbosa 314, Flamengo; ⏲9am-3pm Mon-Fri)

Spanish Consulate (☎21 2543-3200; Room 1601, Rua Lauro Müller 116, Botafogo; ⏲8:30am-1pm Mon-Fri)

UK Consulate (☎21 2555-9600; www.reinounido.org.br; 2nd fl, Praia do Flamengo 284, Flamengo; ⏲8:30am-12:30pm & 1:30-4:30pm Mon-Fri)

Uruguayan Consulate (☎21 2553-6030; www.emburuguai.org.br; 12th fl, Praia de Botafogo 210, Botafogo; ⏲10am-4pm Mon-Fri)

US Consulate (☎21 3823-2000; www.brazil.usembassy.gov; Av Presidente Wilson 147, Centro; ⏲8am-5pm Mon-Fri)

Venezuelan Consulate (☎21 2554-5955; 14th fl, Av Presidente Vargas 463, Centro; ⏲9am-1pm Mon-Fri)

Emergency

You don't need a phone card to call emergency numbers in Rio.

Report robberies to the **tourist police** (☎21 2332-2924; cnr Afrânio de Melo Franco & Humberto de Campos, Leblon; ⏲24hr); no major investigation is going to occur, but you will get a police form to give to your insurance company.

Ambulance	☎192
Fire Department	☎193
Police	☎190

Health

Recommended Vaccinations

Although no vaccinations are required to visit Rio, you should consider getting a yellow-fever vaccination. In 2017 an outbreak of this hemorrhagic fever swept across various parts of the country, reaching the periphery of Rio and over 230 people, including several tourists, died. Note that shortages of the vaccine (particularly in the US) in recent years have made for some long waits, so plan ahead.

The Centers for Disease Control (www.cdc.gov) recommends you stay up to date on all the routine vaccines. These include vaccines for measles-mumps-rubella (MMR), diphtheria-tetanus-pertussis, varicella (chickenpox) and the polio vaccine. The CDC also recommends vaccines for hepatitis A and typhoid.

Since most vaccines don't produce immunity until at least 10 days after they're given, visit a physician well in advance of your departure. Ask your doctor for an International Certificate of Vaccination (otherwise known as the yellow booklet), which will list all the vaccinations you've received. This is mandatory for countries that require proof of yellow-fever vaccination upon entry, but it's a good idea to carry it wherever you travel.

Tap Water

Tap water in Rio is safe to drink but, owing to the treatment process, it may not taste very pleasant. Aside from buying bottled water, you can bring your own filter to improve the taste. Some hotels have their own filtration system to improve the water quality.

Zika Virus

Brazil has experienced several outbreaks of Zika virus since 2015. Transmitted by mosquitoes, Zika rarely causes illness – only one in five infected people will experience the flu-like symptoms. However, the virus has been linked to microcephaly (abnormally small head size with possible brain damage) in babies born to women who were infected while pregnant. Check the latest warnings with the US Centers for Disease Control (CDC) before you travel. If there's an outbreak, pregnant women should consider postponing travel to Brazil.

Internet Access

Most accommodations – including hostels and midrange hotels – provide wi-fi access. It's usually free, though some luxury hotels still charge exorbitant rates for it. You'll also find free wi-fi in most cafes and in many restaurants, as well as in some shopping malls.

Given the widespread availability of wi-fi and the popularity of smartphones, internet cafes are a vanishing breed, though there are still a few scattered around Copacabana and other areas of the Zona Sul. The remaining places charge between R$6 and R$12 an hour.

Blame It on Rio 4 Travel (Map p236; ☎21 3813-5510; www.blameitonrio4travel.com;

Xavier da Silveira 15B, Copacabana; @) offers internet access.

Legal Matters

You are required by law to carry some form of identification. For travelers, this generally means a passport, but a certified copy of the relevant ID page will usually be acceptable.

In the past few years, Rio has gotten serious about drink-driving, and the penalties for driving under the influence are severe. Marijuana and cocaine are plentiful in Rio, and both are highly illegal. An allegation of drug trafficking or possession provides the police with the perfect excuse to lean on you for a bribe – and Brazilian prisons are brutal places. If you are arrested, know that you have the right to remain silent, and that you are innocent until proven guilty. You also have a right to visitation by your lawyer or a family member.

LGBT+ Travelers

Rio is the gay capital of Latin America. There's no law against homosexuality in Brazil. During Carnaval, thousands of gay expatriate Brazilians and foreign tourists fly in for the festivities. Cross-dressers steal the show at all Carnaval balls, especially the gay ones.

Outside Carnaval, the gay scene is fairly subdued. The most gay-friendly street in town is Farme de Amoedo in Ipanema, with cafes, restaurants and drinking spots.

You may hear or read the abbreviation GLS, particularly in the entertainment section of newspapers and magazines. It stands for Gays, Lesbians and Sympathizers, and when used in connection with venues or events basically indicates that anyone with an open mind is welcome. In general the scene is much more integrated than elsewhere; and the majority of parties involve a pretty mixed crowd.

The **Rio Gay Guide** (www.riogayguide.com) has information for gay and lesbian tourists, including sections on Carnaval, nightlife and bathhouses. Its more up-to-date Twitter feed (@riogayguide) lists the night's big parties and other events.

Medical Services

Some private medical facilities in Rio are on a par with US hospitals. The UK and US consulates have lists of English-speaking physicians.

Hospitals

Clinica Galdino Campos (☎21 2548-9966; www.galdinocampos.com.br; Av NS de Copacabana 492, Copacabana; ⏲24hr) The best hospital for foreigners, with high-quality care and multilingual doctors (who even make outpatient calls). The clinic works with most international health plans and travel-insurance policies.

Pharmacies

Pharmacies stock all kinds of drugs and sell them much more cheaply than in the West. However, when buying drugs anywhere in South America, be sure to check the expiration dates and specific storage conditions. Some drugs that are available in Brazil may no longer be recommended, or may even be banned, in other countries. Common names of prescription medicines in South America are likely to be different from the ones you're used to; ask a pharmacist before taking anything you're not sure about.

There are scores of pharmacies in town, a number of which stay open 24 hours.

Drogaria Pacheco (☎21 2521-2124; Visconde de Pirajá 82, Ipanema; ⏲24hr)

Money

The monetary unit of Brazil is the real (R$; pronounced hay-*ow*); the plural is reais (pronounced hay-*ice*).

The real is made up of 100 centavos. Most prices are quoted in reais, though some tour operators and hoteliers prefer to list their rates in US dollars or euros.

ATMs

ATMs are the handiest way to access money in Rio. Unfortunately, there has been an alarming rise in card cloning, with travelers returning home to find unauthorized withdrawals on their cards. This has been especially problematic with Bradesco ATMs, which you should avoid at all costs.

When possible, use high-traffic ATMs inside bank

PRACTICALITIES

Newspapers & Magazines The English-language *Rio Times* (www.riotimesonline.com) maintains a website updated weekly. *Jornal do Brasil* and *O Globo* are Brazil's leading dailies. *Veja* is the country's best-selling weekly magazine. In Rio it comes with the 'Veja Rio' insert, available on Sunday, which details entertainment options for the week ahead.

Smoking Banned in restaurants and bars; some hotels have rooms for smokers.

Weights & Measures Brazil uses the metric system.

buildings during banking hours. Always cover your hands when inputting your PIN, and check your account frequently to make sure you haven't been hacked.

ATMs for most card networks are widely available.

Banco do Brasil has branches with ATM in **Centro** (Av Ataúlfo de Paiva 980, Leblon), **Copacabana** (Av NS de Copacabana 1274; ⏲10am-4pm Mon-Fri) and **Galeão international airport** (1st fl, Terminal 1).

Changing Money

For exchanging cash, *casas de cambio* (exchange offices) cluster behind the Copacabana Palace hotel in Copacabana and along Visconde de Pirajá near Praça General Osório in Ipanema.

Credit Cards

Visa is the most widely accepted credit card in Rio; MasterCard, American Express and Diners Club are also accepted by many hotels, restaurants and shops.

Credit-card fraud is rife in Rio, so be very careful. When making purchases keep your credit card in sight at all times. Have staff bring the machine to your table or follow them to the cashier – don't give them your card.

Tipping

Restaurants *Serviço* (service charge) usually included in bills and mandatory; when *serviço* not included, leave 10%, more if a waiter is friendly and helpful.

Juice stands, bars, coffee corners, street and beach vendors Tipping not customary but a welcome gesture.

Parking assistants Usually about R$4 (these workers receive no wages and are dependent on tips).

Taxi drivers Not usually tipped; round up the fare.

Opening Hours

Standard Rio opening hours:

Restaurants noon–3pm and 7–11pm

Bars noon–2am Monday to Saturday; some open Sunday

Nightclubs 11pm–5am Thursday to Saturday

Shops 9am–6pm Monday to Friday, to 1pm Saturday

Malls 10am–10pm Monday to Saturday, 3–10pm Sunday

Banks 9am–3pm Monday to Friday

Post

Postal services are decent in Brazil, and most mail gets through. Airmail letters to the US and Europe usually arrive in a week or two. For Australia and Asia, allow three weeks.

There are yellow mailboxes on the street, but it's safer to go to a *correios* (post office). Most post offices are open 8am to 6pm Monday to Friday, and until noon on Saturday.

Branches include **Botafogo** (Map p244; Praia do Botafogo 324; ⏲9am-5pm Mon-Fri), **Copacabana** (Map p236; Av NS de Copacabana; ⏲9am-5pm Mon-Fri) and **Ipanema** (Map p228; Prudente de Morais 147; ⏲9am-5pm Mon-Fri).

Public Holidays

New Year's Day January 1

Day of São Sebastião January 20

Carnaval February/March (the two days before Ash Wednesday)

Good Friday & Easter Sunday March/April

Tiradentes Day April 21

May Day/Labor Day May 1

Corpus Christi late May/June (60 days after Easter Sunday)

Independence Day September 7

Day of NS de Aparecida October 12

All Souls' Day November 2

Proclamation of the Republic November 15

Black Consciousness Day November 20

Christmas Day December 25

Telephone

Public phones are nicknamed *orelhões* (floppy ears). They take a *cartão telefônico* (phone card), available from newsstands and street vendors in denominations of R$5 to R$20.

To phone Rio from outside Brazil, dial your international-access code, then 55 (Brazil's country code), 21 (Rio's area code) and the number.

To make a local collect call, dial 9090, then the numbers. For calls to other cities, dial 0, then the code of your selected long-distance carrier, then the two-digit area code, followed by the local number. You need to choose a long-distance carrier that covers both the place you are calling from and the place you're calling to. Carriers advertise their codes in areas where they're prominent, but you can usually use Embratel (code 21) or Telemar (code 31) nationwide.

To make an intercity collect call, dial 9 before the 0xx (the 'xx' representing the two-digit carrier as explained above, ie '21', '31' or a host of other Brazilian carriers). A recorded message in Portuguese will ask you to say your name and where you're calling from, after the tone.

Cell Phones

The *celular* (cell phone) is ubiquitous in Rio. Cell phones have nine-digit numbers beginning with 9.

Brazil uses the GSM 850/900/1800/1900 network, which is compatible with North America, Europe and Australia. The country's

4G LTE network runs on 2500/2690 (for now), which is not compatible with many North American and European smartphones.

Good news for some Americans: if you have an LTE/GSM-capable device (like certain models of the iPhone6) on Sprint or T-Mobile, you can get unlimited texting and data in Brazil on certain plans – though on the 2G network (meaning data is quite slow/nonexistent). You can, however, purchase additional data for better use. Check to see if your iPhone is compatible on www.apple.com/iphone/LTE.

Calls to cell phones are more expensive than calls to landlines. Cell phones have city codes, like landlines, and if you're calling from another city you have to use them. TIM (www.tim.com.br), Claro (www.claro.com.br), Oi (www.oi.com.br) and Vivo (www.vivo.com.br) are the major operators.

Foreigners can purchase a local SIM with a passport instead of needing a Brazilian CPF (tax ID number), though this option is often ignored by cellular providers – prepare for a battle.

If you have an unlocked GSM phone, you can simply buy a SIM card (called a *chip*) for around R$10 to R$20. Among the major carriers, TIM generally has the most hassle-free service. You can then add minutes by purchasing additional airtime from any newspaper stand. Incoming calls are free.

Time

Brazil has four official time zones. Rio, in the southeastern region, is three hours behind Greenwich Mean Time (GMT), four hours behind during the Northern Hemisphere summer. Rio also observes daylight-saving time, pushing the clocks one hour forward from early November to mid-February.

Toilets

➡ Public toilets are available at the *postos* (numbered posts) along the beachfront, and Copacabana has many subterranean bathrooms just off the beach; look for the stairs. It costs around R$2 to use these toilets.

➡ Big shopping centers have (usually well-maintained) facilities.

➡ Staff will generally let you use the toilets in restaurants and bars. Juice bars and other small eateries don't have public toilets.

➡ As elsewhere in Brazil, toilet paper isn't flushed. There's usually a basket next to the toilet to put paper in.

Tourist Information

Riotur's multilingual website (www.visit.rio) is a good source of information. Its offices distribute maps and guides about major events; the main branch is in **Copacabana** (Map p236; ☎21 2541-7522; Av Princesa Isabel 183; ⏲9am-6pm Mon-Fri). There are branches at Galeão airport's **Terminal 1** (Domestic Arrivals Hall ⏲6am-11pm) and **Terminal 2** (International Arrivals Hall; ⏲6am-11pm).

Central 1746 (☎21 2271-7048, 1746; www.1746.rio.gov.br; ⏲24hr) is Rio's City Hall directory assistance. Press 8 for tourist info, then 1 for English.

Visas

Brazil has a reciprocal visa system, so if your home country requires Brazilian nationals to secure a visa, then you'll need a visa to enter Brazil. US, Canadian and Australian citizens need visas, but UK, New Zealand, French and German citizens do not. You can check your status with the Brazilian embassy or consulate in your home country.

If you do need a visa, arrange it well in advance. Note that visas are not issued on arrival. Applying for a visa got easier in 2018 when Brazil rolled out its new e-visa system, which is available to US, Canadian, Australian and Japanese tourists and business travelers. The application fee is $40, plus an online service fee ($4.24).

To apply, visit the official website endorsed by Brazil's Ministry of Foreign Affairs: VFS Global (www.vfsglobal.com/Brazil-eVisa). You will need to upload a passport photograph and a scanned image of your passport bio page. E-visas are valid for two years, for stays of up to 90 days per year.

Once all documents have been submitted, processing time is around five business days. Unfortunately the online application process does not run very smoothly. Many applicants have had problems uploading photos, have had their photos rejected or have experienced website crashes.

After your visa has been approved, you will receive a pdf of your e-visa. Print this out and take it with you on your trip. Without the printed copy, you may not be allowed to board your flight and might be denied entry to the country.

Old-fashioned consular visas are also still available. These are pricier and you'll have to apply in person at a Brazilian consulate in your home country.

Applicants under 18 must also submit a notarized letter of authorization from a parent or legal guardian.

Entry & Exit Card

On entering Brazil, all tourists must fill out a *cartão de entrada/saida* (entry/exit card); immigration officials will keep half, you'll keep the other. Don't lose this card! When you leave Brazil the second half of the card will be taken by immigration officials.

Language

Portuguese is spoken by around 190 million people worldwide, 90% of whom live in Brazil. Brazilian Portuguese today diff ers from European Portuguese in approximately the same way that British English diff ers from American English. European and Brazilian Portuguese have diff erent spelling, pronunciation and, to some extent, vocabulary. For example, in Portugal, the word for 'train' is comboio and in Brazil you'd say trem.

Most sounds in Portuguese are also found in English. The exceptions are the nasal vowels (represented in our colored pronunciation guides by ng after the vowel), which are pronounced as if you're trying to make the sound through your nose, and the strongly rolled r (represented by rr in our pronunciation guides). Also note that the zh sounds like the 's' in 'pleasure'. The stressed syllables (generally the second-last syllable of a word) are indicated with italics. If you keep these few points in mind and read our pronunciation guides as if they were English, you'll have no problems being understood. The abbreviations (m) and (f) indicate masculine and feminine gender, whereas (sg) and (pl) stand for 'singular' and 'plural' respectively.

BASICS

Hello.	*Olá.*	o·*laa*
Goodbye.	*Tchau.*	tee·*show*
How are you?	*Como vai?*	*ko*·mo vai
Fine, and you?	*Bem, e você?*	beng e vo·*se*
Excuse me.	*Com licença.*	kong lee·*seng*·saa
Sorry.	*Desculpa.*	des·*kool*·paa
Yes./No.	*Sim./Não.*	seeng/nowng
Please.	*Por favor.*	por faa·*vorr*
Thank you.	*Obrigado.* *Obrigada.*	o·bree·*gaa*·do (m) o·bree·*gaa*·daa (f)
You're welcome.	*De nada.*	de *naa*·daa

What's your name?
Qual é o seu nome? kwow e o *se*·oo *no*·me

My name is ...
Meu nome é ... *me*·oo *no*·me e ...

Do you speak English?
Você fala inglês? vo·*se faa*·laa eeng·*gles*

I don't understand.
Não entendo. nowng eng·*teng*·do

WANT MORE?

For in-depth language information and handy phrases, check out Lonely Planet's *Brazilian Portuguese Phrasebook*. You'll find it at **shop.lonelyplanet.com**, or you can buy Lonely Planet's iPhone phrasebooks at the Apple App Store.

ACCOMMODATIONS

Do you have a single/double room?
Tem um quarto de solteiro/casal? teng oom *kwaarr*·to de sol·*tay*·ro/kaa·*zow*

How much is it per night/person?
Quanto custa por noite/pessoa? *kwang*·to *koos*·taa porr *noy*·te/pe·*so*·aa

Can I see it?
Posso ver? *po*·so verr

campsite	*local para acampamento*	lo·*kow paa*·raa aa·kang·paa·*meng*·to
guesthouse	*hospedaria*	os·pe·daa·*ree*·a
hotel	*hotel*	o·*tel*
youth hostel	*albergue da juventude*	ow·*berr*·ge daa zhoo·veng·*too*·de
air-con	*ar condicionado*	aarr kong·dee·syo·*naa*·do
bathroom	*banheiro*	*ba*·nyay·ro
bed	*cama*	*ka*·maa
window	*janela*	zhaa·*ne*·laa

KEY PATTERNS

To get by in Portuguese, mix and match these simple patterns with words of your choice.

When's (the next flight)?
Quando é (o próximo vôo)? — kwaang·do e (o pro·see·mo vo·o)

Where's the (tourist office)?
Onde fica (a secretaria de turismo)? — ong·de fee·kaa (aa se·kre·taa·ree·aa de too·rees·mo)

I'm looking for (a hotel).
Estou procurando (um hotel). — es·to pro·koorr·ang·do (oom o·tel)

Do you have (a map)?
Você tem (um mapa)? — vo·se teng (oom maa·paa)

Is there (a bathroom)?
Tem (banheiro)? — teng (ba·nyay·ro)

I'd like (a coffee).
Eu gostaria de (um café). — e·oo gos·taa·ree·aa de (oom kaa·fe)

I'd like to (hire a car).
Eu gostaria de (alugar um carro). — e·oo gos·taa·ree·aa de (aa·loo·gaarr oom kaa·ho)

Can I (enter)?
Posso (entrar)? — po·so (eng·traarr)

Could you please (help me)?
Você poderia me (ajudar), por favor? — vo·se po·de·ree·aa me (aa·zhoo·daarr) por faa·vorr

Do I have to (get a visa)?
Necessito (obter visto)? — ne·se·see·to (o·bee·terr vees·to)

DIRECTIONS

Where is ...?
Onde fica ...? — ong·de fee·kaa ...

What's the address?
Qual é o endereço? — kwow e o eng·de·re·so

Could you please write it down?
Você poderia escrever num papel, por favor? — vo·se po·de·ree·aa es·kre·verr noom paa·pel porr faa·vorr

Can you show me (on the map)?
Você poderia me mostrar (no mapa)? — vo·se po·de·ree·aa me mos·traarr (no maa·paa)

at the corner	*na esquina*	na es·kee·naa
at the traffic lights	*no sinal de trânsito*	no see·now de trang·zee·to
behind ...	*atrás ...*	aa·traaz ...
in front of ...	*na frente de ...*	naa freng·te de ...
left	*esquerda*	es·kerr·daa
near ...	*perto ...*	perr·to ...
next to ...	*ao lado de ...*	ow laa·do de ...
opposite ...	*do lado oposto ...*	do laa·do o·pos·to ...
right	*direita*	dee·ray·taa
straight ahead	*em frente*	eng freng·te

EATING & DRINKING

What would you recommend?
O que você recomenda? — oo ke vo·se he·ko·meng·daa

What's in that dish?
O que tem neste prato? — o ke teng nes·te praa·to

I don't eat ...
Eu não como ... — e·oo nowng ko·mo ...

Cheers!
Saúde! — sa·oo·de

That was delicious.
Estava delicioso. — es·taa·vaa de·lee·see·o·zo

Bring the bill/check, please.
Por favor traga a conta. — porr faa·vorr traa·gaa aa kong·taa

I'd like to reserve a table for ...	*Eu gostaria de reservar uma mesa para ...*	e·oo gos·taa·ree·aa de he·zer·vaarr oo·maa me·zaa paa·raa ...
(eight) o'clock	*(às oito) horas*	(aas oy·to) aw·raas
(two) people	*(duas) pessoas*	(doo·aas) pe·so·aas

Key Words

bottle	*garrafa*	gaa·haa·faa
breakfast	*café da manha*	ka·fe daa ma·nyang
cold	*frio*	free·o
cup	*xícara*	shee·kaa·raa
dessert	*sobremesa*	so·bre·me·zaa
dinner	*jantar*	zhang·taarr
drink	*bebida*	be·bee·daa
entree	*entrada*	eng·traa·daa
fork	*garfo*	gaarr·fo
glass	*copo*	ko·po
hot (warm)	*quente*	keng·te
knife	*faca*	faa·kaa
lunch	*almoço*	ow·mo·so
market	*mercado*	merr·kaa·do
menu	*cardápio*	kaar·da·pyo
plate	*prato*	praa·to
restaurant	*restaurante*	hes·tow·rang·te
spicy	*apimentado*	aa·pee·meng·taa·do
spoon	*colher*	ko·lyerr

vegetarian food	*comida vegetariana*	ko·*mee*·daa ve·zhe·taa·ree·*a*·naa
with/without	*com/sem*	kong/seng

Meat & Fish

beef	*carne de vaca*	*kaar*·ne de *vaa*·kaa
chicken	*frango*	*frang*·go
crab	*siri*	*see*·ree
fish	*peixe*	*pay*·she
fruit	*frutas*	*froo*·tas
lamb	*carneiro*	karr·*nay*·ro
meat	*carne*	*kaar*·ne
oyster	*ostra*	*os*·traa
pork	*porco*	*porr*·ko
seafood	*frutos do mar*	*froo*·tos do maarr
shrimp	*camarão*	ka·ma·*rowng*
tuna	*atum*	aa·*toong*
veal	*bezerro*	be·*ze*·ho
vegetable	*legumes*	le·*goo*·mes

Fruit & Vegetables

apple	*maçã*	maa·*sang*
apricot	*damasco*	daa·*maas*·ko
asparagus	*aspargo*	aas·*paarr*·go
avocado	*abacate*	aa·baa·*kaa*·te
beetroot	*beterraba*	be·te·*haa*·baa
cabbage	*repolho*	he·*po*·lyo
capsicum	*pimentão*	pee·meng·*towng*
carrot	*cenoura*	se·*no*·raa
cherry	*cereja*	se·*re*·zhaa
corn	*milho*	*mee*·lyo
cucumber	*pepino*	pe·*pee*·no
garlic	*alho*	*aa*·lyo
grapes	*uvas*	*oo*·vaas
lemon	*limão*	lee·*mowng*
lettuce	*alface*	ow·*faa*·se
mushroom	*cogumelo*	ko·goo·*me*·lo
nut	*noz*	noz
onion	*cebola*	se·*bo*·laa
orange	*laranja*	laa·*rang*·zhaa
pea	*ervilha*	err·*vee*·lyaa
peach	*pêssego*	*pe*·se·go
pineapple	*abacaxí*	aa·baa·kaa·*shee*
plum	*ameixa*	aa·*may*·shaa
potato	*batata*	baa·*taa*·taa
pumpkin	*abóbora*	aa·*bo*·bo·raa
spinach	*espinafre*	es·pee·*naa*·fre
strawberry	*morango*	mo·*rang*·go
tomato	*tomate*	to·*maa*·te
vegetables	*legumes*	le·*goo*·mes
watermelon	*melancia*	me·lang·*see*·aa

Other

bread	*pão*	powng
cake	*bolo*	*bo*·lo
cheese	*queijo*	*kay*·zho
chilli	*pimenta*	pee·*meng*·taa
eggs	*ovos*	*o*·vos
honey	*mel*	mel
ice cream	*sorvete*	sorr·*ve*·te
jam	*geléia*	zhe·*le*·yaa
lentil	*lentilha*	leng·*tee*·lyaa
olive oil	*azeite*	a·*zay*·te
pepper	*pimenta*	pee·*meng*·taa

CARIOCA SLANG

Making an effort with the language is something Brazilians will greatly appreciate. *Díria* (slang) is a big part of the *carioca* dialect spoken by the residents of Rio. Here are a few words and phrases :

babaca ba·*ba*·ka – jerk

bunda *boon*·da – bottom/bum

Eu gosto de você. *e*·oo *gosh*·too zhi vo·*se* – I like you.

Falou! fa·*low* – Absolutely!/You said it!

Fique à vontade. feek a van·*tazh* – Make yourself at home.

fio dental *fee*·oo den·*tow* – dental floss, aka bikini

gata/gato *ga*·ta/*ga*·too – good-looking woman/man

Nossa! *no*·sa – Gosh!/You don't say! (lit: 'Our Lady')

sunga *soong*·ga – tiny swim shorts favored by *carioca* men

Ta ótimo!/Ta legal! ta *a*·che·moo/ta lee·*gow* – Great!/Cool!/OK!

Tudo bem? *too*·doo beng – Everything OK?

Tudo bem. *too*·doo beng – Everything's OK.

Valeu. va·*le*·o – Thanks.

Vamu nessa! va·moo·*ne*·sa – Let's go!

SIGNS

Banheiro	Bathroom
Entrada	Entrance
Não Tem Vaga	No Vacancy
Pronto Socorro	Emergency Department
Saída	Exit
Tem Vaga	Vacancy

rice	*arroz*	*a·hoz*
salt	*sal*	sow
sauce	*molho*	*mo·lyo*
sugar	*açúcar*	aa·*soo*·kaarr

Drinks

beer	*cerveja*	serr·*ve*·zhaa
coffee	*café*	kaa·*fe*
fruit juice	*suco de frutas*	*soo*·ko de *froo*·taas
milk	*leite*	*lay*·te
red wine	*vinho tinto*	*vee*·nyo *teeng*·to
soft drink	*refrigerante*	he·free·*zhe*·*rang*·te
tea	*chá*	shaa
(mineral) water	*água (mineral)*	*aa*·gwaa (mee·ne·*row*)
white wine	*vinho branco*	*vee*·nyo *brang*·ko

EMERGENCIES

Help!	*Socorro!*	so·*ko*·ho
Leave me alone!	*Me deixe em paz!*	me *day*·she eng paas

Call ...!	*Chame ...!*	*sha*·me ...
a doctor	*um médico*	oom *me*·dee·ko
the police	*a polícia*	aa po·*lee*·syaa

It's an emergency.
É uma emergência. — e oo·maa e·merr·*zheng*·see·aa

QUESTION WORDS

How?	*Como é que?*	*ko*·mo e ke
What?	*Que?*	ke
When?	*Quando?*	*kwang*·do
Where?	*Onde?*	*ong*·de
Which?	*Qual?/Quais?* (sg/pl)	kwow/kais
Who?	*Quem?*	keng
Why?	*Por que?*	porr ke

I'm lost.
Estou perdido. — es·*to* perr·*dee*·do (m)
Estou perdida. — es·*to* perr·*dee*·daa (f)

I'm ill.
Estou doente. — es·*to* do·*eng*·te

It hurts here.
Aqui dói. — a·*kee* doy

I'm allergic to (antibiotics).
Tenho alergia à (antibióticos). — *te*·nyo aa·lerr·*zhee*·aa aa (ang·tee·bee·o·tee·kos)

Where are the bathrooms?
Onde tem um banheiro? — *on*·de teng oom ba·*nyay*·ro

SHOPPING & SERVICES

I'd like to buy ...
Gostaria de comprar ... — gos·taa·*ree*·aa de kong·*praarr* ...

I'm just looking.
Estou só olhando. — es·*to* so o·*lyang*·do

Can I look at it?
Posso ver? — *po*·so verr

How much is it?
Quanto custa? — *kwang*·to *koos*·taa

It's too expensive.
Está muito caro. — es·*taa mweeng*·to *kaa*·ro

Can you lower the price?
Pode baixar o preço? — *po*·de bai·*shaarr* o *pre*·so

There's a mistake in the bill.
Houve um erro na conta. — o·ve oom e·ho naa *kong*·taa

ATM	*caixa automático*	*kai*·shaa ow·too·*maa*·tee·ko
credit card	*cartão de crédito*	kaarr·*towng* de *kre*·dee·to
post office	*correio*	ko·*hay*·o
tourist office	*escritório de turismo*	es·kree·*to*·ryo de too·*rees*·mo

TIME & DATES

What time is it?
Que horas são? — kee *aw*·raas sowng

It's (10) o'clock.
São (dez) horas. — sowng (des) *aw*·raas

Half past (10).
(Dez) e meia. — (des) e *may*·aa

morning	*manhã*	ma·*nyang*
afternoon	*tarde*	*taar*·de
evening	*noite*	*noy*·te
yesterday	*ontem*	*ong*·teng
today	*hoje*	o·zhe
tomorrow	*amanhã*	aa·ma·*nyang*
Monday	*segunda-feira*	se·*goong*·daa·*fay*·ra

Tuesday	*terça-feira*	terr·saa·*fay*·raa
Wednesday	*quarta-feira*	kwaarr·taa·*fay*·raa
Thursday	*quinta-feira*	keeng·taa·*fay*·raa
Friday	*sexta-feira*	ses·taa·*fay*·raa
Saturday	*sábado*	saa·baa·do
Sunday	*domingo*	do·*meeng*·go

January	*janeiro*	zha·*nay*·ro
February	*fevereiro*	fe·ve·*ray*·ro
March	*março*	marr·so
April	*abril*	aa·*bree*·oo
May	*maio*	maa·yo
June	*junho*	zhoo·nyo
July	*julho*	zhoo·lyo
August	*agosto*	aa·*gos*·to
September	*setembro*	se·*teng*·bro
October	*outubro*	o·*too*·bro
November	*novembro*	no·*veng*·bro
December	*dezembro*	de·*zeng*·bro

TRANSPORTATION

boat	*barco*	*baarr*·ko
bus	*ônibus*	o·nee·boos
plane	*avião*	aa·vee·*owng*
train	*trem*	treng

a ... ticket	*uma passagem de ...*	oo·maa paa·*sa*·zheng de ...
1st-class	*primeira classe*	pree·*may*·raa *klaa*·se
2nd-class	*segunda classe*	se·*goom*·daa *klaa*·se
one-way	*ida*	ee·daa
return	*ida e volta*	ee·daa e *vol*·taa

What time does it leave/arrive?
A que horas sai/chega? aa ke *aw*·raas sai/*she*·gaa

Does it stop at ...?
Ele para em ...? e·*le paa*·raa eng ...

Please stop here.
Por favor pare aqui. poor faa·*vorr paa*·re aa·*kee*

bus stop	*ponto de ônibus*	*pong*·to de o·nee·boos
ticket office	*bilheteria*	bee·lye·te·*ree*·aa
timetable	*horário*	o·*raa*·ryo
train station	*estação de trem*	es·*taa*·sowng de treng

NUMBERS

1	*um*	oom
2	*dois*	doys
3	*três*	tres
4	*quatro*	*kwaa*·tro
5	*cinco*	*seeng*·ko
6	*seis*	says
7	*sete*	se·te
8	*oito*	*oy*·to
9	*nove*	*naw*·ve
10	*dez*	dez
20	*vinte*	*veeng*·te
30	*trinta*	*treeng*·taa
40	*quarenta*	kwaa·*reng*·taa
50	*cinquenta*	seen·*kweng*·taa
60	*sessenta*	se·*seng*·taa
70	*setenta*	se·*teng*·taa
80	*oitenta*	oy·*teng*·taa
90	*noventa*	no·*veng*·taa
100	*cem*	seng
1000	*mil*	*mee*·oo

I'd like to hire a ...	*Gostaria de alugar ...*	gos·taa·*ree*·aa de aa·loo·*gaarr* ...
bicycle	*uma bicicleta*	oo·maa bee·see·*kle*·taa
car	*um carro*	oom *kaa*·ho
motorcycle	*uma motocicleta*	oo·maa mo·to·see·*kle*·ta

bicycle pump	*bomba de bicicleta*	*bong*·baa de bee·see·*kle*·taa
helmet	*capacete*	kaa·paa·*se*·te
mechanic	*mecânico*	me·*ka*·nee·ko
petrol/gas	*gasolina*	gaa·zo·*lee*·naa
service station	*posto de gasolina*	*pos*·to de gaa·zo·*lee*·naa

Is this the road to ...?
Esta é a estrada para ...? es·taa e aa es·*traa*·daa *paa*·raa ...

(How long) Can I park here?
(Quanto tempo) Posso estacionar aqui? (*kwang*·to *teng*·po) *po*·so es·taa·syo·*naarr* aa·*kee*

I have a flat tyre.
Meu pneu furou. *me*·oo pee·*ne*·oo foo·*ro*

I've run out of petrol.
Estou sem gasolina. es·*to* seng ga·zoo·*lee*·naa

I've had an accident.
Sofri um acidente. so·*free* oom aa·see·*deng*·te

GLOSSARY

See p34 for more Carnaval terms.

açaí – juice made from an Amazonian berry

baía – bay

baile – dance, ball

baile funk – dance party in the favelas

bairro – neighborhood

baixo – popular area with lots of restaurants and bars

banda – street party

barraca – food stall

berimbau – stringed instrument used to accompany capoeira

bloco – see *banda*

bonde – tram

boteco – small neighborhood bar

botequim – bar with table service

cachaça – potent cane spirit

caipirinha – *cachaça* cocktail

Candomblé – religion of African origin

capoeira – Afro-Brazilian martial art

capela – chapel

carioca – resident of Rio

celular – cellular (mobile) phone

chope – draft beer

chorinho or **choro** – romantic, intimate samba

churrascaria – traditional barbecue restaurant

Cidade Maravilhosa – nickname for Rio de Janeiro (literally 'Marvelous City')

convento – convent

correios – post office

escola de samba – samba school

estrada – road

favela – shanty town

feijoada – black beans and pork stew

feira – open-air market

festa – party

forró – traditional fast-paced music from Northeast Brazil

frescobol – game played on the beach with two wooden racquets and a rubber ball

futebol – football (soccer)

futevôlei – volleyball played without the hands.

gafieira – dance club/dance hall

igreja – church

ilha – island

jardim – garden

lagoa – lake

largo – plaza

limão – lemon

livraria – bookshop

manioc – cassava

mar – sea

maracujá – passion fruit

maté – sweet iced tea

mirante – lookout

moqueca – seafood stew cooked in coconut milk

morro – mountain

mulatto – person of mixed black and white ancestry

museu – museum

onibus – bus

pagode – relaxed and rhythmic form of samba; first popularized in Rio in the 1970s

parque – park

posto – lifeguard station

pousada – guesthouse

praça – square

praia – beach

reais – plural of real

real – Brazil's unit of currency

rio – river

rodoviária – bus terminal

rua – street

salgados – bar snacks

sobreloja – above the store; first floor up

supermercado – supermarket

tacacá – a fragrant soup consisting of manioc paste, jambu leaves and fresh and dried shrimp

tambores – drums

Zona Norte – Northern Zone

Zona Sul – Southern Zone; specifically, the beach- and bay-side neighborhoods of Leblon, Ipanema, Copacabana, Botafogo, Flamengo and Glória.

Behind the Scenes

SEND US YOUR FEEDBACK

We love to hear from travelers – your comments keep us on our toes and help make our books better. Our well-traveled team reads every word on what you loved or loathed about this book. Although we cannot reply individually to your submissions, we always guarantee that your feedback goes straight to the appropriate authors, in time for the next edition. Each person who sends us information is thanked in the next edition – the most useful submissions are rewarded with a selection of digital PDF chapters.

Visit **lonelyplanet.com/contact** to submit your updates and suggestions or to ask for help. Our award-winning website also features inspirational travel stories, news and discussions.

Note: We may edit, reproduce and incorporate your comments in Lonely Planet products such as guidebooks, websites and digital products, so let us know if you don't want your comments reproduced or your name acknowledged. For a copy of our privacy policy visit lonelyplanet.com/privacy.

WRITER THANKS

Regis St Louis

Countless *cariocas* and expats provided help and friendship along the way, and I'm deeply grateful to Cristiano Nogueira, Jackki Saysell, Eduardo Cruxen, Ian Papareskos, Alberto Armendáriz, Bindu Mathur, Tom Lemesurier, German and Daniel Olano, Michael Nagy, Marcelo Esteves, André Paranhos, Toninho, Kevin Raub, Samantha Aquim, Gilson Martins, Antônia Leite Barbosa, and Lenny Niemeyer. As always heartfelt thanks to Cassandra, Magdalena, Genevieve, Rothko and Kazimir for their continued support.

ACKNOWLEDGEMENTS

Cover photograph: Cristo Redentor (Christ the Redeemer) and Sugarloaf Mountain, Flavio Veloso/Getty ©

THIS BOOK

This 10th edition of Lonely Planet's *Rio de Janeiro* guidebook was curated, researched and written by Regis St Louis. The previous two editions were also written by Regis. This guidebook was produced by the following:

Destination Editor Bailey Freeman
Senior Product Editor Saralinda Turner
Product Editor Sandie Kestell
Senior Cartographer Corey Hutchison
Book Designer Gwen Cotter
Assisting Editors Janet Austin, Sarah Bailey, Nigel Chin, Amy Lynch, Claire Rourke, Gabrielle Stefanos
Cover Researcher Naomi Parker
Thanks to Ronan Abayawickrema, Gemma Flynn, Michael Kaplan, Kate Mathews, Virginia Moreno

See also separate subindexes for:
EATING P222
DRINKING & NIGHTLIFE P223
ENTERTAINMENT P224
SHOPPING P224
SPORTS & ACTIVITIES P224
SLEEPING P224

Index

A

accessible travel 205
accommodations 15, 161-70, *see also* Sleeping *subindex*
activities 20, 22-5, 51-3, 110-11, *see also* Sports & Activities *subindex*, *individual activities*
air travel 200-1
Alcione 185, **187**
Alto da Boa Vista 158
AquaRio 13, 128
architecture 20-1, 195-8
Arcos da Lapa 139, **197**
area codes 209-10
art 20-1
ATMs 208-9

B

Bairro Peixoto 93
bargaining 50
Barra da Tijuca 57, 155-60, **155**, **254**
  accommodations 170
  drinking & nightlife 159
  entertainment 159
  food 156, 157-9
  highlights 155
  shopping 156, 159-60
  sights 157
  sports & activities 160
  transportation 156
bathrooms 210
beaches 21, 76-7, 154, 160, **76-7**, *see also individual beaches*
beer 13, 41
Biblioteca Nacional 124
bicycle tours 203
bicycling 13, 51, 111, 201
boat tours 134, 160, 203
boat travel 219
bonde 138
Bonde Station 124
books 172
  architecture 196
  football 191
  history 178
  music 185, 187, 188
Bosque da Barra 157
bossa nova 186-7
Botafogo 13, 56, 101-9, **101**, **244-5**
  accommodations 167-8
  drinking & nightlife 102, 107-8
  entertainment 108-9
  food 102, 104-6
  highlights 101, 103
  shopping 102, 109
  sights 103, 104
  transportation 102
Botafogo football club 192
botecos 39, 41, 147
Boulevard Olímpico 13, 128
budget 14
bus travel 201-2
business hours 209

C

cable cars 103, 124, 138
CADEG 152
Camboinhas 154
Cais do Valongo 128
Campeonato Brasileiro 193
Campeonato Carioca 194
Campo de Santana 125-6
capoeira 52
car travel 202
Carnaval 7, 22, 29-34, **6-7**, **29**, **30**, **33**, **34**
  dates 31
  history 29-30
  tickets 32
Carpintaria 82
Casa de Benjamin Constant 138-9
Casa do Pontal 157
Catacumba 82
Catedral Metropolitana 139
Catete 116-17, 118-19, **241**
caves 158
cell phones 14, 209-10
Centro 56, 121-34, **121**, **246-7**
  accommodations 168
  drinking & nightlife 122, 132-3
  entertainment 133
  food 122, 130-1
  highlights 121, 123
  shopping 122, 133-4
  sights 124-7
  sports & activities 134
  transportation 122
  walking tours 129, **129**
Centro Cultural Banco do Brasil 127
Centro Cultural Correios 127
Centro Cultural Justiça Federal 124
Centro Cultural Laurinda Santos Lobo 138
Centro Cultural Oi Futuro 116
Centro de Arte Hélio Oiticica 125
chemists 208
children, travel with 26-7
Christ the Redeemer, *see* Cristo Redentor
churches, *see individual churches*
Ciata, Tia 186
Cidade do Samba 33
Cinelândia 124-5, 130, **246-7**
cinemas 43
classical music 42-3
climate 15, 22-5
clubs 39-41, *see also* Drinking & Nightlife *subindex*
Coelho, Gonçalo 174
Colônia dos Pescadores 93
Conselheiro, Antônio 180
consulates 206-7
Copa Libertadores 193
Copacabana 56, 90-100, **90**, **236-7**
  accommodations 165-7
  drinking & nightlife 91, 97-9
  entertainment 99
  food 91, 94-7
  highlights 90, 92
  shopping 91, 99-100
  sights 92
  sports & activities 100
  transportation 91
Copacabana Beach 7, 92, **5**, **7**, **76-7**, **92**, **146**
Corcovado 114-15
Cosme Velho 116, **242**
costs 14, 17, 162
  accommodations 162
  drinking & nightlife 40
  food 36
  free attractions 28
courses 205-6
  cooking 205
  dance 47, 145, 206
  language 205
  music 205-6
  surfing 53
  yoga 75
CRAB 125
craft beer 13, 41
credit cards 209
Cristo Redentor 9, 114-15, **8**, **114**
culture 172-3
currency 14
customs regulations 206
cycling, *see* bicycle tours, bicycling

D

da Silva, Leonidas 194
dance 42
  classes 47, 145, 206

dance halls 45
dangers, *see* safety
de Comte, Auguste 175
disabilities, travelers with 205
diving 120
Dom João VI 178
Dom Pedro I 178-9
Dom Pedro II 179
drinking & nightlife 39-41, *see also* Drinking & Nightlife *subindex, individual neighborhoods*
language 214
driving 202

E

economy 172-3
electricity 206
Elevador do Morro do Cantagalo 61
embassies 206-7
emergencies 207
entertainment 42-4, *see also* Entertainment *subindex, individual neighborhoods*
Escadaria Selarón 137, **137**
Espaço Cultural da Marinha 127
etiquette 17, 77
events 22-5, *see also* Carnaval

F

favelas 180, 183
books 185
tours 204
feijoada 37
Feira Nordestina 152
ferry travel 201
Festas Juninas 23, **24**
Festival do Rio 25
festivals 7, 22-5, *see also individual festivals*
films 115, 172, 182, 184
Flamengo 56, 112-20, **112**, **242**
accommodations 168
drinking & nightlife 113, 119-20
entertainment 120
food 113, 117-18
highlights 112, 114-15
shopping 113, 120
sights 114-6
sports & activities 120
transportation 113
Flamengo football club 191
Floresta da Tijuca 12, 89, 158, **12**, **88**
Fluminense football club 192
food 35-8, **35**, *see also* Eating *subindex, individual neighborhoods*
costs 36
courses 205
language 212
tours 204
football 12, 52, 150-1, 191-4, **150**
Forte de Copacabana 93
Forte Duque de Caxias 93
free activities 21, 28
Fundação Eva Klabin 82
Fundição Progresso 139
futevôlei 77

G

gafieiras 45
gardens 21, 88-89, **88-89**
Gávea 56, 78-87, **78**, **234-5**
drinking & nightlife 79, 85
entertainment 86
food 79, 83
highlights 78, 80
shopping 79, 86
sights 80, 81
sports & activities 80, 87
transportation 79
gay travelers 40, 208
Gilberto, João 70, 186
'Girl from Ipanema, the' 70
Glória 116-17, 118-19, **241**
gold mining 176

H

H Stern 61
hang gliding 52, 111, **110**
health 207
helicopter tours 204
hiking 51, 111, **110**
hip-hop 188-90
historical sights 21, 177
history 174-84
19th century 176-9
20th century 181-4
Belle Époque 179-81
Carnaval 29-30
favelas 180
indigenous peoples 174-5
military dictatorship 182
Portuguese colonization 174-5
slavery 175-6
holidays 209
hospitals 208
Humaitá 56, 101-9, **101**, **244-5**
drinking & nightlife 102, 107-8
entertainment 108-9
food 102, 104, 106
highlights 101, 103
shopping 102, 109
sights 103-4

I

Igreja de Nossa Senhora da Glória do Outeiro 117
Igreja de Nossa Senhora de Candelária 127
Igreja de Nossa Senhora do Carmo da Antiga Sé 126
Igreja de Nossa Senhora do Rosário e São Benedito 125
Igreja São Francisco da Penitência & Convento de Santo Antônio 125
Ilha de Paquetá 130
Ilha Fiscal 127, **26**
indigenous peoples 174-5
Instituto de Pesquisa e Memória Presto Novos 128
Instituto Moreira Salles 81
internet access 207-8
internet resources 14, 15, 189
Ipanema 56, 58-75, **58**, **228-9**
accommodations 164-5
drinking & nightlife 59, 69-72
entertainment 73
food 59, 62-5
highlights 58, 60
shopping 59, 73-4
sights 60, 61-2
sports & activities 75
transportation 59
Ipanema Beach 9, 60, **3**, **9**, **55**, **60**, **110-11**
Itacoatiara 154
Itaipu 154
itineraries 18-19

J

Jardim Botânico 81, 89, **88-9**
Jardim Botânico 56, 78-87, **78**, **234-5**
accommodations 165
drinking & nightlife 79, 85-6
entertainment 86
food 79, 83-4
highlights 78, 80
shopping 79, 87
sights 80, 81-2
sports & activities 87
transportation 79
Jobim, Antônio Carlos (Tom) 70, 186
jogging 51
juice bars 36

K

kiosks 97

L

Lagoa 56, 78-87, **78**, **234-5**
drinking & nightlife 79, 86
entertainment 86
food 79, 84-5
highlights 78, 80
nightlife 147
sights 80, 82
sports & activities 80, 87
transportation 79
Lagoa Rodrigo de Freitas 11, 80, **11**, **80**
language 14, 17, 34, 211-16
courses 205
Lapa 56, 135-45, **135**, **250-1**, **10**, **146-7**
accommodations 170
drinking & nightlife 10, 136, 142-3
entertainment 143-4
food 136, 140-1
highlights 135, 137
nightlife 147
shopping 136, 144-5
sights 137, 139
sports & activities 145
transportation 136
Laranjeiras 117, 118, **242**
Largo das Neves 138
Largo do Boticário 115

Largo do Guimarães 138
Leblon 56, 58-75, **58**, **232-3**
accommodations 165
drinking & nightlife 59, 72-3
entertainment 73
food 59, 65-9
highlights 58, 60
shopping 59, 75
sights 60, 61-2
sports & activities 75
transportation 59
legal matters 208
Leme 56, 90-100, **90**, **240**
accommodations 165-7
drinking & nightlife 91, 97-9
entertainment 99
food 91, 97
highlights 90, 92
shopping 91, 99-100
sights 92
sports & activities 100
transportation 91
lesbian travelers 40, 208
LGBT+ travelers 40, 208
Lighting of the Lagoa Christmas Tree 25, **24**
literature, *see* books
Lurixs: Arte Contemporânea 62

M

magazines 208
Maracanã Football Stadium 12, 52, 150-1, **12**, **150**
Marcelo D2 189, **189**
Marina da Glória 117
markets 37, 49, Shopping *subindex*
measures 208
medical services 208
metro travel 202
Mirante do Leblon 61-2
Mirante do Sacopã 82
mobile phones 14, 209-10
money 14, 208-9
Moraes, Vinícius de 70
Morro da Conceição 128, 130
Mosteiro de São Bento 128
motorcycle travel 202
Museu Amsterdam Sauer 61
Museu Casa de Rui Barbosa 104
Museu Chácara do Céu 138
Museu da Imagem e do Som 13, 93
Museu da República 116, **20**
Museu de Arte do Rio 127-8
Museu de Arte Moderna 124
Museu de Arte Sacra 139
Museu de Folclore Edison Carneiro 116
Museu do Amanhã 128, **198**
Museu do Arte Contemporânea 126
Museu do Índio 104
Museu Histórico Nacional 123, **123**
Museu Nacional 153
Museu Nacional de Belas Artes 124
Museu Naval 127
music 42-3, 185-90
courses 205-6
Música no Museu 43
Música Popular Brasileira 187-8

N

newspapers 208
Niemeyer, Oscar 196-7
nightlife 10, 39-41, 146-7, *see also* Drinking & Nightlife *subindex, individual neighborhoods*
Niterói 126

O

Olympics 172
OM.art 82
opening hours 209

P

Paço Imperial 126-7
paddle boarding 52-3
Palácio Tiradentes 126, **28**
Pão de Açúcar 9, 103, **8**, **103**
parks 21, 88-89, **88-89**
Parque da Catacumba 82
Parque da Cidade 81
Parque das Ruínas 138
Parque do Catete 89, 116-17
Parque do Flamengo 89, 116, **88**
Parque Ecológico Chico Mendes 157
Parque Garota de Ipanema 61
Parque Guinle 117
Parque Lage 81-2
Parque Nacional da Tijuca 158, **110**
Parque Natural Municipal de Marapendi 157
Passeio Público 124
Pelé 193
pharmacies 208
Pinheiro, Helô 70
Piratininga 154
Planetário 81
planning
budgeting 14, 36
children, travel with 26-7
festivals & events 22-5
free attractions 21, 28
first-time visitors 16-17
itineraries 18-19
repeat visitors 13
Rio de Janeiro basics 14-15
Rio de Janeiro's neighborhoods 56-7
travel seasons 15, 22-5
websites 14
politics 173
Ponta do Arpoador 61
Ponte Rio-Niterói 126
pop music 188-90
population 173
Portuguese language 14, 17, 34, 211-16
courses 205
Portuguese colonization 174-5
postal services 209
Praça Floriano 125
Praça Mauá 56, 121-34, **121**
drinking & nightlife 122, 132-3
entertainment 133
food 122, 131-2
highlights 121, 123
shopping 122, 133-4
sights 121, 127-30
sports & activities 134
transportation 122
Praça Tiradentes 125-6, 130-1
Praça XV 126-7, 131
Praça XV (Quinze) de Novembro 127
Praça XV (Quinze) de Novembro area 126-7, 131
Praia da Barra da Tijuca 157
Praia de Diabo 93
Praia de Leblon 61
Praia Vermelha 104
Prainha 157
public holidays 209

Q

Quinta da Boa Vista 152

R

Real Gabinete Português de Leitura 125
religion 173
Retrato Espaço Cultural 138
Reveillon 25
rock climbing 52, 111, **111**
rock music 188-90

S

safety 46, 173
samba 45-8, 185-6, **45**
classes 47, 145, 206
language 34
schools 31, 33
Sambódromo 152
Santa Teresa 10, 56, 135-45, **135**, **250-1**, **3**, **11**
accommodations 168-70
drinking & nightlife 136, 142
entertainment 143-4
food 136, 139-40
highlights 135, 137
shopping 136, 144-5
sights 137, 138-9
transportation 136
Seixas, Raul 188
Selarón, Jorge 137
shopping 49-50, 156, *see also* Shopping *subindex, individual neighborhoods*
language 50, 214
opening hours 50
taxes 50
Sítio Burle Marx 89, 157, **89**
slavery 175-6
smoking 208
soccer, *see* football
spas 75
sports 20, 51-3, *see also* football, Sports & Activities *subindex, individual neighborhoods*
Sugarloaf Mountain, *see* Pão de Açúcar
surfing 52-3, 111, **110-11**

T

taxes 17
taxis 202-3
Teatro Popular 126
telephone services 209-10

theater 42
Theatro Municipal 124
time 14, 210
tipping 17, 209
toilets 210
tourist information 14, 210
tours 203-4
train travel 202, 203
tram travel 203
transportation 200-4
langauge 215
travel to Rio de Janeiro 15, 200-1
travel within Rio de Janeiro 15, 125, 201-3
trekking, *see* hiking
tropicália 187

U

Urca 56, 101-9, **101**, **244-5**
accommodations 168
drinking & nightlife 102, 108
entertainment 108-9
food 102, 106-7
highlights 101, 103
shopping 102, 109
sights 103, 104
sports & activities 109
transportation 102
walking tours 105, **105**

V

vacations 209
Vargas, Getúlio 181
Vasco da Gama football club 192
vegetarian travellers 38
visas 14, 210
VLT 125

W

walking, *see* hiking
walking tours 28, 204
Centro 129, **129**
Urca 105, **105**
weather 15, 22-5
websites, *see* internet resources
weights 208
western Rio 57, 155-60, **155**, **254**
accommodations 170
drinking & nightlife 159
entertainment 159
food 156, 157-9
highlights 155
shopping 156, 159-60
sights 157
sports & activities 160
transportation 156
wine bars 13
World Cup 150-1, 194

Z

Zika virus 207
Zona Norte 57, 148-54, **148**, **253**
drinking & nightlife 149, 153-4
entertainment 149, 154
food 149, 152-3
highlights 148, 150-1
sights 150-1, 152
transportation 149

EATING

A

Aconchego Carioca 152
Adega Pérola 95
Alda Maria Doces Portugueses 139
Alessandro E Federico 64
Alquimia 139
Amazônia Soul 65
Amir 96
Ancoramar 131
Antônia Casa e Café 94
Aprazível 140
Arab 95
Arab da Lagoa 84-5
Arataca 96
Armazém do Café 66
ASA Açaí 132
Azteka 63
Azumi 96

B

Bakers 96
Bar do Mineiro 140
Bar Kalango 152
Bar Luiz 131
Bar Urca 107
Barraca da Chiquita 95
Barraca do Uruguai 62
Barsa 153
Bazzar 65
Belga 131
Bibi Crepes 66
Bibi Sucos 94
Bira 159
Bistrô do Paço 131
Botequim Bodega do Sal 132
Botero 118
Braseiro da Gávea 83
Bráz 83-4
Brota 94
Brou 117-18

C

Café Arlequim 131
Café de la Musique 67
Cafe do Alto 139-40
Cafeína 64
Cais do Oriente 131
Capricciosa (Copacabana) 96
Capricciosa (Ipanema) 64
Cariocando 118-19
Carmelo 119
Casa Camolese 13, 83
Casa da Feijoada 65
Casa Ipanema 74
Casa Momus 141
Cervantes 94
Ceviche RJ 104
Churrascaria Palace 96
Cobal do Humaitá 37
Cobal do Leblon 37
Coffeetown 66
Confeitaria Colombo 130
Corrientes 348 119
Cortiço Carioca 141
Cristóvão 130
CT Boucherie 69

D

Da Gema 153
Delírio Tropical 62
Devassa 96
Don Camillo 96-7
Don Pascual 158-9

E

El Born 94
Ella Pizzaria 84
Empório Grão-Pará 95
Empório Jardim na Praia 63
Espaço 7zero6 65
Espaço Lapa Cafe 141
Espetto Carioca 97
Espírito Santa 140

F

Faraj 64
Ferro e Farinha 118
Formidable 69
Fresh Comida Saudável 117
Frontera 64

G

Galeria Bazá 139
Galeto Sat's 94
Garota da Urca 107
Garota de Ipanema 64
Giro 68
Giuseppe Grill 68
Gohan 141
Govardhana Harí 130
Graviola 68
Gringo Cafe 65
Guimas 83
Gurumê 63

I

Imaculada 132
Intihuasi 117

J

Jarbô 83
Joana 62
Joaquina 97
Jojô 84
Julius Brasserie 106-7

K

Koni Store 63, 94
Kurt 66

L

La Bicyclette 84
La Carioca Cevicheria (Ipanema) 63
La Carioca Cevicheria (Lagoa) 85
La Fiorentina 97
La Trattoria 95
La Veronese 62
Lagoon 84
Laguna Restaurante 158
Lasai 106
L'Atelier du Cuisinier 131
Le Blond 67
Le Depanneur 106
LF Café & Bistro 95
Lilia 140
Livraria Prefácio 106
Luigi's 118

M
Majorica 118
Mangue Seco Cachaçaria 141
Marchezinho 104
Massa 67
Maze Inn 118
Mercearia da Praça 64
Meza Bar 106
Miam Miam 106
Mil Frutas 62-3
Mironga 131-2
Momo 66, 94

N
Nam Thai 69
New Natural 65
Nola 67
Nova Capela 141

O
Okanossa 67
Olympe 85
Oteque 106

P
Pabu Izakaya 66-7
Petit Formidable 65-6
Plage Café 83
Porto das Carnes 95
Prana Vegetariano 83
Prima Bruschetteria 68
Principe de Mônaco 95-6
Puro 84

Q
Quitéria 63

R
Rancho Inn 131
Rango Veggie 140
Rascal 68
Refeitório 141
Restaurante Naturaleve 94
Restaurante Os Esquilos 158
Restaurante Quinta da Boa Vista 153

S
Salomé 97
Santa Satisfação 95
Santo Scenarium 141
Shirley 97
Sírio Libaneza 118
Skylab 96
Slow Bakery 104, 106
Sobrenatural 140
South Ferro 106
Stuzzi 67
Sushi Leblon 69

T
Taberna da Glória 119
Tacacá do Norte 117
Taj Mahal 84
Talho Capixaba 68
Térèze 140
TT Burger 95

U
Uruguaiana 130-1

V
Vegetariano Social Club 66
Venga! 63
Vero 62
Vezpa (Copacabana) 94
Vezpa (Ipanema) 62
Vezpa (Lapa) 140
Vezpa (Leblon) 66
Via Sete 64
Void – House of Food 106
Vokos 67

X
Xian 130

Y
Yalla 68

Z
Zazá Bistrô Tropical 65
Zona Sul Supermarket (Ipanema) 63
Zona Sul Supermarket (Leblon) 66
Zuka 68-9

DRINKING & NIGHTLIFE

A
Academia da Cachaça 72
Adega Portugália 119
Alice Bar 108
Amarelinho 132
Antônio's 143
Armazém do Chopp 120
Armazém Senado 142
As Melhores Cervejas do Mundo 98

B
Bar 1928 107
Bar Astor 70
Bar Bukowski 108
Bar da Nalva 143
Bar do Gomes 142
Bar do Horto 85
Bar do Oswaldo 159
Bar do Zé 119
Bar dos Descasados 142
Bar Lagoa 86
Bar Léo 132
Bar Mercadores 133
Bar Surfshop 99
Bar Urca 108
Bar Veloso 71
Baretto-Londra 70-1
Barthodomeu 71
Barzin 70
Bastarda 85
Belmonte 72, 119
Bibi Sucos 73
Blue Agave 71
Bodega 98
Booze Bar 142
Boteco Belmonte 98
Bracarense 72
Brewteco 72
Buraco da Lacraia 143

C
Cafe 18 do Forte 98
Café Secreto 119
Canastra 69
Caverna 108
Champanharia Ovelha Negra 108
Cine Botequim 132
Clássico Beach Club 108
CoLAB 107
Comuna 107
Curto Cafe 132

D
Delirium Cafe 71

E
Empório 37 71
Escondido 98
Explorer Bar 13, 142

F
Fazenda Paradiso Café 142
Fosfobox 99
Fuska 2.0 108

G
Galeria Café 71
Garota de Ipanema 71
Goya-Beira 142

H
Herr Brauer 119-20
Hipódromo 85
Hocus Pocus 107
Hop Lab 154

J
Jobi 72

L
Leviano Bar 143
Lord Jim 72

M
Mud Bug 98

N
Noi 72
Noo Cachaçaria 153-4
Nosso 70

P
Palaphita Gávea 85
Palaphita Kitch 86
Pavão Azul 98
Pizzaria Guanabara 73
Polis Sucos 72
Ponto da Bossa Nova 98

S
Sarau 143
Shenanigan's 71
Sofá Café 98

T
Tap House 71
Tô Nem Aí 71
TV Bar 99

U
Urca Grill 108

V
Vaca Atolada 142

W
Week 132
WineHouse 107
Wood's 72

ENTERTAINMENT

B
Beco das Garrafas 99
Beco do Rato 144
Bip Bip 99
Blue Note Rio 86

C
Carioca da Gema 143
Casa da Cultura Laura Alvim 73
Cidade das Artes 159
Cine Joia 99
Cine Museu da República 120
Cine Odeon 133
Circo Voador 144
Clube dos Democráticos 144, **10**
Clube Manouche 86

E
Espaço Itaú 108
Espaço SESC 99
Estação Net Ipanema 73
Estação Net Rio 109

F
Favela Hype 143
Fundição Progresso 143-4

J
Jockey Club Brasileiro 86

L
Lapa 40 Graus 144

M
Mangueira 154
Maze Inn 120

O
Olho da Rua 109

P
Pedra do Sal 133, **45**

R
Renascença Clube 154
Rio Scenarium 143, **147**

S
Sacrilégio 144
Sala Cecília Meireles 144
Sala Municipal Baden Powell 99
Salgueiro 154
Severyna de Laranjeiras 120

T
Teatro do Leblon 73
Teatro Odisséia 144
Teatro Riachuelo 133
Teatro Rival Petrobras 133
Terra Brasilis 108
Theatro Municipal 133
Trapiche Gamboa 133
TribOz 143

U
UCI – New York City Center 159

SHOPPING

A
Argumento 75
Ateliê Bonifácio 145
Av Atlântica Fair 100

B
Baobá Brasil 145
Baratos de Ribeiro 109
Barra Shopping 159
Botafogo Praia Shopping 109

C
Casa Naara 134
Casa Soma 87
Catherine Labouré 74
Chocolate Q 73
Comparsaria 109
CRAB 134

D
Dona Coisa 87
Draco Store 74

E
Eliane Carvalho 75

F
Fashion Mall 159
Favela Hype 144
Feira do Rio Antigo 145

G
Gabinete 87
Galeria Bazá 145
Galeria River 100
Garota de Ipanema 74
Gilson Martins (Copacabana) 99-100
Gilson Martins (Ipanema) 73-4
Granado 134

H
Havaianas (Copacabana) 100
Havaianas (Ipanema) 74
Hippie Fair 73

I
Isabela Capeto 75

L
La Vereda 144-5
Lenny Niemeyer 73
Livraria da Travessa (Botafogo) 109
Livraria da Travessa (Centro) 134
Livraria da Travessa (Ipanema) 74
Loja Fla 100
Loja Pence 145

M
Maracatu Brasil 120
Maria Oiticica 75
Nova Livraria Leonardo da Vinci 134

O
O Sol 87
Osklen 74
Osklen Surfing 100

P
Parceria Carioca 87
Pé de Boi 120
Pleidisco 134
Praça do Lido Market 100
Praça Santos Dumont Antique Fair 86
Praça São Salvador 120

R
Redley 74
Rio Design Barra 159-60
Rio Sul Shopping 109

S
Shopping Cidade Copacabana 100
Shopping da Gávea 86-7
Shopping Leblon 75

T
Toca do Vinícius 74
Tucum 145

V
Velha Lapa 145
Venda em Garagem 87
Via Parque Shopping 160
Village 159
Void General Store 75

W
Wöllner Outdoor 75

SPORTS & ACTIVITIES

Barra Water Shuttle 160
Fundição Progresso 145
Lagoa Aventuras 87
Mar do Rio 120
Museum of Yoga 75
Passeio Marítimo 134
Rio Electric 100
Spa Maria Bonita 75
Universo Paddle Surf 100

SLEEPING

B
Belga Hotel 168
Belmond Copacabana Palace 167
Blame It on Rio 4 Travel 166
Bonita 164
Books Hostel 170

C
Cabana Copa 165
Casa Áurea 169
Casa Beleza 169
Casa Bianca 169
Casa Caminho do Corcovado 168
Casa Cool Beans 169
Casa da Gente 168-9
Che Lagarto 165

Sights 000
Map Pages **000**
Photo Pages **000**

Che Lagarto Ipanema 164

D

Da Lapa Design Hotel 170
Discovery Hostel 168
Discovery Suites 169
Don Pascual 170

E

El Misti 164, 165

F

Fairmont 167

H

Hotel 55 Rio 170
Hotel Emiliano 13, 166-7
Hotel Fasano 164
Hotel Praia Ipanema 164
Hotel Santa Clara 166
Hotel Santa Teresa 169-70
Hotelinho Urca 168

I

Injoy Hostel 167-8
Ipanema Beach House 164
Ipanema for Rent 161

J

Jucati 166

L

LSH Lifestyle 170

M

Mama Ruisa 170
Mama Shelter 169
Mango Tree 164
Margarida's Pousada 164
Marta Rio Guesthouse 166
Maze Inn 168
Mercure Arpoador 166
Modernistas Hospedagem 169

O

O Veleiro Bed & Breakfast 167
Olinda Rio 166
Orla Copacabana 166

P

Pestana Rio Atlântica 167
Porto Bay Rio Internacional 167
Pouso Verde 165
Pura Vida 165-6

R

Recanto da Urca 168
Rio Design Hotel 166
Rio Spot Homes 166
Rio Surf 'N Stay 170
Ritz Leblon 165

S

Sofitel Rio de Janeiro Ipanema 165
Sol Ipanema 164-5
Solar do Cosme 168

V

Vila Galé 170

W

Walk on the Beach Hostel 165

Y

Yoo2 167

Rio de Janeiro Maps

Sights

- Beach
- Bird Sanctuary
- Buddhist
- Castle/Palace
- Christian
- Confucian
- Hindu
- Islamic
- Jain
- Jewish
- Monument
- Museum/Gallery/Historic Building
- Ruin
- Shinto
- Sikh
- Taoist
- Winery/Vineyard
- Zoo/Wildlife Sanctuary
- Other Sight

Activities, Courses & Tours

- Bodysurfing
- Diving
- Canoeing/Kayaking
- Course/Tour
- Sento Hot Baths/Onsen
- Skiing
- Snorkeling
- Surfing
- Swimming/Pool
- Walking
- Windsurfing
- Other Activity

Sleeping

- Sleeping
- Camping
- Hut/Shelter

Eating

- Eating

Drinking & Nightlife

- Drinking & Nightlife
- Cafe

Entertainment

- Entertainment

Shopping

- Shopping

Information

- Bank
- Embassy/Consulate
- Hospital/Medical
- Internet
- Police
- Post Office
- Telephone
- Toilet
- Tourist Information
- Other Information

Geographic

- Beach
- Gate
- Hut/Shelter
- Lighthouse
- Lookout
- Mountain/Volcano
- Oasis
- Park
- Pass
- Picnic Area
- Waterfall

Population

- Capital (National)
- Capital (State/Province)
- City/Large Town
- Town/Village

Transport

- Airport
- Border crossing
- Bus
- Cable car/Funicular
- Cycling
- Ferry
- Metro station
- Monorail
- Parking
- Petrol station
- Subway/Subte station
- Taxi
- Train station/Railway
- Tram
- Underground station
- Other Transport

Routes

- Tollway
- Freeway
- Primary
- Secondary
- Tertiary
- Lane
- Unsealed road
- Road under construction
- Plaza/Mall
- Steps
- Tunnel
- Pedestrian overpass
- Walking Tour
- Walking Tour detour
- Path/Walking Trail

Boundaries

- International
- State/Province
- Disputed
- Regional/Suburb
- Marine Park
- Cliff
- Wall

Hydrography

- River, Creek
- Intermittent River
- Canal
- Water
- Dry/Salt/Intermittent Lake
- Reef

Areas

- Airport/Runway
- Beach/Desert
- Cemetery (Christian)
- Cemetery (Other)
- Glacier
- Mudflat
- Park/Forest
- Sight (Building)
- Sportsground
- Swamp/Mangrove

Note: Not all symbols displayed above appear on the maps in this book

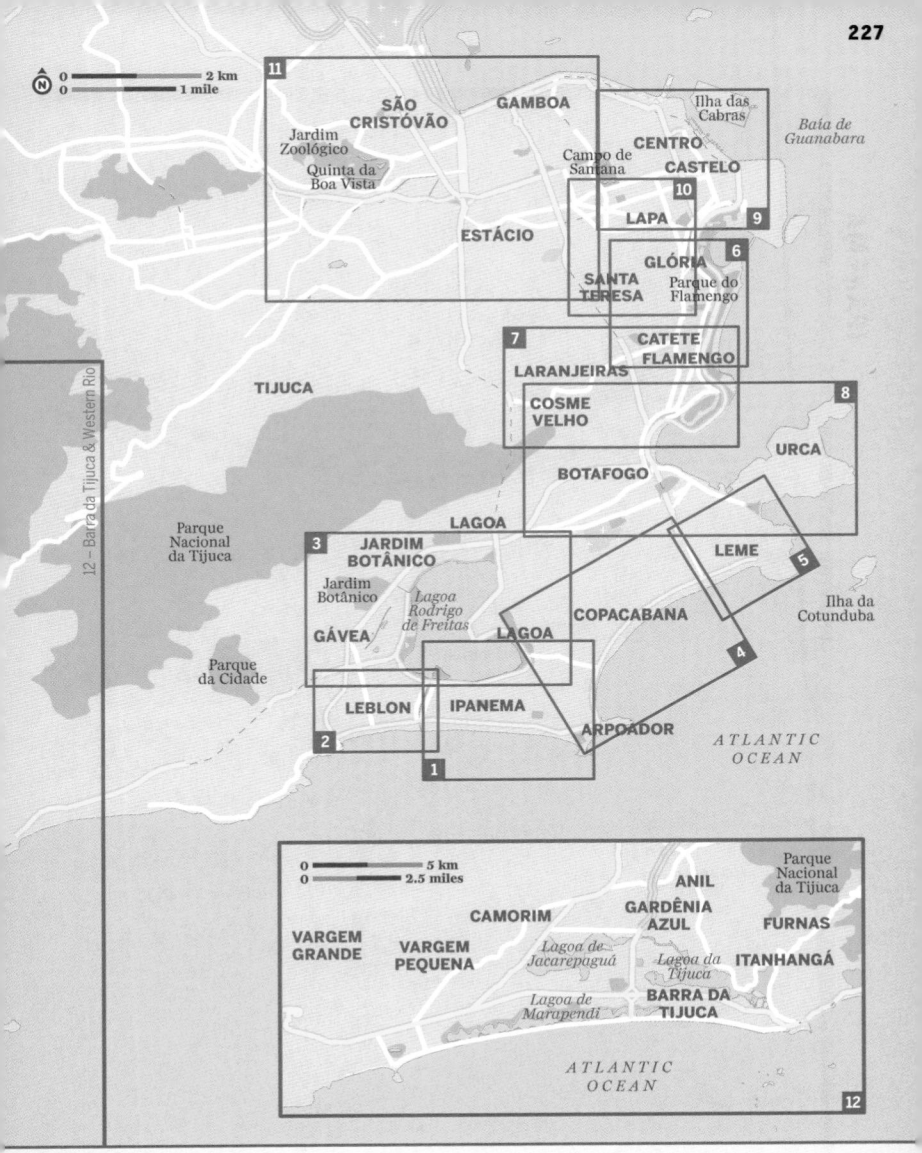

MAP INDEX

Ipanema (p228)
Leblon (p232)
Gávea, Jardim Botânico & Lagoa (p234)
4 Copacabana (p236)
5 Leme (p240)
6 Catete & Glória (p241)
7 Flamengo, Laranjeiras & Cosme Velho (p242)
8 Botafogo, Humaitá & Urca (p244)
9 Centro & Cinelândia (p246)
10 Santa Teresa & Lapa (p250)
11 Zona Norte (p253)
12 Barra da Tijuca & Western Rio (p254)

Key on p230

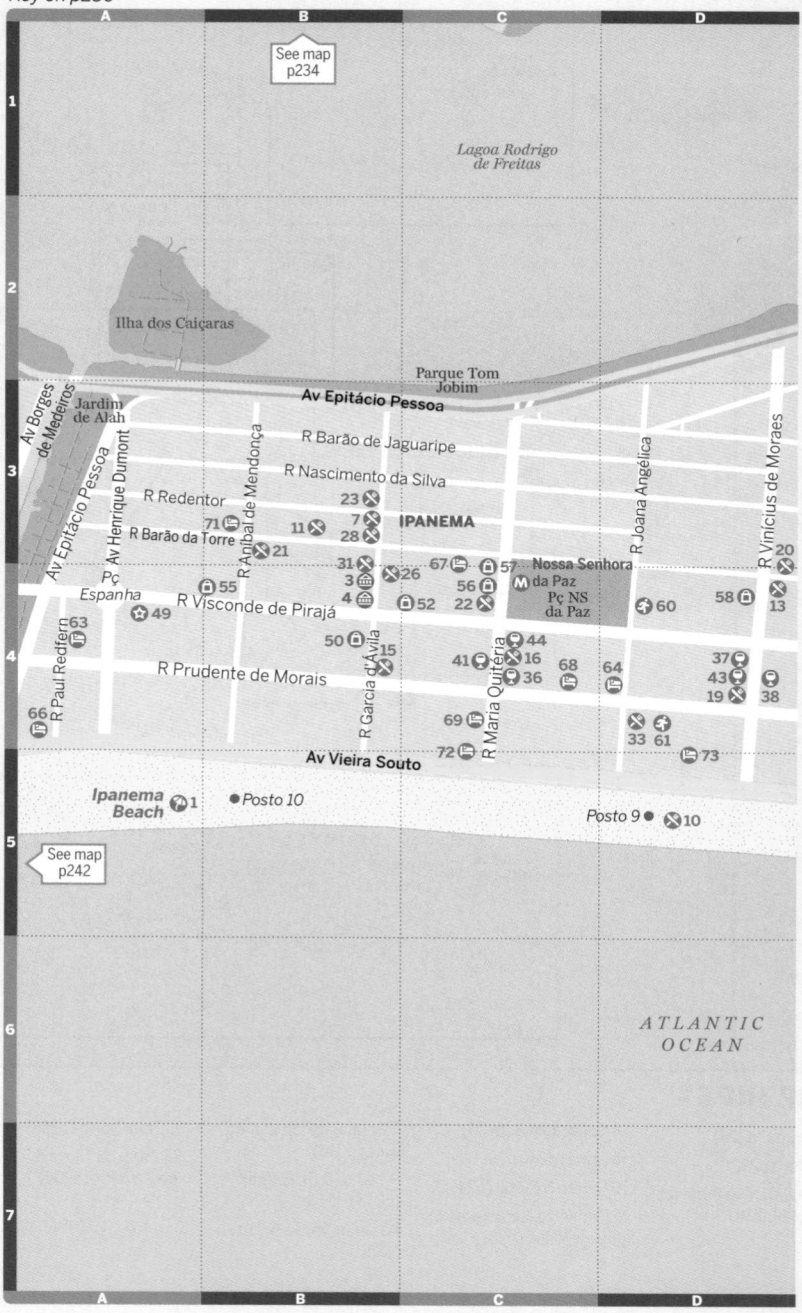
IPANEMA
A
B
C
D
1
2
3
4
5
6
7
See map p234
See map p242
Lagoa Rodrigo de Freitas
Ilha dos Caiçaras
Parque Tom Jobim
Av Epitácio Pessoa
Av Borges de Medeiros
Jardim de Alah
Av Epitácio Pessoa
Av Henrique Dumont
R Barão de Jaguaripe
R Nascimento da Silva
R Redentor
R Barão da Torre
R Aníbal de Mendonça
IPANEMA
R Joana Angélica
R Vinícius de Moraes
Nossa Senhora da Paz
Pç NS da Paz
Pç Espanha
R Visconde de Pirajá
R Paul Redfern
R Prudente de Morais
R Garcia d'Ávila
R Maria Quiteria
Av Vieira Souto
Ipanema Beach
Posto 10
Posto 9
ATLANTIC OCEAN
1
10
13
15
16
19
20
21
23
26
28
31
33
36
37
38
3
4
7
11
41
43
44
50
52
55
56
57
58
60
61
63
64
66
67
68
69
71
72
73
22
49

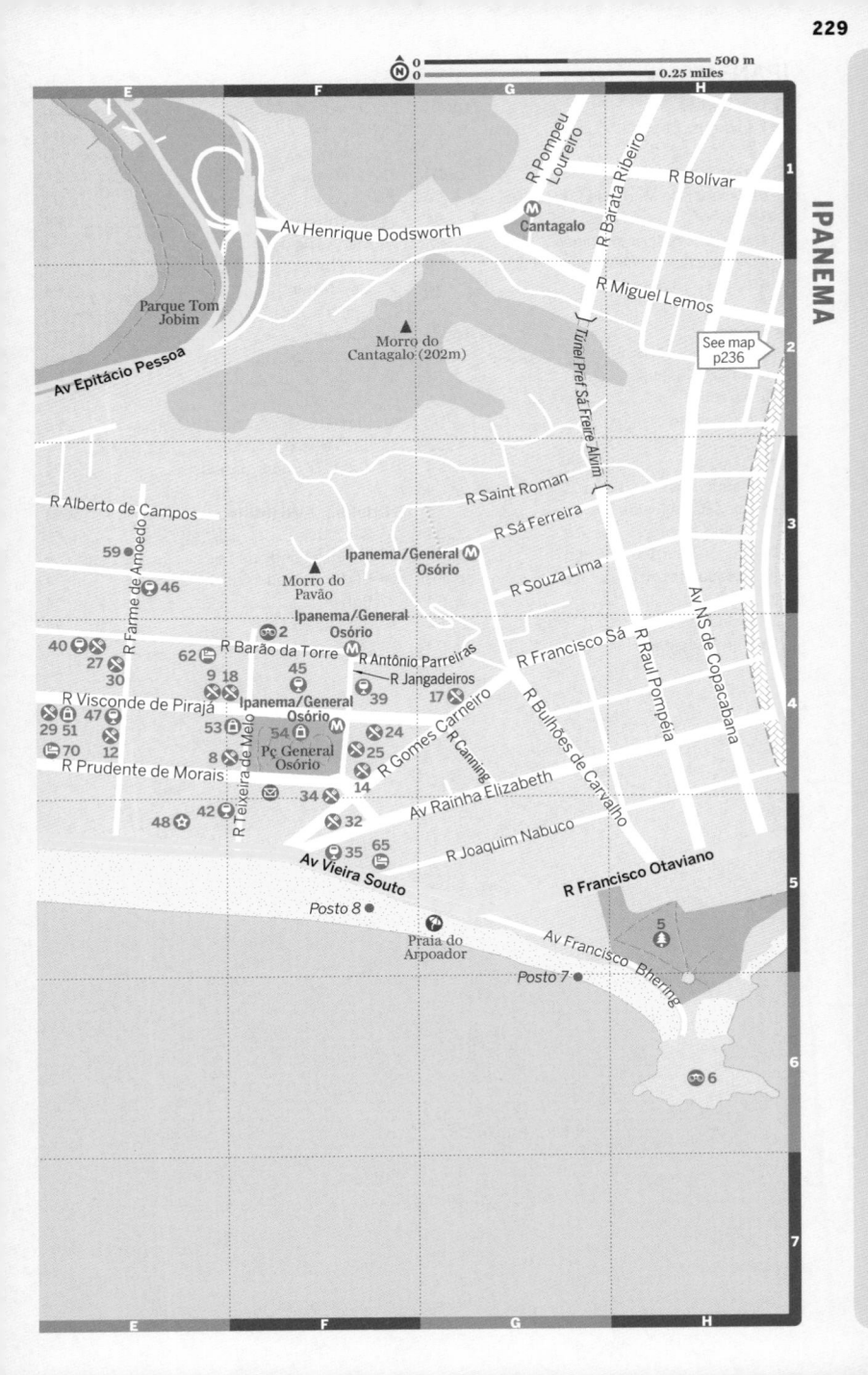
0 500 m
0 0.25 miles
E F G H
1 2 3 4 5 6 7
IPANEMA
R Pompeu Loureiro
R Barata Ribeiro
R Bolívar
Av Henrique Dodsworth
Cantagalo
R Miguel Lemos
Parque Tom Jobim
Morro do Cantagalo (202m)
Av Epitácio Pessoa
Túnel Pref Sá Freire Alvim
See map p236
R Saint Roman
R Alberto de Campos
R Sá Ferreira
Ipanema/General Osório
R Souza Lima
Morro do Pavão
R Farme de Amoedo
Ipanema/General Osório
R Barão da Torre
R Antônio Parreiras
R Jangadeiros
R Francisco Sá
R Raul Pompéia
Av NS de Copacabana
R Visconde de Pirajá
Ipanema/General Osório
R Gomes Carneiro
R Canning
R Bulhões de Carvalho
R Prudente de Morais
Pç General Osório
R Teixeira de Melo
Av Rainha Elizabeth
R Joaquim Nabuco
Av Vieira Souto
R Francisco Otaviano
Posto 8
Praia do Arpoador
Av Francisco Bhering
Posto 7
2 5 6 8 9 12 14 17 18 24 25 27 29 30 32 34 35 39 40 42 45 46 47 48 51 53 54 59 62 65 70

IPANEMA *Map on p228*

Top Sights **(p60)**

1 Ipanema Beach A5

Sights **(p61)**

2 Elevador do Morro do Cantagalo F4
3 H Stern B4
4 Museu Amsterdam Sauer B4
5 Parque Garota de Ipanema H5
6 Ponta do Arpoador H6

Eating **(p62)**

7 Alessandro E Federico B3
8 Amazônia Soul F4
9 Azteka E4
10 Barraca do Uruguai D5
11 Bazzar B3
12 Cafeína E4
13 Capricciosa D4
14 Casa da Feijoada F4
15 Delírio Tropical B4
16 Empório Jardim na Praia C4
Espaço 7zero6 ..... (see 66)
17 Faraj G4
18 Frontera F4
19 Garota de Ipanema D4
20 Gringo Cafe D3
21 Gurumê B3
Joana ..... (see 64)
22 Koni Store C4
23 La Carioca Cevicheria B3
24 La Veronese F4
25 Mercearia da Praça F4
26 Mil Frutas B4
27 New Natural E4
Quitéria ..... (see 69)
28 Venga! B3
29 Vero E4
30 Vezpa E4
31 Via Sete B3
32 Via Sete Arpoador F5
33 Zazá Bistrô Tropical D4
34 Zona Sul Supermarket F4

Drinking & Nightlife **(p69)**

35 Bar Astor F5
Baretto-Londra ..... (see 65)
36 Barthodomeu C4
37 Barzin D4
38 Blue Agave D4
39 Canastra F4

40 Delirium Cafe E4
41 Empório 37 ..... C4
42 Galeria Café E5
43 Garota de Ipanema D4
Lord Jim ..... (see 63)
Nosso ..... (see 56)
44 Polis Sucos C4
45 Shenanigan's F4
46 Tap House E3
47 Tô Nem Aí E4

Entertainment **(p73)**
48 Casa da Cultura Laura Alvim E5
49 Estação Net Ipanema A4

Shopping **(p73)**
50 Casa Ipanema B4
51 Catherine Labouré E4
Chocolate Q ..... (see 28)
Draco Store ..... (see 53)
Garota de Ipanema ..... (see 43)
52 Gilson Martins C4
53 Havaianas F4
54 Hippie Fair F4
Lenny Niemeyer ..... (see 28)
55 Livraria da Travessa B4
56 Osklen C4
57 Redley C4
58 Toca do Vinícius D4

Sports & Activities **(p75)**
59 Caminhos Language Centre E3
60 Museum of Yoga D4
61 Spa Maria Bonita D4

Sleeping **(p164)**
62 Bonita E4
63 Che Lagarto Ipanema A4
64 El Misti D4
65 Hotel Fasano F5
66 Hotel Praia Ipanema A4
67 Ipanema Beach House C3
68 Ipanema For Rent C4
69 Ipanema Inn C4
70 Mango Tree E4
71 Margarida's Pousada B3
72 Sofitel Rio de Janeiro Ipanema C4
73 Sol Ipanema D5

LEBLON

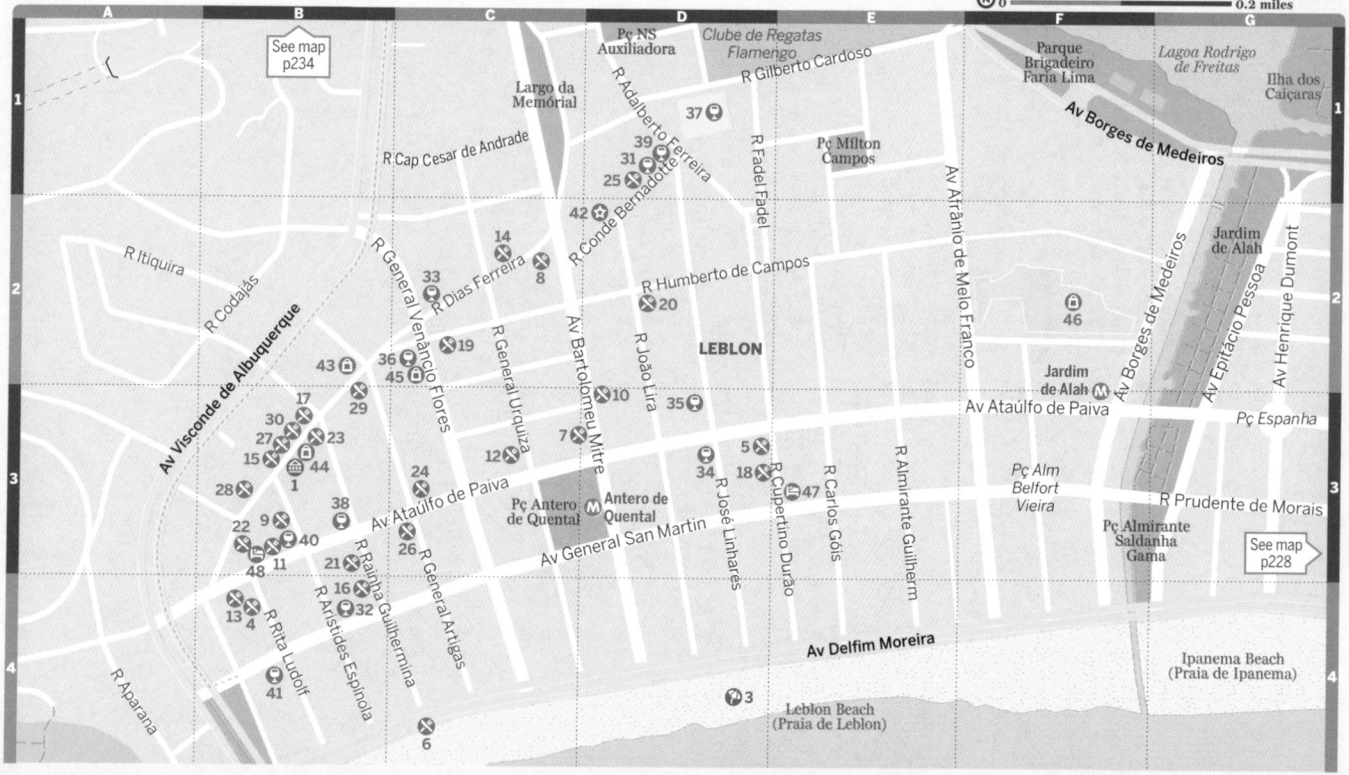
0 400 m
0 0.2 miles
A B C D E F G
1 2 3 4
See map p234
See map p228
Pç NS Auxiliadora
Clube de Regatas Flamengo
Parque Brigadeiro Faria Lima
Lagoa Rodrigo de Freitas
Ilha dos Caiçaras
Largo da Memórial
R Gilberto Cardoso
R Adalberto Ferreira
R Cap Cesar de Andrade
Pç Milton Campos
Av Borges de Medeiros
R Fadel Fadel
Av Afrânio de Melo Franco
R Conde Bernadotte
R Itiquira
R Codajás
R General Venâncio Flores
R Dias Ferreira
R Humberto de Campos
Jardim de Alah
Av Borges de Medeiros
Av Epitácio Pessoa
Av Henrique Dumont
LEBLON
Av Visconde de Albuquerque
R General Urquiza
Av Bartolomeu Mitre
R João Lira
Jardim de Alah
Av Ataúlfo de Paiva
Pç Espanha
R Carlos Góis
R Almirante Guilherm
Pç Alm Belfort Vieira
R Prudente de Morais
Pç Antero de Quental
Antero de Quental
Av Ataúlfo de Paiva
Av General San Martin
R José Linhares
R Cupertino Durão
Pç Almirante Saldanha Gama
R Rainha Guilhermina
R Aristides Espinola
R General Artigas
R Rita Ludolf
Av Delfim Moreira
Ipanema Beach (Praia de Ipanema)
R Aparana
Leblon Beach (Praia de Leblon)

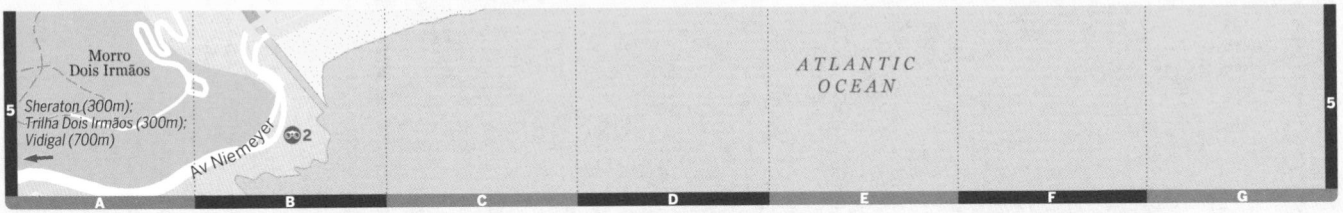

Sights (p61)

1 Lurixs: Arte Contemporânea B3
2 Mirante do Leblon B5
3 Praia de Leblon D4

Eating (p65)

4 Armazém do Café B4
5 Bibi Crepes D3
6 Café de la Musique C4
7 Coffeetown C3
8 CT Boucherie C2
Formidable ..... (see 20)
9 Giro B3
10 Giuseppe Grill D3
11 Graviola B3
12 Kurt C3
13 Le Blond B4
14 Massa C2
15 Momo B3
16 Nam Thai B4
17 Nola B3
18 Okanossa D3
19 Pabu Izakaya C2
20 Petit Formidable D2
21 Prima Bruschetteria B3
Rascal ..... (see 46)
22 Stuzzi B3
23 Sushi Leblon B3
24 Talho Capixaba C3
25 Vegetariano Social Club D1
26 Vezpa C3
27 Vokos B3
28 Yalla B3
29 Zona Sul Supermarket B3
30 Zuka B3

Drinking & Nightlife (p72)

31 Academia da Cachaça D1
32 Bar Veloso B4
33 Belmonte C2
34 Bibi Sucos D3
35 Bracarense D3
36 Brewteco C2
37 Cobal do Leblon D1
38 Jobi B3
39 Noi D1
40 Pizzaria Guanabara B3
41 Wood's B4

Entertainment (p73)

42 Teatro do Leblon D2

Shopping (p75)

43 Argumento B2
44 Eliane Carvalho B3
45 Isabela Capeto C2
Maria Oiticica ..... (see 46)
46 Shopping Leblon F2
Void General Store ..... (see 38)
Wöllner Outdoor ..... (see 46)

Sleeping (p165)

47 Lemon Spirit Hostel E3
48 Ritz Leblon B3

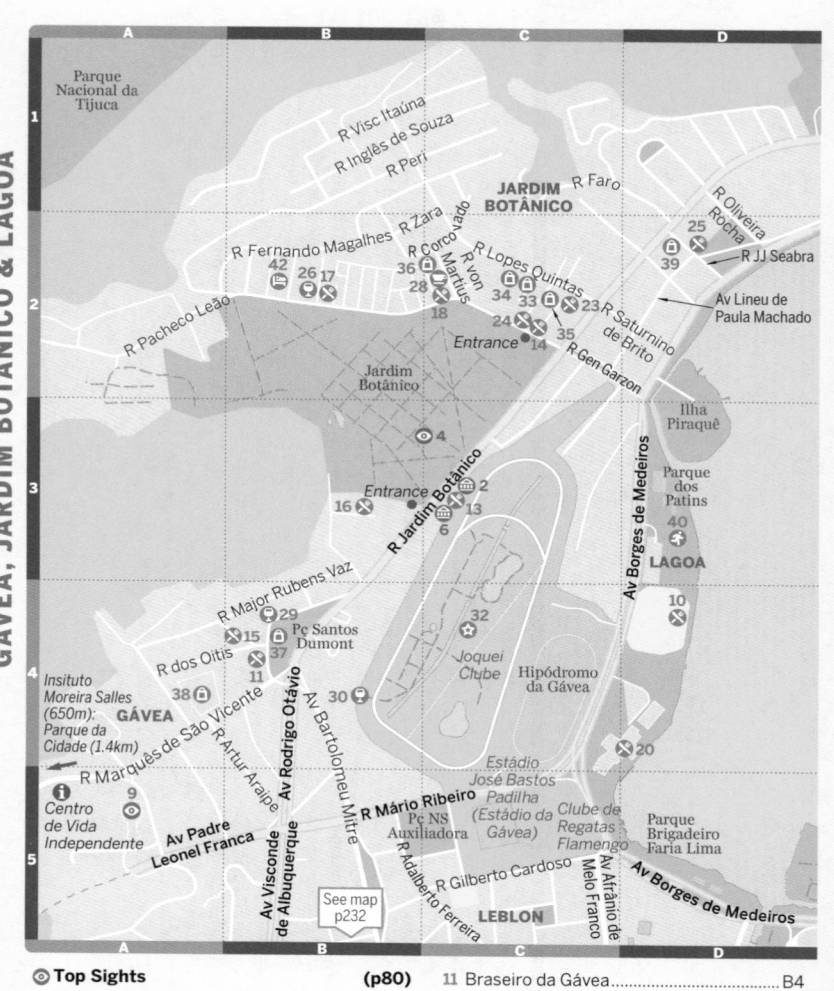

Top Sights (p80)

1 Lagoa Rodrigo de Freitas E4

Sights (p81)

2 Carpintaria C3
3 Fundação Eva Klabin G4
4 Jardim Botânico C3
5 Mirante do Sacopã F3
6 OM.art C3
7 Parque da Catacumba G4
8 Parque Lage E1
9 Planetário A5

Eating (p83)

10 Arab da Lagoa D4
11 Braseiro da Gávea B4
12 Bráz E1
13 Casa Camolese C3
14 Ella Pizzaria C2
15 Guimas B4
16 Jarbô B3
17 Jojö B2
18 La Bicyclette C2
19 La Carioca Cevicheria E1
20 Lagoon D4
21 Olympe F1
22 Plage Café E1
23 Prana Vegetariano C2
24 Puro C2
25 Taj Mahal D2

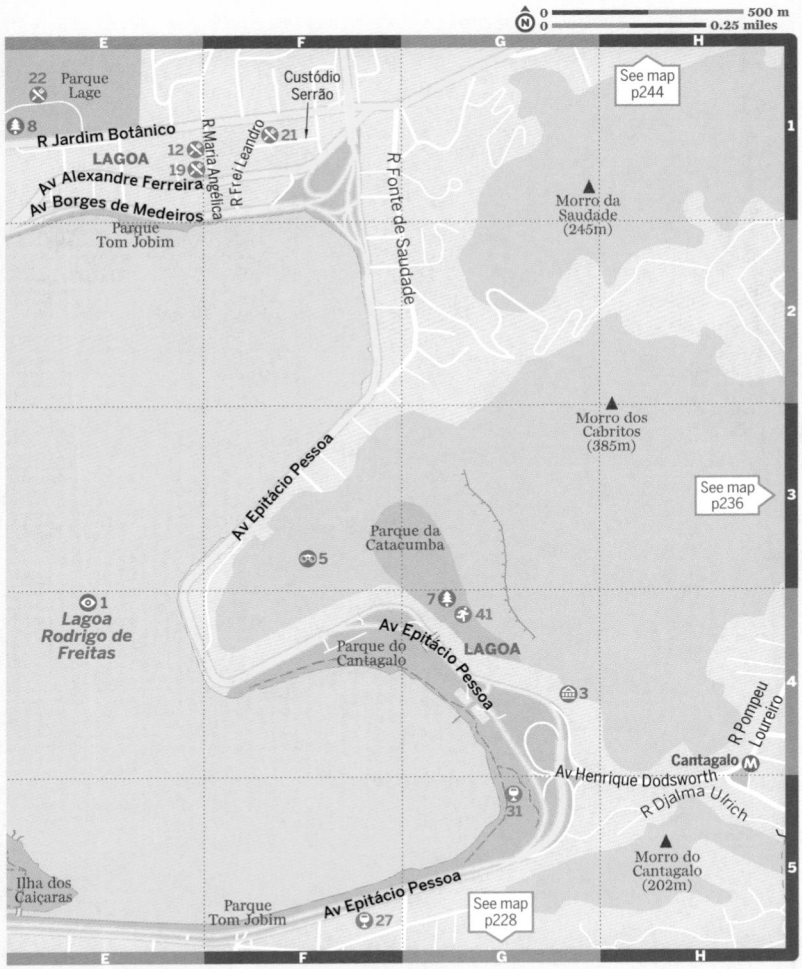

Drinking & Nightlife (p85)

26 Bar do Horto B2
27 Bar Lagoa F5
28 Bastarda C2
29 Hipódromo B4
30 Palaphita Gávea B4
31 Palaphita Kitch G5

Entertainment (p86)

Blue Note Rio ..... (see 20)
Clube Manouche ..... (see 13)
32 Jockey Club Brasileiro C4

Shopping (p86)

33 Casa Soma C2
34 Dona Coisa C2
35 Gabinete C2
36 O Sol C2
Parceria Carioca ..... (see 38)
37 Praça Santos Dumont Antique Fair B4
38 Shopping da Gávea A4
39 Venda em Garagem D2

Sports & Activities (p87)

40 Helisight D3
41 Lagoa Aventuras G4

Sleeping (p165)

42 Pouso Verde B2

Key on p238

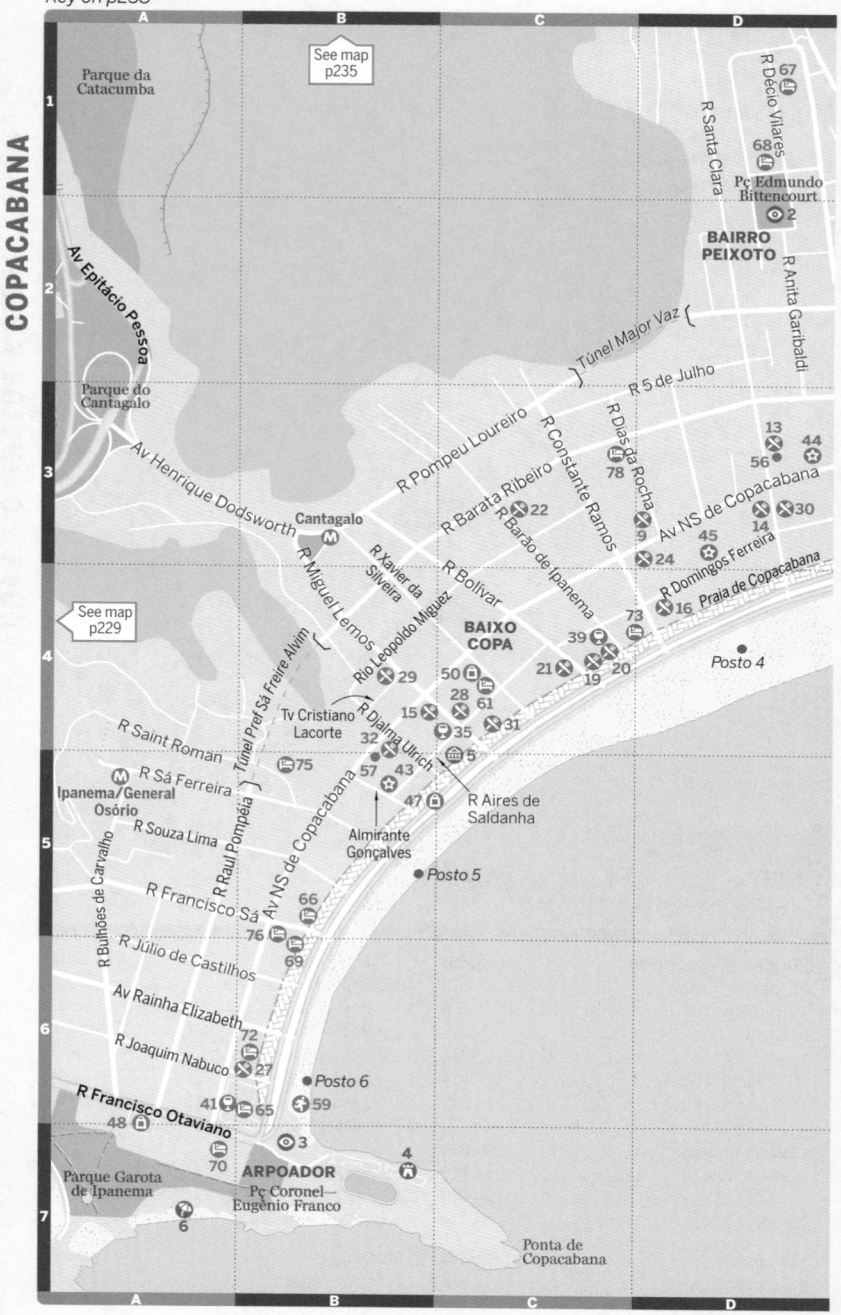
COPACABANA
A
B
C
D
1
2
3
4
5
6
7
See map p235
See map p229
Parque da Catacumba
Parque do Cantagalo
Av Epitácio Pessoa
Av Henrique Dodsworth
Cantagalo
R Miguel Lemos
R Xavier da Silveira
Rio Leopoldo Miguez
R Pompeu Loureiro
R Barata Ribeiro
R Constante Ramos
R Dias da Rocha
R Barão de Ipanema
R Bolivar
BAIXO COPA
Av NS de Copacabana
R Domingos Ferreira
Praia de Copacabana
Posto 4
Túnel Major Vaz
R 5 de Julho
R Santa Clara
R Décio Vilares
Pç Edmundo Bittencourt
BAIRRO PEIXOTO
R Anita Garibaldi
Tv Cristiano Lacorte
R Saint Roman
R Sá Ferreira
Túnel Pref Sá Freire Alvim
Ipanema/General Osório
R Souza Lima
R Raul Pompéia
R Bulhões de Carvalho
R Francisco Sá
R Júlio de Castilhos
Av Rainha Elizabeth
R Joaquim Nabuco
R Francisco Otaviano
R Dialma Ulrich
Almirante Gonçalves
R Aires de Saldanha
Posto 5
Posto 6
ARPOADOR
Pç Coronel Eugênio Franco
Parque Garota de Ipanema
Ponta de Copacabana

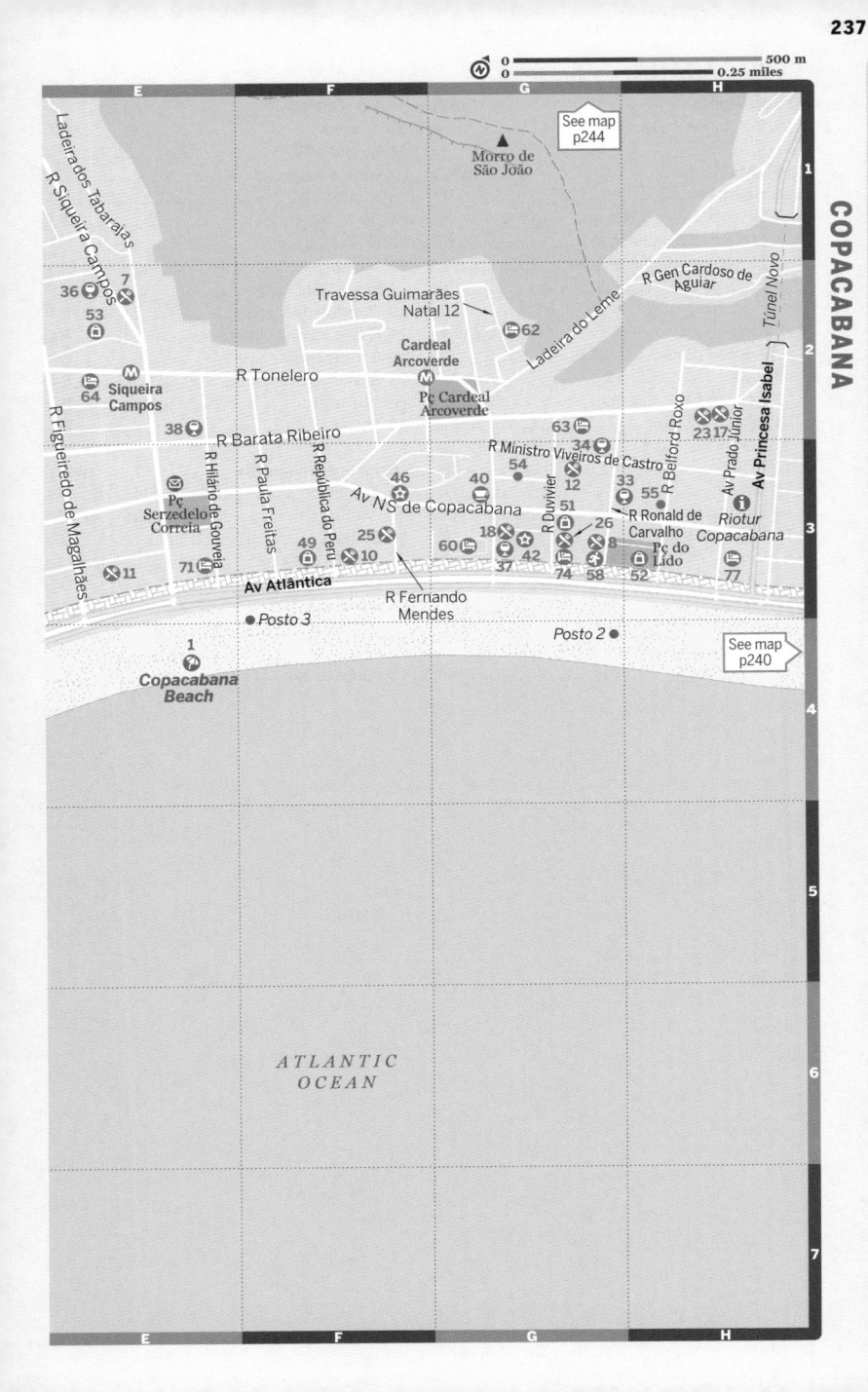
0 500 m
0 0.25 miles
E
F
G
H
1
2
3
4
5
6
7
See map p244
Morro de São João
Ladeira dos Tabaraias
R Siqueira Campos
36
7
53
64
Siqueira Campos
R Figueiredo de Magalhães
38
R Tonelero
Travessa Guimarães Natal 12
62
Cardeal Arcoverde
Pç Cardeal Arcoverde
Ladeira do Leme
R Gen Cardoso de Aguiar
Túnel Novo
Av Princesa Isabel
63
34
R Ministro Viveiros de Castro
54
12
40
46
Av NS de Copacabana
R Barata Ribeiro
R Hilário de Gouveia
R Paula Freitas
R República do Peru
Pç Serzedelo Correia
R Duvivier
51
26
33
55
R Belford Roxo
R Ronald de Carvalho
Pç do Lido
52
23
17
Av Prado Júnior
Riotur Copacabana
77
18
42
37
60
74
58
8
25
10
49
71
11
Av Atlântica
R Fernando Mendes
Posto 3
Posto 2
1
Copacabana Beach
See map p240
ATLANTIC OCEAN

COPACABANA *Map on p236*

Top Sights **(p92)**
1 Copacabana Beach E4

Sights **(p93)**
2 Bairro Peixoto D2
3 Colônia dos Pescadores B7
4 Forte de Copacabana B7
5 Museu da Imagem e Som C5
6 Praia de Diabo A7

Eating **(p94)**
7 Adega Pérola E2
8 Amir G3
9 Antônia Casa e Café D3
10 Arab F3
11 Arataca E3
12 Azumi G3
13 Bakers D3
14 Barraca da Chiquita D3
15 Bibi Sucos B4
Brota ..... (see 48)
Cafe Colombo ..... (see 4)
16 Capricciosa D4
17 Cervantes H2
18 Churrascaria Palace G3
19 Devassa C4
20 Don Camillo C4
21 El Born C4
22 Empório Grão-Pará C3
23 Galeto Sat's H2
24 Koni Store D3
25 La Trattoria F3
26 LF Café & Bistro G3
Momo ..... (see 60)
27 Porto das Carnes B6
28 Principe de Mônaco C4
29 Restaurante Naturaleve B4
30 Santa Satisfação D3
31 Skylab C4
TT Burger ..... (see 48)
32 Vezpa B4

Drinking & Nightlife **(p97)**
33 As Melhores Cervejas do Mundo H3
Bar Surfshop ..... (see 48)
34 Bodega G3
Cafe 18 do Forte ..... (see 4)
35 Escondido C4
36 Fosfobox E2
37 Mud Bug G3
38 Pavão Azul E2
39 Ponto da Bossa Nova C4

40 Sofá Café G3
41 TV Bar A6

Entertainment (p99)
42 Beco das Garrafas G3
43 Bip Bip B5
44 Cine Joia D3
45 Espaço SESC D3
46 Sala Municipal Baden Powell F3

Shopping (p99)
47 Av Atlântica Fair B5
48 Galeria River A6
49 Gilson Martins F3
50 Havaianas C4
51 Loja Fla G3
Osklen Surfing ..... (see 48)
52 Praça do Lido Market H3
53 Shopping Cidade Copacabana E2

Sports & Activities (p100)
54 Bike in Rio G3
55 Cook in Rio H3
56 Instituto Brasil-Estados Unidos D3
57 Rio by Bike B5
58 Rio Electric G3
59 Universo Paddle Surf B6

Sleeping (p165)
60 Belmond Copacabana Palace G3
61 Blame It on Rio 4 Travel C4
62 Cabana Copa G2
63 Che Lagarto G2
64 El Misti E2
65 Fairmont B6
66 Hotel Emiliano B5
67 Hotel Santa Clara D1
68 Jucati D1
69 Marta Rio Guesthouse B6
70 Mercure Arpoador A7
71 Olinda Rio E3
72 Orla Copacabana B6
73 Pestana Rio Atlântica C4
74 Porto Bay Rio Internacional G3
75 Pura Vida B5
76 Rio Design Hotel B5
77 Rio Spot Homes H3
78 Walk on the Beach Hostel C3

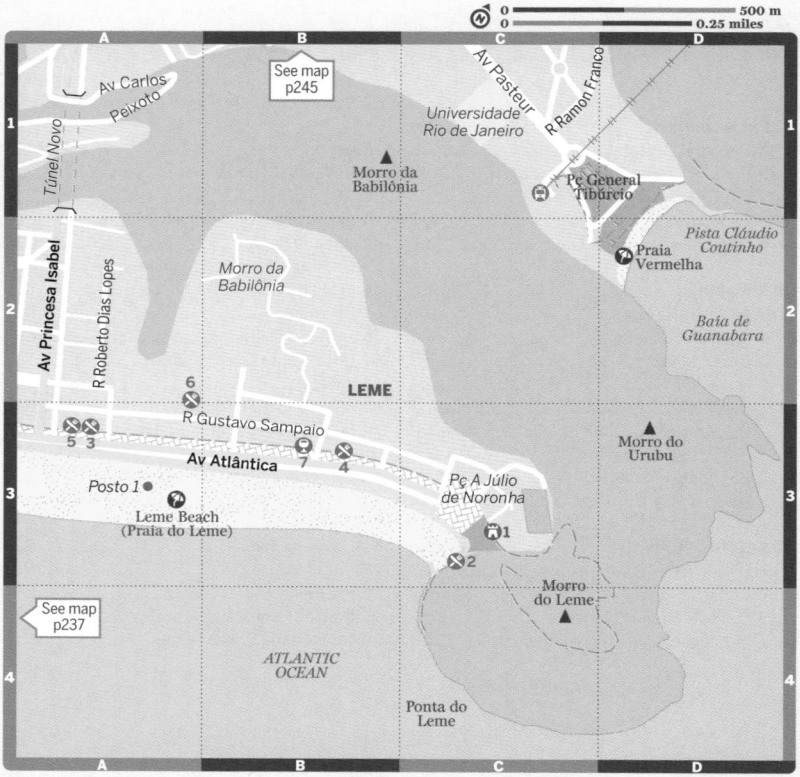

Sights **(p93)**

1 Forte Duque de Caxias C3

Eating **(p97)**

2 Espetto Carioca C3
3 Joaquina A3
4 La Fiorentina B3
5 Salomé A3
6 Shirley A2

Drinking & Nightlife **(p97)**

7 Boteco Belmonte B3

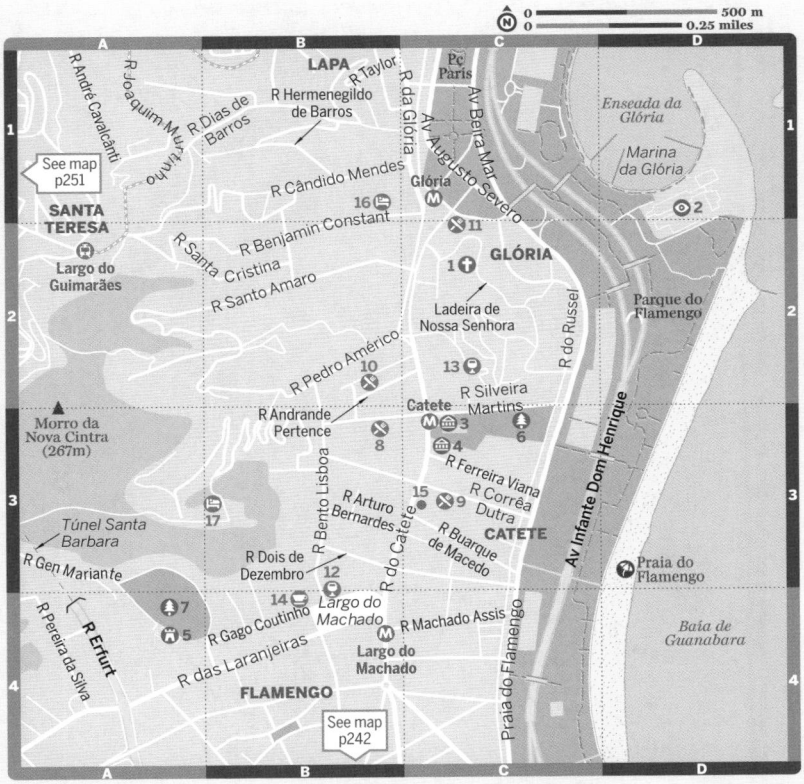

CATETE & GLÓRIA

Sights (p116)

1 Igreja de Nossa Senhora da Glória do Outeiro C2
2 Marina da Glória D1
3 Museu da República C3
4 Museu de Folclore Edison Carneiro C3
5 Palácio das Laranjeiras A4
6 Parque do Catete C3
7 Parque Guinle A4

Eating (p118)

8 Cariocando B3
9 Carmelo C3
Corrientes 348 ..... (see 2)
10 Ferro e Farinha B2
Maze Inn ..... (see 17)
11 Taberna da Glória C2

Drinking & Nightlife (p119)

12 Adega Portugália B3
13 Bar do Zé C2
14 Café Secreto B4

Entertainment (p120)

Cine Museu da República ..... (see 3)
Maze Inn ..... (see 17)

Sports & Activities (p120)

Bem Brasil ..... (see 2)
15 Carioca Languages C3
Mar do Rio ..... (see 2)

Sleeping (p168)

16 Discovery Hostel B1
17 Maze Inn B3

FLAMENGO, LARANJEIRAS & COSME VELHO

FLAMENGO, LARANJEIRAS & COSME VELHO

Top Sights (p114)
1 Cristo Redentor A4

Sights (p116)
2 Centro Cultural Oi Futuro F1
3 Largo do Boticário A3
4 Parque do Flamengo G2

Eating (p117)
5 Botero E1
6 Brou F2
7 Fresh Comida Saudável F1
8 Intihuasi F2
9 Luigi's E2
10 Majorica F2
11 Sírio Libaneza E1
12 Tacacá do Norte F2

Drinking & Nightlife (p119)
13 Armazém do Chopp F2
14 Belmonte F2
Herr Brauer ..... (see 8)

Entertainment (p120)
15 Severyna de Laranjeiras E2

Shopping (p120)
16 Maracatu Brasil E2
17 Pé de Boi E2
18 Praça São Salvador E2

Sleeping (p168)
19 Casa Caminho do Corcovado A4
20 Solar do Cosme A3

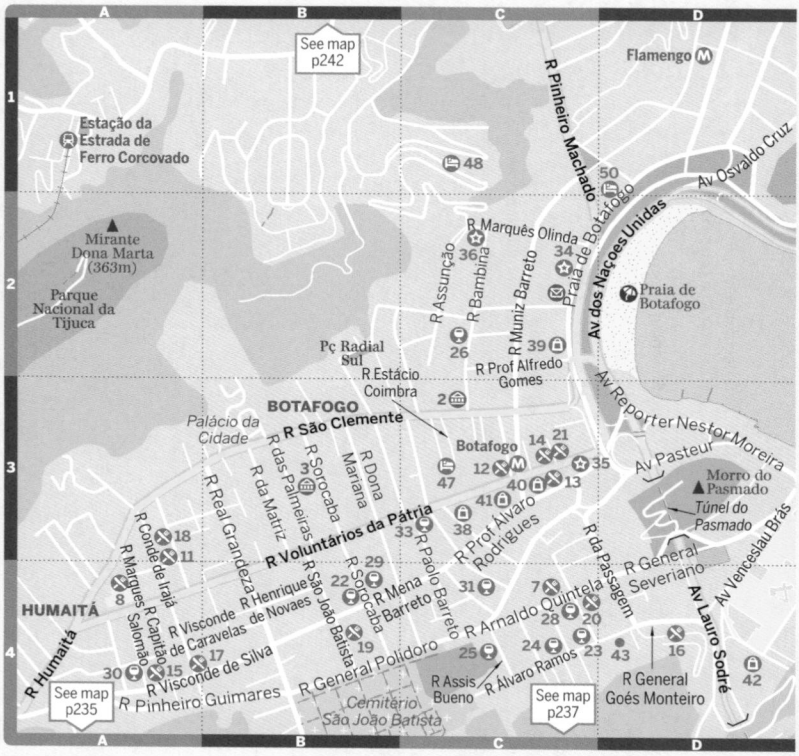

Top Sights (p103)

1 Pão de Açúcar G2

Sights (p104)

2 Museu Casa de Rui Barbosa C3
3 Museu do Índio B3
4 Praia da Urca F2
5 Praia Vermelha F4

Eating (p104)

6 Bar Urca G2
7 Ceviche RJ C4
8 Cobal do Humaitá A4
9 Garota da Urca G2
10 Julius Brasserie F3
11 Lasai A3
12 Le Depanneur C3
13 Livraria Prefácio C3
14 Marchezinho C3
15 Meza Bar A4
16 Miam Miam D4
17 Oteque A4
18 Oui Oui A3
19 Slow Bakery B4
20 South Ferro C4
21 Void – House of Food C3

Drinking & Nightlife (p107)

22 Alice Bar B4
23 Bar 1928 ..... C4
24 Bar Bukowski C4
Bar Urca ..... (see 6)
25 Caverna C4
26 Champanharia Ovelha Negra C2

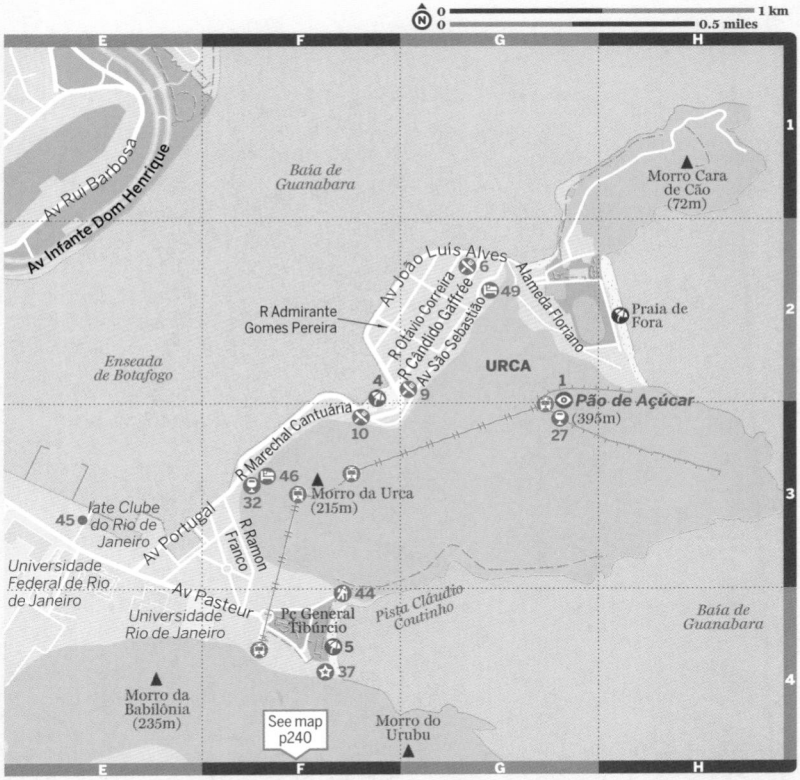

27 Clássico Beach Club G3
28 CoLAB C4
29 Comuna B4
30 Fuska 2.0 ..... A4
31 Hocus Pocus C4
32 Urca Grill F3
33 WineHouse C3

Entertainment **(p108)**
34 Espaço Itaú C2
35 Estação Net Rio C3
36 Olho da Rua C2
37 Terra Brasilis F4

Shopping **(p109)**
38 Baratos da Ribeiro C3
39 Botafogo Praia Shopping C2
40 Comparsaria C3
41 Livraria da Travessa C3
42 Rio Sul Shopping D4

Sports & Activities **(p109)**
43 Casa de Dança Carlinhos de Jesus D4
44 Pista Cláudio Coutinho F4
45 Sail in Rio E3

Sleeping **(p167)**
46 Hotelinho Urca F3
47 Injoy Hostel C3
48 O Veleiro Bed & Breakfast C1
49 Recanto da Urca G2
50 Yoo2 ..... D1

Key on p248

A
B
C
D
1
2
3
4
5
6
7
Av Venezuela
Av Barão Tefé
AquaRio (800m)
Blvd Olímpico
Parada dos Museus
SAÚDE
PÇ MAUÁ
Instituto de Pesquisa e Memória Presto Novos (350m)
Pç Jornal do Comércio
R Coelho e Castro
Morro de São Bento
R Sacadura Cabral
Ladeira do João Homem
LIESA
R Dom Gerardo
R Acre
R Primeiro de Março
Ladeira Pedro Antônio
R do Jogo da Bola
Pç Major Valô
R Mairink Veiga
São Bento
Av Rio Branco
R Viscon de Inhaúma
Pç dos Estivadores
R Sen Pompeu
R Major Daemon
Largo de Santa Rita
R Teófilo Otoni
R Alexandre Mackenzie
R Camerino
R da Conceição
R Uruguaiana
Pç Pio X
Candelária
R da Alfândega
Av Marechal Floriano
Av Presidente Vargas
R dos Andradas
CENTRO
R Miguel Couto
R do Ouvidor
See map p253
Presidente Vargas
Uruguaiana
R do Rosário
SAARA
R da Alfândega
R Senhor dos Passos
R da Conceição
Pç Monte Castelo
R Gonçalves Dias
Colombo
Sete de Setembro
R de Buenos Aires
R Gonçalves Ledo
Av Passos
R Luís de Camões
Largo de San Francisco de Paula
Saara
Campo de Santana
Pç da República
R Tomé de Souza
R Regente Feijó
Tiradentes
R da Constituição
Pç Tiradentes
R da Carioca
Carioca
Largo da Carioca
R Pedro I
Av República do Paraguai
Av 13 de Maio
Av República do Chile
R Lélio Gama
R Senador Dantas
Bonde to Santa Teresa
R Visconde de Itaboraí
R Primeiro de Março
Av Gomes Freire
R do Lavradio
R Evaristo da Veiga
Travessa do Comércio
R do Mercado
R do Ouvidor
R dos Arcos
Av Mem de Sá
Arcos do Lapa
CINELÂNDIA
R do Passeio
R Joaquim Silva
Largo da Lapa
R Teixeira de Freitas
0
100 m
See map p250

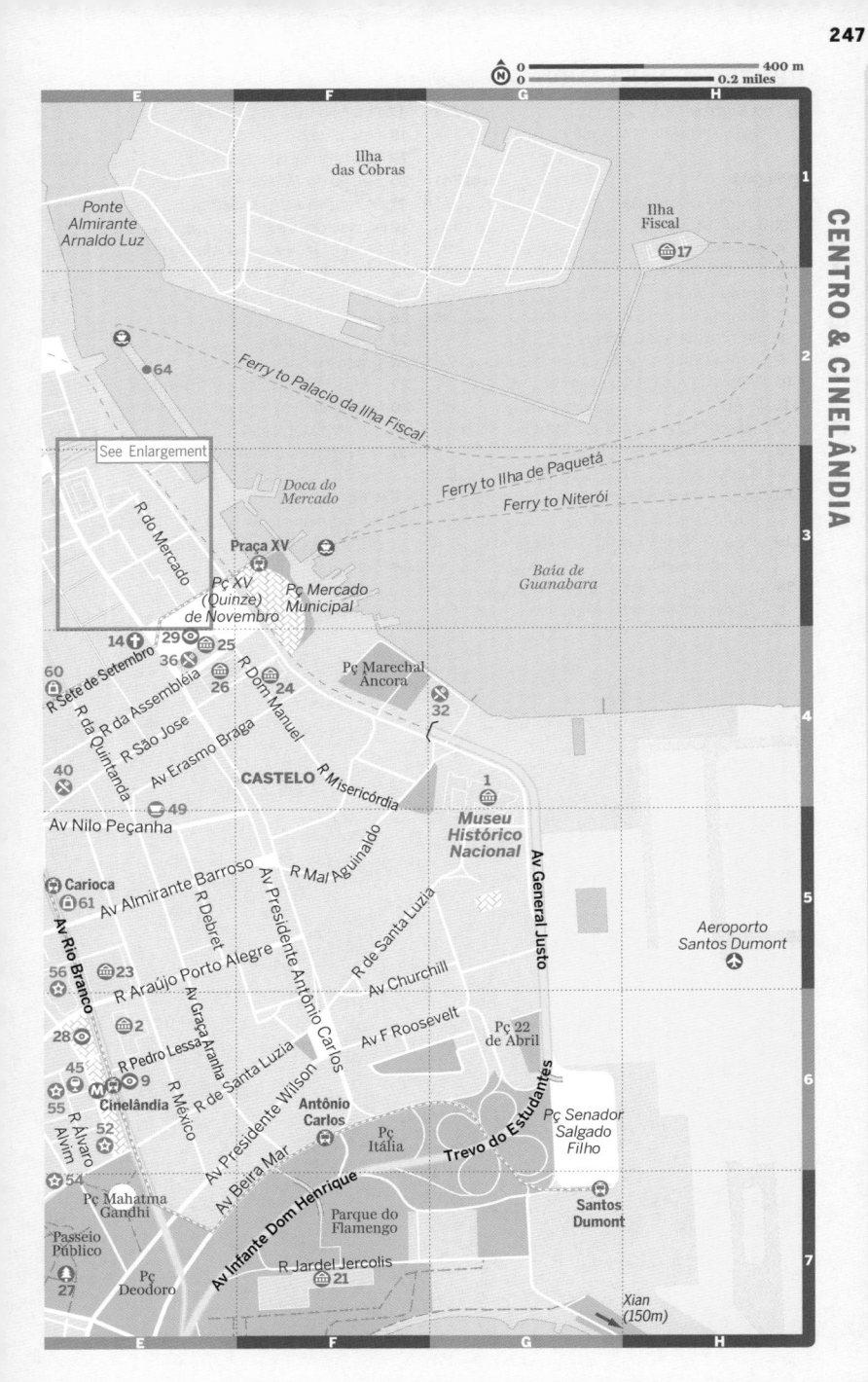
0 400 m
0 0.2 miles
E F G H
1 2 3 4 5 6 7
CENTRO & CINELÂNDIA
Ilha das Cobras
Ponte Almirante Arnaldo Luz
Ilha Fiscal
17
64
Ferry to Palacio da Ilha Fiscal
See Enlargement
Doca do Mercado
Ferry to Ilha de Paquetá
Ferry to Niterói
R do Mercado
Praça XV
Pç XV (Quinze) de Novembro
Pç Mercado Municipal
Baía de Guanabara
14
29
25
36
26
24
60
R Sete de Setembro
R da Assembléia
R da Quintanda
R São José
Av Erasmo Braga
R Dom Manuel
Pç Marechal Ancora
32
40
CASTELO
R Misericórdia
1
Museu Histórico Nacional
49
Av Nilo Peçanha
Carioca
61
Av Almirante Barroso
R Mal Aguinaldo
Av Presidente Antônio Carlos
Av General Justo
Av Rio Branco
R Debret
R de Santa Luzia
Aeroporto Santos Dumont
56
23
R Araújo Porto Alegre
Av Graça Aranha
Av Churchill
28
2
Av F Roosevelt
Pç 22 de Abril
45
R Pedro Lessa
9
R de Santa Luzia
R México
55
Cinelândia
Antônio Carlos
Av Presidente Wilson
Pç Itália
Trevo do Estudantes
Pç Senador Salgado Filho
R Álvaro Alvim
52
Av Beira Mar
54
Pç Mahatma Gandhi
Parque do Flamengo
Santos Dumont
Av Infante Dom Henrique
Passeio Público
R Jardel Jercolis
21
27
Pç Deodoro
Xian (150m)

CENTRO & CINELÂNDIA *Map on p246*

Top Sights (p123)

1 Museu Histórico Nacional G4

Sights (p124)

2 Biblioteca Nacional E6
3 Bonde Station D6
4 Boulevard Olímpico B1
5 Cais do Valongo A1
6 Campo de Santana A4
7 Centro Cultural Banco do Brasil A6
8 Centro Cultural Correios A6
9 Centro Cultural Justiça Federal E6
10 Centro de Arte Hélio Oiticica C4
11 CRAB B5
12 Espaço Cultural da Marinha B6
13 Igreja de Nossa Senhora de Candelária D3
14 Igreja de Nossa Senhora do Carmo da Antiga Sé E4
15 Igreja de Nossa Senhora do Rosário e São Benedito C4
16 Igreja São Francisco da Penitência & Convento de Santo Antônio D5
17 Ilha Fiscal H1
18 Morro da Conceição C2
19 Mosteiro de São Bento D1
20 Museu de Arte do Rio C1
21 Museu de Arte Moderna F7
22 Museu do Amanhã D1
23 Museu Nacional de Belas Artes E5
24 Museu Naval F4
25 Paço Imperial E4
26 Palácio Tiradentes E4
27 Passeio Público E7
28 Praça Floriano E6
29 Praça XV (Quinze) de Novembro E4
30 Real Gabinete Português de Leitura C4
Theatro Municipal ..... (see 56)
31 Travessa do Comércio B7

Eating (p130)

32 Ancoramar G4
33 ASA Açaí B2
34 Bar Luiz C5
Belga ..... (see 65)
Bistrô do Paço ..... (see 25)

35 Botequim Bodega do Sal B2
36 Café Arlequim E4
37 Cais do Oriente A6
38 Casa Paladino C3
39 Confeitaria Colombo D4
Cristóvão ..... (see 39)
40 Govardhana Harí E4
41 Imaculada C2
42 L'Atelier du Cuisinier D3
43 Mironga D2
44 Rancho Inn D3

Drinking & Nightlife **(p132)**
45 Amarelinho E6
46 Bar Léo B6
47 Bar Mercadores B7
48 Cine Botequim D2
49 Curto Cafe E4
50 Week B2

Entertainment **(p133)**
51 Casa do Choro D5
52 Cine Odeon E6
53 Pedra do Sal B2
Teatro do Centro Cultural Banco do Brasil ..... (see 7)
54 Teatro Riachuelo E7
55 Teatro Rival Petrobras E6
56 Theatro Municipal E5
57 Trapiche Gamboa A2

Shopping **(p133)**
58 Casa Naara C3
CRAB ..... (see 11)
59 Granado A7
60 Livraria da Travessa E4
61 Nova Livraria Leonardo da Vinci E5
62 Pleidisco C5

Sports & Activities **(p134)**
63 Free Walker Tours D5
64 Passeio Marítimo E2

Sleeping **(p168)**
65 Belga Hotel C3

SANTA TERESA & LAPA

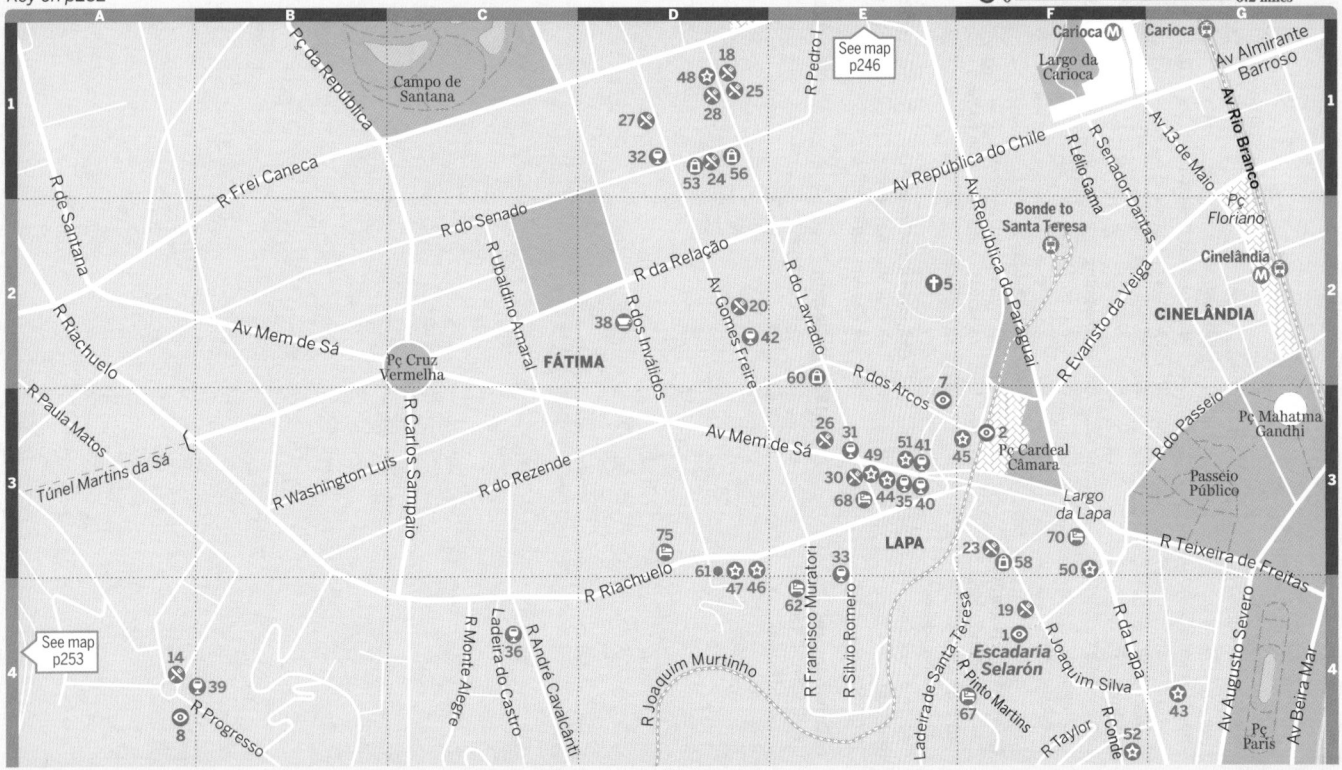

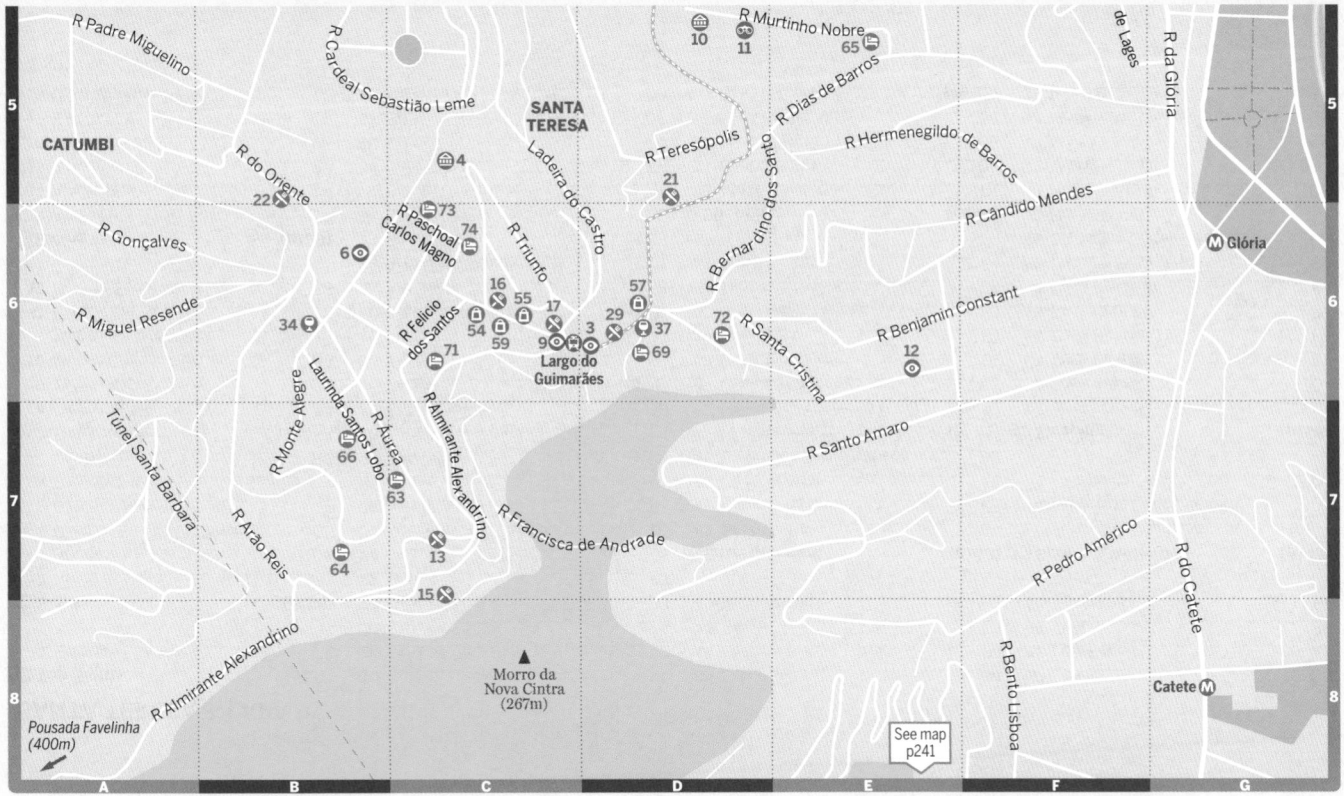
R Padre Miguelino
R Cardeal Sebastião Leme
CATUMBI
SANTA TERESA
R Murtinho Nobre
R Dias de Barros
R Hermenegildo de Barros
R Teresópolis
Ladeira do Castro
R do Oriente
R Gonçalves
R Paschoal Carlos Magno
R Triunfo
R Bernardino dos Santos
R Cândido Mendes
Glória
R Miguel Resende
R Felício dos Santos
Largo do Guimarães
R Santa Cristina
R Benjamin Constant
R Monte Alegre
Laurinda Santos Lobo
R Áurea
R Almirante Alexandrino
R Santo Amaro
Túnel Santa Bárbara
R Francisca de Andrade
R Pedro Américo
R do Catete
R Aarão Reis
R Almirante Alexandrino
Morro da Nova Cintra (267m)
R Bento Lisboa
Catete
Pousada Favelinha (400m)
See map p241
R da Glória
de Lages

SANTA TERESA & LAPA *Map on p250*

Top Sights (p137)
1 Escadaria Selarón F4

Sights (p138)
2 Arcos da Lapa F3
3 Bonde D6
4 Casa de Benjamin Constant C5
5 Catedral Metropolitana E2
6 Centro Cultural Laurinda Santos Lobo B6
7 Fundição Progresso E3
8 Largo das Neves A4
9 Largo do Guimarães C6
10 Museu Chácara do Céu D5
Museu de Arte Sacra ..... (see 5)
11 Parque das Ruínas D5
12 Retrato Espaço Cultural E6

Eating (p139)
13 Alda Maria Doces Portugueses C7
14 Alquimia A4
15 Aprazível C7
16 Bar do Mineiro C6
17 Cafe do Alto C6
18 Casa Momus D1
19 Cortiço Carioca F4
20 Espaço Lapa Cafe D2
21 Espírito Santa D5
22 Galeria Bazá B5
23 Gohan F3
24 Lilia D1
25 Mangue Seco Cachaçaria D1
26 Nova Capela E3
Rango Veggie ..... (see 58)
27 Refeitório D1
28 Santo Scenarium D1
29 Sobrenatural D6
Térèze ..... (see 71)
30 Vezpa E3

Drinking & Nightlife (p141)
31 Antônio's E3
32 Armazém Senado D1
33 Bar da Nalva E3
34 Bar do Gomes B6
Bar dos Descasados ..... (see 71)
35 Booze Bar E3
36 Buraco da Lacraia C4
37 Explorer Bar D6
38 Fazenda Paradiso Café D2
39 Goya-Beira B4
40 Leviano Bar E3
41 Sarau E3
42 Vaca Atolada D2

Entertainment (p143)
43 Beco do Rato G4
44 Carioca da Gema E3
45 Circo Voador F3
46 Clube dos Democráticos D3
Favela Hype ..... (see 55)
Fundição Progresso ..... (see 7)
47 Lapa 40 Graus D3
48 Rio Scenarium D1
49 Sacrilégio E3
50 Sala Cecília Meireles F3
51 Teatro Odisséia E3
52 TribOz F4

Shopping (p144)
53 Ateliê Bonifácio D1
54 Baobá Brasil C6
55 Favela Hype C6
56 Feira do Rio Antigo D1
Galeria Bazá ..... (see 22)
57 La Vereda D6
58 Loja Pence F3
59 Tucum C6
60 Velha Lapa E2

Sports & Activities (p145)
Fundição Progresso ..... (see 7)
61 Núcleo de Dança Renata Peçanha D3

Sleeping (p168)
62 Books Hostel E4
63 Casa Áurea C7
64 Casa Beleza B7
65 Casa Bianca E5
66 Casa Cool Beans B7
67 Casa da Gente F4
68 Da Lapa Design Hotel E3
69 Discovery Suites D6
70 Hotel 55 Rio F3
71 Hotel Santa Teresa C6
72 Mama Ruisa D6
73 Mama Shelter C6
74 Modernistas Hospedagem C6
75 Vila Galé D3

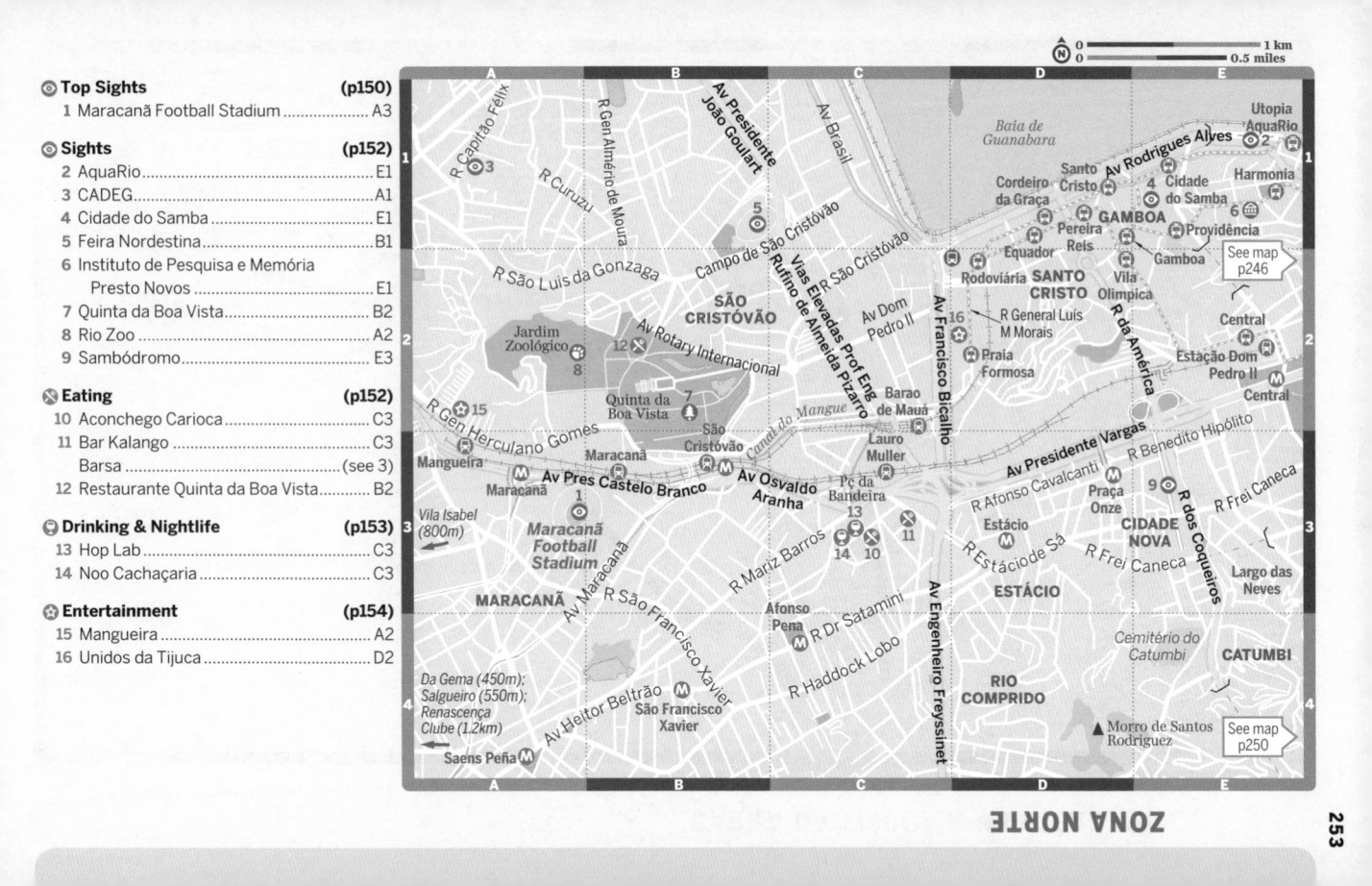
0 1 km
0 0.5 miles
Top Sights (p150)
1 Maracanã Football Stadium A3
Sights (p152)
2 AquaRio E1
3 CADEG A1
4 Cidade do Samba E1
5 Feira Nordestina B1
6 Instituto de Pesquisa e Memória Presto Novos E1
7 Quinta da Boa Vista B2
8 Rio Zoo A2
9 Sambódromo E3
Eating (p152)
10 Aconchego Carioca C3
11 Bar Kalango C3
Barsa (see 3)
12 Restaurante Quinta da Boa Vista B2
Drinking & Nightlife (p153)
13 Hop Lab C3
14 Noo Cachaçaria C3
Entertainment (p154)
15 Mangueira A2
16 Unidos da Tijuca D2
Baía de Guanabara
Utopia AquaRio
Av Rodrigues Alves
Harmonia
Santo Cristo
Cordeiro da Graça
Cidade do Samba
GAMBOA
Pereira Reis
Providência
Equador
Gamboa
Rodoviária
SANTO CRISTO
Vila Olímpica
See map p246
R Capitão Félix
R Gen Almério de Moura
Av Presidente João Goulart
Av Brasil
R Curuzu
Campo de São Cristóvão
R São Luis da Gonzaga
SÃO CRISTÓVÃO
Vias Elevadas Prof Eng Rufino de Almeida Pizarro
R São Cristóvão
Av Dom Pedro II
Av Francisco Bicalho
R General Luís M Morais
Praça Formosa
R da América
Central
Estação Dom Pedro II
Jardim Zoológico
Av Rotary Internacional
Quinta da Boa Vista
Canal do Mangue
Barão de Mauá
Lauro Muller
R Gen Herculano Gomes
Mangueira
Maracanã
São Cristóvão
Av Pres Castelo Branco
Av Osvaldo Aranha
Pç da Bandeira
Av Presidente Vargas
R Benedito Hipólito
R Afonso Cavalcanti
Praça Onze
R dos Coqueiros
R Frei Caneca
Vila Isabel (800m)
Maracanã Football Stadium
R Mariz Barros
Estácio
CIDADE NOVA
R Estácio de Sá
R Frei Caneca
Largo das Neves
MARACANÃ
Av Maracanã
R São Francisco Xavier
Afonso Pena
R Dr Satamini
ESTÁCIO
Av Engenheiro Freyssinet
Cemitério do Catumbi
CATUMBI
R Haddock Lobo
RIO COMPRIDO
Da Gema (450m); Salgueiro (550m); Renascença Clube (1.2km)
Av Heitor Beltrão
São Francisco Xavier
Morro de Santos Rodrigues
See map p250
Saens Peña
ZONA NORTE

BARRA DA TIJUCA & WESTERN RIO

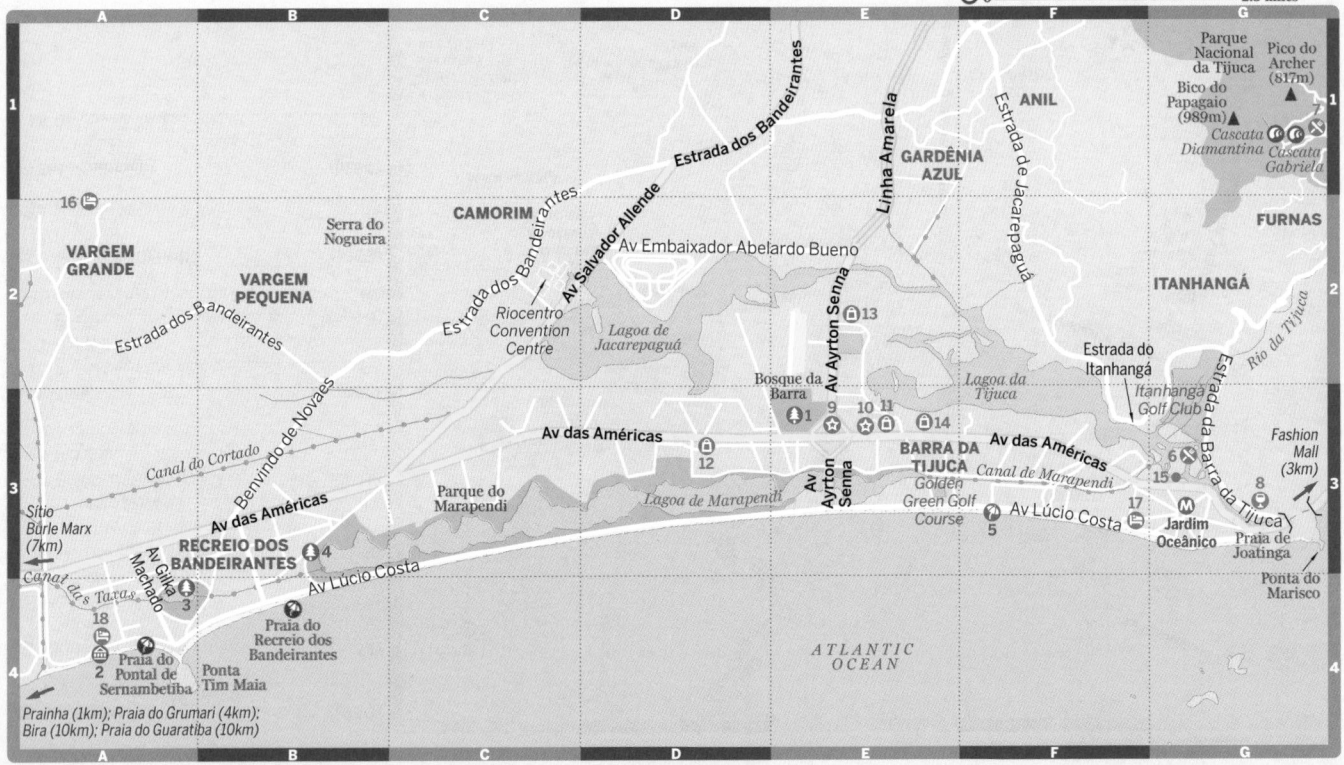